Praise for *Management 3.0*

"I don't care for cookbooks, as in '5 steps to success at whatever.' I like books that urge you to think—that present new ideas and get mental juices flowing. Jurgen's book is in this latter category; it asks us to think about leading and managing as a complex undertaking—especially in today's turbulent world. Management 3.0 offers managers involved in Agile/lean transformations a thought-provoking guide how they themselves can 'become' Agile."
—**Jim Highsmith**, Executive Consultant, ThoughtWorks, Inc.,
    www.jimhighsmith.com, author of *Agile Project Management*

"An up-to-the-minute, relevant round-up of research and practice on complexity and management, cogently summarized and engagingly presented."
—**David Harvey**, Independent Consultant, Teams and Technology

"Management 3.0 is an excellent book introducing agile to management. I've not seen any book that comes near to what this book offers for managers of agile teams. It's not only a must read, it's a must share."
—**Olav Maassen**, Xebia

"If you want hard fast rules like 'if x happens, do y to fix it' forget this book. Actually forget about a management career. But if you want tons of ideas on how to make the work of your team more productive and thereby more fun and thereby more productive and thereby more fun and…read this book! You will get a head start on this vicious circle along with a strong reasoning on why the concepts work."
—**Jens Schauder,** Software Developer, LINEAS

"There are a number of books on managing Agile projects and transitioning from being a Project Manager to working in an Agile setting. However, there isn't much on being a manager in an Agile setting. This book fills that gap, but actually addresses being an effective manager in any situation. The breadth of research done and presented as background to the actual concrete advice adds a whole other element to the book. And all this while writing in an entertaining style as well."
—**Scott Duncan**, Agile Coach/Trainer, Agile Software Qualities

"Don't get tricked by the word 'Agile' used in the subtitle. The book isn't really about Agile; it is about healthy, sensible and down-to-earth management. Something, which is still pretty uncommon."
—**Pawel Brodzinski**, Software Project Management

"When I first met Jurgen and learned he was writing a book based on complexity theory, I thought, 'That sounds good, but I'll never understand it.' Books with words like entropy, chaos theory, and thermodynamics tend to scare me. In fact, not only did I find Management 3.0 accessible and easy to understand, I can [also] apply the information immediately, in a practical way. It makes sense that software teams are complex adaptive systems, and a relief to learn how to apply these ideas to help our teams do the best work possible. This book will help you whether you're a manager or a member of a software team".
—**Lisa Crispin**, Agile Tester, ePlan Services, Inc., co-author of *Agile Testing*

"This book is an important read for managers who want to move beyond 'managing by hope' and understand the underpinning of trust, motivation, and the complexity that exists in nearly every team out there."
—**Cory Foy**, Senior Consultant, Net Objectives

"This book is a very accessible compendium of team management practices based on scientific research. It's not only the tremendous value in each page of this book, but also Jurgen's typical sense of humor that turns this book into a pleasant read."
—**Ruud Cox**, Test Manager, Improve Quality Services

"The very heart of software development is to get people to recognize they are in a complex system that should be managed accordingly. Management 3.0 addresses both the recognition and the concomitant transformative aspects. By so doing, Jurgen Appelo provides a bridge between theory and practice that has so far been considered too far away."
—**Israel Gat**, Founder, The Agile Executive, author of *The Concise Executive Guide to Agile*

"If you really want to know about Agile management, read Jurgen's book. He explains why looking for results is key to involving the team and for a great outcome. As Jurgen says, management is not simple and this book explains why. With humor and pragmatism, Jurgen shows you how you can think about management."
—**Johanna Rothman**, Consultant, Rothman Consulting Group, Inc., author of *Manage It!*

"In this book, Jurgen does a great job of explaining the science behind complexity and how Agile management methods have arisen from the need to manage in complex, dynamic, and unpredictable circumstances. If you're leading Agile development teams and interested in developing your management skills, this book is a must-read."
—**Kelly Waters**, Blogger, Agile Development Made Easy!

"I firmly believe that Management 3.0 will become the 'Bible' of Agile management books in the decade ahead."
—**Ed Yourdon**, IT Management/Software Consultant, Nodruoy, Inc., author of *Death March*

"This book is not written for those who want a quick fix. This book is written for serious students who have a passion and love for management. This book is written for management craftsmen."
—**Robert C. Martin**, Owner, ObjectMentor, Inc., author of *Clean Code*

"Every 21st century Agile (or non-Agile) manager needs to read Jurgen Appelo's Management 3.0. With an engaging and accessible style, Appelo outlines current theories from complexity science, management, leadership, and social systems [and] then pulls them all together with practical examples. Then he throws in reflective questions to assist managers in applying it all to their current situations. Whenever I work with a manager, executive, or leadership team, I'll recommend this book."
—**Diana Larsen**, Consultant, FutureWorks Consulting LLC, co-author of *Agile Retrospectives*

"Jurgen takes his readers on a wide-ranging romp through system theory, complexity theory, management theory—and distills it for practical application. His book will help managers think about their work differently and expand their options for effective action in the workplace."
—**Esther Derby**, Consultant, Esther Derby Associates, Inc., co-author of *Behind Closed Doors: Secrets of Great Management*

"Jurgen managed to write a book that links the tons of books he has read. Although there were a few moment I did not agree with him, I loved the way this book challenged my thinking. This is the perfect book if you want to know how to create your own answers in this complex world."
—**Yves Hanoulle**, Agile Coach, PairCoaching.net

"Management 3.0 brings together the best thinking in the fields of complex adaptive systems, Agile management, and Lean product delivery to suggest a pragmatic framework for effective management in the 21st century. To be successful in the face of rapidly changing market conditions, we must create organizations that enable our people to adapt, with a minimal amount of oversight and direction. Management 3.0 gives us a roadmap for leading teams in the face of profound uncertainty. Jurgen has made a significant contribution to the field of Agile management and leadership."
—**Mike Cottmeyer**, Agile Coach, LeadingAgile

"Too many Agile practitioners ignore the realities of the real world. But in the real world Agile projects must be managed, directed, and moved forward. This benefits both the company and the team, and Jurgen has done a great job of bringing those practices into focus in a real and practical way. If you're involved with Agile software in a shop of any size, or if you're a manager (or executive) who's seen the benefits of Agile and want to bring them into your shop, you owe it to yourself to read this book."
—**Jared Richardson**, Agile Coach, Logos Technologies, co-author of *Ship It!*

"I had felt quite well-equipped to manage teams adopting an Agile software development approach, having read works like Managing Transitions, Leading Change, and Behind Closed Doors, until I began to read Management 3.0. Appelo's compendium works at a variety of levels: It helps novice managers with a diverse collection of easy-to-apply models, it helps experienced managers see what they need to unlearn, and I assume it will help even expert managers adapt to contemporary styles of leadership and governance. Management 3.0 has opened my eyes to the vast world of modern-day management whose surface I see I have only scratched so far, and I look forward to Appelo's work guiding me along as I learn."
—**J.B. Rainsberger**, Consultant, Coach, Mentor, jbrains.ca, author of *JUnit Recipes*

"Software projects are complex living systems; knowledge loss happens as soon as you manage them. Make your life easier, minimize the loss: Read this book!"
—**Jacopo Romei**, Agile Coach, co-author of *Pro PHP Refactoring*

"For people who 'get' the message, this book may prove to be as valuable as Darwin's book On the Origin of Species."
—**Florian Hoornaar**, Entrepreneur, Octavalent

MANAGEMENT 3.0

MANAGEMENT 3.0

Leading Agile Developers, Developing Agile Leaders

JURGEN APPELO

✦✦Addison-Wesley

Upper Saddle River, NJ • Boston • Indianapolis • San Francisco
New York • Toronto • Montreal • London • Munich • Paris • Madrid
Cape Town • Sydney • Tokyo • Singapore • Mexico City

The publisher offers excellent discounts on this book when ordered in quantity for bulk purchases or special sales, which may include electronic versions and/or custom covers and content particular to your business, training goals, marketing focus, and branding interests. For more information, please contact

    U.S. Corporate and Government Sales
    (800) 382-3419
    corpsales@pearsontechgroup.com

For sales outside the United States, please contact

    International Sales
    international@pearson.com

Visit us on the Web: www.informit.com/aw

Library of Congress Cataloging-in-Publication Data

Appelo, Jurgen, 1969-
  Management 3.0 : leading Agile developers, developing Agile leaders / Jurgen Appelo. -- 1st ed.
    p. cm.
  Includes bibliographical references and index.
  ISBN 978-0-321-71247-9 (pbk. : alk. paper) 1. Management information systems. 2. Agile software development--Management. 3. Leadership. I. Title.
  HD30.213.A67 2011
  658.4--dc22
                  2010041778

ISBN-13: 978-0-321-71247-9
ISBN-10: 0-321-71247-1

Text printed in the United States on recycled paper at R.R. Donnelley in Crawfordsville, Indiana.
Third Printing: January 2012

Editor-in-Chief
Mark Taub

Executive Editor
Chris Guzikowski

Development Editor
Sheri Cain

Managing Editor
Kristy Hart

Project Editor
Andy Beaster

Copy Editor
Apostrophe Editing Services

Indexer
Cheryl Lenser

Proofreader
Jennifer Gallant

Publishing Coordinator
Raina Chrobak

Cover Designer
Alan Clements

Compositor
Bumpy Design

To Raoul,
For nearly ten years as a team.

Contents

Forewords

By Robert C. Martin

I hate management books. I do. People give them to me all the time saying: "You should read this one, it changed my life!" These books are all about 150 pages. They have 14 point type, double-spaced. They have lots of pictures. They have titles like: *Open Locker Management, Management by not Managing, First Clean All The Glasses, Now Discover Your Knees, The Power of Positive Penalties,* and *Tnemeganam!* They sit on my shelves. I sometimes read them in the John.

They all tell the same story. The author is always some guy who was running a company and failing horribly. When he reaches "bottom" (remember, I read them in the John) he has a critical insight that no human has ever had before. When he describes this idea to others, they think he's crazy; but he tries it anyway, and makes a $1,000,000,000,000 (one trillion dollars—billions are so passé nowadays). And now, out of the goodness of his heart, he wants to share that idea with you (for a small fee) so that you can make your trillion.

These books are usually repetitive, simple-minded, and inane. They are written at a third-grade level for poor saps who think that *one simple insight* is all they need to fix their problems. These unfortunate dweebs hope, against all hope, that if they just read the latest blockbuster: *Blue Pants Management,* and then have everyone in the office wear blue pants on Thursdays, that their management problems will go away.

Like I said, I hate management books. So why am I writing the foreword to a management book? I am writing the foreword to *this* management book because *this* book has the word *Eukaryotic* in it! What does "Eukaryotic" mean? That's not important. The point is that this book has words in it that have more than three syllables! This book talks about the *Red Queen Race* hypothesis. This book has depictions of *tesseracts.* This book talks about *Drunkard's Walks.* In short, this book is *smart!*

Just take a look at the table of contents. You'll see topics like *Complex Systems Theory, Game Theory, Cybernetics, Self-Organization,* and *The Darkness Principle.* You'll see that the author covers issues from team-size and motivation to scaling organizations up vs. scaling them out.

When you read this book you can tell that the author has done his homework. This is not just a simple-minded anecdote about how some old football player turned a department around. Rather, this book is a serious compilation of management ideas, techniques, and disciplines that have been accumulating for over a century. The author has taken these ideas and synthesized them with the *Agile Software Development* movement to form a *memeplex*, an interconnected system of ideas that every student of management will want to absorb. This book is not written for those who want a quick fix. This book is written for *serious* students who have a passion and love for management. This book is written for management craftsmen.

By Ed Yourdon

A long time ago, in a galaxy far far away, my colleagues and I proudly proclaimed that we were the young revolutionaries of the computer field, ushering in a new generation of methods and techniques for software programming, design, and analysis—which seemed to go hand-in-hand with the top-down, command-and-control management approach that prevailed at the time. We weren't clever enough to label our ideas "Software 2.0" in the fashion that subsequent advocates of "Web 2.0" and "Enterprise 2.0" have done ... but in any case, Jurgen Appelo's new book, *Management 3.0*, tells me that my generation has been consigned to the dustheap of history.

The issue here, and the subject of Jurgen's book, is not really about software development techniques—though the "Agile" development approach that has been growing ever more popular during the past decade does reject the idea that the requirements and architecture for a complex system can be developed in a strictly linear fashion, by following a top-down, hierarchical, deterministic approach. In a complex world where the end-users are not really sure what they want their system to do, and where everything around the users is changing all during the development of that system, we do need an orderly (dare I say "structured"?) approach to develop the boundaries and overall framework of the user's system—but many of the details will remain unknown and unknowable unless an "emergent" approach allows them to be discovered at the right time.

If that is true of the technical job of analyzing, designing, and implementing systems—and I firmly believe it is—then it is also true of the management approach that organizes, motivates, monitors, constrains, and (hopefully) rewards the people who carry out those technical tasks. So the top-down hierarchical style of management that corresponded to our top-down hierarchical "structured" approach to analysis and design in the 1970s is now being referred to as "Management 1.0"; and Jurgen tells us that there was also a phase known as "Management 2.0" that largely consisted of fads (like "Business Process Reengineering" and "Six Sigma") and add-ons to the earlier Management 1.0 approach.

But Management 3.0, which Jurgen's book discusses in detail, is based on complexity theory. It's something that mathematicians and biologists have been studying for the past few decades, and it's now becoming a central part of economics and sociology—and, more generally, management of people and their relationships in an organization. You really need to read Jurgen's summary of this concept—and the related ideas of causality, determinism, and reductionism – because almost anyone whose education has focused on engineering, mathematics, and/or computer science has been inculcated with these ideas from an early age.

With this grounding, you'll be ready for Jurgen's "model" of modern management, which he portrays as a six-eyed monster named Martie—with a separate "eye" for viewing people, empowerment, alignment, improvement, competence, and structure. You'll need to plow through two more introductory chapters in which Jurgen summarizes Agile software development and complex systems theory, but after that he devotes two full chapters to each of these six components of the Management 3.0 approach.

You won't find any of the "traditional" project-management stuff about risk management, estimating, scheduling, and monitoring progress with Microsoft Project; indeed, there is no mention at all of Microsoft Project in this book, and you won't find any references to the standard textbooks on risk management or estimating of schedules and budgets for projects. Those traditional activities still have to be carried out in most cases, and you probably should take a Project Management 101 course to make sure you understand them; but the essence of Jurgen's presentation is that even if you do a perfect job at carrying out the basics of Project Management 101, it's not enough to guarantee success. (Indeed, it may even aggravate the problem of complexity, and help you arrive at a disaster sooner than before!)

You can read the chapters of Jurgen's book somewhat independently, and perhaps even out of sequence—but I recommend that you read them all, and digest them slowly. There is an enormous amount of good advice, practical checklists, and wise counsel (how did someone so young become so wise?) on the nuances of leading, motivating, coaching, and communicating with individual developers, project teams, and the higher-level executives who are often still "stuck" in older ways of managing (e.g., the ones who insist on referring to the employees in their organization as "resources"). You may be tempted to treat some of his advice as glib one-liners (e.g., the advice in Chapter 4 that innovation is a bottom-up phenomenon, and that it cannot be mandated from the top), but if you read the book carefully, you'll see that it's a very sophisticated (and well-researched) discussion of the nuances involved in balancing things like self-organization versus anarchy.

I was amused to see Jurgen's statement, relatively early in his book, that he "wish[ed] a book like this had been available (or known) to me when I created my Internet start-up ten years ago. But then I might have become a millionaire and probably wouldn't have bothered writing this book in the first place." I feel the same way: I wish this book had been available (or known) to me when I first stumbled into the software field some 45 years ago, or at least when someone foolishly promoted me into a project-management position two years later. But then I too might have become a millionaire and probably wouldn't have bothered writing the foreword for this book.

Seriously, the only real problem I foresee with Jurgen's book is that the managers of my generation are still alive, and because the recent financial crisis reduced their 401(k) pension plans to a 201(k) or a 101(k), they're still working—and they're still doing their best to impose a rigid, top-down hierarchical management style on their subordinates. It's also problematic that managers of Jurgen's generation are moving into positions of power—because many of them have been brainwashed into following a top-down hierarchical management approach for such a long time, and they, too, may resist the ideas of Management 3.0.

But if the growing popularity of Agile software development techniques is any indication, it's only a matter of time before the equally Agile management techniques espoused by Jurgen Appelo in Management 3.0 become equally popular. And if you're determined to become an "Agile manager" for dealing successfully with today's ever-more-complex projects, then while Jurgen's book will certainly not be the only book you read, it may well be the first book that you read on the subject.

And more important, it's likely to be the book that you return to, over and over again. I firmly believe that Management 3.0 will become the "Bible" of Agile management books in the decade ahead.

Acknowledgments

Thank you. These are perhaps the only two words in the English language that can never be wrong. Never inappropriate. Never useless. And all too often forgotten. But not this time.

Thank you, Mike Cohn, for reading my blog and asking me to be the sixth author in your great signature series and for answering each of my many questions (sometimes within the hour.)

Thank you, fellow authors, Lyssa Adkins, Lisa Crispin, Janet Gregory, Clinton Keith, Roman Pichler, and Kenny Rubin, for making me feel part of a team. And for sharing your experiences, so I could learn without stumbling (too much).

Thank you, early reviewers of my book: Andrew Woodward, Angelo Anolin, Cory Foy, David Harvey, David Moran, Diana Larsen, Esther Derby, Florian Hoornaar, Geoffrey Lowney, Israel Gat, J.B. Rainsberger, Jacopo Romei, Jared Richardson, Jens Schauder, Jim Highsmith, Johanna Rothman, John Bauer, Kelly Waters, Lisa Crispin, Louis Dietvorst, Marcin Floryan, Markus Andrezak, Mendelt Siebenga, Mike Cohn, Mike Cottmeyer, Nico van Hemert, Olav Maassen, Paul Klipp, Paul Stalenhoef, Pawel Brodzinski, Phillip Ghadir, Radu Davidescu, Ramkumar KB, Robert van Kooten, Russell Healy, Ruud Cox, Scott Duncan, Stephen Hill, Vasco Duarte, Yves Hanoulle, and Zachary Spencer. Your valuable (and sometimes painful) contributions made this book, and its accompanying website, a whole lot better. There were times I even agreed with you.

Thank you, Chris Guzikowski, Raina Chrobak, Sheri Cain, Andy Beaster, and all other smart people at Addison-Wesley, for your patience in working with this first-time author and explaining how book production works (probably for the 1,000th time.)

Thank you, Stephan Meijer, Lennert Ouwerkerk, Raj Menon, and other friends, colleagues, and contacts for your help during the writing of this book. Many little favors together are one big contribution.

Thank you, Mrs. Stappers, for teaching me English. Fortunately, the online dictionaries made up for the many times I didn't learn my words.

Thank you, my friends, Amnon, Floris, Erik, Femke, Nadira, Devika, Rudie, Niels, Hanneke, Trudie, Jeroen, and Arno. It is rare to find people genuinely interested in another person's passion.

Thank you, my (former) colleagues at ISM eCompany. I spent seven years learning how (not) to manage software teams. Sorry about my crappy code and email bombs.

Thank you, Alistair Cockburn, Artem Marchenko, Brian Marick, Christopher Avery, Corey Haines, Dennis Stevens, Elisabeth Hendrickson, George Dinwiddie, Joseph Pelrine, Karl Scotland, Mike Vizdos, Philippe Kruchten, Ron Jeffries, and many, many other bloggers and writers I've had the pleasure of meeting in person. You've all been inspiring and extremely helpful for this weird new kid on the block.

Thank you, Ed Yourdon and Bob Martin, for supporting this first-time author with your generous forewords. Someday I will return the favor. (If you need a cartoon, let me know.)

Thank you, blog readers and Twitter followers. Your continued support, and your many questions and answers, helped me to keep going.

Thank you, Raoul, for giving me the time and space to write this book. A system can only self-organize within boundaries. I'm sure my project was able to grow and flourish because of your gentle boundaries.

And thank you, dear reader, for opening this book. If you like it, please tell me. If not, please don't.

About the Author

Jurgen Appelo is a writer, speaker, trainer, developer, entrepreneur, manager, blogger, reader, dreamer, leader, and freethinker. And he's Dutch, which explains his talent for being weird.

After studying software engineering at the Delft University of Technology, and earning his Master's degree in 1994, Jurgen busied himself either starting up or leading a variety of Dutch businesses, always in the position of team leader, manager, or executive.

Jurgen's most recent occupation was CIO at ISM eCompany, one of the largest e-business solution providers in The Netherlands. As a manager, Jurgen has experience in leading software developers, development managers, project managers, quality managers, service managers, and kangaroos, some of which he hired accidentally.

He is primarily interested in software development and complexity theory, from a manager's perspective. As a writer, he has published papers and articles in many magazines, and he maintains a blog at www.noop.nl. As a speaker, he is regularly invited to talk at seminars and conferences.

Last but not least, Jurgen is a trainer, with workshops based on the Management 3.0 model. His materials address the topics of energizing people, empowering teams, aligning constraints, developing competence, growing structure, and improving everything.

However, sometimes he puts all writing, speaking, and training aside to do some programming himself, or to spend time on his ever-growing collection of science fiction and fantasy literature, which he stacks in a self-designed book case that is four meters high.

Jurgen lives in Rotterdam (The Netherlands)—and sometimes in Brussels (Belgium)—with his partner Raoul. He has two kids and an imaginary hamster called George.

Preface

This book is about **Agile management**, the managerial counterpart to Agile software development. I believe that Agile management is under-represented in the Agile world. There are many dozens of books for Agile developers, testers, coaches, and project managers, but next to none exist for Agile managers and team leaders. However, when organizations adopt Agile practices, it is imperative that team leaders and development managers learn a better approach to leading and managing their teams.

Studies indicate that management is the biggest obstacle in transitions to Agile software development [VersionOne 2009]. For software teams, it is hard to be Agile and implement processes such as Scrum, XP, or Kanban when their "leaders" are stuck in old-fashioned management styles. Managers need to understand what their new role is in the 21st century, and how to get the best out of Agile software teams. This book aims at managers who want to become agile, and Agile developers who want to learn about management.

What makes this a unique management book is that it is grounded in science and leans heavily on complex systems theory. Unlike other (general) management books, it will not ask you to open your heart, hold hands, and sing "Kumbaya." Many managers, particularly in technical businesses, are "left-brainers," with a preference for logical, rational, analytical thought. So I wrote a book that appeals, hopefully, to left-brainers. But the right-brainers among you shouldn't fear! The scientific references in this book are explored in a casual manner, with plenty of explanations, metaphors, pictures, and at least two jokes that are actually funny.

One important goal I had for this book was to be *descriptive*, instead of *prescriptive*. Its purpose is to make you understand how organizations and Agile teams work, so you can solve your own problems. The world is too complex to give you merely a list of practices to follow. What managers in the 21st century need most is *insight* so that they can develop their own prescriptions for their own particular needs [Mintzberg 2004:252].

Story of This Book

It took me ten years to produce this book. In the first half of that decade, I took an interest in both Agile software development, and complexity theory (I can't remember which was first,) and the authors of books on Agile and complexity could hardly keep up with my thirst for inspiration. While reading their materials I started seeing a bigger picture. I saw that Agile software development was the practical implication of treating software teams and projects as complex systems, and that few authors used or even acknowledged that link in their writings (with Jim Highsmith and Ken Schwaber as notable exceptions). And so, somewhere in 2005, I tried writing my own book about it. But I failed, miserably. I had texts, but no readers. New ideas, but no feedback. Many theories, but little experience. And great enthusiasm, but no stamina.

In the meantime, throughout that decade, I managed software development teams and gained a lot of experience in the many ways to do this wrong. And while being a manager, and introducing Agile practices in several organizations, I wondered about management in Agile software development. I was certain that managers and team leaders had important roles to play. But the books didn't tell me what they were.

Then in January 2008, I started writing my blog, NOOP.NL, with the explicit purpose of getting feedback from people about my ideas on software development, management, and complexity, and to check whether people were interested in that kind of stuff. And they were! Within 1½ years readership grew to 4,000 subscribers. I participated in inspiring discussions with many experts around the world, and my appearances at various conferences in Europe and the United States were also well received. And so it appeared I had found my niche.

In August 2009, just after the global financial crisis hit us, I saw the time was right for a second attempt at writing a book. This time it was easy. I had an archive of blog posts, useful feedback from readers, a decade of management experience (mostly of things that *didn't* work,) plenty of time (because business was slow), and a large enough following to motivate several publishers to send me a contract. Then, after signing my first book contract ever, it was only a matter of doubling my research, tripling my thinking, and quadrupling my output. (Somehow this sounds easier than it was.)

You will notice that I am neither an Agile consultant nor a complexity scientist, and this is both my strength and weakness. My strength is that I rarely suffer from tunnel vision. My thinking is not "tainted" or steered by specific sciences, methods, or preferred solutions. I was always good at seeing patterns across multiple domains, ever since I was ten years old and my teacher advised me to seek a career in problem analysis. My weakness is that I sometimes suffer from helicopter vision. I lack the detailed knowledge of scientists, and the deep experience of consultants who've seen dozens of businesses from the inside. Fortunately, I seem to have developed a knack at writing simple, unexpected, concrete, credible, and emotional stories. An imperfect message told well is more useful than a perfect message nobody cares to read.

While I wrote this book, I used my blog to get feedback on my imperfect messages, and my readers made sure that I was going in the right direction, helping me to improve my thinking, and telling me which of my ideas were useful, and which were not. This is the book I wanted to write for ten years. But, in a way, it is also the book my readers wanted to read.

Structure of This Book

You will not see case studies in this book or an extensive list of "standard" practices. Instead, you can read about research, metaphors, ideas, and suggestions. This won't make the book less useful. On the contrary, it is claimed that the biggest advancements are made when ideas from one domain are copied and adapted in another. You can learn at least as much from survival strategies in biological ecosystems as you can from case studies in other software businesses. Ideas are rarely a perfect match for your situation. It is you who can see if, and how, these ideas can be applied in your context.

This book is simple to use. You start at the front. That's the side with the picture on it. Then you start flipping and reading pages. Every time you finish reading a page, you flip it and continue with the next. At some point, you will arrive at a sturdy page that is completely blank. That is the end of the book.

Chapter 1 is the *introduction*. It describes how linear thinking often leads to incorrect conclusions. And it introduces the core idea of this book: the six views of the *Management 3.0 model*.

Chapters 2 and 3 give you an *overview* of *Agile software development* and *complex systems theory* respectively. They lay a double-sided foundation for Agile management, and the six views that follow in the next chapters.

Chapters 4 and 5 describe *Energize People*, the first view of the Management 3.0 model. One chapter does this from a theoretical side, and the other from a practical side. They describe that people are the most important parts of an organization and that managers must do all they can to keep people active, creative, and motivated.

Chapters 6 and 7 describe *Empower Teams*, the concept that teams can self-organize, which is the second view of the *Management 3.0 model*. This view requires empowerment, authorization, and trust. Again, the first chapter is mainly about theory, and the second is mainly about practice.

Chapters 8 and 9 explain the concept of *Align Constraints*, which is the realization that self-organization can lead to anything, and that it's therefore necessary to protect people and shared resources, and to give people a clear purpose and defined goals. It is the third view of the Management 3.0 model.

Chapters 10 and 11 present the problem that teams can't achieve their goals if team members aren't capable enough. Managers must therefore contribute to the development of people's skills and discipline. *Develop Competence* is the fourth view of the Management 3.0 model.

Chapters 12 and 13 describe that many teams operate within the context of a complex organization, and that it is important to consider the form of the social network through which communication flows. *Grow Structure* is the fifth view of the *Management 3.0 model*.

Chapters 14 and 15 address *Improve Everything*, the sixth and last view of the Management 3.0 model. This view, separated in a theoretical and practical chapter, just like the ones before, explains that people, teams, and organizations need to improve continuously to defer failure for as long as possible.

Finally, Chapter 16 is the *conclusion* of the book, in which the Management 3.0 model is reviewed and compared with a few other management models.

As you can see, the six views of the Management 3.0 model are described in two chapters each, where every time the nature of the first is more theoretical and the second is more practical. Though it is possible to read only the practical chapters about the "how" of Agile management, this means you'd miss the "why" described in the other ones.

There are few dependencies between the chapters. And so, *in theory*, you could read about the six management views in any order. However, *in practice*, it is probably easiest simply to start with the first one. I have not personally checked the flow of all 720 permutations of reading the six views in any order.

Within each chapter, you may sometimes notice that different topics are only weakly connected. This is by design. I found it important that the six views of the Management 3.0 model, and the separation of theory versus practice, were the constraints for the structure of this book. Self-organization within each chapter, and tightening the seams between topics, was sometimes a challenge. But I think I succeeded well enough. And I hope that the eyes of the viewers are, as with many other creative products, more forgiving than those of the creator.

Contents of This Book

The text of this book was written with the beta version of Microsoft Word 2010. The illustrations have all been hand drawn by me, scanned into the computer, and colored with Paint.NET. Sometimes you see a grey box showing a question or remark, followed by a brief answer. Most of these are based on feedback I got from readers of my blog and reviewers of early drafts of the book. I also included plenty of footnotes with hyperlinks to external resources. I took control of external hyperlinks by using a URL shortener, so I can update them whenever a resource has moved elsewhere. Among these hyperlinks are many links to the Wikipedia website. Some people believe linking to Wikipedia is bad practice, but I disagree. I'd rather link directly to a topic that is continuously being improved than referring to part of a dead tree that is hard to obtain because it is either expensive or out of stock.

To prevent accusations of flying high without getting my feet dirty, I made sure that the "practical" chapters are, in total, bigger than the "theory" chapters. Furthermore, at the end of each chapter, you can find suggestions for "reflection and action," which should make the book even more practical.

It is often said that metaphors greatly improve people's ability to understand abstract concepts, which is why I use so many of them. In this book you see development managers compared to gardeners, wizards, traffic managers, and other interesting people. The original title for this book was *The Abstract Gardener*. But I decided to replace that title, because metaphors tend to break when stretched too far, which is why I now prefer to use different ones in different situations.

This book has an accompanying website at management30.com. On this website, you can find additional materials (that didn't make it into the book), the original illustrations (which you are free to steal for your own purposes), contributions from readers, and links to other resources related to Agile management, software development, and complexity theory. Best of all, the site enables you to discuss each individual topic of this book with other readers, which turns this static book into the social conversation and opportunity for learning that it intends to be. Go to mgt30.com/toc/ and add your own comments, ideas, and links for the many topics discussed in this book.

About the Title

Management 3.0 is a strange name. But I believe that the "3.0" number conveys the right message about the direction that management is taking in the 21st century.

Management 1.0 = Hierarchies

Some people call it scientific management, whereas others call it command-and-control. But the basic idea is the same: An organization is designed and managed in a top-down fashion, and power is in the hands of the few. Those at the top of the hierarchy have the highest salaries, the biggest egos, and the most expensive chairs. Those at the bottom have little money, few responsibilities, and no motivation to do a good job.

To compensate for the danger of their high positions, the top executives are allowed to play with bonuses that, in many cases, have far more effect on personal wealth than organizational performance. As a side effect, dangerous bonus schemes also contributed to a worldwide financial implosion. Oops.

We can safely conclude that Management 1.0, even though it is still the most widespread version of management in the world, has a number of serious flaws. It is old, outdated, and in need of an upgrade.

Management 2.0 = Fads

Some people realized that Management 1.0 doesn't work well out-of-the-box, so they created numerous add-on models and services with a semi-scientific status, like the Balanced Scorecard, Six Sigma, Theory of

Constraints, and Total Quality Management. Being add-ons to Management 1.0, these models assume that organizations are managed from the top, and they help those at the top to better "design" their organizations. Sometimes it works; sometimes it doesn't.

In the meantime other models and services focus on the craft and art of management. Many books, such as *The One-Minute Manager*, *The 21 Laws of Leadership*, and *Good to Great*, have presented basic principles and guidelines for managers, and tell them to practice and build experience. Again, they are sometimes right, and sometimes not. And they replace each other faster than the diapers on a toddler.

Management 2.0 is just Management 1.0 with a great number of add-ons to ease the problems of an old system. But the architecture of Management 2.0 is still the same outdated hierarchy.

Management 3.0 = Complexity

The last few decades saw the birth and rise of complexity theory, first applied to mathematics and biology and later to economics and sociology. It was a major breakthrough. Stephen Hawking thought it was so important that he called the 21st century the "century of complexity."

One important insight is that all organizations are networks. People may draw their organizations as hierarchies, but that doesn't change that they are actually networks. Second, social complexity shows us that management is primarily about people and their relationships, not about departments and profits.

Many of us already knew that "leadership" is just a trendy name for managers doing the right thing and doing things right. But complexity thinking adds a new dimension to our existing vocabulary. It makes us realize that we should see our organizations as living systems, not as machines.

It is nice to have a new name. Names can be powerful. The "3.0" version indicates that management needs changing. It usually takes Microsoft three major releases of a product to get things right. I believe that management has, in its third incarnation, finally found a solid scientific foundation. The earlier add-ons are still valuable. But we have to replace assumptions of hierarchies with networks, because the 21st century is the Age of Complexity.

About the Subtitle

The subtitle of this book, "Leading Agile Developers, Developing Agile Leaders" points at the topic of *leadership*…a term often used incorrectly. There are two kinds of people misinterpreting leadership. I call them the "princes" and the "priests."

Leadership Princes

Some people claim that "leadership is different from management," in the sense that leadership is about inspiration, whereas management is about execution. They suggest leadership takes place on a "higher level" than management. And I cringe every time I see a company presenting their executives as "our leadership."

This view disregards that any person can be a leader in some way. Every employee, from the top executive to the bottom developer, can inspire others and give them direction. It also ignores that shareholders need executives to *manage* their business. By definition, leaders have no power of authority over their followers. Why would a shareholder give money to a "leader" with no authority? It makes no sense.

Unfortunately, for executives it is trendy to call themselves "leaders," no matter whether anyone is following them. Top managers use "leadership" as a social myth to reinforce their positions in the management hierarchy [Hazy 2007:110]. I call them *leadership princes* (and princesses) because they think their position makes them more qualified than others to lead people and because they value shiny objects over common sense.

Leadership Priests

Other people claim that "management is not needed." They refer to social networks, Wikipedia, Linux, and other great achievements of social groups that shared a purpose and made things happen. They suggest that "self-organizing" people don't need managers, only leaders with a vision.

Unfortunately, this view ignores that none of these examples are about businesses. If nobody *owns* the assets of an organization, nobody is needed to *manage* them. But a business does have assets. Shareholders won't appreciate it when self-organization spontaneously changes their biotech business into a catering service. Whether employees need managers is irrelevant. It is the shareholders who need managers of their business. Self-organization is devoid of value. It takes someone with an interest in its outcomes to decide whether the results of self-organization are "good" or "bad."

But alas, some people think hierarchies are "bad," and self-organization is "good." I call them leadership priests (and priestesses) because they preach a belief in something that is "good," whereas (as this book shows you) there are no scientific grounds for that belief.

Leadership Pragmatists

Reality requires us to be pragmatic about management and leadership. Every business has to be managed on behalf of its owners. And yes, managers *should* have leadership capabilities. But many leadership roles can be assumed by self-organizing (nonmanaging) people throughout the organization. And these informal leaders should understand that self-organization is subject to a little direction from the owners. This happens by passing authority around, through managers.

If you're like me, neither a prince nor a priest, you're among the commoners. I will call you a leadership pragmatist. You understand that the management hierarchy is a basic necessity (but nothing to brag about) and that the bulk of the work is done in a social network of peers: leaders and followers. Communication flows through the network. Authorization flows through the hierarchy.

I wrote this book for the pragmatists....

Chapter 1

Why Things Are Not That Simple

For every complex problem there is an answer that is clear, simple, and wrong.

—H.L. Mencken, journalist, writer (1880–1956)

On paper, I was once a millionaire. Informal investors valued my Internet start-up at 10 million Euros, and I owned 70 percent of the financial fiction they created around me. I was even awarded the title of *Entrepreneur of the Year,*[1] because I was so good at conveying my vision. And my colorful diagrams of expected revenues and profits looked fabulous, on paper.

But the money that the investors and I put in did not result in more profits. The extra content we created did not bring more visitors to our site. The programmers we hired did not significantly increase our speed of development. And the deals we made with other sites did not result in increased revenues. Actually, we were earning *less* than before the first round of investments. I'm sure you wouldn't even know the name of our less-than-glorious site if I told you. We created as much buzz as a fruit fly in a hurricane. And when the dot-com bubble burst, it wiped out our little venture, including all the other startups around us.

But we had fun. And we learned. Oh, how we learned! If it's true that people learn from mistakes, then by now, I must be quite close to the status of an Omniscient Being. As a development manager, team leader, project manager, and software developer, I made so many mistakes that I find it strange I didn't bring the entire Internet down with me. But learn we did.

And that is also my hope for you when you read this book. That you learn from my mistakes and from the mistakes of many others before me. One of the things I learned this past decade is that **Agile software development**[2] (see Chapter 2, "Agile Software Development") is the best way

---

1   Dutch press release of Millidian, dated December 15, 1999, is available via http://www.mgt30.com/millidian/.
2   http://www.mgt30.com/agile/.

to develop software. But I've also learned that old-style management is the biggest obstacle to the adoption of Agile software development around the world. Well, I assume that you are either a manager or someone interested in management. Perhaps you are a software developer, a CTO, a team leader, or a tester with management capabilities. It doesn't matter for now. What's important is that you want to learn about management–*Agile* management. And you will, I promise. This book teaches you how to be a good Agile manager and how to grow an Agile organization. We'll get there soon enough, but *not* without a solid foundation, which requires that you first learn about people and systems. And the way people *think* about systems. Why, you may wonder? Well, because doctors learn how human bodies work. Because pilots learn how planes work. And because software engineers learn how computers work. That's why managers must learn how social systems work.

One thing *I* learned, painfully, is that no matter what you plan for the system, it is not going to happen. The world doesn't work that way. The system you live in doesn't care about your plans. You may think that A leads to B, and in theory, you might even be right. But theory rarely works in practice, and *predictability* has a devious sister named *complexity*.

But I'm getting ahead of myself. As I explain later, humans prefer to understand things in a linear way, which means it might be best to use a linear approach for this story. And the story of this book starts with causality. This chapter investigates causality and nonlinearity and ends with the introduction of the Management 3.0 model.

Causality

The idea that things happen as we've planned (as I had hoped when I was a paper millionaire) has its roots in our innate preference for **causal determinism**. This is "the thesis that future events are necessitated by past and present events combined with the laws of nature."[3] Causal determinism tells us that each thing that happens is caused by other things that happened before. Logically this means that if we know all about our current situation, and we know all variants of one thing leading to another, we can predict future events by calculating them from prior events and natural laws. You can catch a ball when it is thrown at you because you can predict in which direction it is going. It is how you know what little

---

3 http://www.mgt30.com/determinism/.

will be left of your monthly salary after going out with your friends; or how you learned the best ways to make your brother or sister mad and get away with it.

In the scientific world, causal determinism has been a tremendous success, enabling scientists to accurately predict a huge range of events and phenomena. For example, using Newtonian physics, they predict that Halley's Comet will return to our solar system in 2061.[4] Such a scientific prediction is astronomically more reliable than the doomsday predictions that keep shifting every time the last one failed. The scientific method of calculating future events from past events and natural laws was so successful that philosopher Immanuel Kant promoted universal causal determinism as a necessary condition for all scientific knowledge [Prigogine, Stengers 1997:4].

Causal determinism enables software developers to design, plan, and predict what their software will do in its production environment. They write or modify their code to define or change the future behavior of the system after compilation and deployment. If we ignore bugs, operating system crashes, power failures, account managers, and other environmental hazards for the moment, we can say that these developers' predictions are often quite accurate. Causality enabled me to predict, quite accurately, that my startup would go under if we didn't find more customers.

But strange as it seems, causality is not enough. Although we can predict the return of Halley's Comet, and the behavior of a piece of software when it's in production, we cannot accurately predict next month's weather. And neither can we predict the full combination of features, qualities, time, and resources of a software project, or (pity me) the time of arrival of new customers.

What is the difference?

Complexity

If predictability is the friendly and reliable son of the neighbors next door, **complexity** is his unfathomable and unruly little sister. Predictability enables you to go to work, make appointments, play sports, and watch TV, whereas complexity frequently turns that same interaction between you and the world into an unpredictable and unmanageable mess, full of unexpected issues and surprises.

---

4 http://www.mgt30.com/halley/.

People sometimes confuse complexity with large numbers (like many things going on at the same time), but complex things aren't always large. Take one water molecule, for example. (Figuratively speaking of course, or else it would require a significant amount of practice.) The water molecule is made up of only two hydrogen atoms and one oxygen atom. That's not really a big thing, is it? Still, the combination of just those three atoms leads to unexpected behavior of water molecules in the form of strange effects in fluidity, density, and other physical and chemical phenomena [Solé 2000:13], that cannot be (easily) explained in terms of the individual atoms (see Figure 1.1). Complexity doesn't necessarily follow from large numbers. Only three water molecules are enough to produce complex behavior, as indicated by the famous **three–body problem**.[5]

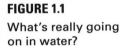

FIGURE 1.1

What's really going on in water?

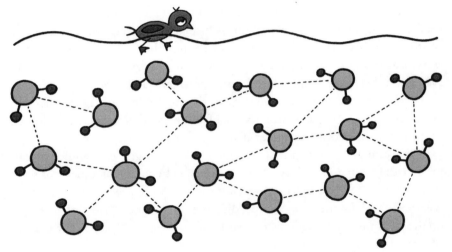

Fortunately, science hasn't stood still since Kant's enthusiastic support of causal determinism. Dynamical systems theory, chaos theory, network theory, game theory, and several other branches of science have made great strides in explaining *why* some phenomena are unpredictable, and why many events simply cannot be planned or calculated and just have to be experienced and observed. The total body of scientific research into complex systems is sometimes collectively referred to as the **complexity sciences** (see Chapter 3, "Complex Systems Theory").

Although causality successfully ruled the sciences from as early as the 17th century, complexity is a product of the 20th century that significantly

---

5   http://www.mgt30.com/euler/.

gained momentum since **complexity theory**[6] became a scientific discipline in its own right near the end of the century. Theoretical physicist Stephen Hawking was quoted as saying that the 21st century is the century of complexity [Chui 2000].

Complexity theory is good news for managers, team leaders, and project managers (and all other kinds of "leaders" and "managers") in software development organizations. It means that there's a new *scientific* way of looking at complex systems, a topic that includes the problem of building software and managing organizations. Though I'm afraid this revelation came 10 million Euros too late for me, I agree with Stephen Hawking that complexity is one of the most important concepts for the 21st century.

Our Linear Minds

Unfortunately, we are faced with a slight inconvenience when applying complexity theory to problem solving: Our minds prefer causality over complexity. The article *"Born Believers: How your brain creates God"* [Brooks 2009] describes how the human mind has an overdeveloped sense of cause and effect, which primes us to see purpose and design everywhere, even where there is none. The article describes that children believe pointy rocks exist for animals to scratch themselves on, and rivers exist so boats have something to float on. It appears that the human brain is wired to find purpose and causality in everything. We attribute cause and effect to all things around us, even when there's no reason to.

> "You see bushes rustle, you assume there's somebody or something there"[....] This over-attribution of cause and effect probably evolved for survival. If there are predators around, it is no good spotting them 9 times out of 10. Running away when you don't have to is a small price to pay for avoiding danger when the threat is real.[7]

Our minds are wired to favor what I call "linear thinking" (assuming predictability in cause and effect) over "nonlinear thinking" (assuming things are more complex than that.) We are accustomed to stories being told linearly, from start to finish. School taught us linear equations and

---

6   http://www.mgt30.com/complex-systems/.
7   Brooks, Michael. "Born believers: How your brain creates God." New Scientist, February 4, 2009. http://www.mgt30.com/believers/. [Brooks 2009:32]

largely ignored the much more ubiquitous nonlinear equations simply because they're too hard to solve. We accept "he did it" much more easily than "well, some things just happen." Whenever there's a problem B, we assume that event A caused it. The financial crisis is caused by bankers; the loss of jobs is caused by immigrants; the bad atmosphere at work is caused by the manager; the melting polar ice is caused by CO2 emissions; and the team didn't make the deadline because someone screwed things up. Our linear thinking minds see the world as a place full of easily explainable events with simple causes and simple effects. Gerald Weinberg called it the **Causation Fallacy** [Weinberg 1992:90].

Our mental addiction to causal determinism has led people to use *control* in their attempts to make sure that the *right* events are separated from the wrong ones. After all, if we know that situation A leads to event B, while situation A' leads to event C, and C is better than B, then we have to only force A into A' and things will turn out for the better. Or so it seems.

Engineers and other people with technical minds are particularly susceptible to the concept of control. It was engineers who developed **scientific management**,[8] the command-and-control style of management that has been all the rage since the early 20th century. And it was engineers who devised the kind of control systems that we still find in many organizations today [Stacey 2000a:7]. We all know by now that these control systems work adequately only with repetitive tasks that don't require much thinking. But they *don't* work with creative product development! It seems fair to expect from engineers that they try to pull people out of the management swamp that they got everyone into.

Causality in management makes managers look for causes that would produce the outcomes exactly as they need them, through careful upfront design, and meticulous top-down planning. The bigger the organization, the larger the effort to deconstruct and reconstruct the entire system to achieve the desired goals.

In the past, I have willfully created my own illusions of upfront design and top-down planning. My award-winning business plan was at least 30 pages of carefully crafted nonsense. It described in detail how we were going to get rich. We believed in it then. I had written it myself, so it had to be true.

---

8 http://www.mgt30.com/scientific-management/.

Reductionism

The approach of deconstructing systems into their parts and analyzing how these parts interact to make up the whole is called **reductionism**.[9] It is the idea that "phenomena can be explained completely in terms of other, more fundamental phenomena." We can deconstruct an airplane and understand how it works by studying all its parts; we can understand a software system by analyzing its code; and nowadays scientists attempt to understand diseases and defects by analyzing the human genome, hoping to find individual genes that are "responsible" for all kinds of "problems."

The reductionist approach works well but only down to a point (see Figure 1.2). After many decades of study, scientists still don't understand how human consciousness works. Despite more than a hundred years of economic theories, economists still don't have models that accurately predict a financial crisis. The many theories used to model climate change vary immensely in their predicted consequences of global warming. And though we have plenty of models for software development, projects all over the world are still suffering from unpredictable results. Organisms, human consciousness, economies, climates, and software projects all behave in ways that cannot be predicted by deconstructing them and studying the parts.

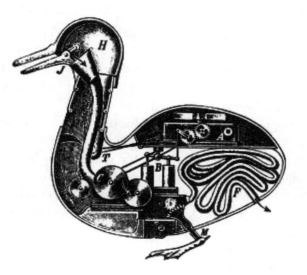

FIGURE 1.2
Reductionism
taken a bit too far.[10]

---

9 http://www.mgt30.com/reductionism/.
10 Figure from Wikipedia, in the public domain: http://www.mgt30.com/duck/.

AND PEOPLE ARE BAD INTERPRETERS, TOO

Several of my book reviewers pointed out to me that people are notoriously bad at interpreting their environment. We humans tend to ignore the things we don't believe in, and we disregard anything that doesn't match our mental models. This also contributes to us not accurately predicting what is actually going to happen.

Holism

Holism[11] is the idea that the behavior of a system cannot be fully determined by its component parts alone. Instead, the system as a whole determines in an important way how the system behaves. It is often seen as the opposite of reductionism, although complexity scientists believe that complexity is the bridge between the two, and both are necessary but insufficient [Corning 2002:69].

Even some of the staunchest of reductionists discard the idea that all phenomena can be explained in terms of their parts. Philosopher Daniel Dennet coined the term **greedy reductionism**[12] [Dennett 1995] to mean the forms of reductionist thinking where a phenomenon is explained *away* in favor of its underlying parts. For example, the argument that hyperlinks are "nothing more than electrons and hyperlinks don't really exist" would be a form of greedy reductionism. My own counter-argument to greedy reductionism would be that, if greedy reductionists are right, then greedy reductionists don't really exist either, which would annul their ridiculous arguments. But I digress.

The concept of **hierarchical reductionism**, a term suggested by evolutionary biologist Richard Dawkins [Dawkins 1996], aims for a middle ground with the view that complex systems can be described as a hierarchy, wherein each level can be described in terms of parts one level down in the hierarchy but not lower. This would effectively deny you the possibility of explaining that your project went all wrong because a bunch of quarks and leptons got in your way.

Many people falsely believe that the reductionist hypothesis implies a "constructionist" one, which would say that any system can be

---

11 http://www.mgt30.com/holism/.
12 http://www.mgt30.com/greedy-reductionism/.

constructed once we understand its parts. This is false because even if we fully understand all parts of a system, that doesn't mean that the whole is simply the sum of the parts [Miller, Page 2007:41]. Knowledge of the lower-level parts doesn't imply our ability to reconstruct the higher-level system. Even though we can apply reductionism to trace a problem back to its origins (of which the *root-cause analysis technique*[13] would be a fine example), interestingly enough we cannot apply a constructionist approach to build a system that *prevents* such problems from happening in the first place. For example, we can figure out why a human heart fails (reductionism) but we can never create a heart that won't fail (constructionism).

IS THERE NO VALUE IN ROOT-CAUSE ANALYSIS?

There is *plenty* of value in root-cause analysis. I mean that root-cause analysis can only look to the past. It helps you to fix problems that have already happened, so they won't happen again. But it won't help you to predict what *will* go wrong in the future.

Hierarchical Management

The holistic view and the hierarchical reductionist view both agree that not everything in a complex system can be explained by seeking causes in the lower levels within the system. They allow each level to have novel and *irreducible* properties. For example, no matter how hard you look, you won't find easily identifiable levers, knobs, and gears for walking, swimming, and quacking in a deconstructed duck (refer to Figure 1.2). Nevertheless, when you see it in the park, you will recognize it as a duck.

This has far-reaching consequences for managers of complex systems, like you and me, and many other development managers, project managers, and team leaders. It means that those who know all about one level of a hierarchical system may be unqualified to deal with lower or higher levels in that same system because those other levels require different kinds of knowledge. A molecular biologist may be "unqualified" as a gardener because understanding how biology works on the level of eukaryotic cells, genes, and RNA does not imply an understanding of how to tend a garden; whereas a gardener need not know a thing about chromosomes and genomes to do a good job at gardening. Similarly, the

---

13 http://www.mgt30.com/root-cause/.

CEO of an organization needs to know a lot about managing businesses, but he could be a complete no-no when it comes to coaching and other people management skills. (I'm sure plenty of readers can acknowledge firsthand experience with such circumstances.)

Managing organizations requires other kinds of knowledge and experience than managing people, although *some* knowledge of the underlying levels *might* be useful. Software engineer Joel Spolsky proposed the **Law of Leaky Abstractions** [Spolsky 2002] as an explanation of how parts in a system can manifest themselves in counterintuitive ways in the higher levels, which are supposed to abstract away the lower-level implementation details. Higher-level programming layers that suffer from events in their underlying implementations are considered leaky. Obscure error messages presented to users are another common effect of leaky abstractions in software (see Figure 1.3).

FIGURE 1.3
The result of a
leaky abstraction?

We can see similar problems in other complex systems. My conscious mind occasionally suffers from blackouts, déjà-vus, forgetfulness, random memories, and other weird effects that can be explained only as lower-level irregularities in my neural network leaking through to the higher level that I call my mind. But I don't have to analyze my neural pathways to put my consciousness to good use, although it is nice to learn from neurologists that the embarrassing quirks in my mind are actually quite common. Likewise, you don't need to fully understand assembly programming to write good higher-level programs, although *some* lower-level knowledge could make your life easier at times. With management, it is the same. A CEO doesn't need to be a great people manager to manage an organization when all the "people stuff" is delegated to a trusted management team. (Unlike development managers, project managers, and team leaders who need to be people managers on a daily basis.) But at least *some* people skills could come in handy for anyone in case lower-level problems come to the surface at higher levels (in other words, when things get leaky).

Agile Management

When hierarchical management embraces complexity and nonlinear thinking, we arrive at what I call **Agile management**. It is the logical companion to **Agile software development**, which is an approach to software development independently developed by several groups and individuals throughout the 1990s (see Chapter 2). It grew out of discontent with the many failures of the deterministic approach to software development, where tight control, upfront design and top-down planning resulted in many intensively managed but disastrously performing software projects.

Agile software development has (some of) its roots in complexity theory, acknowledging that causal determinism is insufficient when trying to deliver successful projects. Well-known Agile concepts such as *self-organization* and *emergence* are copied straight from complexity science literature [Schwaber, Beedle 2002], and Agile practitioners these days understand that it is impossible to prevent failure using a constructionist approach. Only by repeatedly accepting failure and subsequently purging its causes from the system you can steadily grow a software project and allow it to perform successfully. It's almost like growing up and raising children.

Despite tremendous success in terms of return on investment of Agile software projects [Rico 2009], many managers are responsible for obstructing the adoption of Agile project management and Agile software development in organizations around the world. Surveys on Agile adoption indicate that change management, organizational culture, managerial support, team education, and external pressure are the main obstacles to further Agile adoption and causing software projects to fail [VersionOne 2009]. And most of these are management responsibilities. Assuming the reports are correct (and I have no reason to believe they are not), it seems that managers all over the world are posing a problem instead of participating in the solution. And sadly, this is not a problem unique to Agile software development. It is the same with almost any substantive organizational change.

In this book, I take the stance that traditional management is usually the problem, not the solution, in any kind of change management, which is a view expressed many years earlier by W. Edwards Deming. That's why we need a theory for Agile management: a management theory closely fitting Agile software development.

My Theory of Everything

Is there some theory that can help managers by telling them what to do in an Agile environment? Over a number of decades, many management theories have been proposed, although most of those are not theories at all in the scientific sense [Lewin, Regine 2001:5]. A real scientific theory would not only identify some natural phenomena, but would also make assertions about observations in the real world, explaining what things to expect *before* they can be observed. This is where most management "theories" fall short. They are often not theories but techniques. Instead of offering a description of how the world works, they offer (useful) advice for dealing with problems and situations. The Theory of Constraints (TOC) is a good example. It is not a scientific theory but a management philosophy offering a process improvement technique for achieving goals by continuously focusing on constraints.

Does that mean I can now propose my own "theory" of Agile management, secretly hoping for a position among the likes of Porter, Deming, and Drucker? I'm afraid not.

Once I hoped to find a *Theory of Everything* for managing software teams. The theory would have described the principles of all software teams and would have helped people with a complete unified model for managing those teams. In hindsight, I think my mind suffered a giant leaky abstraction at the time.

Fortunately, I soon discovered that this goal was out of reach for two reasons. First, plenty of theories for people working together in teams are already available. The field is known as **social complexity**: the study of social groups as complex systems. (The book, *Small Groups as Complex Systems* [Arrow 2000] and the magazine, *Emergence: Complexity & Organization*[14] are recommendable publications in this field.) Second, complexity theory itself tells us that unified models of complex systems are impossible to create. Any attempt to create one model to fully describe a class of complex systems will always fail. It is a topic that I touch upon in Chapter 16, "All Is Wrong, But Some Is Useful," and one that made me feel a wave of relief when I discovered it: *It's not possible. Great! That means I can work on something else!* I can hardly think of a better example of failing early. (**Gödel's incompleteness theorems**[15] have shown that the same

---

14 The magazine E:CO is published by Emergent Publications; see http://www.mgt30.com/eco/.

15 http://www.mgt30.com/godel/.

impossibility applies to *all* unified theories. Perhaps we should be glad that scientists don't give up as easily as I do.)

The Book and the Model

This book can help you to become a better manager. In particular, it tells you what your responsibilities are as an *Agile manager* in an *Agile* organization executing Agile software development projects. And it gives you plenty of techniques to translate theory into daily practice. It shows you how to manage teams knowing that systems are usually complex, not linear, and how to focus on adaptability, not predictability. It doesn't make much difference if you are a development manager, team leader, CTO, or software developer. In the end we are all managers of the environment around us. Let's try and understand how to do that well.

The model used for this book is depicted in Figure 1.4. I call it Martie, the Management 3.0 model. Martie has six views on organizations. Each of these six views is described separately, in two chapters, from a theoretical side and a practical side. The Management 3.0 model is my representation of the different aspects of Agile management. But before we discuss its details, I think it is important to review the basics of its two

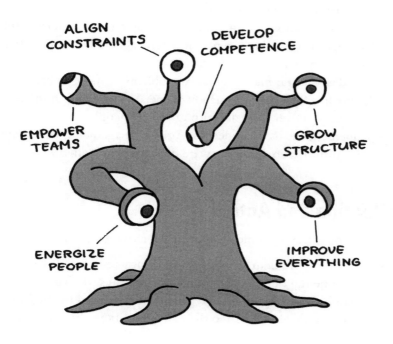

FIGURE 1.4

Martie, the Management 3.0 model.

components, *agility* and *complexity*, and to review a bit of their respective histories. Chapter 2 gives you a brief overview of Agile software development, whereas Chapter 3 takes a look at the foundations of complex systems theory. The "real meat," or how to manage software development teams using the six views of the Management 3.0 model, is discussed in the core of the book, which starts with Chapter 4, "The Information-Innovation System" and ends with Chapter 15, "How to Improve Everything." Finally, Chapter 16 provides a brief conclusion.

I only wish a book like this had been available (or known) to me when I created my Internet startup ten years ago. But then I *might* have become a millionaire and probably wouldn't have bothered writing this book. This seems to prove that career planning is often useless, and that failure can be a blessing in disguise.

Summary

The human brain is wired to assume that every event has an identifiable cause. This is called causality and is useful for prediction and planning. However, quite often things are more complex than they seem. Complexity science teaches us that applying linear thinking to complex problems can lead to painful mistakes.

Although reductionism (understanding a system by understanding its parts) has been successful in science, it is now generally accepted that reductionism can be taken too far.

For understanding many complex problems, a more holistic view is needed, which is the goal of the study of social complexity. It offers a holistic view on whatever happens with groups of people.

Management 3.0 is a model for Agile management, which applies complexity thinking to Agile software development teams.

Reflection and Action

Let's see if you can apply some ideas from this chapter to your organization:

- Review a problem on your list of things-to-solve. Try to imagine the cause of the problem. Are you sure that is the sole reason? How do you know? Have you discussed the problem with all stakeholders? Do they all agree about the single cause?

Try this simple mind exercise for each of your most important problems. Make sure you're not oversimplifying the complexity of the problems and that you're not addressing the wrong cause.

- If people in your organization use a root-cause analysis technique (like 5 Whys[16]) engage in a discussion with them about the bias these techniques have for simplistic cause-and-effect relationships. Many effects in complex systems have *multiple* causes and circular relationships between causes and effects. None of the causes are actually the root; therefore, root-cause analysis techniques may not capture the complexity of the world you live in. But a discussion with your competent colleagues can. Organize it.

---

16 http://www.mgt30.com/5-whys/

Chapter **2**

Agile Software Development

I get up every morning determined to both change the world and have one hell of a good time. Sometimes this makes planning my day difficult.

— E.B. White, American writer (1899–1985)

This chapter is optional reading for some of you. If you're familiar with Agile software development, you already know much (if not all) of what this chapter has to offer. The goal is to provide a concise overview of Agile software development, specifically for the readers who want to know a little more about the background and fundamentals of Agile *before* we start exploring what the role is of managers in Agile organizations (in Chapter 4, "The Information-Innovation System").

Throughout this book, I assume that you *do* know a little of the basics of Agile software development. But for now, just pretend that you believe XP is an old operating system, and keep on reading.

Prelude to Agile

Counting money is for me almost as much fun as spending it. In the early 1990s, when I studied at the Technical University in Delft, I created a bookkeeping program in my spare time. I did this because it was fun, despite the smallish inconvenience that I had no money to count at that time. Perhaps a dark corner of my mind secretly hoped that the millions would arrive automatically when I was ready to count them. But alas, they never did.

The product (about 30,000 lines of code) was created only by me. I had no formal methodology, little experience with building software, and no manager, coach, or mentor. But I had time, a computer, a vision, and an intense motivation to make a great product (see Figure 2.1).

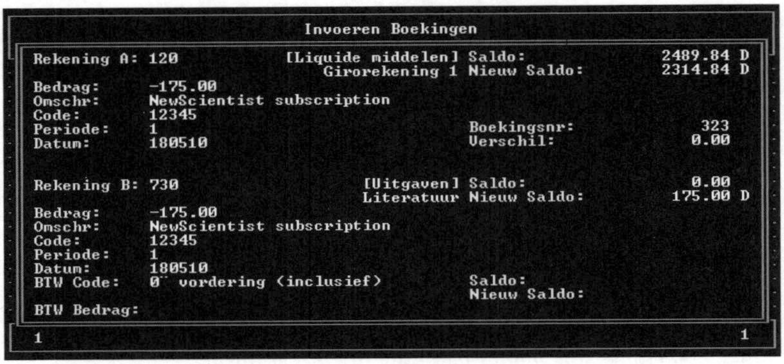

FIGURE 2.1

JEBS 2.0, my 20-year old bookkeeping program (in Dutch).

Amazingly, I sold the software to a few dozen customers, some of whom were astonished that bookkeeping software could be simple, friendly, and good-looking (for a program in 1990). And now, 20 years later, I am *still* using the same old program for my own bookkeeping. And in those 20 years that I've been using it, I found only three minor bugs.

How is this possible? How can an inexperienced programmer build something of such high quality that it works almost flawlessly for 20 years?

I have absolutely no idea.

But…I can list some circumstances that Agilists can recognize:

- **I built my product passionately**. I had some experience with bookkeeping applications and was convinced that they were digital minions from hell, trying to suck the life and soul out of users with each of their keystrokes. I had a vision that my program would be *different*. Unlike the other software in that business, mine would be a pleasure to use.

- **I was my own critical customer**. I built the program for *myself*, not for others. Sure, I was happy that I found some customers, even though they didn't bring me the millions that the dark part of me had been hoping for. But with everything I did, I made sure the product worked like *I* wanted it to work.

- **I had no plan, only a list of features**. I started with the features that I would need every day such as entering new transactions. Then I moved on to less-critical stuff such as balances and corrections. I ended with nice-to-haves such as Help pages and exports until I got tired of it all and simply announced that the product was ready.

- **I grew the process while building the product**. I followed a simple checklist for each procedure that I wrote, and that checklist steadily grew over time. I had never heard of unit testing, but with my checks and double-checks, my daily discipline could rival that of an airplane pilot.

So there you have it. I had motivation, a critical customer, no upfront plan, discipline, and a self-organized process. It didn't matter that I had never done something like that before. What mattered was that I was eager to learn.

Ten years after creating my bookkeeping program, I found out that (part of) the process I had used back then was suddenly being called "Agile software development." And now, ten years after learning about this, I am writing a book on one of Agile's missing ingredients. The scope of the book is about the same as the scope of my old bookkeeping program. And, like before, the dark part of my mind is ready to start counting.

The Book of Agile

In the beginning, engineers created computers and software. The software was formless and bad, and darkness was over the faces of users. And the engineers said, "Let there be structure," and there was structure.

Quite a lot of structure, actually.

In the last five or six decades, many software engineers have been concerned about the huge variety in quality of software produced with people's *ad-hoc* approaches to software development. And so they started creating. And what they came up with were *formal* approaches. The profession of **software engineering**[1] was born. It assumed that software development is an *engineering* effort, and it introduced many models, methods, frameworks, languages, patterns, and techniques that were supposed to help programmers produce better software. But strangely enough, for most projects they didn't. More often, what the formal approaches *did* introduce was bureaucracy. Software products typically took so long to build, and required so much paperwork to be passed around, that their "formal" requirements had changed long before the systems were delivered. In the meantime, some small teams of passionate and disciplined programmers, with ad-hoc processes and flexible requirements, delivered products of higher quality, at a fraction of the cost, and in a fraction of the

---

1   http://www.mgt30.com/software-engineering/.

time. Creation had produced dinosaurs, but the ants were running away with the food.

In the early 1990s, a new approach called **Rapid Application Development (RAD)**[2] was devised. It combined some of the formal techniques from "heavyweight" software engineering (such as change boards, inspections, and metrics) with down-to-earth practices (such as prototyping, evolutionary delivery, and intensive customer collaboration) as found in many of the more successful ad-hoc project teams [McConnell 1996]. This cross-breeding of formal and ad-hoc development approaches culminated in the first named methods for "lightweight" software development, including **Evo**[3] (1988), **Scrum**[4] (1995), **DSDM**[5] (1995), **Crystal**[6] (1997), **Extreme Programming (XP)**[7] (1999), **Feature Driven Development (FDD)**[8] (1999), **Pragmatic Programming**[9] (1999), and **Adaptive Software Development**[10] (2000).

The Cambrian explosion of methods, articles, books, and seminars for lightweight software development gave some experts the idea to organize a meeting with the leading figures of that movement at the time. In 2001, they got together in a ski resort in Utah. They choose the word "agile" to replace "lightweight," and the Agile Manifesto[11] was born (see Figure 2.2).

The Agile Manifesto was primarily seen by many as a reaction against the bureaucracy of the formal approaches, which were clearly too "ordered." But few people realized that it was also taking a stance against undisciplined programmers, "chaotic" processes, and low-quality products, which clearly dominated the ad-hoc side of the software development world. The leaders in this new movement figured out that there is a middle road between structure and nonstructure, between order and chaos. In a way, it was a heroic attempt to go back to the early days of passionate pioneering but without the monstrosities that anarchies so often came up with.

---

2 http://www.mgt30.com/rad/.
3 The EVO Manuscript, dated August 21, 1997, is available at http://www.mgt30.com/evo/.
4 http://www.mgt30.com/scrum/.
5 http://www.mgt30.com/dsdm/.
6 http://www.mgt30.com/crystal/.
7 http://www.mgt30.com/xp/.
8 http://www.mgt30.com/fdd/.
9 http://www.mgt30.com/prag/.
10 http://www.mgt30.com/asd/.
11 The Manifesto for Agile Software Development can be found at http://www.mgt30.com/manifesto/.

FIGURE 2.2

The Manifesto for Agile Software Development.

A number of the Agile gurus subsequently formed the Agile Alliance,[12] a nonprofit organization with the purpose to promote Agile software development around the world. A new ecosystem of conferences, consultants, books, and magazines was born. And software development became **Agile**, with a capital A, signifying that it is something deeper than just a collection of practices for software development. By discovering and acknowledging that software projects, similar to living creatures, exist between order and chaos, Agile became a Way of Life.

---

12 The Agile Alliance has its own website: http://www.mgt30.com/agilealliance/.

The Fundamentals of Agile

Nowadays, the number of **Agilists** (people who attempt to adhere to the values and principles of Agile) has grown into the millions. And surveys confirm that the majority of software developers around the world practice at least some of the "core Agile practices" [VersionOne 2009].

The fundamentals of Agile have been described many times, and plenty of authors are better at explaining them than I am. Still, I feel it is necessary to include a brief overview in this book. Being an Agilist myself, I prefer to do things my way, and therefore I will describe the Agile basics using my own "seven dimensions of software projects," a topic that I return to in Chapter 11, "How to Develop Competence".

People

First and foremost, Agile recognizes that people are unique individuals instead of replaceable resources and that their highest value is not in their heads but in their interactions and collaboration. Agile calls for small teams where different roles (developers, designers, testers, and so on) form cross-functional units, preferably colocated (located in the same room). These teams are then required to self-organize, meaning that no method or process is imposed on them. They are trusted to get the work done in ways that they think are best, assuming that they know how to do that, with accountability for their results.

Functionality

Agile understands that the best products are created when customers are directly involved with the teams creating them. A team collaborates with the customer (or a customer representative) to maintain and continually reprioritize an ever-changing backlog of features. These features are described in a concise format, or "inch-deep," and more extensive exploration and documentation starts only as soon as they are selected for immediate implementation by the team. Simplicity is the key to good design of each feature, and after their implementation the usefulness of features is immediately verified by the customer.

Quality

For successful products a focus on quality is crucial, and therefore technical excellence finds itself at the core of Agile. It is achieved through

Test-Driven Development[13] (writing test code *before* writing production code), code reviews (often through pair programming), Definition-of-Dones (checklists), iterative development (adapting code due to changes or new insights), and refactoring (improving code even when no features have changed). Agilists recognize the need for emergent design, meaning that the best architectures are not defined up-front (or only in a basic form) and are allowed to further emerge while developing a product.

Tools

Agilists believe that tools are among the least important contributors to successful products, yet plenty of tools are described and promoted in Agile literature. Experienced Agile teams prefer tools for daily builds, continuous integration, and automated testing. Agile software development *needs* teams to be motivated. But repetitive tasks are boring, not motivating, so they should be automated. Many Agilists also call for supportive environments, such as open office layouts, and tools that "radiate" information, such as big task boards and burn charts. In an Agile context, tools are meant to strengthen motivation, communication, and collaboration in a team.

Time

Agile has a special relationship with time. In Agile projects, delivery dates and deadlines as much as budgets can be chosen almost arbitrarily. Software is produced in short time frames, often in time boxes or "sprints," and delivered in many incremental releases, where each release is a potentially shippable product. This enables business owners to take control of timing, moving release dates back and forth, depending on what features they want to make available and when. In the meantime, the team always strives for a sustainable pace so that it can maintain its development speed almost indefinitely.

Value

One of the primary reasons the Agile Manifesto was crafted was to address the need to respond to change. The environment is never static. Features that were valuable yesterday may be useless tomorrow, *including* the features that were already successfully delivered to users. Agilists try to cope with this challenge by nurturing short feedback and delivery cycles.

---

13 http://www.mgt30.com/tdd/.

Frequent product releases are not only meant to invite feedback from the environment and feed the findings back into the development process, but also to deliver new and updated features to users as soon as the need is detected, thereby optimizing their business value.

Process

Even though Agile suggests a people-over-process paradigm, this doesn't mean that process is unimportant. Far from it. Some essential processes in an Agile context are minimal planning (or "rolling-wave planning"), daily face-to-face communication (often in the form of standup meetings), and measurement of progress by evaluating working software (features accepted by the customer). Agilists also acknowledge the need for continuous improvement, whereby the processes themselves are repeatedly evaluated and tuned through regular reflection or retrospectives.

Conflict

These are what I believe to be the fundamentals of Agile. And of course, they are just my words. Some Agilists might disagree with the brief descriptions I have offered here. But that is also part of being Agile. I might even call "conflict" the eighth dimension of Agile software development. As you see later, internal conflict is a natural aspect of complex systems and a prerequisite for creativity and innovation. It is a great privilege to be among people who enjoy few things more than trying to improve on one another.

The Competition of Agile

There are few games without competition and few systems without conflict. Our world wouldn't be interesting without some dissenting views. Fortunately there is plenty of healthy competition within the Agile world, such as Scrum versus Extreme Programming, Scrum versus Kanban, and even Scrum[14] versus Scrum![15] But the various Agile methods are not the only players in this game. There are a couple of powerful and promising contestants offering ideas that are sometimes analogous, sometimes complementary and sometimes downright contradictory.

---

14 The Scrum Alliance has its own website: http://www.mgt30.com/scrumalliance/.
15 Scrum.org was founded by Scrum creator Ken Schwaber: http://www.mgt30.com/scrumorg/.

One of the bigger players is **Lean software development**,[16] which is a translation of the concepts of Lean manufacturing to the domain of software development. The seven principles of Lean [Poppendieck 2009:193] are based on the 14 principles of the Toyota Way[17] (the management philosophy of the Toyota corporation), and the 14 points for Management by W. Edwards Deming.[18] There is significant overlap between the worlds of Lean and Agile, which is why they often play on the same side, with the same experts, sharing the same fan base, and being covered in the same blogs, magazines, and TV shows. Lean software development has made considerable contributions to the Agile world from a managerial perspective, with its clear focus on removing waste and optimizing the whole. And although Lean joined the software development league a few years later than Agile, the Lean movement has caught up by evolving its own conferences, consultants, coaches, and consortiums.[19]

A smaller but capable player is the **Software Craftsmanship** movement, guided by the Manifesto for Software Craftsmanship[20] (see Figure 2.3), which is said to both challenge and extend the original Agile Manifesto. The software craftsmanship proponents take the stance that software developers are not engineers but craftsmen (and craftswomen). (Some people draw on the apprenticeship model of medieval Europe as a fitting metaphor.) The Craftsmanship movement is the nimble and fearless new co-player of Agile and Lean, with its own (smaller) events, books, and forums. Together, on the lightweight side of software development, the three of them seem to form a great team—despite the occasional fist fights in the locker rooms.

But the heavyweight methods and frameworks have not remained idle either. Possibly the most famous of these players, and one of the most controversial, is the **Capability Maturity Model Integration (CMMI)**.[21] Since 1987, it has been developed and maintained by the Software Engineering Institute, a research and development center headquartered at the Carnegie Mellon University. It started out as a process improvement description for software engineering but has grown into a more abstract framework that now covers other professions besides software

---

16 http://www.mgt30.com/lean/.
17 http://www.mgt30.com/toyota/.
18 http://www.mgt30.com/deming/.
19 The Lean Software and Systems Consortium can be found via http://www.mgt30.com/leanssc/.
20 The Manifesto for Software Craftsmanship can be found via http://www.mgt30.com/craftsmanship/.
21 http://www.mgt30.com/cmmi/.

development. The CMMI is an approach that aims to provide guidance by describing five maturity levels and 22 process areas. The CMMI tells you only *which* process areas can be addressed in your process improvement efforts. It doesn't prescribe *how* to implement them. For this reason some Agilists believe that the CMMI, even though its full description spans many hundreds of pages, is still compatible with Agile software development because Agile methods complement the CMMI by describing the "how" of process improvement. But Agilists wouldn't be Agilists if they didn't disagree with each other. And thus some believe that the gravity of the CMMI, despite its good intentions, pulls organizations in the direction of bureaucracy and crippled teams with high ratings for looks and outfits but low scores for actual game play.

FIGURE 2.3

The Manifesto for Software Craftsmanship.

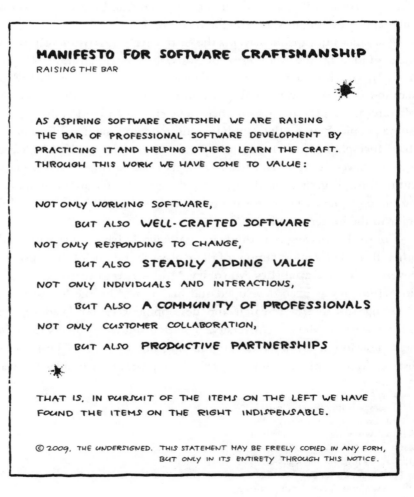

MANIFESTO FOR SOFTWARE CRAFTSMANSHIP
RAISING THE BAR

AS ASPIRING SOFTWARE CRAFTSMEN WE ARE RAISING THE BAR OF PROFESSIONAL SOFTWARE DEVELOPMENT BY PRACTICING IT AND HELPING OTHERS LEARN THE CRAFT. THROUGH THIS WORK WE HAVE COME TO VALUE:

NOT ONLY WORKING SOFTWARE,
    BUT ALSO **WELL-CRAFTED SOFTWARE**
NOT ONLY RESPONDING TO CHANGE,
    BUT ALSO **STEADILY ADDING VALUE**
NOT ONLY INDIVIDUALS AND INTERACTIONS,
    BUT ALSO **A COMMUNITY OF PROFESSIONALS**
NOT ONLY CUSTOMER COLLABORATION,
    BUT ALSO **PRODUCTIVE PARTNERSHIPS**

THAT IS, IN PURSUIT OF THE ITEMS ON THE LEFT WE HAVE FOUND THE ITEMS ON THE RIGHT INDISPENSABLE.

© 2009, THE UNDERSIGNED. THIS STATEMENT MAY BE FREELY COPIED IN ANY FORM, BUT ONLY IN ITS ENTIRETY THROUGH THIS NOTICE.

Similar conflicting signals have been heard about the **Guide to Project Management Body of Knowledge (PMBOK)**,[22] which is published and maintained by the Project Management Institute. Interestingly enough, this guide started as a description of best practices for project management in general. But since its first publication in 1987, it has been revised several times and has been made more "agile," in response to successes achieved by Agile project managers. Contrary to the CMMI, the PMBOK specifically suggests, with many processes, *how* project managers can do their jobs. And though the suggested practices don't always fit well with Agile principles, many project managers actively try to resolve the discrepancies. Though, it must be said, most of the PMBOK covers different territory than Agile does. Exactly the same can be said for **PRINCE2**,[23] a project management method in a similar vein, published and maintained by the Office of Government Commerce in the UK and mainly practiced in Europe.

Last but not least is the **Unified Process**,[24] and its more well-known refinement called the **Rational Unified Process (RUP)**.[25] It was developed in 1997 by Rational Software (now IBM). The RUP is to software developers what the PMBOK is to project managers. It defines a considerable framework of processes that can (and should) be tailored to specific project situations, but its documentation is delivered in such a way that the entire framework is often seen as bureaucratic. Agilists believe that a process should be grown throughout a project, beginning with a bare minimum of a few practices. RUP tried the opposite approach, defining many practices and then suggesting that the unneeded ones can be removed. (I have often compared this approach to the purchase and subsequent dismantling of a Boeing 747 with the purpose to turn it into a bicycle for shopping. For many projects it seemed smarter to me to simply use a bicycle.) Not surprisingly, in response to Agile's many victories around the world, several more Agile alternatives to the RUP have been proposed, including the **Agile Unified Process (AUP)**,[26] the **Open Unified Process (OpenUP)**,[27] and the **Essential Unified Process (EssUP)**.[28] But none of these players seem to have fared well in the global league of Agile methods.

---

22 http://www.mgt30.com/pmbok/.
23 http://www.mgt30.com/prince2/.
24 http://www.mgt30.com/up/.
25 http://www.mgt30.com/rup/.
26 http://www.mgt30.com/aup/.
27 http://www.mgt30.com/openup/.
28 http://www.mgt30.com/essup/.

The Obstacle to Agile

Again and again, empirical evidence has shown that Agile software development, when done well, shows a tremendous return on investment [Rico 2009]. But if Agile methods have such positive effects, why doesn't everyone use them? Why are so many software projects around the world still failing?[29]

The report *State of Agile Development Survey 2009* by VersionOne listed "management opposed to change," "loss of management control," "lack of engineering discipline," "team opposed to change," and "quality of engineering talent" as the main concerns about adoption of Agile, together with many organizations' "needs" for planning, predictability, and documentation [VersionOne 2009].

Hold on…. Let's review those concerns again: We're talking about various managerial controls, organizational change management, and engineering talent….

Forgive me if I'm wrong, but…aren't they all…ehm…*management* responsibilities? Doesn't this simply mean that *managers* around the world are the biggest obstacles to Agile software development?

As a manager, this conclusion doesn't make me happy.

As a writer, it does.

I believe that Agile software development has overlooked the importance of (line) management. If managers don't know what to do and what to expect in an Agile organization, how are they supposed to feel involved in a transition to Agile software development? What is the message of Agile here? If it's just "we don't need managers," it's no wonder Agile transitions are obstructed all over the world.

So to have organizations enjoy the benefits of Agile transitions, they have to know the answer to an important question: What *is* the future of the manager in an Agile world?

Line Management versus Project Management

My first name is not common in my country. But somehow, I have ended up working with several instances of Jurgen, Jurjen, and Jörgen throughout my career. This has led to a lot of confusion. When names are similar, people tend to ignore all other distinctions. If Ella Fitzgerald had

---

29 The press release for the CHAOS Summary 2009 report is available via http://www.mgt30.com/chaosreport/.

been named Jurgen, I'm sure my colleagues would have asked me to sing for them.

I see the same problem with people who are called "managers."

In 2005, a number of people who specialized in managerial work (project managers, line managers, and others) got together and fashioned **The Declaration of Interdependence (DOI)**[30] (see Figure 2.4).

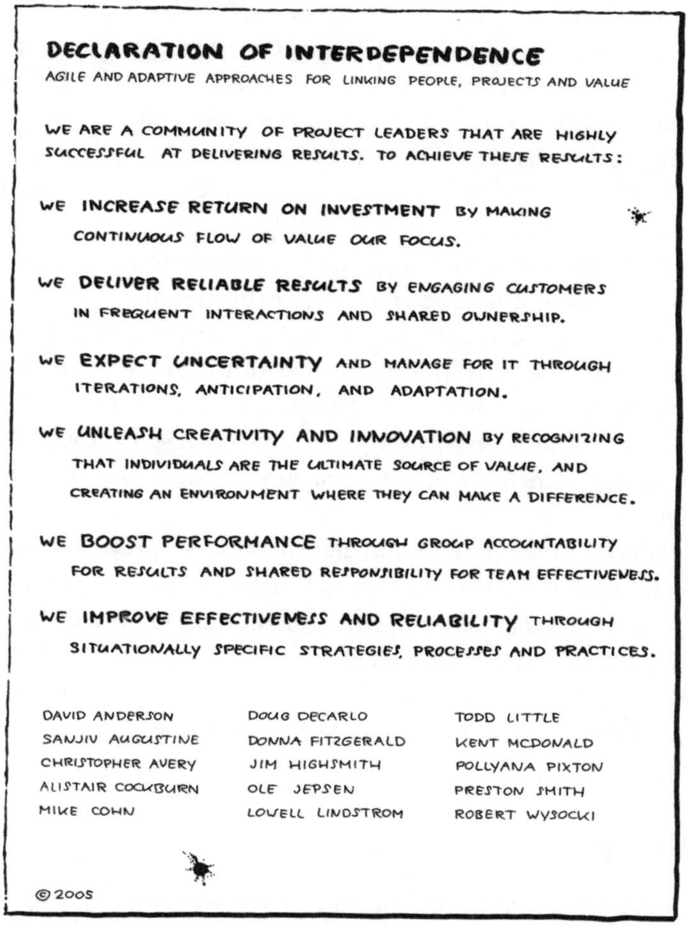

FIGURE 2.4

The Declaration of Interdependence.

DECLARATION OF INTERDEPENDENCE

AGILE AND ADAPTIVE APPROACHES FOR LINKING PEOPLE, PROJECTS AND VALUE

WE ARE A COMMUNITY OF PROJECT LEADERS THAT ARE HIGHLY SUCCESSFUL AT DELIVERING RESULTS. TO ACHIEVE THESE RESULTS:

WE **INCREASE RETURN ON INVESTMENT** BY MAKING CONTINUOUS FLOW OF VALUE OUR FOCUS.

WE **DELIVER RELIABLE RESULTS** BY ENGAGING CUSTOMERS IN FREQUENT INTERACTIONS AND SHARED OWNERSHIP.

WE **EXPECT UNCERTAINTY** AND MANAGE FOR IT THROUGH ITERATIONS, ANTICIPATION, AND ADAPTATION.

WE **UNLEASH CREATIVITY AND INNOVATION** BY RECOGNIZING THAT INDIVIDUALS ARE THE ULTIMATE SOURCE OF VALUE, AND CREATING AN ENVIRONMENT WHERE THEY CAN MAKE A DIFFERENCE.

WE **BOOST PERFORMANCE** THROUGH GROUP ACCOUNTABILITY FOR RESULTS AND SHARED RESPONSIBILITY FOR TEAM EFFECTIVENESS.

WE **IMPROVE EFFECTIVENESS AND RELIABILITY** THROUGH SITUATIONALLY SPECIFIC STRATEGIES, PROCESSES AND PRACTICES.

DAVID ANDERSON · DOUG DECARLO · TODD LITTLE · SANJIV AUGUSTINE · DONNA FITZGERALD · KENT MCDONALD · CHRISTOPHER AVERY · JIM HIGHSMITH · POLLYANA PIXTON · ALISTAIR COCKBURN · OLE JEPSEN · PRESTON SMITH · MIKE COHN · LOWELL LINDSTROM · ROBERT WYSOCKI

© 2005

In its first incarnation the declaration was primarily intended for project management. Later it was realized that its principles could be interpreted more broadly and applied to "management in general." However, the declaration is oriented primarily toward *managing software projects* and

---

30 The Declaration of Interdependence is available via: http://www.mgt30.com/doi/.

not *managing teams of people*. This is underlined because the authors of the DOI also founded the Agile *Project* Leadership Network.[31]

Unfortunately, project management and functional (or line) management are often mixed up. Excellent books by leading experts, including *Agile Management* [Anderson 2004], *Managing Agile Projects* [Augustine 2005], and *Agile Project Management* [Highsmith 2009], discuss both project management and line management issues. And a similar situation is found in many forums, blogs, and magazines. I wish it were different, because project management and line management are not the same. It's like confusing software developers with system administrators. They might be sharing the same ideas, the same jokes, the same haircuts, and the same clothes (figuratively speaking) but they should *not* be treated as the same people. (I'm serious. Just try and ask any software developer to fix your computer. Or better, don't!)

By not clearly distinguishing line management from project management, we're making it hard for both line managers and project managers to understand what their roles are in an Agile organization. Fortunately, I have not been the only one to realize this. Several books came before mine, including *Behind Closed Doors* [Rothman, Derby 2005] and *Leading Lean Software Development* [Poppendieck 2009], in which responsibilities of line managers in software development organizations were better outlined.

In this book, I separate line management from project management. My primary goal is to help *line managers* (including development managers and team leaders) understand their role in their organizations. But I'm sure project managers, system managers, service managers, office managers, and coffee managers can also find some of my material interesting.

And for those of you who thought I was DJ Jurgen…sorry.

Summary

Agile software development is an approach to software development that originated in the 1990s. It was a response to both bureaucratic and ad-hoc development methods that were unable to deliver software products successfully in a consistent manner.

Agile software development, with values and principles expressed in the Agile Manifesto, has a focus on people and teams, frequent delivery of

---

31 http://www.mgt30.com/apln/.

high-quality releases, intensive customer collaboration, and responding to change, with minimal upfront planning.

The Agile values and principles have been implemented through various Agile methods, such as Scrum and Extreme Programming. However, none of the Agile methods address the role of line management (not to be confused with project management) in Agile organizations. This has led to the problem of line management often being identified as the biggest obstacle to the adoption of Agile practices.

Reflection and Action

Let's see if you can apply some ideas from this chapter to your organization:

- Review the seven dimensions of software projects (people, functionality, quality, tools, time, value, process). Do your software projects take all these into account? Are your teams Agile in every dimension? If not, what do you plan to do about it?

- Think about the managers in your organization. Which ones might form an obstacle to the adoption of Agile software development? Is there something you can do about it? Make sure you know what you need from *them* to make *your* Agile management approach a success.

- Is it clear for everyone who is a line manager of who and who is not? Are there uncertainties or disagreements about line managers versus project managers? If there are, what will you do about it?

- Develop your Agile management skills by subscribing to blogs and groups about Agile teams and organizations. You can find an up-to-date list on the Management 3.0 website at http://www.management30.com.

Chapter 3

Complex Systems Theory

Wonder is what sets us apart from other life forms. No other species wonders about the meaning of existence or the complexity of the universe or themselves.

—Herbert W. Boyer, professor of biochemistry (1936–)

Many Agile software development experts agree that a software development team is a **complex adaptive system**[1] because it is made up of multiple interacting parts within a boundary, with the capacity to change and learn from experience. [Highsmith 1999:8] [Schwaber 2002:90] [Larman 2004:34] [Anderson 2004:11] [Augustine 2005:24]. And who am I to claim otherwise?

The magazine *Emergence: Complexity & Organization* once conducted an extensive study of management books referencing complexity with experts from various sciences, including the hard ones like physics and mathematics. It turned out that the reviewers agreed on the usefulness of complexity theory when applied to organizations and management:

> One finds widespread agreement [among reviewers] on the existence of a significant potential for the study of complex systems to inform and illuminate the science and management of organizations.[2]

But, as you see later, the real debate among experts is about *which* scientific terms can be applied *where*.

Like the previous chapter, this one is an introductory overview. Only this time it is about complexity theory. Or perhaps I should make that plural because you will notice that ideas about systems have grown into a body of knowledge comprising multiple theories over a period of more than a hundred years.

---

1   http://www.mgt30.com/cas/.
2   Maguire, Steve. and Bill McKelvey. "Complexity and Management: Moving from Fad to Firm Foundations". Emergence. Vol. 1, Issue 2, 1999. Used with permission. [Maguire, McKelvey 1999:23].

It is good to know a little of context and history. And it's nice to look smart the next time you're at a party when you can recite the difference between general systems theory and dynamical systems theory, while pointing out that your host's recipe for her delicious lemon pie is not complex but complicated.

I have just one word of warning for you. This overview is necessarily incomplete, oversimplified, and at times subjective. Though I'm sure those are exactly the reasons why it will be understandable.

Cross-Functional Science

Chapter 13, "How to Grow Structure," discusses organizational silos, or the idea of separating people who are doing different kinds of work, and why this often negatively impacts the performance of an organization. Interestingly enough, a similar situation has existed in science for many decades.

Most universities and research institutes are organized in scientific silos. Physicists work with physicists, biologists with biologists, and mathematicians with mathematicians. This has led to scientific fragmentation and tunnel vision among scientists and researchers. The different scientific disciplines are so isolated from each other that they usually don't know what the others are doing [Waldrop 1992:61].

Scientific silos can be a problem because many phenomena in the world, across different scientific disciplines, are similar to each other. For example, economists were baffled in the past by a phenomenon known as "local equilibriums," which happened to be something that physicists were already familiar with at the time [Waldrop 1992:139]. And phase transitions in physics look suspiciously similar to punctuated equilibriums in biology. And biologists have noticed that mathematics can help them analyze ecologies of species [Gleick 1987:59]. And "discoveries" made by mathematicians turned out to have been discovered years earlier by meteorologists. [Gleick 1987:31].

For many decades, scientists in different disciplines have struggled with complex phenomena that they could not explain. But when the dots were connected *between* the sciences, and systems across all disciplines were understood to be *complex systems*, suddenly things began to make more sense. I once read the suggestion that the biggest leaps in science happened when scientists worked in fields they were unfamiliar with, because they brought with them the knowledge and experience (and fights and failures) of another field that they *were* familiar with!

Like Agile software development, complex systems theory favors a cross-disciplinary approach to problem solving. Complexity thinking is the antidote to specialization in science. It recognizes patterns in systems across all scientific disciplines and promotes problem solving involving concepts from different fields. But complexity theory has not been the first attempt at cross-breeding the sciences. Let's have a brief look at history to see what happened before.

General Systems Theory

In the late 1940s, a number of scientists and researchers, led by biologist Ludwig von Bertalanffy, created an area of study called **general systems theory**[3] (sometimes simply called *systems theory*). Their studies were based on the idea that most phenomena in the universe can be viewed as webs of relationships among elements. And no matter whether their nature is biological, chemical, or social, these systems have common patterns and behaviors that can be studied to develop greater insight into systems in general. The grand goal of systems theory was to form a unity of science that was interdisciplinary: a common language of systems across all sciences.

One of the achievements of systems theory, which continued to be studied and expanded until at least the 1970s, was shifting the focus from *elements* in a system to *the organization of elements*, thereby recognizing that relationships among elements are dynamic, not static. Scientists studied concepts like **autopoiesis** (how a system constructs itself), **identity** (how a system is identifiable), **homeostasis** (how a system remains stable), and **permeability** (how a system interacts with its environment). [Mitchell 2009:297].

The recognition that a software development team can construct itself, that it can define its own identity, that it needs to interact with its environment, and that interactions among team members are just as important as the team members themselves (or even more so) can all be attributed to general systems theory.

Regrettably, the unification was never fully achieved, which should come as no surprise to software developers with experience in attempts at

---

3   http://www.mgt30.com/systemstheory/.

unification. But the legacy of general systems theory is significant. Almost all laws for system theory also turn out to be valid for complex systems [Richardson 2004a:75], which is more than various unification frameworks in software engineering have achieved.

Cybernetics

Around the time when general systems theory was conceptualized by biologists, psychologists, economists, and other researchers, a similar area of study called **cybernetics**[4] was created by a similarly diverse group of neurophysiologists, psychiatrists, anthropologists, and engineers, with mathematician Norbert Wiener as a leading figure.

Cybernetics is the study of regulatory systems that have **goals** and interact with their environment through **feedback mechanisms**. The goal of cybernetics itself is to understand the processes in such regulatory systems, which include **iterations** of *acting* (having an effect on the environment), *sensing* (checking the response of the environment), *evaluating* (comparing the current state with the system's goal), and back again to acting. This circular process is a fundamental concept in the study of cybernetics.

From cybernetics, we have adopted the view that a software development team is a goal-directed system that regulates itself using various feedback cycles. We have learned that in a self-regulating system like a software team, rather than energy and force, it is information, communication, and purpose that are the most important factors. And cybernetics helped us understand that feedback plays a crucial role in the development of complex behavior [Mitchell 2009:296].

General systems theory and cybernetics are often confused. This is not surprising because they both influenced each other; they both have difficult names; they both tried to work toward a unified science for systems; and they both proved unable to live up to their original goals. Nevertheless, each is responsible for carrying the body of knowledge of systems, which later theories could benefit from and build upon.

---

4 http://www.mgt30.com/cybernetics/.

Dynamical Systems Theory

When we see systems theory and cybernetics as the two legs of the body of knowledge of systems, one of its arms is certainly **dynamical systems theory.**[5]

Grown out of applied mathematics in the 1960s, dynamical systems theory explains that dynamic systems have many **states**, some of which are stable and some of which are not. When parts of a system never change over time, or when they always settle back to original values after having been disturbed, we say that the stable states are acting as **attractors**.

The relevance of dynamical systems theory to software development is that it helps explain why some projects are stable and why others are not. And why sometimes it seems impossible to change an organization because it always reverts back to its original behavior.

Dynamical systems theory played a pivotal role in later theories by offering mathematics as a helping hand when dealing with hard-to-measure concepts from systems theory and cybernetics. (And it is a comforting thought that part of what was to become complexity theory was not just a brain wave but was instead solid math.)

Game Theory

If we consider dynamical systems theory as one arm of the body of knowledge of systems, **game theory**[6] must certainly be the other one. Multiple systems often compete for the same resources—or try to have each other for lunch. Game theory indicates that, in such cases, systems may develop competing strategies.

As another branch of applied mathematics, game theory attempts to capture behavior of systems in strategic situations, where the success of one depends in part on the choices made by others. Game theory was developed in the 1930s and introduced to biology and evolutionary theory in the 1970s when it was recognized that it applied to the strategies of organisms for catching prey, evading predators, protecting territories, and dating the other sex.

Game theory has turned out to be an important tool in many fields, including economics, philosophy, anthropology, and political science. And of course software development, where it not only helps software

---

5 http://www.mgt30.com/dst/.
6 http://www.mgt30.com/gametheory/.

developers to build games, electronic markets, and peer-to-peer systems, but also explains the behavior of people in teams, and the behavior of teams in organizations.

Evolutionary Theory

It is hard to imagine anyone not being familiar with **evolutionary theory**,[7] which became well-known ever since Charles Darwin published *The Origin of Species*, one of the most famous books ever, in 1859. What virtually all biologists agree on are the basic concepts of evolution: gradual genetic changes in species and survival of the fittest by natural selection.

Of course, agreement on the basics doesn't prevent biologists from bickering endlessly about the details. The importance of random genetic drift (species changing for no reason), punctuated equilibriums (sudden drastic changes instead of gradual change), selfish genes (selection at the gene level instead of organisms or groups), and horizontal gene transfer (species exchanging genes with each other) have all been discussed, embraced, and disputed vigorously [Mitchell 2009:81–87]. (But confront them with Intelligent Design[8] and suddenly biologists are united in their rejection of such unscientific nonsense.)

Evolutionary theory has contributed significantly to the study of all kinds of systems, whether they are biological, digital, economical, or sociological. It is said that teams, projects, and products evolve while adapting to their changing environments. And even though the kind of "evolution" in software systems is not the same as Darwin described, evolutionary thinking has helped in understanding growth, survival, and adaptation of systems over time. And this is why I consider evolutionary theory to be the brains of the body of knowledge of systems.

Chaos Theory

Although a number of discoveries about chaos were made earlier, the real breakthrough of **chaos theory**[9] happened in the 1970s and 1980s with Edward Lorenz and Benoit Mandelbrot being the leading figures at the time.

---

7 http://www.mgt30.com/evolution/.
8 http://www.mgt30.com/intelligent-design/.
9 http://www.mgt30.com/chaos/.

Chaos theory taught us that even the smallest changes in a dynamic system can have tremendous consequences at a later time. This means that the behavior of many systems is ultimately unpredictable because minor issues can turn into big problems, as any software team is eager to acknowledge. This innate unpredictability of dynamic systems has far-reaching consequences for estimation, planning, and control, which is a well-known concern among climate scientists and traffic experts but less readily accepted among project managers and line managers.

Another topic addressed by chaos theory was the discovery of *fractals* and *scale invariance*, which is the concept that the behavior of a system when plotted in a graph looks similar on all scales.

Chaos theory is seen by some as *the* predecessor to complexity theory and shares with it an appreciation for uncertainty and change, which is why I like to see it as the heart of the body of knowledge of systems.

The Body of Knowledge of Systems

There is not a single definition of complexity, and there is not a single theory covering all complex systems [Lewin 1999:x]. Scientists have been looking for fundamental laws that are true for all systems for ages, but so far they have been unsuccessful.

> It seems reasonable to ask—exactly what is this thing called "complexity theory?" For although there are many definitions of CT [complexity theory], it has been suggested, that there is no unified description.[10]

Each system is different, and lessons learned with past results are no guarantee of future performance. And so it appears that what we have is a collection of theories that are sometimes complementary, sometimes overlapping, and sometimes contradictory.

Furthermore, there are plenty of smaller studies that, each in their own right, have brought significant contributions to the field of complex systems. We could call them the eyes, ears, fingers, and toes of the body of knowledge. For example, the work on **dissipative systems**[11] gave us insight into *spontaneous pattern-forming* and how systems can *self-organize*

---

10 Wallis, Steven E. "The Complexity of Complexity Theory: An Innovative Analysis"
E:CO Vol. 11, Issue 4, 2009. Used with permission. [Wallis 2009:26].
11 http://www.mgt30.com/dissipative-system/.

within *boundaries*. The work on **cellular automata**[12] taught us how *complex behavior* can result from *simple rules*. From the study of **artificial life**[13] we learned how *information processing* works in *agent-based systems*. Thanks to **learning classifier systems**[14] we came to understand how *genetic algorithms* enable living systems to be capable of *adaptive learning*. And thanks to developments in **social network analysis**[15] we now understand how *information propagates* among people in a network.

Despite the problem that the body parts don't match properly in some places, and that the figure looks uglier than a zombie in a tutu, the body of knowledge of systems is alive and kicking (see Figure 3.1). And when applied to *complex* systems, we call it complex systems theory. But…what does it mean for a system to be complex?

FIGURE 3.1

The Body of Knowledge of systems.

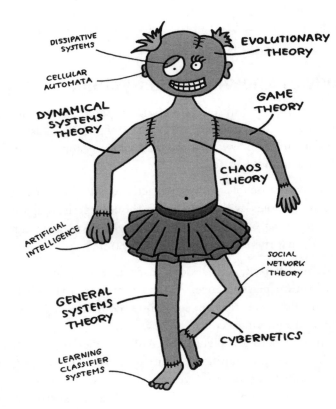

---

12 http://www.mgt30.com/cellular-automaton/.
13 http://www.mgt30.com/artificial-life/.
14 http://www.mgt30.com/lcs/.
15 http://www.mgt30.com/social-network/.

Simplicity: A New Model

Many experts have discussed simplicity and complexity. But their contributions have often confused various terms, which hasn't led to a simplification of the discussion itself. Here is my attempt to clear things up a little. What is simplicity?

> Simplicity usually relates to the burden which a thing puts on someone trying to explain or understand it. Something which is easy to understand or explain is simple, in contrast to something complicated.[16]

If you're going to discuss simplicity, it is useful to know the difference between *complex* and *complicated*. Not knowing the difference means you might apply exactly the wrong approach to the right problem (or the right approach to the wrong problem).

I believe the difference needs to be explained using two dimensions, depicted in the model in Figure 3.2. The first dimension is about the *structure* of a system and how well we *understand* it:

- **Simple** = Easily understandable
- **Complicated** = Very hard to understand

The second dimension is about the *behavior* of the system, and how well we can *predict* it:

- **Ordered** = Fully predictable
- **Complex** = Somewhat predictable (but with many surprises)
- **Chaotic** = Very unpredictable

My underpants are simple. I found it easy to understand how they work. But my watch is complicated; if I took it apart it would take me a long time to understand its design and its components. And yet, neither my watch nor my underpants hold any surprises. (At least not for me.) They are ordered, predictable systems.

A three-person software development team is simple, too. It takes only a few meetings, dinners, and beers to get to know everyone on a team. A city is not simple but complicated. It takes taxi drivers years to know all its streets, alleys, hotels, and restaurants. And yet, both teams and cities are complex. No matter how well you know them, there will always be surprises. They are predictable to a degree, but you never know for sure what will happen tomorrow.

---

16 http://www.mgt30.com/simplicity/.

FIGURE 3.2

The Structure-Behavior Model of systems.

A double pendulum (two pendulums attached to each other) is also a simple system. It is easy to make and easy to understand. And yet, it undergoes unpredictable chaotic motion due to a high sensitivity to the initial setup of the pendulum. And stock markets are also chaotic. They are by definition unpredictable, or else everyone would know how to make money on stock exchanges, and the entire system would collapse. But, unlike pendulums, stock markets are also extremely complicated. The many different businesses and types of financial properties and transactions make them utterly incomprehensible for a simple guy like me.

HOW DOES THIS DIFFER FROM OTHER MODELS?

Cynefin[17] is a framework devised by knowledge management scholar David Snowden (see Figure 3.3a). It describes a typology of contexts using four domains: Simple, Complicated, Complex, and Chaotic (with Disorder as a fifth domain in the middle) and is used to guide approaches to decision making and policy making [Snowden 2010b].

Management professor Ralph Stacey created something similar, called the Agreement & Certainty Matrix (see Figure 3.3b). It shows Simple, Complicated, Complex, and Anarchy (Chaos) as four areas based in two dimensions: the degree of agreement and the degree of uncertainty [Stacey 2000b].

In Chapter 16, "All Is Wrong, But Some Is Useful," you learn that all models are wrong, but some are useful. And each of the three

17 http://www.mgt30.com/cynefin/.

models mentioned here is wrong, but each can be useful. The main difference between my model and the other two is that I don't see complicated and complex as two separate domains. My Structure-Behavior Model has led me to identify six domains instead of four, with some overlap of complicated and complex systems. If you find this useful, you can use my model in your evaluation of systems. If not, feel free to use the other ones. They aren't that bad either.

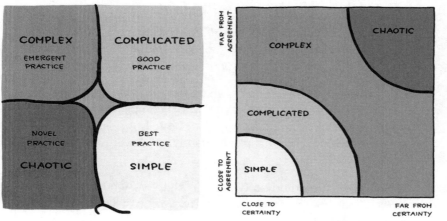

FIGURE 3.3A

The Cynefin model (by David Snowden).[18]

FIGURE 3.3B

The Agreement & Certainty model[19] (by Ralph Stacey).

Complicated refers to a system's *construction* being too intricate to understand, unless you're an expert, whereas *complex* and *chaotic* refer to a system's *behavior*, which is unpredictable to a small or large degree. What is complicated is not necessarily complex, like two cars in a garage. And what is complex need not be complicated, like two people in a bedroom. (But these people's behavior in their bedroom *can* be quite unpredictable.)

- **Simplification** is the act of making the structure better understandable (moving it from top to bottom in my model).

- **Linearization** is the act of making behavior better predictable (moving it from right to left in the model).

Unfortunately, linearization is (in laymen's terms) usually confused with simplification. And that's where the complications start.

---

18 Figure from Wikipedia, in the public domain: http://www.mgt30.com/cynefin-img/.
19 Stacey, Ralph D., Strategic Management and Organisational Dynamics: The Challenge of Complexity, First Edition, ©2000. Reprinted by permission of Pearson Education, Inc., Upper Saddle River, NJ. [Stacey 2000b].

WHAT ABOUT COMPLEXITY IN SOFTWARE SYSTEMS?

Many people agree that software should be as simple as possible. And when software isn't simple enough, some speak of the need to "reduce complexity."[20]

This is a bit confusing because the terminology used in that way does not match the scientific use of the word "complexity." And neither does it distinguish between the structure and behavior of a software system.

However, honesty requires me to admit that the terms "complex" and "complicated" existed long *before* scientists started assigning different meanings to them. So in that respect, the laymen are right and the scientists are wrong.

Nevertheless, when it requires an expert to understand the structure of your software, *I* prefer to say it is complicated. And when the behavior of your software cannot be fully predicted (as in AI, neural networks, or multiplayer games), I say the software is complex.

Simple well-structured software can show very complex behavior, whereas complicated messy software can still behave orderly and fully predictable.

Revisiting Simplification

I believe my Structure–Behavior Model can simplify discussions around simplicity, and clear up some misunderstandings…

> Everything should be made as simple as possible, but no simpler. (Albert Einstein)

With this quote Einstein meant that a system must be made understandable, which means moving it vertically, from the top of my model to the bottom (simplification). However, his addition "but no simpler" seems to map to the behavior of the system. Einstein tried to warn not to change

---

20 The Definition of Common Terms of the Consortium for Untangling Enterprise Complexity can be found via http://www.mgt30.com/cuec/.

the system horizontally because that would change the *kind* of system (which, in my opinion, is linearization, not simplification).

> Simplicity is a myth whose time has passed, if it ever existed [Norman 2007].

In his inspiring article "Simplicity Is Highly Overrated," Don Norman discussed the value of having more features in a product instead of fewer. More features means different/enhanced behavior and (often) also a different structure. In my diagram it is both a horizontal and vertical issue. (For example: When Google added Priority Inbox to Gmail, this made Gmail's behavior more complex. It also complicated the user interface, but I still could understand it well enough.)

Unfortunately, Don Norman used the term simplification both for linearization of behavior (horizontally) and simplification of structure (vertically). And so Don complicated his message, which is exactly why many people didn't understand him. Maybe it would have helped if Don had used pictures:

> The goal of visual thinking is to make the complex understandable by making it visible, not by making it simple.[21]

In his bestselling book, *The Back of the Napkin*, Dan Roam suggests to use pictures to make things understandable. He clearly refers to moving things from complicated to simple (vertically). However, his warning "not to make things simple" seems to me, again, a confusion of terms. What Dan means is that pictures should not change the complexity (behavior, meaning) of something because that would mess up people's ability to predict what the pictures are trying to say.

And therefore, by all means, simplify everything that is hard to understand. But be careful not to linearize ("simplify") something because the reduced behavior of what you offer may not be what your user had expected.

Nonadaptive versus Adaptive

What none of the models show you is that many systems can navigate themselves in that interesting area right between order and chaos.

---

21 Roam, Dan. The Back of the Napkin (Expanded Edition). City: Portfolio Hardcover, 2009. [Roam 2009].

When I was a little boy sitting in the bath tub, playing with the many things I found tumbling about in the water, one thing that fascinated me was the little whirlpool that arose when the plug was pulled from the bottom of the tub. I played with these whirlpools and learned that I could make them disappear, reappear, and rotate in both directions. They had to suffer my presence, and they were clearly not able to adapt to my playful moods. Whirlpools are an example of *nonadaptive* complex systems. They are complex, but they don't adapt [Lewin 1999:15].

Somewhat more interesting is the category of **complex adaptive systems (CAS)**. These systems *are* able to adapt to their environments, for example, an infant learning to walk, a strain of bacteria becoming resistant to an antibiotic, car drivers evading a traffic jam, an ant colony learning about the location of a peanut butter and jelly sandwich, and a software team adapting to what their customer *really* wants.

The systems that I refer to in this book, including software development teams, are in most cases complex *adaptive* systems. They move themselves toward the sweet spot between order and chaos. They learn and adapt, and navigate their way with "chaordic processes" that are neither fully ordered nor truly chaotic [Highsmith 2002].

In that little bath tub several decades ago, the whirlpools were stupid nonadaptive systems. The real complex adaptive system in that bath tub was *me*. I adapted my behavior to whatever the little whirlpools were doing. And it was me who learned how to control them.

But, assuming that software teams are systems, can we actually call them complex adaptive systems? Can we compare team members to children playing in bath tubs?

Are We Abusing Science?

In Agile software development, we regularly hear references to scientific terms such as *self-organization* and *emergence*.

> At the heart of complex adaptive systems theory's relevance to software development is the concept of emergence and the factors leading to emergent results.[22]

---

22 Highsmith, Jim. Adaptive Software Development. New York: Dorset House Pub, 1999. [Highsmith 1999].

For example, an ant colony, the brain, the immune system, a Scrum team, and New York City, are self-organizing systems.[23]

Scrum is not a methodology, a defined process, or set of procedures. It's an open development framework. The rules are constraints on behavior that cause a complex adaptive system to self-organize into an intelligent state.[24]

Is it justified to apply complex systems theory to software development? Do the complexity scientists themselves agree that words like *self-organization* and *emergence* not only apply to ant hills, the brain, and the immune system, but also to Agile teams?

Some scientists have not so nice things to say about people like us borrowing their scientific terms. They say we use scientific terminology without bothering about what the words mean. They say we import scientific concepts without any conceptual justification. And they say some of us are intoxicated with words, indifferent to what they actually mean [Sokal 1998:4].

OK, I cheated a little. Sokal's rant was not directed at Agilists using (or abusing) complexity science but at people in general. Still, the signal here is clear. To hammer it in, here's a quote that hits closer at home:

Not unexpectedly, the complexity gurus are most upset with how complexity science terms are loosely, if not metaphorically, defined and tossed into our managerial discourse—one [guru] goes as far as to suggest that the book[s] offer many insights for managers, but one should simply black out all references to complexity science.[25]

Ouch!

Alright, I cheated again. This rant was directed at *management literature* abusing terms from complexity science, not Agile literature. But...we are warned.

---

23 Schwaber, Ken and Mike Beedle. Agile Software Development with Scrum. Englewood Cliffs: Prentice Hall, 2002. [Schwaber, Beedle 2002].

24 Taken from Tom Hume's blog entry about Jeff Sutherland's presentation: http://www.mgt30.com/shock-therapy/.

25 Maguire, Steve. and Bill McKelvey. "Complexity and Management: Moving from Fad to Firm Foundations". Emergence. Vol. 1, Issue 2, 1999. Used with permission. [Maguire, McKelvey 1999:55].

We have to be careful when carrying over terms from complexity science to other disciplines, including management and software development. For example, when a small issue in a software project unexpectedly turns out to have big consequences, it is all too easy to say that this is typical "chaotic" behavior of the system. But without understanding what chaos actually *means* from a scientific viewpoint, we might be making ourselves the laughing stock among complexity scientists around the world....

So, is the term *self-organizing team* an example of abuse of science?

And what about *emergent design*? Is that abuse of science as well?

Personally, I don't think so. But it may be wise to remain critical and skeptical at all times.

In this book I write about ideas and concepts found in complex systems theory that we *might* apply to managing software development teams. And though admittedly I *do* have a veritable intoxication with words, I intend to do this with proper regard to their scientific *meaning* and by providing ample *justification*.

A New Era: Complexity Thinking

When you apply complex systems theory to software development and management, you are treating your organization as a system.

This is not new. **System dynamics**,[26] originally developed in the 1950s (and not to be confused with dynamical systems theory) is a technique developed to help managers understand and improve their industrial processes. System dynamics was one of the first techniques to show how even seemingly simple organizations can have unexpected nonlinear behaviors [Stacey 2000a:64]. System dynamics recognized that the structure of an organization, with its many circular, interlocking, and sometimes time-delayed relationships between organizational parts, is often a more important contributor to an organization's behavior than the individual parts themselves. System dynamics has helped managers to improve their understanding of business processes, while at the same time pointing out that the properties of an organization are often a result of the entire system and cannot be traced back to individuals in the organization. System dynamics is not part of the body of knowledge of systems. Instead it is a tool,

---

26 http://www.mgt30.com/system-dynamics/.

like a 60-year old calculator, to make the body of knowledge interesting for managers who like using numbers.

A newer but similar technique is called **systems thinking**,[27] developed in the 1980s and popularized by Peter Senge's book *The Fifth Discipline* [Senge 2006]. It is about understanding how things influence each other within a whole. Systems thinking is a problem-solving mindset that views "problems" as parts of an overall system. Instead of isolating individual parts, thereby potentially contributing to unintended consequences, it focuses on cyclical relationships and nonlinear cause and effect within an organization. Systems thinking is similar to system dynamics, though the latter typically uses actual simulations and calculations in an attempt to analyze the impact of alternative policies objectively. Systems thinking is said to be more subjective in its evaluation of complex structures because it has no clear definition of usage [Forrester 1992]. Its main contribution is for people to concentrate on problematic systems instead of problematic people. I would say that systems thinking is like a 30-year old camera that can give managers a more complete picture of their organization from various interesting but subjective angles.

The study of complexity in social systems is called **social complexity**. Unfortunately, neither system dynamics nor systems thinking recognize that social complexity cannot realistically be analyzed and adapted in a top-down fashion [Snowden 2005]. Simulating organizations with simplistic models, or drawing teams and people with bubbles and arrows, falsely suggests that managers can analyze their organization, modify it, and then steer it in the right direction. System dynamics and systems thinking recognize nonlinearity, but they are still grounded in the idea that top management can somehow construct a "right" kind of organization that can produce the "right" kind of results. In their approach to applying the body of knowledge of systems to organizations, they are little more than 19th century deterministic thinking in a 20th century jacket [Stacey 2000a]. The 21st century is the age of complexity. It is the century where managers realize that, to manage social complexity, they need to understand how things *grow*. Not how they are *built*.

This book applies complex systems theory in a way that does not contradict its own message of nonlinearity, nondeterminism, and uncertainty. The Management 3.0 model applies **complexity thinking**. It assumes that managers *cannot* construct and steer a self-organizing team. Instead such a team must be grown and nurtured. It acknowledges that productive

---

27 http://www.mgt30.com/systems-thinking/.

organizations are *not* managed with models and plans. Instead it must emerge through the power of self-organization and evolution. I like to see complexity thinking as the light that feeds all that grows. It is the energy source from which everything is derived and produced. Calculators and cameras are interesting, but they are useless without light.

In Chapter 4, we start shining that light on software development teams and how the first view of the Management 3.0 model supports them as growing, self-organizing, adapting systems.

Summary

Complexity science is a multidisciplinary approach to research into systems, which builds on earlier achievements in the fields of general systems theory, cybernetics, dynamical systems theory, game theory, evolutionary theory, and game theory.

It is widely acknowledged that findings in complexity science can be applied to social systems, like software development teams and management, though it is still unclear how far we can go in copying system concepts from one discipline to another.

One important finding is that complexity (an indication of predictability) is different from complicatedness (an indication of understandability). Another finding is that many complex systems can adapt to changing environments, in which case we call them complex adaptive systems (CAS).

Social complexity is the study of social groups as complex adaptive systems.

Reflection and Action

Let's see if you can apply some ideas from this chapter to your organization:

- Nourish and develop your ability for complexity thinking by subscribing to blogs and groups about self-organizing teams and complexity in organizations. You can find an up-to-date list on the Management 3.0 website, http://www.management30.com.

Chapter **4**

The Information-Innovation System

When an actor comes to me and wants to discuss his character, I say, "It's in the script." If he says, "But what's my motivation?" I say, "Your salary."

—Alfred Hitchcock, filmmaker (1899–1980)

Software projects are **complex adaptive systems**. It is a view shared by many software development experts and Agile/Lean evangelists. But what makes those systems work?

M. Mitchell Waldrop, author of *Complexity: the Emerging Science at the Edge of Order and Chaos*, describes that systems composed of "agents" are at the heart of every discussion at the Santa Fe Institute, the world's leading institute on complexity science. These agents can be molecules, or neurons, or web servers, or fish, or people, always organizing and reorganizing themselves into larger structures, and thereby forming new emergent structures with new emergent behaviors [Waldrop 1992:88].

When I look at software projects I see *people* who are constantly *organizing and reorganizing themselves into larger structures (project teams, social groups, task forces, committees, and so on).* And at the project team level, new *emergent structures* form and engage in new *emergent behaviors.* Clearly, like any other complex system, a software project consists of interconnected agents (people) that interact with each other and form an integrated whole. (Note that the term *agents* in complex systems has nothing to do with *software agents* programmed by developers. In complexity theory it's just another word for *interacting elements* or *parts.*)

Even though software projects have many elements, only people are the real agents, or the *active* elements (see Figure 4.1). (We can consider teams themselves to be agents on the next higher level.) Requirements, features, artifacts, deliverables, tools, technologies, and processes are not agents because they cannot *actively* organize and reorganize themselves or initiate interaction with any of the other elements in the project. People have the right capabilities of interaction and organization, but they also need energy to make proper use of those capabilities. Therefore, *Energize People* is the first view of the Management 3.0 model, and most of this chapter is about people. But before talking about people, we first have to talk about organizations.

FIGURE 4.1

Agents in a social complex system.

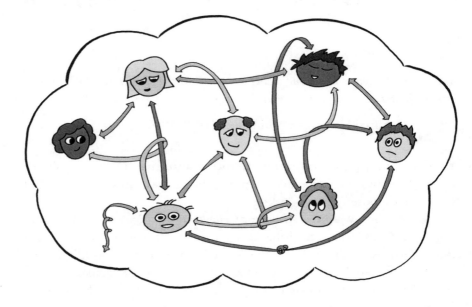

Innovation Is the Key to Survival

In any competitive environment, **innovation** is the key to survival. It is a matter of life and death for companies around the world [Davila 2006:6]. Innovation usually offers the highest levels of value creation in a company [Highsmith 2009:31]. Knowledge–creating organizations (including software development companies) should be focused primarily on innovation, wrote Professor Ikujiro Nonaka in *The Knowledge Creating Company* [Nonaka 2008]. And not only knowledge companies, says Robert D. Austin, professor of creativity and innovation. When technologies keep lowering the cost of iteration, more and more industries can increasingly compete on innovation [Austin, Devin 2003:53].

Well, isn't that a coincidence….

Innovation happens to be a concept at the heart of complexity science. Researchers found that complex adaptive systems actively *seek* a position between order and chaos because innovation and adaptation are maximized when systems are at "the edge of chaos" [Kaufmann 1995]. The world's biosphere came up with innovations such as the White-faced Saki Monkey, the Pink Fairy Armadillo, the Aye-Aye, and the Dumbo Octopus (see Figure 4.2). And of course, poodles (which proves that the biosphere has a crazy sense of humor). Researchers say that complexity—that interesting state between order and chaos—is the root of innovation, in physics, biology, psychology, and beyond.

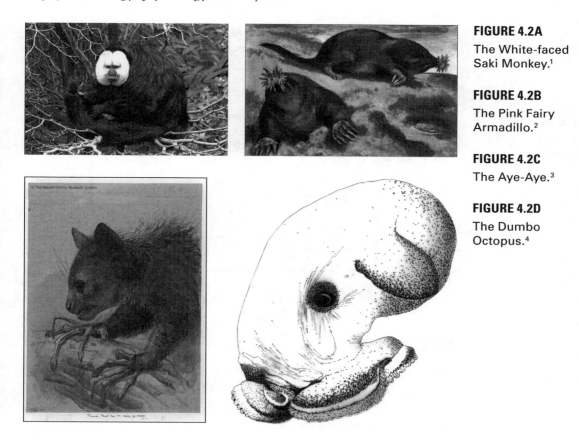

FIGURE 4.2A

The White-faced Saki Monkey.[1]

FIGURE 4.2B

The Pink Fairy Armadillo.[2]

FIGURE 4.2C

The Aye-Aye.[3]

FIGURE 4.2D

The Dumbo Octopus.[4]

1   Copyright photo by Skyscraper: http://www.mgt30.com/saki-monkey/. Reprinted under the Creative Commons License. Please visit http://creativecommons.org/.
2   Picture in public domain: http://www.mgt30.com/armadillo/.
3   Picture in public domain: http://www.mgt30.com/ayeaye/.
4   Copyright drawing by Amélie Onzon: http://www.mgt30.com/octopus/. Reprinted under the Creative Commons License. Please visit http://creativecommons.org/.

Innovation is a typical bottom-up phenomenon, according to publications such as *Complexity and Innovation in Organizations* [Fonseca 2002] and *Complexity Perspectives in Innovation and Social Change* [Lane 2009]. They emphasize that innovation is doomed to fail when launched by upper-management as top-down programs of special people assigned with the exclusive and difficult task of inventing something new. This approach reflects the causal deterministic view of trying to take charge of what's going to happen in the future. It doesn't work.

The complex systems approach says that innovation is not a planned result but an emergent result. However, for things to *emerge* there has to be something to emerge *out of.* This led me to identify the **Five Cogs of Innovation** (see Figure 4.3), which are discussed next.

FIGURE 4.3

The Five Cogs of Innovation.

Knowledge

There is a strong link between innovation and **knowledge workers**, said Don Tapscott and Anthony D. Williams in *Wikinomics* [Tapscott, Williams, 2008]. Developers, designers, architects, analysts, testers, and all other types of software creators are known to be knowledge workers. The term was coined by management guru Peter Drucker, who needed a way to emphasize that the main job of many workers is to work with information. Many other business experts, like Ikujiro Nonaka, later supported the idea that knowledge is the fuel for innovation [Nonaka 2008].

This is exactly what happens in our software projects. Knowledge enables us to deliver new software features to our users, and we attempt to deliver business value to our customers: value that they didn't have before. Our project teams therefore turn knowledge into innovation.

Knowledge itself is built from the continuous input of **information** from the environment in the form of education and learning, requests and requirements, measurements and feedback, and the steady accumulation of experience. In short, a software team is the kind of system that consumes and transforms information and produces innovation.

Neuroscientists have known for some time that knowledge is not stored in individual locations in a human brain. Unlike binary data, which is stored in specific locations in a computer memory, knowledge is stored as patterns over large portions of a person's brain. If a small portion of that brain is somehow disabled, chances are good the knowledge is still largely intact. It seems like knowledge in a human brain is a bit like information on the Internet: a parallel distributed system with things redundantly stored in multiple locations and with no one in control [Kelly 1994:454]. Some call it "holographic memory," after the technique of holograms, which store information about a whole image in every little piece of a film [Hunt 2008:48].

This means that nodes in a knowledge network (a human brain, the Internet, a social group) can work with only partial access to the whole network, but performance declines with the number of connections. Exactly the same conclusion was made in research by Rob Cross and Andrew Parker, published in their book *The Hidden Power of Social Networks*. They found that people's expertise is not the most important indicator of their performance. Instead, what actually makes a difference is their connectivity in the organization [Cross 2004:11].

Given that much of the knowledge used in projects is tacit knowledge (undocumented and hard to transfer), the people in an organization need to share it through "osmotic communication" and working together [Cockburn 2007:202]. And therefore it is imperative that our software teams consist of people who *want* to share and work together. (We revisit the communication issue in Chapters 12, "Communication on Structure," and 13, "How to Grow Structure". For now, we concentrate on the people part.)

Software developers convert information into innovation, which coincides nicely with fact 22 of Robert Glass' *Facts and Fallacies of Software Engineering*:

> Eighty percent of software work is intellectual. A fair amount of it is creative. Little of it is clerical.[5]

5   Glass, Robert. Facts and Fallacies of Software Engineering. Boston: Addison-Wesley, 2003. [Glass 2003:60].

Software creators are problem solvers. Glass has measured that system analysts spend 80 percent of their time thinking. I believe this also applies to each of the other types of team members in software projects (maybe with the exception of some business consultants).

The same study carried out by Glass also showed that 16 percent of the intellectual tasks are creative, indicating that creativity plays an important role in the process of converting knowledge into innovation.

Creativity

The crucial variable in the process of turning knowledge into value is **creativity** [Kao 2007]. Creativity is about producing new things, diverging from conventional approaches, inventing new answers with old information, and seeing solutions where others didn't see them before. (And sometimes it is about stealing old things and cloaking them in a smart way so that nobody finds out.)

The importance of knowledge as input for creativity is now widely accepted among social researchers [Runco, Pritzker 1999]. They found evidence that creativity is primarily based on people's knowledge and the combination of dissimilar ideas, which enables the emergence of new perspectives. To the inexperienced and naive, creativity often looks like magic. But in truth creativity is rooted in the fertile grounds of knowledge and many hours of hard work and thinking.

There is no single, authoritative perspective or definition of creativity. At least 60 different definitions can be found in psychological literature. However, a widespread conception of creativity is that it manifests itself in the production of things that are both *original* and *useful*.[6]

Original

The intention (or hope) of many software developers is to *solve problems with code that has not been produced before* (by themselves and preferably also not by others). Techniques such as object-orientation, component-based design, service-oriented architecture, and refactoring are all there to help developers in making each line of code unique. Ultimately, software developers think that, in a perfect world, each piece of code would exist only once. In their quest for this utopia, trying to prevent any repetition of work, software developers have far more possibilities than, say, writers,

---

6   http://www.mgt30.com/creativity/.

painters, architects, and hairdressers. None of these other creative people have a similar array of techniques for abstraction and indirection. (They probably don't even know what it is.)

Useful

Likewise, to *produce useful results* is another intention of many software developers. Quite possibly, no other type of creative activity in business has increased global productivity levels as much as software development has. I've heard people say that the business value of software exceeds that of every other creative product by several orders of magnitude. Developers can hardly be compared to writers, painters, architects, or even hair dressers for that matter. (Though I might make an exception for rock stars.) They often don't even think of themselves as "creative," with all the wishy-washy connotations often associated with that term. Most software developers are not of the poem–writing, ballet-dancing kind. They just want to make things that are *used*. (For the sake of the argument, I am ignoring the vast number of unused features of which developers *thought* they were going to be used.)

It appears that creativity, the production of things both *original* and *useful*, is at the core of software development. The best-known model for the creative process was proposed by Graham Wallas and Richard Smith in their 1926 publication *The Art of Thought*. Their five-step process is just as applicable to software development as to any other creative activity. For example, suppose you are responsible for improving the performance of a website. The five-step creative process might look like the following:

1. **Preparation**: Finding out what the location and dimension of the problem is, such as the time it takes for (some) queries to execute on the database server.

2. **Incubation**: Pondering on the performance problem, both consciously and unconsciously, while taking a shower, playing poker and discussing the latest Batman movie with friends (possibly all at the same time).

3. **Intimation**: Realizing that the solution might have to be found in a better data model, and not as you thought earlier, in more efficient queries or better hardware.

4. **Illumination**: Suddenly having the insight that a solution can be realized by "denormalizing" some database tables which allows for faster data retrieval.

5. **Verification**: Trying out the new solution and verifying and improving it until it has the intended results.

This is creativity. People use this process during requirements gathering, analysis and design, construction, testing, and all the other areas of software engineering.

And for book writing, too.

Motivation

People are the only elements in a software project capable of initiating interaction. The agents in a complex system interact with each other by exchanging signals and messages. They receive each other's input, they process it, and they transform it into the output of their choice. (It may not always be the output you had hoped for, but output it is….)

People are also the only elements capable of developing knowledge, exhibiting creativity, and performing the activities needed to take their ideas to the market place. And people happen to be the only ones capable of controlling software projects because only people have the level of complexity required to manage complex systems.

One conclusion is becoming more and more evident: The primary focus of any manager should be to *energize people*, to make sure that they actually *want* to do all that stuff. And doing all that stuff requires **motivation**.

Like a gardener looking after his plants in the garden, a manager looks after the employees on his teams. To fully support his people's capabilities for knowledge, creativity, and control, a manager must *keep his people motivated*.

In *The One-Minute Manager*, one of the best selling management books of the 20th century, Kenneth H. Blanchard said it like this:

> People who feel good about themselves produce good results.[7]

In *First, Break All the Rules*, a popular book based on one of the most extensive management research projects ever performed, Marcus Buckingham and Curt Coffman suggested a manager should select people, set expectations, motivate them, and develop them. Those are, in their

---

7 Blanchard, Kenneth and Spencer Johnson. The One Minute Manager. New York: Morrow, 1982. [Blanchard 1982:19].

words, the four core activities of the manager as a "catalyst." [Buckingham, Coffman 1999:61].

Finally, in June 2008, Forrester released a report that concluded that *IT projects are people projects* [Sheedy 2008]. Everyone except five pygmies locked in a sauna already knew that, but it's nice that Forrester supported this conclusion with solid research.

Then why is it that, in many organizations, models, methods, and process descriptions, continuous motivation of people is often overlooked or ignored? Many times I listened to job candidates complaining about bad levels of people management in their former employer's organizations. Clearly many managers still need to learn the basics of management.

To be fair, although the CMMI for Software Development [Chrissis 2007] does not have any process areas listed for people management, the Software Engineering Institute did address this by releasing a separate People Capability Maturity Model [Curtis 2001], which might help organizations to successfully address their critical people management issues.

Motivation is *"the activation or energization [sic] of goal-oriented behavior."*[8] It is therefore crucial for managers to activate or energize the people in the complex systems that we call our software teams. Of course, many people are already active and energetic. The point is that they need to work in a system that should *continue* to energize them and not take energy away from them. Managers are responsible for that system and therefore for people's continued motivation.

> The creation of novelty requires not only appropriate thinking and personality, but also the desire or at least the readiness to diverge, take risks, defy conventional opinion, or expose oneself to the possibility of being wrong, in other words, appropriate motivation.[9]

Sometimes people love pointing out that you cannot *make* people motivated. We also cannot make people happy. And we cannot make people feel proud. Motivation, happiness, and pride are states of people's minds, and (sometimes regrettably) we cannot program them directly. But we can certainly *try* to achieve the desired effect. Stand-up comedians do this every day. They try to make people laugh, and some are better at it than others. And they know that the jokes that work for some have no effect

---

8   http://www.mgt30.com/motivation/.
9   This text was published in the Encyclopedia of Creativity, Arthur Cropley, Definitions of Creativity, page 521, Copyright Academic Press 1999. Used with permission. [Cropley 1999:521].

on others. But these comedians also know that, given some types of audiences, some types of jokes work most of the time. With motivation it is exactly the same.

Motivation is a fine example of social complexity. It is nonlinear and sometimes unpredictable. It cannot be defined or modeled with a single diagram.

The most widely used model of motivation is Maslow's hierarchy of needs.[10] It depicts motivation as a five-level hierarchy, with survival instincts (or *physiological needs*) at the bottom and personal development (or *self-actualization*) at the top. (And in between we find *safety/security, love/belonging*, and *self-esteem*, in that order.) However, I concur with a number of researchers who believe that the diagram is flawed. Maslow's hierarchy of needs makes it seem as if motivation is a fairly straightforward layered and linear phenomenon. But it is not. Motivation is much more complex than that.

In the next chapter, we discuss various approaches to people motivation in more detail. However, first we need to complete the picture of the information–innovation system.

Diversity

Seven years ago, when I started working for my most recent employer, the entire organization (about 30 people at that time) consisted only of 20-something, white, straight, single males. The atmosphere was what you would expect from such an environment: conversations on football/soccer, lewd jokes, the smell of beer, and trash in every corner. In short, the perfect place to work, if you were a 20-something, white, straight, single male. But our projects ran into many problems—until the organization started changing.

The subculture of 20-something, white, straight, single males in our region could not keep up with the rapid growth of our company. And so the women arrived. And the married guys. And people with kids. And people older than 40. And people from all sorts of ethnic, religious, sexual, and disabled minorities. Before we knew it, the organization had grown to 200 people, and the group of 20-something, white, straight, single males had dwindled to just another minority. And the company is still a great place to work, particularly for the large majority of people representing one or two minorities.

---

10 http://www.mgt30.com/maslow/.

In biological ecosystems, genetic diversity is one of the most important principles. Biodiversity (the variation of species) is the most obvious form of it, but there's also diversity within species themselves. Did you know that honey bees are slightly different from each other? That's how they regulate the temperature in their beehives. When a hive gets too cold, the bees start huddling together, buzzing their wings. And when it gets too hot, the bees spread out, and they start fanning their wings. Now, if the bees would respond to the same specific temperatures, they would all start buzzing or fanning their wings at the same time, resulting in a wildly oscillating temperature in the hive. Therefore, to improve stability, the bees respond to different temperature levels. When the temperature rises, one by one the bees will start fanning their wings. And the more bees join in, the slower the temperature rises until it stops completely. Diversity among bees smoothes and stabilizes the temperature in the beehive [Miller, Page 2007:15].

Diversity (officially: **heterogeneity**) in a complex system is important because the many benefits far outweigh the costs (of variation within the system). Scientists have found that diversity can stabilize a system and make it resilient to environmental changes. Diversity helps a system to survive in tough environments. It increases flexibility and feeds innovation. [Stacey 2000a:7].

Diversity also means that in a complex system, you cannot use averages. A thousand clones of one average honey bee cannot ensure stability in the beehive. Or consider this other example: There is no average virus that gives you the common cold. There are at least 200 known viruses that can give you a cold and probably even more unknown ones. This diversity is the viral system's way of being successful in making you sick, year after year.

Jim Coplien and Neil Harrison listed Diversity as a pattern in *Organizational Patterns of Agile Software Development* [Coplien, Harrison 2005:135]. They recognized that diversity is a good way to stimulate innovation and the ability to find solutions to problems. Tom DeMarco and Timothy Lister, in *Peopleware*, named the Uniform Plastic Person as Diversity's antipattern. They referred to the problem of managers trying to impose uniformity on people and teams. Furthermore, it has been found that diverse teams often outperform homogeneous teams [Cockburn 2007:70].

Managers have the tendency to hire lookalikes of themselves, as pointed out by John Maxwell in *The 21 Irrefutable Laws of Leadership* [Maxwell 1998]. The 20-something, white, straight, single males typically hire other 20-something, white, straight, single males, simply because they can get along so well. It's a natural thing easily explained by the selfish-gene theory put forward by Richard Dawkins [Dawkins 1989]. Our genes have programmed us to favor other people with copies of the same genes and to dislike others whose DNA differs more. Over tens of thousands of years, our genes have been busy waging wars against each other and turned us into bigots. In sociology this is called **homophily**,[11] the tendency of individuals to associate with similar others.

Unfortunately, our genes don't care about the success of our software projects, but we do! Favoring similar people is a trap that managers must try to avoid. That's why I nowadays prefer new people with different educations, experiences, technical skills, people skills, viewpoints, skin colors, ages, genders, personalities, and you-name-it. It's how I try to enforce stability, flexibility, resilience, and innovation in projects.

Creative solutions that people come up with are largely dependent on their backgrounds. This means that diversity in a team can significantly enhance a team's creative powers. However, this doesn't mean that greater diversity *always* leads to greater creativity. Putting together a police agent, a Dutchman, a ballet dancer, and a toddler possibly wouldn't give you the level of innovation you had been hoping for. There has to be some balance and sufficient common ground so that all diverging views are still connected in a bigger pattern. Lewin and Regine call this **inclusive diversity** [Lewin, Regine 2001:44].

Personality

Agile and Lean brought wonderful things to the world of software development. But I sometimes cringe when I see enumerations of "Agile values" or "Lean principles." Every time they are different, and every time they make no sense to me.

The Agile Manifesto[12] mentions *trust* in its twelve principles. But Mary and Tom Poppendieck have a special place for *respect* among their seven principles of Lean software development [Poppendieck 2007:36]. There is no mention of trust in the Lean principles, and there is no mention of respect in the Agile principles. Why the difference? I'm quite certain that trust and respect are *not* synonyms. I trust my dictionary. But I don't respect it.

---

11 http://www.mgt30.com/homophily/.
12 http://www.mgt30.com/agile-principles/.

Unfortunately, the confusion doesn't stop there…Kent Beck's short list of five values of Extreme Programming contains *communication, simplicity, feedback, courage,* and *respect* [Beck 2005:18-21]. (Note that *trust* is not among them!) But Ken Schwaber's list of five values of Scrum has replaced three of those with *commitment, focus,* and *openness* [Schwaber, Beedle 2002]. What are the Agile gurus trying to accomplish here? Should we now discuss which values are better than other values? Or should we just merge them all into one big list and get it over with?

When you dig a bit deeper into this topic, you quickly figure out that *trust, respect, courage, simplicity, commitment, focus,* and *openness* are all examples of human virtues. They are personality traits that we value as being good. But there are more! There's a whole legion of them, including *appreciation, assertiveness, benevolence, caution, chastity, cleanliness, cooperativeness, curiosity, determination, encouragement, excellence, fairness, fitness, flexibility, generosity, honesty, honor, humor, integrity, loyalty, nonviolence, patience, resilience, respectfulness, responsibility, restraint, self-discipline, sincerity, skill, sympathy, truthfulness, wisdom,* and many more.

Does Agile place "trust" on a higher level than the other virtues? Is "respect" singled out in Lean because it is the mother of everything? Does Scrum have a better list than XP because the communication and feedback mentioned by XP are actions, rather than human virtues? Are other virtues, such as excellence, flexibility, honesty, humor, responsibility, self-discipline, and skill somehow less important in Agile and Lean?

I think four times "no." The gurus probably never actually took a chance to dig deeper into this topic. They could have picked some other set of five virtues, such as *excellence, honesty, responsibility, self-discipline,* and *humor* (I would definitely leave out *chastity*), and it wouldn't have made a difference for Agile and Lean adoption around the world. Or would it? On my blog and in my talks around the world, I have repeatedly claimed that excellence and self-discipline are wrongfully *assumed* by Agile and rarely made explicit (see Chapter 10, "The Craft of Rulemaking"). But I digress….

Researchers found that creativity is a product of knowledge, motivation, and personality [Runco, Pritzker 1999]. In any project team, knowledge can only lead to innovation when people's personalities and motivations are properly addressed. *That* is one of the main reasons why virtues are important. They determine people's behavior and have big consequences for other people's motivations.

Choosing either trust or respect, or some other limited set of virtues, is a too simplistic approach to address personalities and motivations.

Software projects benefit from some virtues being shared by all team members. But as we've seen in the previous section, creativity also benefits when there is a healthy dose of diversity of personalities (and virtues) in the team. And what a good thing that is! Agile recognizes that we're all human. We're not saints, nor robots. We cannot be virtuous in every dimension. (Nonviolence is the one I struggle most with, when government officials are around.)

Don't be fooled by arbitrary sets of values or principles. As a manager, depending on the context, you should pick your own set of human virtues to focus on in your teams. Just remember that Agile values are not a fixed set of five, seven, or twelve items. This book is about complexity, not about simple answers.

Virtues are attributes of **personality**. And with this we arrive back at the topics of creativity and innovation, which were the main themes in this chapter. Without the right "team personality," it is hard to get any creativity out of a team. And that's why focusing on the right virtues is so important: Virtues shape the personality of a team and therefore the creativity in their work.

Finally, we end up with a system shown in Figure 4.3. Information flows into the system, where a combination of knowledge, creativity, motivation, diversity, and personality triggers people to do work, which results in what we were aiming for…innovation. Innovation is crucial for businesses, and it turns out that its components are all about people. That's why *being in business means you're dealing with people*.

Only People Are Qualified for Control

People are the only elements in a software project with the ability to initiate interaction and to convert information into innovation. But there was another reason for people being the center of attention in this chapter. It has to do with the **Law of Requisite Variety**[13] defined by W. Ross Ashby:

> If a system is to be stable the number of states of its control mechanism must be greater than or equal to the number of states in the system being controlled.[14]

---

13 http://www.mgt30.com/requisite-variety/.
14 Reprinted under the Creative Commons License. Please visit http://creativecommons.org/.

Simply put, this law states that a system can be controlled by another system only when the other system is just as complex as or more complex than the first one. (This is actually an oversimplification, but there's no need to get too technical at this time.)

People are the most complex elements in any software project. This makes them best qualified to directly control their own projects because people (not processes) are the only parts with sufficient complexity to deal with the variety of states that they are confronted with. And any complex system, if it is to produce useful results, needs some level of control.

Neither documented processes, nor code generators, nor project management tools, nor the most exquisite upfront designs can ever hope to have the amount of complexity that any ordinary software project possesses. Processes, tools, and designs cannot outperform their masters. Without people, they are useless.

The Law of Requisite Variety makes it quite clear that if *some* level of control is needed in a project, you had better select people as the control mechanisms. They are the only ones complex enough to actually pull it off.

WHAT ABOUT TOOLS?

Tools are like sensors and emitters. They are useful for input and output so that people can better control their projects.

Tools can be necessary but are never sufficient for success. Human analysis of the information gained with tools is required before people can take action, given a certain context.

From Ideas to Implementation

Innovation is not only useless without people but it's also useless without implementation. It doesn't matter how creative people are; if the ideas that they generate are never used to implement new products or services, they are merely interesting artifacts [Phillips 2008]. Business value is generated by taking the results of creativity and applying processes and **activity** to convert those results into a working business model and bringing those creative ideas to the market. Or in the words of Theodore Levitt:

> A powerful new idea can kick around unused in a com-
> pany for years, not because its merits are not recognized,
> but because nobody has assumed the responsibility for
> converting it from words into action.[15]

For an organization to be innovative, managers and team members must actively cultivate knowledge, creativity, motivation, diversity, and personality. Brainstorm sessions, pizza nights, out-of-the-box thinking, mind maps, crazy ideas on whiteboards, and large quantities of alcohol (for some people) are helpful but not enough. There must be an organizational focus on *actionable* items that push the ideas from conception to introduction into the market place. This, of course, is the reason why many people do *projects*. It is also the reason why, in many places in this book, I assume that software teams are busy doing projects.

Creativity is also reflected in the way I chose to structure my book project. I decided to split each of its six main themes in two chapters, where the first has a focus on theory and the second has a focus on practice. In this chapter, we have seen that various theories underlying the idea of the information–innovation system require the *energization of people*. It is the first view of the Management 3.0 model. The next chapter discusses that important view from a more practical side.

Summary

In a software development organization, people are the only elements with the ability to manage projects. That's why it's important to energize people. This happens by allowing them to participate in innovative organizations.

For many organizations, innovation is the key to survival, which we can break down into five crucial "cogs" of innovation: *Knowledge* is needed to enable knowledge workers to be productive. *Creativity* is needed to produce results that are original and useful. *Motivation* of employees is important so that they actually do something worth doing. *Diversity* of people adds robustness and flexibility to an organization. And *personality* is the result of people embracing a number of basic virtues.

These five cogs of innovation all need to be in place to energize knowledge workers and to have them produce innovative products and services.

---

15 Levitt, Ted. Ted Levitt on Marketing. Boston: Harvard Business School Press, 2006. [Levitt 2006:172]

Reflection and Action

Let's see if you can apply some ideas from this chapter to your organization:

- Get some colleagues together, and review the five cogs of innovation (knowledge, creativity, motivation, diversity, personality). Is your organization actively addressing all of these? Is every wheel in the information-innovation system running smoothly? If not, what do you plan to do about it?

- Discuss the *identifiable* results of innovation in your organization. Can you name any results? If not, why not? If all the prerequisites (knowledge, creativity, motivation, diversity, personality) are in place, why are no innovations implemented? Are there any actionable items missing?

Chapter 5

How to Energize People

Creative powers can just as easily turn out to be destructive. It rests solely with the moral personality whether they apply themselves to good things or to bad. And if this is lacking, no teacher can supply it or take its place.

—Carl Jung, psychiatrist (1875–1961)

In the previous chapter, we identified a software team as a system that consumes information and produces innovation. The system has people as its important agents, and therefore Energize People is the first view in the Management 3.0 model. We have also identified five criteria that must be met to make this system of people work: *knowledge, creativity, motivation, diversity,* and *personality*. In this chapter, we elaborate on four of these topics, discussing them from a more practical side. However, the scope of this book required me to let the *knowledge* topic rest for now. Knowledge management in organizations is a topic too vast to squeeze into a few pages. (And you could argue that knowledge better fits the fourth view of the Management 3.0 model, which is about developing competence.) So let's save that topic for a rainy day and focus on *creativity, motivation, diversity,* and *personality*.

Creative Phases

Research into creativity resulted in me finding the article "Definitions of Creativity," by Arthur J. Cropley [Cropley 1999:511], which provides interesting material on this topic. Cropley writes that there are three phases of creativity:

- **Preconventional creativity** is the kind commonly exhibited by children younger than 7 years old. It is mainly formed using visual perception and involves spontaneity, emotional involvement, and sometimes the repainting of a child's bedroom walls.

- **Conventional creativity** is the second phase of creativity. It is often found in children between 7 and 11 years old and involves actual thinking, but this is dominated by constraints and conventions imposed by the child's skills that are being developed.

- **Postconventional creativity** is the last phase and is found in children older than 11 years and in adults. In this phase people can produce new things *despite* knowing what the constraints and conventional approaches are.

The important difference between preconventional and postconventional creativity is that small children produce novelty because they are *ignorant* of the constraints, whereas adults can produce novelty *despite* knowing the constraints. For example: My first printed publication as a 4 year old was a wedding card I designed for my kindergarten teacher (see Figure 5.1a). My preconventional creativity made me depict my teacher about five times bigger than her new husband. (Maybe because in my mind she was about five times more important.) Later, in my conventional creative phase, I learned to draw humans in more reasonable shapes and sizes (see Figure 5.1b). But much later, when I was a student, my talents had entered the postconventional phase, and my drawings reverted to the same distortions I had unknowingly experimented with when I was 4 years old. Only this time it was intentional (see Figure 5.1c).

I believe the three phases of creative thinking are a useful tool, but I don't believe they have anything to do with the minds of children. Let me explain this with another example: In the old days of Windows 3.1, I once showed a friend of mine some printed pages of text I had created using a cool font. I told him I had somehow lost the font and was unable to find it. My friend, who was blissfully ignorant of anything related to computers, looked strangely at the printed text and said he didn't understand my problem. "But you have the font on paper here," he said. "Yes," I answered, "but it's not in my computer." At this he replied with a puzzled look: "But yesterday you showed me your new scanner. Why don't you scan the font back into the computer?"

The three-phase approach to creativity applies to *everyone*, adult or not, who is not familiar with the constraints of a certain problem domain. Anyone of us can be naïve and ignorant, and all of us can come up with ideas too far-fetched to be considered by experienced people whose creative thinking takes place in the conventional phase. The idea of scanning a font from printed paper into a computer was an original and creative solution—for someone who is too ignorant to understand that it is also a ridiculous idea. As a software developer, I couldn't have imagined this even if I wanted to.

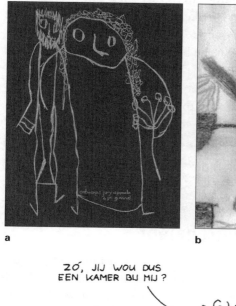

FIGURE 5.1

Drawings made when I was a) 4 years, b) 8 years, c) 19 years old.[1]

a

b

c

The problem with knowledge is that, at first, it *constrains* people's views of the world. They lose their childlike and uninhibited talent to make ridiculous connections between unrelated things. The challenge is

---

1 Irrelevant translation: "So, you want to rent a room with me?" "Hmmm, there's not much meat here, is there?"

to regain that talent by moving to the phase of postconventional creativity, which enables a person to be as imaginative as a child, but *with* the knowledge of what the real constraints are. Only then can they achieve the highest levels of creativity and make drawings even more bizarre than mine. This concept is sometimes referred to as having a "beginner's mind" and is nicely described in the book *Zen Mind, Beginner's Mind* [Suzuki 1980].

In many organizations, employees get stuck in the conventional creative phase. They aren't challenged to get to the next level. It is a manager's job to make sure that employees advance to the level of postconventional creativity, developing a beginner's mind, for the sake of innovation and organizational survival—for example, by exposing them to environments that stimulate reflection and inspiration.

Manage a Creative Environment

Creativity requires the availability of information and knowledge and a diverse bunch of motivated people with a good mix of personalities. These prerequisites should be sufficient for teams to generate creative ideas. But there are a few things a manager can do to turn up the heat and stimulate creativity in the team. A manager should not only look at the development of a beginner's mind, but also at the environment. A person is likely to be more creative when his environment breathes creativity.

Safety

People are creative only when they feel it is safe to express their ideas. There must be *freedom* to be creative and freedom to take *risks* when talking about new ideas and acknowledgment that *failure* is OK. When people know that they are free to take risks and fail, they are more inclined to come up with new ideas. Feeling safe means not being afraid to express ideas and ask questions (W. Edwards Deming) [Austin, Devin 2003:118].

Play

There is plenty of creativity involved when people play games. By turning ordinary activities into little games, or by playing games during lunch breaks, you can challenge people's minds and allow them to practice their creative talents.

Variation

Routine work kills creative thinking. Organize a meeting in the local park, give each product release the name of a funny animal, or put someone's drawings on the cover of your monthly progress reports. You can open people's minds and spur associative thinking by making sure that there is always sufficient variation, even in routine work.

Visibility

I once worked in an environment where cartoons were put on the wall; people were working while lying on a couch; paper, markers, scissors, dossiers, and confetti were strewn across the floor; some people were completing a 5,000-piece puzzle; and teabags were dangling from the ceiling. (You can ask me another time how they got up there.) It was one of the most creative times of my life. You can instill creativity just by making other people's creative results visible. (And in the case of the teabags, palpable.)

Edge

I once went hang gliding in Rio de Janeiro. Rarely had I been so nervous. But as soon as we were in the air, I was glad that I did it. And I am happy to have tried camping in the wild. And talking in front of big audiences. And eating piranhas in the Amazon. And riding stark naked on a bike through a city. And handing over draft chapters of this book to critical reviewers. But you will *not* find me bungee-jumping any time soon. I only do things that are barely in reach of my courage.

The *edge* can be compared to a good work out, which has to hurt a little to be effective.

> If you want to become adept at any activity involving change, innovation, or creativity, you'll eventually face up to the fact that edge discomfort is a part of your life. You'll need to be OK with that. You don't want to learn to stretch painlessly. You want to learn to accept the discomfort of an edge as a condition of your work, a sign that you're doing it well.[2]

---

2   Austin, Robert and Lee Devin. Artful Making. New York: *Financial Times*/Prentice Hall, 2003. Used with permission.[Austin, Devin 2003:123].

In practice, the *edge* doesn't mean that you should give people too much work to do. It means that real challenges for the human mind should be a little scary. And you can help people to find their edge.

Although teams are responsible for the projects they are working on, managers are responsible for the environment they work in. Because people's behavior depends (in part) on their environment, it is imperative that you tweak the environment to get the best out of your teams. Regularly check the list of *safety, play, variation, visibility,* and *edge,* and ask yourself whether you've done enough to give your team the best possible environment to work in.

Creative Techniques

You can employ literally hundreds of techniques to stimulate creativity in your teams. I cannot possibly list them all. It would require a book all by itself. (Fortunately, such books already exist [Clegg, Birch 2006].) However, on a meta-level, it is interesting to note that creative techniques can be divided into several categories[3]:

- **Processes**: Some creative techniques, such as Creative Problem Solving, Productive Thinking Model, and Synectics, describe the process to follow to generate creative solutions. Most of them involve a number of steps that can be repeated until sufficient ideas have been generated. They can encompass other more specific techniques for the execution of individual steps.

- **Problem Definition**: Some techniques deal specifically with problem analysis and redefinition to make it better understandable. They include techniques such as Chunking (dividing a problem in smaller chunks), Five Ws and H (asking Who? Why? What? Where? When? And How?), and Boundary Examination (refining the problem).

- **Idea Generation**: These are techniques that concern themselves with finding as many potential solutions as possible for the problem. Both Brainstorming (generating ideas in a group while suspending judgment) and Talking Pictures (generating ideas through association with pictures) are examples of this category.

---

3   Creative techniques are available at the Mycoted website:
http://www.mgt30.com/mycoted/.

- **Idea Selection**: The ideas that have been generated need to be selected at some point. Anonymous Voting (making people feel safe about expressing their opinions), Consensus Mapping (sequencing ideas into a usable plan), and Sticking Dots (determining priorities) are examples of this category.

Extrinsic Motivation

Now that we have discussed *creativity*, it is time to turn to the practical side of *motivation*, the next of the cogs of innovation. And I must admit that I cheated a little. I didn't cover all relevant theories in the previous chapter. On the topic of motivation, there is still a little background to cover.

Management professor Douglas McGregor devised a model of motivation he called **Theory X and Theory Y**[4] [McGregor, Cutcher-Gershenfeld 2006]. Theory X says that people in general prefer not to work. (Theory Y is discussed in the next section.) Theory X says that money, managerial controls, and the proverbial carrots and sticks are the best ways to get people to do their jobs; and even more of the same is needed to have them do their jobs *well*. It holds that a certain amount of **extrinsic motivation** is needed to make people operate at peak performance.

External motivation in the form of financial benefits, such as merit raises, incentive pay, and bonuses, can *sometimes* work. For example: stock options among employees can, occasionally, work well for startup companies with little funds [Yourdon 2004:94]. And nonmonetary rewards are another well-known form of extrinsic motivation. Steve McConnell wrote that these have worked quite well for him while he was working for Microsoft [McConnell 2004:139].

Praise and compliments are an even more subtle form of motivation but also extrinsic in nature. While writing the previous sentence, I received an email message from a reader telling me that my blog posts are "brilliant stuff." (This was apparently a smart person.) I can hardly think of better ways to motivate me, considering that I once wrote that I'm a compliment junkie. You can make me do almost anything, and I will enjoy it, too, as long as you make me feel that I'm good at it. But that's just me. Other people might be normal.

---

4 http://www.mgt30.com/theory-xy/.

The extrinsic approach to motivation is quite common in western civilizations. It is a direct result of the causal deterministic fallacy in that it assumes that for every desired situation B there must exist a cause A that will make it happen. Yet complexity showed us that the world isn't as linear as people often think. B could very well never happen, despite all the money and energy that people waste on A.

Unfortunately, nonlinearity not only means that desired effects don't come about. It also means that *undesired* side effects *do* come about, as Tom DeMarco and Timothy Lister nicely described in Peopleware:

> These *motivational accessories*, as they are called (including slogan coffee mugs, plaques, pins, key chains, and awards), are a triumph of form over substance. They seem to extol the importance of Quality, Leadership, Creativity, Teamwork, Loyalty, and a host of other organizational virtues. But they do so in such simplistic terms as to send an entirely different message: Management here believes that these virtues can be improved with posters rather than by hard work and managerial talent.[5]

Many experts acknowledge and agree that a lot of damage can be created by merit raises, incentive pay, and bonuses:

> Deming believed that every business is a system, and the performance of individuals is largely the result of the way the system operates. In his view, the system causes 80 percent [other sources claim an even higher percentage] of the problems in a business, and the system is management's responsibility. He wrote that using exhortations and incentives to get individuals to solve management problems simply doesn't work. Deming opposed ranking because it destroys pride in workmanship, and he opposed merit raises because they address the symptoms, rather than the causes, of problems.[6]

---

5   DeMarco, Tom and Timothy Lister. Peopleware: 2nd Edition. New York: Dorset House Pub, 1999. [DeMarco, Lister 1999:178].

6   Source: Poppendieck, Mary. "Unjust Deserts" Better Software. July/August 2004, page 34. Used with permission. [Poppendieck 2004:34].

Clearly Deming had an interesting view of teams and organizations, perfectly in line with systems thinking and complexity theory, and far before such scientific schools of thought were in vogue. One cannot help but understand that in the 1950s when people's opinions were still firmly rooted in causal deterministic thinking, American businesses collectively rejected Deming's ideas. Consequently, Deming went to Japan where his ideas had a tremendous effect on the competitiveness of Japanese businesses.

Extrinsic motivation is a problem because of the nonlinear behavior of complex adaptive systems. The pushing and prodding of individual elements in such a system has unexpected consequences and side effects that are (for someone outside the system) often too complex to be foreseen. For example: The American government created policies to promote home ownership among "lower class" citizens in the United States (extrinsic motivation). And combined with financial bonuses in the banking world (also extrinsic motivation), this caused the whole financial system to inflate and subsequently collapse, pushing the world into a recession [Norberg 2009]. Another example on a smaller scale: One CEO saw the stock of his company losing 22% of its value after an internal email was made public in which he told employees that he expected all parking lots to be full at 7:30 a.m. [Austin, Devin 2003:119].

Different authors have jointly identified multiple, dangerous side effects of extrinsic motivation. These include suboptimization of key processes, destroyed intrinsic motivation, addiction to extrinsic stimuli, reduced performance in problem solving, and unintended competition between colleagues [Austin 1996] [Poppendieck 2004] [Pink 2009].

However, I want to stress that extrinsic motivation is not always a bad thing. Reading through the extensive literature, you could get the impression that the Theory X approach is to be avoided at all times. This is simply not true. There is nothing inherently wrong with the concepts of bonuses, rewards, and T-shirts. Like there's also nothing intrinsically wrong with cars, knives, and pesticides. It is only a problem when naïve people are unaware of their dangers. Unfortunately, when it comes to complex systems, most people are naïve and unaware. So the bottom line is this: If you don't know what you're doing, steer clear of Theory X and extrinsic motivation.

Intrinsic Motivation

The Theory Y-part of Douglas McGregor's model of motivation assumes that people enjoy their mental and physical duties, and that they think work is as natural as play. This part of McGregor's model is all about **intrinsic motivation**, and people's innate desire to do well, and their eagerness for self-control and self-direction in accomplishing objectives.

IS THERE A THEORY Z?

Actually, there is. Developed by William Ouchi, it is seen by many as a derivative of Theory Y. It seems to go one step further in suggesting that employees want to build happy working relationships with their colleagues and want to feel appreciated.

Personally, I don't distinguish between Theory Y and Theory Z because they are both about intrinsic motivation.

A position that is widely accepted in recent writing is that creativity is based on intrinsic motivation—the wish to carry out an activity for the sake of the activity itself, and not in the hope of obtaining external rewards. Extrinsic motivation can inhibit creativity or even be fatal to it [Runco, Pritzker 1999:521].

Intrinsic motivation does not suffer from the nonlinear side effects so often experienced with extrinsic motivation. In the case of intrinsic motivation, it is not a matter of we-want-results-B-so-we-must-give-an-incentive-for-A. With intrinsic motivation A *equals* B: The things we do are themselves the rewards!

We have identified two important reasons for managers to focus on intrinsic motivation. It turns out that, in complex systems, the side effects of extrinsic motivation are unpredictable and often outweigh the benefits. Furthermore, researchers have found that creativity, that crucial link between knowledge and innovation, is best served by intrinsic motivation, not by extrinsic motivation.

The path for managers is clear: When they care about organizational survival, they need to care about innovation. When they care about innovation, they need to care about creativity. When they care about creativity, they need to care about intrinsic motivation. It's almost like a Natural Law.

---

7 http://www.mgt30.com/theory-z/.

Demotivation

Sometimes people claim that you cannot motivate a person and that you can only remove the impediments that prevent a person from being motivated. Or in other words, you cannot introduce motivation; you can only eliminate demotivation (is this a valid Scrabble word?). Fortunately, this is not true.

Can you make a person happy? Or can you eliminate only the things that make her unhappy? Can you make a person laugh? Or can you only eliminate the things that make him cry?

Two-factor theory[8] (or Motivator-Hygiene theory), is a model proposed by psychologist Frederick Herzberg, who found that satisfaction and dissatisfaction are independent of each other [Herzberg 2008]. The things that motivate people on the job are different from the things that demotivate them. Bad environments, low salaries, and bureaucratic rules are examples of things that make people unhappy. But even when managed well, they don't motivate anyone to do a better job. Have you ever heard someone say, "Gosh, this comfortable chair is really motivating me to do my job as best as I can?" I think not. Instead, people are motivated by other things, such as increased responsibilities, their ability to do a good job, the opportunity to make their own decisions, and the sense of belonging to a group.

Herzberg makes a distinction between motivators and hygiene factors:

- **Motivators**: Challenging work, achievement, personal growth, recognition, responsibilities, and so on.
- **Hygiene factors**: Job security, salary, status, working conditions, policies, fringe benefits, and so on.

Herzberg used the name "hygiene factors" because, like hygiene, these factors don't make people healthier or happier. It is their *absence* that can cause deterioration of health or happiness.

According to this theory, you cannot motivate a person by "eliminating demotivation." Taking away the things that make people dissatisfied, or introducing hygiene factors, can at most result in people having neutral feelings toward their jobs. But that's not enough. It follows from Herzberg's theory that you also have to introduce motivators: the things that really motivate people. They are different from mere hygiene factors. And they are the topic of the next section.

---

8 http://www.mgt30.com/two-factors/.

Ten Desires of Team Members

We've seen that intrinsic motivation is preferred over extrinsic motivation. Now we go a step further, and we investigate what intrinsic motivation is made of, starting with **Self-determination theory**.[9]

Self-determination theory is a general model of intrinsic motivation that differentiates between three main intrinsic needs. These needs are universal, innate, and psychological [Deci, Ryan 2004]:

- **Competence**: The need for a person to experience oneself as capable in coping with the environment
- **Autonomy**: The need for someone to actively participate in determining one's own behavior, with autonomous choice of actions
- **Relatedness**: The need to care for and be related to others, and to be involved in the social world

Professor Steven Reiss proposed a similar theory. He found that 16 basic desires guide nearly all human behaviors.[10]

Acceptance	The need for approval
Physical Activity	The need for exercise
Curiosity	The need to think
Power	The need for influence of will
Eating	The need for food
Romance	The need for love and sex
Family	The need to raise children
Saving	The need to collect
Honor	Being loyal to a group
Social Contact	The need for friends
Idealism	The need for purpose
Status	The need for social standing
Independence	Being an individual
Tranquility	The need to be safe
Order	Or stable environments
Vengeance	The need to strike back

---

9 http://www.mgt30.com/self/.
10 Source: Reiss, Steven. Who Am I? The 16 Basic Desires That Motivate Our Actions and Define Our Personalities. City: Berkley Trade, 2002. Used with permission. [Reiss 2002].

Some businesses are adept at providing opportunities for eating, sex, and vengeance. (I'm just joking, of course.) But I would prefer to ignore those and focus on some of the other innate human desires. I believe a number of them can be directly targeted by managers. Both self-determination theory and the 16 basic desires explain how we can motivate people and we can turn these theories into the 10 Desires of Team Members:

1. Make sure that people **feel competent** at what they are doing. Give them work that challenges their abilities but that is still within their grasp.

2. Try to let people **feel accepted** by you and the group. Compliment them on their achievements (but only if you mean it).

3. Make sure that their **curiosity** is addressed. Even though some activities can be boring, there should always be something new for them to investigate.

4. Give people a chance at satisfying their **honor**. You must allow teams to make their own rules, which team members will follow happily (or sometimes grudgingly).

5. Infuse the business with some **idealism** (purpose). You're not just there to make money. You're also making a (small) contribution to make the world a better place. (Note: Be careful with this one. It is often abused by top management in an attempt to obfuscate its real purpose, which is simply to make money.)

6. Foster people's **independence** (autonomy). Allow them to be different from other people, with their own tasks and responsibilities. And compliment them on their original and interesting hair style.

7. Make sure that some level of **order** is maintained in the organization. People work better when they can rely on some (minimal) company rules and policies.

8. Make sure that people have some **power** or influence over what's happening around them. Listen to what they have to say and help them in making those things happen.

9. Create the right environment for **social contacts** (relatedness) to emerge. There's usually no need to venture into the romance area, but friendships can easily arise, provided that managers take care of a fertile context.

10. Finally, it is important for people to feel that they have some **status** in the organization. They shouldn't feel like dangling somewhere at the bottom of a big hierarchy.

Make it a regular activity to review all ten items on the list of ten desires, and remind yourself that you need to do something about one thing or another. The tasks typically fall in the *important-but-not-urgent* range [Covey 2004], meaning that it is easy to forget about them. But in the long run, they can help you much more than a salary raise.

BUT WHAT IF EMPLOYEES WANT EXTRINSIC MOTIVATORS?

Some employees specifically ask for bonuses, rewards, or incentive pay. What can you do about this?

If there is no way around the extrinsic motivation, you could ask employees to be creative and describe all the possible ways that they can think of to rig the system. Then ask them how the extrinsic motivators should be (re)defined to prevent these same problems.

When the employees ask for external motivators, *they* have to solve the problem of undesired side effects because *you* don't want them.

And if you don't know how to target people's intrinsic desires, you can always ask. Scott Berkun suggests there's one simple question that a manager can ask every person in a team:

"What can I do to help you do your best work?"[11]

Just by asking this simple question, you do three things:

- You acknowledge that the person is at least capable of doing her best.
- You make the person evaluate her own performance.
- You initiate a discussion about possible further improvements.

---

11 Berkun, Scott. *Making Things Happen: Mastering Project Management.* Sebastopol: O'Reilly Media, Inc, 2008. [Berkun 2008:186].

Scott's single question is easy to ask on a regular basis. And hard for older guys, like me, to forget.

What Motivates People: Find the Balance

People's motivation is personal and as indefinable, unpredictable (and ridiculous) as their tastes in food, music, and (wo)men. I once asked the readers of my blog what motivated them. They answered they are motivated when

- They created a product that made a difference for someone.
- They have a feeling of control over their computer.
- They have the ability to build stuff that makes people's lives easier.
- They can improve themselves, professionally and personally.
- They are allowed to order books because they love reading.
- They realize that four hours went by while it felt like ten minutes.
- They are treated as a human being, and not as another resource.
- Their product achieves success, and success boosts confidence.
- They feel their product is an expression of themselves.
- They feel a rush of finding solutions to difficult problems.
- They revel in creating simple solutions while still delivering value.
- They have a job that earns them money.
- They are trusted with critical projects.
- Their passion for software engineering is rewarded.
- They can use the newest technologies.
- They got a token of appreciation from all stakeholders.
- A user said "thank you."

As you can see, there are many ways to motivate (and demotivate) people. As a development manager or project manager, it might help to use a mental balance sheet in your head for each person in your team to monitor their motivation. Here's how it works…

When I was 12 years old, one of my teachers told my mother that my attitude was like that of a territorial animal. I hated sharing my comfort space. I didn't like it when pencils and other stuff (of the kids next to me) occupied some inches of my desk. And I also kept pushing away the schoolbags that were invading my territory on the floor. This attitude has never changed. I still don't like it when people trespass on my belongings, my living space, or the results of my creative efforts. I once had a partner who carelessly opened my mail. He still carries my bite marks. And I feel no shame in admitting that it took me three years to agree on a shared bank account with my current spouse. With hesitation.

Not surprisingly, I also don't like sharing my code with other people. That's why I consider collective code ownership, as promoted by Extreme Programming, to be in direct violation with my personal well-being. My code is mine. Your code is yours. Sure, I'd love to interface, and I'm eager to make improvements, but for my code, it will happen under my conditions. I don't want other people to touch my stuff. My code is not available for a collective rewrite. (Surely, I hope you're not suggesting that others can rewrite my book, too, are you?)

So, if you think some practice (like collective code ownership) is required (as it often is), how are you going to handle the motivation of a stubborn guy like me?

Imagine a balance sheet (see Figure 5.2) that lists the things that motivate and demotivate a person on your team. "Best" practices have different effects on different people. Collective code ownership demotivates me. Therefore, it subtracts one point from my motivational balance sheet. But my good friend Niels, who is the truest socialist I ever allowed to come close to my private life, would probably be delighted to hand over his code to the collective. Therefore, a collective code ownership policy might motivate him tremendously, and his motivational balance sheet would earn a big point.

We should treat other debates on practices in a similar way. For example, I like working in a large open space so that I can see everyone and always know who stole my chair. But I understand that other people prefer a private office so that they can enjoy some peace and quiet while they work. Fortunately, that was one positive point for me on my balance sheet, when I was working on one big open floor, shared with 80 people, three printers, a big red balloon, and a ship's bell. However, I think my friend Niels values his privacy more than I do, so maybe he would score a negative point on this issue. If he were to work in that office. Which he isn't. So, good for him!

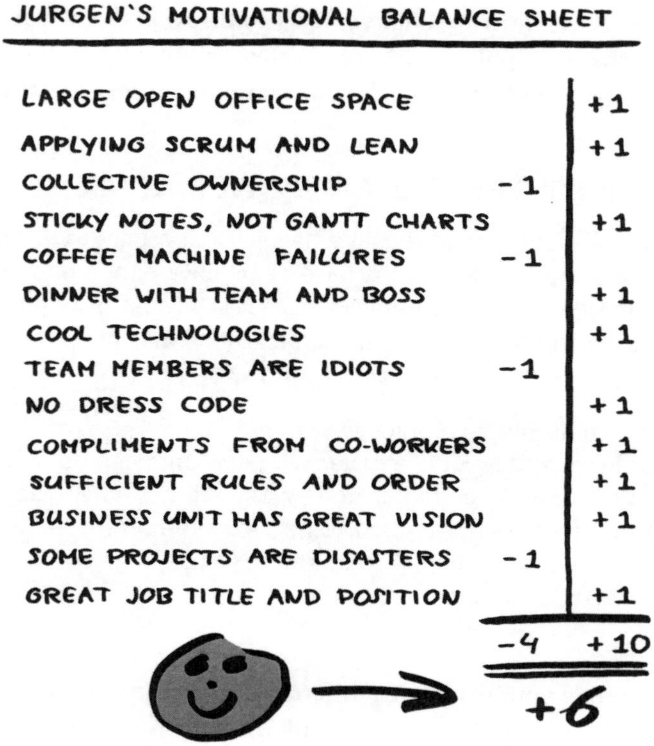

JURGEN'S MOTIVATIONAL BALANCE SHEET

LARGE OPEN OFFICE SPACE	+1
APPLYING SCRUM AND LEAN	+1
COLLECTIVE OWNERSHIP	-1
STICKY NOTES, NOT GANTT CHARTS	+1
COFFEE MACHINE FAILURES	-1
DINNER WITH TEAM AND BOSS	+1
COOL TECHNOLOGIES	+1
TEAM MEMBERS ARE IDIOTS	-1
NO DRESS CODE	+1
COMPLIMENTS FROM CO-WORKERS	+1
SUFFICIENT RULES AND ORDER	+1
BUSINESS UNIT HAS GREAT VISION	+1
SOME PROJECTS ARE DISASTERS	-1
GREAT JOB TITLE AND POSITION	+1

$$-4 \quad +10$$
$$+6$$

FIGURE 5.2

My Motivational Balance Sheet is positive!

Likewise, in Scrum, we could discuss whether to estimate features using "story points" versus "ideal days" versus "T-shirt sizes" versus "bananas," and whether the iteration length should be one week or four weeks, and whether to use a fancy electronic tool or pink paper sticky notes as an Agile planning tool, and so on, and so on…. But the best thing is this: By simply supporting your team members in having these discussions, you score positive points on every motivational balance sheet in the team. It's like creating wealth for free!

Many roads lead to Rome. And although the ways leading to successful software projects might be somewhat less numerous, there are still plenty of choices along the way. On the forks in the roads, I often come across discussions and heated debates on "best" practices that don't take into account the first value of the Agile Manifesto, which is still "People over Process." Motivating your people is always more important than establishing your own favorite processes. Just face it, if you are ever unfortunate enough to be managing a project team full of people like me, they are never going to like the collective code ownership policy, no matter how many Kent Beck Signature books you try to throw at them. You will have to balance that new policy with some other convincing and motivational practices, or you will have to lick your wounds and try something else.

WHAT IF SOMEONE HAS A NEGATIVE BALANCE?

When someone has a negative balance I see only two options: Work together on making the balance positive or agree to replace the employee. A person who does not like most of what's happening on the team and in the organization can bring down the motivation of everybody else working with her.

I would confront this employee with her own balance of likes versus dislikes, and I would ask her what we both can do, together, to turn the tide. When things don't work out, it is time to acknowledge that there is not a good fit between the employee and the team or the organization. And this needs to be done sooner rather than later.

Every person on your team has a different motivational balance sheet. The processes and tools you introduce will score both positive and negative points across the team. Sure, it might be necessary to introduce a new rule that sends most of your team into turmoil—like writing time sheets or taking turns listening to a customer. Sometimes there's no gain without a little pain. Whatever practices you preach, motivate your people, and keep their sheets balanced.

Make Your Rewards Intrinsic

In your attempts at rewarding people, aim for intrinsic motivation by linking your actions to innate human desires. For example: Do not buy arbitrary books for someone as a cheap (extrinsic) reward. Buy books that are meant to satiate someone's curiosity and his need for competence. Do not pay for a team dinner as a way of saying "thank you" for achieving a milestone. Pay for a team dinner if it is meant to address people's needs for social contact and relatedness (and eating). And do not introduce rules, practices, or policies just to please people who ask for them. Again, that would be an extrinsic reward. The real purpose must be to introduce order and stability.

Your interviews and discussions with employees will result in them expressing their desire for rewards and incentives. But whether it is the elimination of demotivation or the introduction of motivation, either way you must try to address only their intrinsic needs.

Diversity? You Mean Connectivity!

After *creativity* and *motivation*, the next of the cogs of innovation to discuss is *diversity*. When people ask me to discuss diversity, and how to promote it in software teams, I sometimes refer to a blog post I wrote a while ago. It paints a picture from the perspective of an employee:

> I am ____. It's not by choice. That's how I was born. I am perfectly happy being ____. It's no big deal. It's just the way it is. But other people are making a fuss about it.
>
> Some say there ought to be more people who are ____ in software development. They say we must invite people who are ____ to try a technical career, because there aren't enough of them in our industry. And some say we should hire people who are ____ because they "add diversity" to our teams.
>
> I don't see why.
>
> Either people who are ____ like software development, or they don't. (It's unlikely they've never heard of it. Unless they are ★★★) I don't favor an annual celebration day for ____ people in software development. And I don't need awards or programming languages named after people who are ____. I certainly don't like government subsidies for people who are ____. And I *definitely* don't like positive discrimination (affirmative action) in favor of people who are ____. Because I think it is an insult to people like me who are both ____ *and* competent enough to create a career on their own.
>
> And besides, if we make exceptions for people who are ____, then we should do the same for people who are @@@, ###, &&&, --- and ===. And where does that end?

> Of course, when some #*! people are negatively discriminating against ____ people, we should fight them. But that's all there is to it. Neutrality is our end goal. It's not a stop somewhere halfway.
>
> I'm very happy that I am where I am today because I am competent. Not because some people hired me because I am ____.

The approach some people have to the issue of social diversity is rather simplistic. Their idea of "adding diversity" to a software team is often limited to attracting more women. It is an approach based on stereotypes about gender differences, and from a scientific perspective, it is completely outdated [Eliot 2010:26]. There's a lot more to diversity than "the shape of one's genitals." [Hamel 2007:158].

It has been noted by management experts and complexity scholars that a person's performance is determined, to a large extent, by the system in which he (or she) is set to work. And social network analysis has revealed that this performance also depends on the person's connectivity with other people in the social network [Cross 2004:11].

This means that when you hire a new person one of the important things to watch out for is *how this person will connect to other people in the organization*. Preferably, you want these connections to be of a different kind than the connections the existing team members have established because diversity in connectivity has the highest impact on competence and performance on your team. Of course, there's much more to diversity than just connectivity. But the impact of connectivity is certainly higher than the impact of gender.

This means, when hiring a new team member, right after checking for competence, you should check for a person's connection-making capabilities. For example, check what kind of connections she made in her previous job; the kind of connections she prefers in her social life; the sources she uses to increase her knowledge; the way she approaches the receptionist, the HR manager, and other people in your organization; and the way this person can get along with the team she is likely to join. That means you check this stuff *before* you sign the contract because these are all indicators of the real diversity the person can add to your team.

Personality Assessments

In this chapter, we have discussed *creativity, motivation*, and a tiny bit about *diversity*. We can discuss the remainder of the diversity issue by combining it with the topic of *personality*. A diversity of personalities on a team stimulates stability, resilience, flexibility, and innovation. On the other hand, there must be sufficient common ground (or inclusive diversity) among team members to ensure cohesiveness and for them to resolve conflicts. But how do you know if a team is both diverse and cohesive enough? Enter personality tests. There are several ways to assess people's personalities:

The **Sixteen Personality Factor Questionnaire**[12] is a tool developed by psychologist Raymond B. Cattell. Empirical research has confirmed that this model, which distinguishes between 16 personal traits, is useful in predicting a person's behavior in many settings. It provides an integrated picture of an individual's whole personality. My suggestion is to have a look at the 16PF model when you are most serious about personality tests and when people have sufficient time available to do the tests.

The **Myers-Briggs Type Indicator** (MBTI)[13] assessment is the most widely used personality assessment tool in the world, although its effectiveness has been disputed in scientific circles. The MBTI model sorts a number of psychological differences into four opposite pairs (*Extraversion* versus *Introversion*, *Sensing* versus *Intuition*, *Thinking* versus *Feeling*, and *Judging* versus *Perceiving*.) The model is sometimes accused of suffering from the **Forer Effect** (people believing that statements reflect their personality, whereas in reality they apply to almost everyone). I would advise you to consider this test if you care more about people's enthusiasm than scientific justification. The results are fun to discuss, and they enable easy comparisons, if you don't take the results too seriously.

The **Enneagram of Personality**[14] proposes nine personality types, represented with a nine-pointed diagram in a circle. It is said that the tool is an effective method for self-development, although it is sometimes criticized for not being falsifiable (meaning it is unscientific) and accused of having its roots in mysticism. Nevertheless, such a test can be fun to do with a team. And if team members are reluctant to have their personalities assessed scientifically, this unscientific Enneagram can be a welcome compromise. A bit of relativism and a good laugh are worth sharing with

12 http://www.mgt30.com/16pf/.
13 http://www.mgt30.com/mbti/.
14 http://www.mgt30.com/enneagram/.

team members, even if it's only to stimulate team ~~building~~ growing[15] and awareness of differences.

The last model in this list is the **Big Five Factors of personality**.[16] It's a model that consists of five personality traits (*Openness, Conscientiousness, Extraversion, Agreeableness*, and *Emotional Stability*) and is considered to be the most comprehensive model available, providing a conceptual framework that integrates all earlier findings and theory in personality psychology. However, a common complaint about the Big Five model is that it is too high level to be useful. Several studies have confirmed that models of lower-level traits, such as 16PF, Myers–Briggs, and the Enneagram, can be more powerful in predicting actual behavior of people. But they are also more controversial than the Big Five, which is seen as the first (and only) scientific consensus in personality psychology. The Big Five model is a great choice if you want a personality assessment that is scientific in its approach, like the 16PF model, but that doesn't dig too deep. This could draw in some people who would otherwise feel uncomfortable about such a test, or who lack the time to do a full 16PF assessment.

Four Steps toward Team Personality Assessment

There are four things you can do when assessing diversity and coherence of personalities in software development teams.

First, *take the tests yourself*. Get to know yourself. When you understand your own personality, you will better understand what kind of manager you are and how you are likely to be perceived by your teams. For example: The tests showed me that I'm very interested in high-level analysis of ideas, patterns, and designs, and usually not very concerned with pragmatic little rules and details. This means I could be a weak manager when a team is uncaring of daily discipline, orderliness, and cleanliness. And I might have too little patience for (and too much criticism of) other people's solutions.

Second, *share your own test results with your teams*. Show them what they can expect from you as a person. When you are secretive about yourself,

---

15 Mike Cohn suggested that I should use the term "team growing" instead of "team building," which would better reflect my organic view of organizations. Unfortunately, the term "team building" is so deeply ingrained that I keep correcting myself.
16 http://www.mgt30.com/big-five/.

you can expect team members to be secretive toward you. And you don't want that, I'm sure. So don't be coy, and show them your strengths *and* your weaknesses. Yes, this takes some courage. You harden yourself by exposing your vulnerability. You want people to respect and trust you. Openness and honesty can achieve exactly that (and much more).

Third, *ask team members to do a personality test, privately.* There are plenty of free tests to choose from on the Internet, but you can get more elaborate and professional test reports when you are prepared to pay for them. It is not unreasonable to require that team members understand themselves. When they know their own strengths and weaknesses, they are in a better position to behave accordingly. And as a manager you earn some extra points when you show them that you're willing to invest in their self-development.

Now, you *can* stop here. It's great when you know yourself, the team members know you, and the team members know themselves. You will have solved 75% of the team personality issue, which may be enough for your situation. On the other hand, you *might* want to go for the full 100%...

Fourth, you can *suggest that the team members share their results with each other.* This can only be done voluntarily, and only when there's a high level of trust in the team. Naturally, you will have preceded this question by giving them your own test scores, so they know what to expect and might be more willing to follow your lead. Arrange a meeting in a warm, relaxed, nonthreatening atmosphere, and have team members talk freely about their test results. Emphasize that scores are not meant to be good or bad. One cannot be both left- and right-handed at the same time, and neither can someone be both shy *and* bold, or grounded *and* abstracted. And even if people don't really care for the personality models, which, it must be stressed, are not without controversy and dispute, the exercise itself can be a great way to do some team ~~building~~ growing.

When team members better understand each other's personalities, they (and you) can identify any deficiencies in diversity or cohesiveness on the team. And you can discuss what to do about that. It also means the team is in a perfect position for the next step: choosing their team values.

One final note: Some states and countries restrict the use of personality tests by employers, although the legal restrictions are usually directed at employers requiring such tests in the process of hiring new employees. You may want to check this first for your situation and legal environment.

Do-It-Yourself Team Values

The Team Personality Assessment exercise shows a team what kind of people they have on the team. This knowledge can be useful in the following exercise, where the team decides what their core values need to be.

Agile principles, Lean principles, Scrum values, XP values…. Anyone who wants to guide and motivate a software development team seems to come up with his own set of standard values or principles, but I believe that every project is different, and every team may need its own customized value system.

I hereby give you the *Do-It-Yourself Team Values Kit*. Now you can create your own set of values. The idea is simple. It works like this:

1. Print the Big List of 50 Virtues (see Table 5.1) and give a copy to each of your development team members. (Note: Some of the "standard" Agile, Lean, Scrum, and XP values are printed in bold letters.)

2. Tell your team that, together, they must select between three and seven virtues from this list. These must be the virtues that they consider to be the most important, given their current project, situation, and personalities. They *can* choose some standard Agile values, but they can also select some other ones.

3. Optionally, do exactly the same with the stakeholders *outside* the team (functional managers, users, and so on). Get a representative number of them together and have them select between three and seven items that the stakeholders think would be the most important values for the project.

4. Then get together with the team and compare the lists, which must have been created independently. Most selected virtues will probably be different, but some choices will be the same or very similar. It is likely that the environment and the system itself have different views on what's important. Talk about the mutual expectations until you reach consensus on a merged list of three to seven values ("five plus or minus two").

5. You now have agreed on the final team values. Make them clear to all team members and stakeholders by displaying them on posters, mugs, task boards, coffee machines, screensavers, and lunch menus.

TABLE 5.1

Big List of 50 Virtues (Agile Values in Bold)

Accuracy	Creativity	Honesty	Persistence	**Simplicity**
Assertiveness	Curiosity	Humor	Pragmatism	Skill
Aesthetics	Decisiveness	Industriousness	Purposefulness	Stewardship
Balance	Determination	Initiative	Rationality	Tactfulness
Caution	Endurance	Integrity	Reliability	Thoroughness
Cleanliness	Enthusiasm	Joyfulness	Resilience	Tolerance
Commitment	Excellence	Knowledge	**Respect**	**Trust**
Confidence	Flexibility	Mindfulness	Responsibility	Trustworthiness
Cooperation	**Focus**	**Openness**	Self-discipline	Unity
Courage	Helpfulness	Orderliness	Service	Vision

The Big List of 50 Virtues was inspired by the *Wisdom Commons* website[17] where you can find many more virtues applicable to everyday work and life. Of course, teams are free to augment the list with other virtues that they consider essential.

A good list of team values originates from the team and its environment. Many initiatives for "company values" fail because they are devised by top management and imposed on the work floor, and because they do not take into account that different teams may need different values. For example: A creative team may need some more *decisiveness*, whereas a pragmatic team could be in need of a bit more *cleanliness*.

WHAT IF YOU MANAGE MULTIPLE TEAMS?

Good question. I see the same balancing act happening here as many parents are struggling with. They want to treat each of their children equally, but given different personalities some children may be "more equal" than others.

---

17 Descriptions of virtues and morality are available via http://www.mgt30.com/wisdom/.

> My mother sometimes had to be very strict with my brother, while he complained that the same rules never applied to me. And for good reason, as my track record of mischief could fit on half a sticky note.
>
> Likewise, managers will find that they have to treat different teams, and different people, in different ways. And they must be prepared to explain why.

The Big List of 50 Virtues also gives people a chance to introduce some items often forgotten in standard lists of Agile principles, such as the values for craftsmanship (*excellence*, *skill*, and *self-discipline*).

Consensus with management (the environment) on the final list can be vital. The team is embedded in an organization and therefore might have to agree with the organization on the set of team values.

Finally, teams change, projects change, and organizations change. This could necessitate that you redo this exercise once in a while. Teams cannot focus on too many team values at the same time. After having followed certain values for some time, it might be wise to refocus on other ones.

Define Your Personal Values

There are not only team values to concern yourself with. You also have some personal virtues to care about.

When you read many management books, as I do, you quickly end up with an impossible list of important virtues. The authors tell you to be honest and tactful and cautious and assertive and committed and flexible and determined and pragmatic and trustworthy and helpful and open and reliable and tolerant and thorough. And you must have a vision. Oh, and humor, too.

That's not hard. That's inhuman.

It is impossible to be virtuous in 50 dimensions. Trying many things at the same time equals not trying anything at all. It is better to choose a small set of values to focus on. Don't worry too much about the others. Their time will come, too.

I suggest you start by measuring yourself against the same values that were selected by the teams. If *respect* is on the team values list, treat each team member as your equal. If *decisiveness* is important for the team, make sure never to delay any of your decisions that the team depends on. When you want people to be *self-disciplined*, make sure that you honor your meetings and that you're always there on time. Don't use a different value system than the one the team is using. Don't focus on creativity, humor, and tolerance when a team agreed to be self-disciplined, responsible, and orderly. Leading should be done by example, and seeing is believing.

DO YOU MEAN I CANNOT BE MYSELF?

Not at all. You must stay true to your own nature because people easily see through falsely assumed values.

But I'm sure there's room to switch focus to any of your natural behaviors that most closely matches what you expect of the team. (And if one of the values does not come naturally to you, you can at least show them how you're *trying* to self-improve and make things work.)

If one or two values on the team values list come natural to you, feel free to replace them (only for yourself) with some others that you find more challenging. You've done the tests, so you should know your personality by now, and one or two problematic virtues should be easy to choose.

The No Door Policy

And now that we have almost finished this chapter with a bit of self-reflection, I believe a final word is in order for the relationship between a manager and his team.

One of the management concepts I dislike the most, is the **Open Door Policy**. The idea of this policy is that every manager's door is open to all employees, and each of them is encouraged to have open discussions with any manager; and not just at the next management level, but at *all* management levels.

I dislike this policy for three reasons:

- It communicates that managers have a door, and ordinary employees don't. Have you ever heard of an Open Door Policy for ordinary workers? I haven't. Apparently, some top managers think that normal employees have less need for privacy than managers do. A door emphasizes a separation, even when it is open.

- It communicates that it is OK for employees to ignore their own manager and to discuss and negotiate matters with the superiors of their superiors. The policy encourages people to skip nodes in the line of command (both upward and downward). They can circumvent people with a strong opinion (usually me), and deal with the ones who are more pliable and who often lack the context to make proper decisions.

- It communicates that, at any time, employees can peek in the top manager's private room and see his personal secretary, mahogany desk, private Nespresso coffee machine, and titanium golf clubs.

I think the Open Door Policy communicates and emphasizes *distance*, whereas organizations are better off emphasizing *closeness* and *togetherness*. I can hardly think of a better example of "people management" gone wrong (except perhaps for the phrase "people are our greatest assets," which I dislike even more).

We need a different policy, one that emphasizes that managers should not be separated from other kinds of employees, and that managers are people, just like all the others in the organization.

In my last job as a manager I preferred to have a desk somewhere among my teams. It was the same kind of desk that they had. And I wanted to drink the same miserable goo that was being passed off as coffee. I appreciated that important decisions (like architecture and interface choices) were shared with me before people made them final. Which is why I did the same: I asked people for feedback on stuff like brand names, logo designs, company rules, and tool selection, before I made the decisions.

We could call this approach the No Door Policy. When there are no doors you share the same air and the same rules. No one is more important than any of the others. It doesn't mean there needs to be a physical open space. (Although it can help.) And it doesn't mean a manager must be seated directly next to his people. The only purpose of the policy is to communicate that everyone is in it together. We're the same kind of people. We just have different jobs, with different responsibilities. Nothing should be separating us.

This chapter discussed how to "energize the agents" in our complex system. But we haven't finished talking about people. On the contrary, the subsequent chapters also have *people* as their underlying theme. In Chapters 6 and 7, we look at people organizing themselves and how the second view of the Management 3.0 model sees this as a crucial part of Agile management.

Summary

Postconventional creativity is about doing things in unusual ways, while fully understanding what's considered "normal." Such a creative mindset can be supported by teaching people creative techniques and giving them a creative environment to work in.

Extrinsic motivation of people rarely works well because it suffers from unexpected side effects. Intrinsic motivation works much better, though it is important to distinguish motivators (like personal growth) from mere hygiene factors (like job security.)

The connectivity of people is one of the most important aspects of diversity. Diversity in connectivity, not diversity in gender, is one of the best predictors of competence and performance in a team.

People and teams can learn about themselves, and about each other, through personality assessments. When shared and discussed *voluntarily*, such assessments can be great contributors to trust and respect in a team.

Team values can be picked to reflect the attitude a team needs most. It is wise to select personal values that closely match those of the team, so you can lead by example.

Reflection and Action

Let's see if you can apply some ideas from this chapter to your organization:

- Discuss with your team the concept of "beginner's mind" (postconventional creativity). What are you doing to develop and support this kind of mindset?

- Consider the creative environment in your organization. Are you actively addressing safety, play, variation, visibility, and edge?

- Discuss various creative techniques with your team. Which ones are used right now? Do people need to learn more of them?

- Identify forms of extrinsic motivation in your organization and come up with a plan to eliminate them—in particular the financial ones.

- Review the list of ten intrinsic desires. Are you trying to address motivation of team members by relating your efforts to these basic desires?

- Regularly use Scott Berkun's one simple question if you're serious about motivation.

- Learn about personalities and diversity in your team by taking the four steps toward a team personality assessment.

- Use the Do-It-Yourself Team Values list to generate a small list of values that can guide your team in their daily decision making.

- Consider thinking about your own personal values. Are they in line with what you expect from your team? Are they different? Can you lead by example?

- Move your desk to the same area where your team is. If this is not possible, move only your chair.

Chapter 6

The Basics of Self-Organization

Science is organized knowledge. Wisdom is organized life.

> —Immanuel Kant, philosopher (1742–1804)

For centuries, mathematicians have preferred to work with *linear (ordered) systems*, and they considered *nonlinear (complex) systems* to be a special group. But reality is full of paradoxes. Nonlinear systems are the norm and abundant throughout the universe, whereas linear systems are a rare and special breed. Someone once said that distinguishing between linear and nonlinear systems is like dividing all species into two groups: fruit flies and non-fruit flies. And humans, together with whales, tigers, and woodpeckers, would be part of the non-fruit flies group. Could it be that mathematicians are, quite literally, a bit simple-minded? Or might this indicate that they are only human and also part of the group of non-fruit flies?

This chapter focuses on the concept of **self-organization** in nonlinear systems. This topic is fundamental to both management and software development. Therefore I intend to discuss it quite rigorously. And I will make it clear why Empower Teams is the second view of the Management 3.0 model.

Self-Organization within a Context

In the beginning, there was nothing. And then there were membranes or strings, which formed quarks and gluons. And the quarks and gluons organized themselves into composite particles, such as protons and neutrons. And these guys, with the help of some friends called electrons, subsequently organized themselves into atoms. Then these atoms got together one day and decided to take self-organization to yet another level, and they formed molecules. Millions of different molecules were created that way, and they created communities, forming stars, planets, comets, and other crazy objects.

Then some of the molecules, swimming around in a warm and cozy pool, thought they were the coolest of the lot, and they decided to replicate themselves. They adopted the trendy name RNA. The copying frenzy quickly went in many directions, and soon there were prokaryotes and eukaryotes (and viruses, too). And boy, it didn't stop there either.

These biological cells self-organized into millions of different species, and it didn't take long for the brain of one of those species ("humans") to form consciousness. This new aggregate system subsequently decided to take self-organization to even higher levels. It formed tribes, societies, cities, businesses, and (as one of its least successful ideas) governments.

From the beginning of the universe, everything in it was shaped by self-organization:

> Self-organization is the process where a structure or pattern appears in a system without a central authority or external element imposing it through planning.[1]

Self-organization is the norm. It is the *default* behavior of dynamic systems, whether these systems consist of atoms, molecules, viruses, species, or businesses. Or software developers....

It is a bit silly that self-organization of teams is regularly hailed as a "best practice" in Agile software development. Self-organization cannot be a best practice. It is the "default practice" of any system, including teams. No matter how you manage a team, there *will* be self-organization. People will discuss and agree on lunch meetings, folder structures, workplace territories, and birthday parties. Everything that management does not constrain (and much that it attempts to) will self-organize. Humans have behaved that way for 200,000 years.

But is what happens also happening in the "right direction?"

Though every self-organizing system can have its own direction, the possible directions are limited by its environment. The latest theories of the universe suggest that ours is just one out of many, and that our specific universe is "special" (for us) in that it has some specific cosmological parameters. It is these cosmological constants that have constrained and given direction to the self-organization of quarks, protons, atoms, molecules, and the whole shebang.

Likewise, the earth's environment has constrained and given direction to the formation of biological cells. And these cells in their turn have

---

1 http://www.mgt30.com/self-organization/. Reprinted under the Creative Commons License. Please visit http://creativecommons.org/.

constrained and given direction to the formation of viruses. And so on, and so on.... No self-organizing system exists without context. And the context constrains and directs the organization of the system.

Self-Organization toward Value

Some people would argue that animals know the meaning of value. After all, monkeys are reluctant to give up bananas when they possess them. But I beg to differ. Behavior of animals, as programmed by their genes, follows evolutionary strategies. From an evolutionary perspective, it makes perfect sense not to throw away a banana. Scientists can explain almost all social behaviors in animals from an evolutionary perspective. They can explain why I don't like throwing away my old shoes, even when there's no reason to keep them. It's just the beast in me.

What makes humans unique is that, with the introduction of consciousness, we invented morality, laws, and authority. We defined *preferred directions* for self-organizing systems because we see some results as valuable and other results as harmful. We value human lives; therefore, we consider malaria parasites and HIV viruses an undesirable result of self-organization. From an evolutionary perspective, it might seem strange to extend the lives of 80-year old people. But (fortunately), we still do it. We value lots of other irrational and unnatural things, too, like nondiscrimination, peace, and monogamy.

Self-organization makes no distinction between good or bad, between virtues or vices, between valuable or harmful. Systems simply do whatever the environment allows them to do. Whatever they can get away with. And so, humans embraced the concept of **command-and-control**.

In their attempts to steer self-organizing systems (businesses, teams, countries) in the direction that *stakeholders* considered to be valuable, people started assuming command and resorted to a command-and-control style of giving direction. That's how managers got their positions. And that's why governments try to run countries. They care about results, and they want to make sure that self-organizing systems either *produce* valuable things (products and services) or *refrain* from harming valuable things (human lives, economic growth, natural resources). Managers want software teams to create valuable software and make money, and they don't want teams to run away with the cash register. Sometimes the managers succeed. Sometimes they don't.

The funny thing is that many people think command-and-control has always been the norm, and that "self-organizing teams" are a new and interesting concept. But that's just the common "simple-mindedness" again. Self-organization is the formation of things without top-down direction, and it pervades the universe. Conscious command-and-control (imposed order) was invented 13.7 billion years after self-organization, by humans, in their attempts to protect what they believe is valuable. Self-organization is the norm. And command-and-control is the special case.

In his 2001 paper, "Agile Processes and Self-Organization," Ken Schwaber wrote the following:

> Agile processes employ self-organizing teams to handle the complexity inherent in systems development projects. A team of individuals is formed. They organize themselves into a team in response to the pressure of a deadline, reminding me of the saying, "Nothing focuses the mind like a noose!" The pressure cooker of the deadline produces cooperation and creativity that otherwise is rare. This may seem inhumane, but compared with non-agile practices for dealing with complexity, self-organization is a breath of fresh air.[2]

Indeed, for *some* people, locked up in command-and-control organizations, self-organization is like a breath of fresh air. But the fresh air existed long before humans came on stage and invented stifling bureaucracy. And I don't believe that cooperation and creativity are otherwise rare. I just spent several pages of this book explaining that the *whole universe*, and everything in it, is the product of cooperative and creative self-organization. That's not rare. That's ubiquitous.

Self-Organization versus Anarchy

Some experts think that self-organization is different from **anarchy** [Highsmith 2009:60]. Jim Highsmith says that self-organization (in a social context) *implies* some form of leadership, and that it otherwise degenerates into anarchy. I respectfully disagree, although my disagreement is only about semantics.

---

2   Schwaber, Ken. "Agile Processes and Self-Organization"
http://www.mgt30.com/agile-processes/. 2001. Reprinted by permission of Ken Schwaber.
[Schwaber 2001].

The origin of the word "anarchy" is *anarchia*, from Greek, and from *anarchos*, which means "having no ruler." Various dictionaries list two meanings for anarchy:

- Absence of order (or presence of disorder)
- Absence or denial of any authority or established order

This means either of two things: chaos (no order) or complexity (order but not *imposed* by an authority). This is depicted in Figure 6.1. Governance stretches from complexity into order. And anarchy, the absence of governance, stretches from complexity into chaos. (Note: It is merely a simplified, metaphorical picture. But it works for me.)

FIGURE 6.1

Governance versus anarchy.

Anarchy has a bad name, which is undeserved. In the minds of most people, anarchy equals chaos. This misconception is probably the main reason why some experts don't like associating self-organization with anarchy. But galaxies behave in an anarchistic manner, and yet they are not chaotic. Ecosystems are anarchistic, but they are also not chaotic. And countries without (working) governments are anarchies but are also not necessarily chaotic.[3]

A self-organizing system can be the complex variant of anarchy. This is true in physics, in chemistry, in biology, and in sociology. There are many definitions of self-organization, and none of them require leadership, management, or authority. It makes no sense to change the meaning of self-organization when applied in a social context.

The real issue that some people have with anarchy is that such unmanaged systems can behave in a way that the stakeholders don't value. When my children are playing a game, running around me and yelling in my ears, I would eagerly agree that this is anarchy. But the children are self-organizing. It just means their way of self-organizing is not appreciated by me as their primary stakeholder. It's the same with software developers playing football in the office while people are working. (I'm

---

3 http://www.mgt30.com/anarchies/.

serious, I've seen this happen.) Then yes, I will enforce some governance. As Dave Snowden said in a conference session, "Then you draw a line on the floor, and you tell those kids: if you cross this line, you're dead."[4]

Self-Organization versus Emergence

When a property of a system cannot be traced back to any of the individual parts in the system, it is called an **emergent** property. Your personality is an emergent property of your brain. It cannot be traced back to individual neurons. Likewise, fluidity is an emergent property of water, and culture is an emergent property of a group of people.

Three aspects are important for a property to be emergent:

- **Supervenience** is the observation that the property will no longer exist if you take away the individual parts of the system. For example, your personality disappears when I remove your neurons. (Relax; I won't try to prove it.)

- The property is **not an aggregate**, meaning that it is not simply the result of adding up the properties of the individual parts. For example, a single water molecule has no fluidity. So you cannot simply add up the fluidities of a billion individual molecules to determine the fluidity of water.

- There must be **downward causality**, meaning that the emergent property should influence the behavior of the individual parts. For example, the culture of a group of people influences the behavior of its members.

In short, emergent properties are global (to the system), irreducible, and noticeable (to the parts). See Figure 6.2.

The boundaries of the sciences rely on emergent levels. Physics resolves into chemistry, which resolves into biology, which resolves into psychology, which resolves into economics. And each science works with the emergent properties generated by previous levels [Miller, Page 2007:45]. It also means that each level gives rise to new laws and new insights. Psychology is more than just applied biology; biology is more than just applied chemistry; and chemistry is more than just applied physics [Waldrop 1992:82]. This is why **greedy reductionism** doesn't work.

---

4 Copied from David Snowden's speech at the Scandinavian Agile Conference 2009: http://www.mgt30.com/snowden-speech/.

You cannot explain a failed software project in terms of one person's brain waves, or forgetting your spouse's birthday in terms of faulty atoms or string theory. Trust me, I tried. Didn't work.

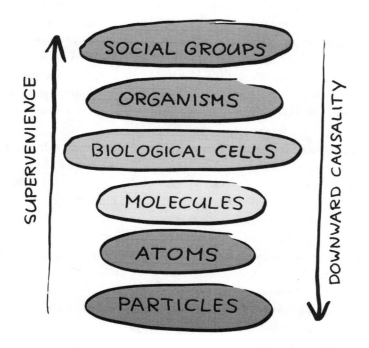

FIGURE 6.2

Emergence (supervenience and downward causality).

Throughout literature, there has been some confusion (and disagreements) about self-organization and emergence [De Wolf, Holvoet 2005]. Some scientists defined one in terms of the other, whereas others claimed they are separate concepts [Corning 2002]. I agree with Peter Corning in that there may be self-organizing systems without emergent properties and emergent properties in systems that are human-created instead of self-organizing. But it is just a matter of definition. In this book, I choose to use the term emergence for "organized 'wholes' composed of functionally distinct 'parts' that produce irreducible combined effects" [Corning 2003:23]. Even though this book is not a self-organizing system, the impression it will make on you will definitely be an emergent property: The impression is global to book, irreducible to the individual pages, but quite noticeable to these pages if you choose to burn the book after reading.

Emergence in Teams

When trying to translate the concept of emergence to teams, we can recognize a host of interesting phenomena. The first is the possibility of *collective decision making* without central planning. Swarm raids of army ants are reported to be among the largest organized operations carried out by any animal [Solé 2000:166]. But not a single ant has a picture of the entire operation in its mind. Likewise, no team member may have a complete picture of the whole project. And yet it is common for good plans to emerge from the interaction of team members, where each can only work with incomplete information.

From research into human consciousness, we learn that multiple conflicting views can result in a (seemingly) *singular view* of the entire system. Daniel Dennett and Marvin Minsky both suggested that "one stream of consciousness" is an illusion. According to Dennett there are actually "multiple drafts" of consciousness [Dennett 1992]. Our brain resolves these multiple competing interpretations of the world into something that we call one identity, or a "self." For an illusion, it works remarkably well. And Minsky described similar ideas, which he called the "society of mind" [Minsky 1986].

There are plenty more theories and models of the human mind, but many of them share the idea of multiple parts resolving into a single consciousness. Likewise, the multiple views of the world in a team can resolve into a singular team view. The team identity is an illusion, and yet it works by having a real impact on their projects. Paradoxically, human consciousness works *because* of the underlying multiple drafts. And the team identity works *because* of the underlying disparate views. I am sure some people will be glad to know that their diverging opinions may turn out to be crucial for a team identity to emerge. (Just don't blame me next time you get into a fight.)

It is also known that a system can be *more than the sum of the parts*. Our brains have a stable "alpha wave" of between 8–12 Hz. It is an accurate clock, although it is constructed from many sloppy ones because all the individual neurons have their own rates of discharging, varying between 8 to 12 times per second. And yet the emergent alpha rhythm is more reliable than that of any of the neurons [Strogatz 2003:42]. Similarly, it is not uncommon for a whole team to perform better than the best performance of any of the individual team members. DeMarco and Lister call this a "jelled team." It is a group of people so strongly linked that the whole is more than the sum of the parts. The productivity of such a group is greater than what the same people can do in unjelled form [DeMarco, Lister 1999:123].

Finally, the nature of emergent properties is often unpredictable [Solé 2000:20]. Water, consisting of two hydrogen atoms and one oxygen atom per molecule, is subject to state changes like freezing and cooking. There is nothing in the properties of hydrogen and oxygen atoms predicting these properties of water [Waldrop 1992:82]. It is the same with teams. You cannot predict the behavior of a team by analyzing individual team members separately. The emergent behavior of the team is a result of the interactions between the team members. Teams are responsible for their own team culture, their own process, their own image in the organization, and sometimes even their own name. You cannot predict these emergent properties when you put a team together. The only thing you can predict is that they will always try to undermine your profitability by asking for expensive tools and seminars.

Self-Organization versus Self-Direction versus Self-Selection

Besides self-organization, a few similar terms are sometimes associated (or confused) with Agile software development teams. Table 6.1 reviews them.

Term	Description
Self-organized/ self-managed	The team organizes its own activities.
Self-selected/ self-designed	The team is self-organizing *and* creates and maintains itself.
Self-directed/ self-governed	The team is self-selected *and* there is no outside management.

TABLE 6.1

Differences Between the Self-* Terms

Closely related to self-organization is **self-selection**. A self-selecting team is a team that selects its own team members. Professor J. Richard Hackman calls it a self-designing team [Hackman 2002:53]. Such a team is an emergent team because the property "team" was not put in place by a manager [Lewin, Regine 2001:282-284]. A startup business consisting of just a few founders is an example of a self-selected team. They manage their own business, although they still operate within the parameters of the law.

Self-direction, which is the same as **self-government** [Hackman 2002:53], is a special form of self-organization and self-selection, in that no management from outside the team is directing it [Lewin, Regine 2001:282-284]. A group of friends playing volleyball on a beach is a self-directing team. They make their own laws for the game. A criminal organization is self-directed, too. It intentionally breaks the laws imposed on it by the environment.

Apparently, a self-directing team is a special type of self-organizing team. Every group of people doing something together is self-organizing. They always fit the scientific definitions of self-organization. In an organizational context, the really interesting question is how much these self-organizing teams are also allowed to be self-directing.

Finally, the term **self-managed** is rather ambiguous. Most people see it as the equivalent of self-organized, but some people consider it to be the same as self-directed. I prefer not to use it.

Darkness Principle

Now that we've looked at the meaning of self-organization, let's look at some conclusions that researchers were able to draw from this.

From a complexity perspective, there is a good reason why teams in an organization must make decisions together. This follows logically from the **Darkness Principle**. This principle states that each agent in a system is ignorant of all behaviors of the system. If an agent "knew" the entire system, the complexity of the whole system would have to reside in that agent. [Cilliers:1998:4-5].

What we learn from the Darkness Principle is that each team member can only have an incomplete mental model of the whole project. That is why they have to plan and decide together. It is why Scrum and Extreme Programming require the whole team to be present during planning meetings and daily stand-ups. The team members must aggregate their limited mental models and agree on a joint approach (see Figure 6.3).

FIGURE 6.3
Team members aggregating their mental models.

Some managers are not comfortable with the idea of allowing a team to make decisions together. They feel they lose control over what's happening when teams make decisions without them. Managers assume that decisions must be enforced, or otherwise anarchy unfolds. But that same anarchy has just constructed an entire universe, all by itself. So it cannot be all that bad. The move to self-organized teams occurs because it is a way to *increase control* over the uncertainties facing a work team [Thomas 2000:35]. Managers must learn that they are "in charge, but not in control" [Stacey 2000a:4]. Any attempts to "control and contain" usually don't work and sometimes even have counterproductive consequences. For example, it is found that attempts of the police to control and contain crowds can *cause* the problems that the police are trying to prevent. [Bond 2009b:41].

Nobody on a team (or in a crowd) has a complete picture of all that's happening in the entire group. By letting them solve their problems and make decisions together you actually *increase* control over the situation. On Twitter, Mike Cohn suggested that Agile software development is *micromanagement* by the team. The Darkness Principle makes it clear that it is this micromanagement that must be delegated from the manager to the team.

Conant-Ashby Theorem

Delegation of control is the best way to keep projects manageable. We can deduce this in a few easy steps, starting with the **Conant-Ashby Theorem**[5]:

> Every good regulator of a system must have a model of that system.

When we want to control something, we need a model of it. That's what this theorem says. To construct such a model (our mental representation) we use the information that the system provides:

- A pilot uses the information in a cockpit to understand what the aircraft is doing and to control it.
- A traffic controller uses information on radar screens to envision the air space around an airport and to control the traffic in it.
- And a manager uses meetings and reports to try and understand the dynamics of a project ("Controlling & Monitoring" [Pmi 2008]).

However, control of a system can only be as good as the quality of the information available from the system. The less information there is about a system, or the less accurate it is, the worse our ability to create a proper mental model of it. And without a good model, the Conant-Ashby Theorem says, we cannot be good regulators.

To make matters worse, complexity adds some fuel to the fire. The more complex a system is, the less capable we are to construct a working model of it. It is hard enough (but not impossible) to understand how a computer works and how to control it. Or how a car works and how to control it. But with complex systems the available information for a controller is either *too complex to comprehend* or *not enough to construct a proper model of it*.

As an example, try to imagine a map of London that should help you control everything in the city, from traffic to communication, from families to businesses. Either way, you have way too much information to fit in your brain, or you have too little to do a reasonable job. With complex systems, as a controller, you're doomed!

---

5   Taken from the Distributed and Complex Systems Wiki, at: http://www.mgt30.com/ashby/.

The more complex a system is, the less we can control it. (And software projects can be complex.) Fortunately, there is a simple solution:

- Traffic controllers don't manage the aircraft. They let the pilots do that.
- Pilots hardly do any controlling themselves. Much of it is delegated to automated systems.
- And (wise) managers delegate most activities to team members.

Delegation of control is a manager's way of controlling complex systems. You push decisions and responsibilities down to a level where someone has information that is *smaller in size* and *more accurate*. Smart managers understand that they must try to make as few decisions as possible. For better overall control of a complex system, most of the decisions should be made in the subsystems.

Distributed Control

I do not actively control my own heart rate, my digestive system, my breathing, my blood pressure, my sleep, or my immune system. These activities are all taken care of by subsystems within the bigger system that I call "me." I would even dare to suggest that "me" is little more than a virtual system. It thinks it is in control, and it communicates with other virtual systems that think they are in control. But at the end of the day, our bodily subsystems are doing all the work, on their own. And they leave only a minor window open for what we like to call "free will."

This delegation of control does not stop at the subsystems either. My immune system has no central control. There is no master neuron in my brain to control my thinking, and there is no master pacemaker cell to regulate my heartbeat. All control is distributed again among the parts. And for a good reason: A single controlling authority makes a system neither robust nor resilient.

If there were a clear advantage to central control, natural selection wouldn't have resulted in distributed control as the principle design philosophy for organisms. This is easy to understand: If my immune system were controlled by a central authority, it would be much easier for viruses to take it down. It wouldn't be as robust and resilient as it is now.

Kevin Kelly, writer and expert in digital culture, listed nine "Laws of God" in his book Out of Control [Kelly 1994:469]. These are the first two:

- **Distribute being**: A complex system is more than the sum of its parts. The "extra" part is distributed among the system. It cannot be attributed to any single authoritative part.

- **Control from the bottom up**: In a complex system, everything happens at once, and problems ignore any central authority. Therefore overall governance must be spread among all the parts.

Distributed control is crucial for the survival of complex systems. For the Internet, this has been achieved by ensuring that there are many so-called "root name servers" all over the world, which makes it practically impossible to take down the Internet.

For organizations, we can achieve something similar. The way to distribute control in an organization is through *empowerment*.

THIS DELEGATION STUFF ISN'T REALLY NEW, IS IT?

True, much of what I write about delegation isn't new. Experts like W. Edwards Deming and Peter Drucker have discussed decentralization and delegation of control decades ago.

I am only trying to describe and summarize these ideas against the backdrop of social complexity.

Empowerment as a Concept

Empowerment is a recurring theme in management literature. It has been described and promoted many times before. Some authors have suggested not using the word "empowerment" anymore [Thomas 2000] [Pink 2009]. They say the word has a negative connotation, which hints at subordinates being "disempowered" by default, after which they need to be "given power" by their managers [Lewin, Regine 2001]. Their preferred approach is not to call people subordinates but "associates" or "partners" [Stallard 2007:76].

Using the word "partners" instead of "subordinates" is a nice idea, but empowerment is still a core responsibility of managers. Ultimately, the way an organization is structured, and how it operates, is the responsibility of its owners. Only they can decide which employees (or "partners") can be given the freedom of hiring people, the power of signing contracts with customers and vendors, the right to negotiate salaries, or access to the corporate bank account. We often call these people *managers*. Managers to which such powers have been extended may have the option of further extending these powers to other people. Or not. It depends on the instructions they got with their powers.

So yes, there is empowerment, and it starts with the owner of the business, but it doesn't mean the organizational structure is necessarily a hierarchy. Empowerment can be extended throughout an organization in several other ways.

I gave the keys of my house to my cleaner. I pay her to clean every week, but I gave no specific instructions. (I admit that I wouldn't even know how to do it myself.) I don't feel that I'm her boss. We are simply in an economical relationship, through the delegation of work in exchange for a fee. One time, when I came home early, I noticed she had her teenage daughter helping her with the cleaning. Apparently, she had delegated some of the work herself. And though it meant that there were now two persons wandering around my house, touching my stuff, and putting clothes in the wrong closets, I decided to trust her judgment in this. That is empowerment.

Empowerment as a Necessity

I remember a decision I once had to make. The company I worked for had three big new projects and two locations in which to execute these projects (Ukraine and Holland). Obviously, our teams needed to know in which location we would be doing which project, and several people turned to me for a decision. I had no idea why. I tried to be inconspicuous and wasn't wearing anything remarkable. But clearly, they found me and expected my influence or control.

Twenty-six hundred years ago, the Chinese philosopher Laozi referred to influence and control in his famous work *Dao De Jing*:

> Intelligent control appears as uncontrol or freedom. And for that reason it is genuinely intelligent control. Unintelligent control appears as external domination. And for that reason it is really unintelligent control. Intelligent control exerts influence without appearing to do so. Unintelligent control tries to influence by making a show of force.

Unfortunately, in my position, I had no useful information about these projects. So I found some people to give me information that I could use to compare the projects. It was the typical problem of any complex organization: Information flows everywhere, except to the top. Or rather, information flows around central authorities, and therefore governance should arise from localized activities [Kelly 1994].

As a manager, I had two goals: The first one was that as many projects as possible must be done in Ukraine (for financial reasons). The second one was that the risks for us and our customers should be minimized. Actually no, I had three goals. The third one was that I wanted people not to bother me with questions that I had no answer to.

My directives should have been sufficient for our people to make a decision themselves. But either I had not communicated my goals clearly, or they preferred to let me think for them. I should have refused.

Intelligent control means exerting influence without appearing to do so. And rulemaking should arise from our people's own interactions, not from my authority. So…if I had done my job well, I would have said, "These are my goals. Figure it out." Instead, I stupidly reviewed the information I got about technologies, dependencies, available resources, and knowledge. I then thought of a (simple) optimal solution, presented it to those involved as a suggestion, and asked everyone if they agreed. And of course, they agreed. It was a terrible waste of my time. It cost me at least six games of Minesweeper (expert level).

Paradoxically, to better steer an organization, a manager has to give up the illusion of control. Empowerment is often seen as a tool to motivate people. But that is incorrect. The reason to empower people is not to improve motivation but to *improve manageability*. The information in the network is much better than the information available in any individual node, including the fat and expensive one that thinks of itself as the "control center." People must be empowered to make their own decisions with the information they already have, whether they like it or not.

Fortunately, I didn't completely fail as an intelligent manager. After sending them my suggestion for the three projects, one project manager asked me which people to assign to these projects. I told him that I didn't know, and that I was sure he could figure that out by himself. I was not sure whether he liked that answer, and frankly I didn't care (much). I don't empower people to please them. I empower them to make better decisions than me.

You Are (Like) a Gardener

There is a big difference between managing constructed systems and managing complex systems. Constructed systems (airplanes, bridges, coffee machines) are lifeless things built from scratch, piece by piece, until they're ready for use. Complex systems (gardens, households, chickens) are often things that grow, day by day, until they're mature, and then (some time later) they die.

People are careless in their use of language, and they often make a mess of terminology. They tend to talk about building living things, which is impossible. We don't build cities, we grow them. What we build are the individual houses, roads, and trash cans. What we grow are families, businesses, trees, and large populations of ugly pigeons. The sum of all that is a city, and it grows. It is not just a construction. Likewise, we don't build companies. We grow them. And we don't build relationships. We grow them.

People also talk about building software. And (in many cases) that's incorrect, too. What we build are lines of code, design documents, and compiled assemblies. What we grow are user interaction, data repositories, social networks, and (for the systems that I created) extensive bug databases. We don't build software systems; we grow them.

Unfortunately, I cannot claim this brilliant piece of reasoning as my own. It was already documented 35 years ago by Frederick P. Brooks:

> The building metaphor has outlived its usefulness. It is time to change again. If, as I believe, the conceptual structures we construct today are too complicated to be accurately specified in advance, and too complex to be built faultlessly, then we must take a radically different approach. [...] Let us turn to nature and study complexity in living things, instead of just the dead works of man. Here we find constructs whose complexities thrill us with awe. The brain alone is intricate beyond mapping, powerful beyond imagination, rich in diversity, self-protecting, and self-renewing. The secret is that it is grown, not built. So it must be with our software systems.[6]

---

6   Brooks, Jr., Frederick P. The Mythical Man-Month: Essays On Software Engineering, © 1995, Addison Wesley Longman Inc., Reproduced by permission of Pearson Education. [Brooks 1995:201].

When it comes to managing teams the terminology is again not properly applied. It's better to talk of team growing instead of team building.

> We stopped talking about building teams, and talked instead of growing them. The agricultural image seemed right. Agriculture isn't entirely controllable. You enrich the soil, you plant seeds, you water according to the latest theory, and you hold your breath. You just might get a crop. You might not. If it all comes up roses, you'll feel fine, but next year you'll be sweating it out again. That's pretty close to how team formation works.[7]

Again, my thinking turns out to be devoid of originality. DeMarco and Lister already saw things correctly 23 years ago. And, since then, the agricultural metaphor has been used many times to explain how to manage people. For example, analogies have been used for the hiring and firing of people (which was compared to the selection of appropriate plants for locations in a garden, and the removal of weeds that deplete energy away from the useful plants) [Bobinski 2009]. And the analogies don't stop there. I will try and add three more:

- Living systems grow fast in the beginning and then reach a level of maturity. Mature systems don't need to be looked after as often as the young systems. Mature teams don't need to be looked after that much either. They are experienced enough to fix most of their own problems. An occasional checkup is sufficient to keep things running smoothly.

- When a garden is not managed, it will simply keep growing but in another direction than what was intended. It's the same with software systems and teams. If you don't manage them, they will grow in a direction that was never planned. And the result might not be as pretty as you had hoped for.

- Many growing systems have a certain life expectancy. They have a tendency to wither away and die. There's nothing wrong with that. It is part of nature. When living systems get old, more and more time and energy are needed to sustain them. Gardeners know that there comes a time to replace the old with the new, by digging out the old, roots and all, throwing it on the compost heap, and making room for new seeds to grow.

---

7 DeMarco, Tom and Timothy Lister. Peopleware: 2nd Edition. New York: Dorset House Pub, 1999. [DeMarco, Lister 1999].

Developers and managers have a lot in common. We are all gardeners. We all use the same kinds of tools (see Figure 6.4). We seed, feed, and nurture our systems. We know young systems need more care than mature ones. We weed out everything that draws energy away from our healthy growing systems, and, when the time has come, we recognize when to replace the old with the new.

FIGURE 6.4
Your management tools.

Chapter 8, "Leading and Ruling on Purpose," discusses another important responsibility of managers: putting up fences and boundaries, and positioning the system so that it can grow in the right direction. But first, we will have a more detailed look at the practical side of *Empower Teams*, the second view of the Management 3.0 model.

Summary

Self-organization, the process of something structuring itself, is the default behavior of many kinds of systems. And because people tend to attribute value to the results (considering them either "good" or "bad") they can discuss whether these systems are self-organizing in the right direction.

Other terms often associated with self-organization are anarchy, emergence, self-selection, self-direction, and self-management. Their meanings are all similar but have subtle and important differences.

In a software team, like in any other self-organizing system, none of the participants can fully understand the entire system. That's why they must aggregate their mental models. And because a good mental model is needed to control a system, control must be delegated and distributed over all team members. This is why empowerment of people is not merely a luxury but a necessity to increase control over a project.

Reflection and Action

Let's see if you can apply some ideas from this chapter to your organization:

- Try to list the emergent properties of your team. Which properties of the team exist only at the team level and do not relate to any specific individual? Or would you say that your team is merely a group of individuals with no emergent properties? Why is that?

- Imagine a list of decisions that your team is allowed to make without you. And imagine a list of decisions that you make without your team. Which list is bigger? And why?

Chapter 7

How to Empower Teams

Ultimately, the only power to which man should aspire is that which he exercises over himself.

— Elie Wiesel, writer, political activist, Nobel Laureate (1928–)

Sir Francis Bacon once wrote the famous words "knowledge is power." (Actually, he wrote "for also knowledge itself is power," but history decided that wasn't catchy enough.) This resonates with the idea that *knowledge workers* are *(em)power(ed) workers*. They have the knowledge, so they are the ones wielding the real power in their organizations. Yet they often don't realize this.

Though managers still have the power to hire and fire employees, in knowledge-rich environments, knowledge workers have the most critical jobs. Management is nowadays often compared to leading a sports team, in which the manager is the facilitator and coach, and the real work is done by star players. As a manager you must learn what it takes to empower your team to make your players score. But first, let's look at what you should *not* do.

Don't Create Motivational Debt

It is easy to solve problems by being bossy. You can tell people to switch desks, to take on another project, or to join another team. However, it is much better to solve those same problems by *asking* people to move around. Unfortunately, this is also much more difficult.

I would be the first to admit that I've done my share of bossing people around. *"You, go sit over there! You there, finish this project! And you, make me a caffè latte, and go clean my desk!"* This kind of management is easy. And the sense of power can be addictive. But smart managers understand that they create *motivational debt* by being bossy. Because people don't want to be told what to do. They want to be asked.

I frequently remind managers (and myself) that people must be asked to do a job. When people have not agreed to do something, you don't have their commitment. And when you don't have their commitment, you have a motivational problem on your hands. Telling people to do something they don't want is a sure-fire way to build up motivational debt. And debts need to be paid back, or else people will leave you standing in the cold. With no coffee. And a dirty desk.

Some years ago, a few managers and I asked two employees to switch to another team. In both cases, we thought the work in the new team was more challenging, and the two candidates would be nuts to turn down this great offer. But both of them did! They were happy with their teams and the jobs they were doing. I was glad we didn't just assume they would be happy with the transfer because we would have created bigger problems than we had tried to solve. Still, it came as a surprise, and having to look for other solutions didn't make our mission any easier. But I am confident that the two candidates felt good about having been considered for the other team. And if not, they will certainly have felt good about being able to say "No."

Good management can make short-term problems harder to solve, whereas it makes long-term problems easier. Good managers even tend to make each other's job more difficult now and then. I am sure that the rejection by both candidates could be attributed, in part, to the leadership skills of their team manager. I can imagine no better compliment for a manager than team members unwilling to leave the team. As the manager in question said, "Well, it seems I'm doing at least something right!"

I still catch myself being (moderately) bossy every now and then. Not long ago I told some business consultants that they were required to deliver their requirements to the teams in the form of user stories. Sorry folks, that was me being bossy again! I could also have *asked* them to do this. While at the same time, I could have told the teams that they would have the freedom to refuse any requirements not delivered as user stories. And I could have sat back and enjoyed the commotion from my comfortable chair. With a caffè latte. At a clean desk.

OK, so I told you what *not* to do. Now let's look at what you *should* do when empowering teams. That's what this chapter is all about.

> ### AREN'T YOU SETTING UP PEOPLE AGAINST EACH OTHER?
>
> No, I'm just encouraging them to resolve their differences together. Managers cannot prevent employees from having arguments and disagreements. But they also shouldn't always see themselves as judges.

Wear a Wizard's Hat

I was catapulted into my first management job 15 years ago, and I didn't like it one bit. At the time, my employer wanted me to build a new business out of an interesting idea that my friend Floris and I had developed together. Our idea turned into a successful venture, and I was suddenly faced with managing 20 developers and designers. It was a painful experience. I preferred working on my own ideas, solving problems, and not bothering with the mundane details of customer projects. My co-founder and I quickly created a layer of project managers so that I could be shielded from all that boring stuff.

Once, when one of the project managers was on a vacation, I had to descend from my ivory tower to take over his job. Annoyed, and with a deep frustrated sigh, I invited the team members for a short meeting. We quickly went through the stuff they were doing, I pointed out a few risks in their priorities, gave some pointers about a possible solution, told them to buzz off, and I quickly flew back up to my magic orbs and vials. A couple of days later I descended again to check on their progress, and we went through the same procedure. I never wanted to be a full-time manager, so I turned myself into a "one-minute manager," a term suggested by Ken Blanchard [Blanchard, Johnson 1982].

Two weeks later, after the project manager had returned, I was surprised to hear from a team member that he had preferred my management style over the way the project manager was managing the team. It turned out that he was always micromanaging everything, whereas I just communicated a direction and let the team figure out the details that I didn't want to be bothered with. The project manager had a politician's hat. He loved talking, meeting, documenting, and socializing. I had a wizard's hat. I just liked problem solving and conjuring spells to scare away all kinds of evil.

No matter whether your favorite character is Gandalf, Merlin, or Dumbledore, the wise wizard seems like a good metaphor for a manager. (Yes, I know we already had a gardening metaphor. Just indulge me for a moment.) In every fantasy story I've read (which is a large number, I admit), no matter how formidable the characters, the wise wizards never do the real work. They are not supposed to join in the full adventures themselves. They are only there to help the real heroes succeed. And, as a manager, the same applies to you.

Pick a Wizard, Not a Politician

I prefer to give the job of managing a technical team to someone in the team who never cared about that kind of stuff. I want him to be a person who is so concerned about building great solutions that he cannot be bothered to spend time micromanaging other people. But because he has a passion for doing things right, he will commit to this assignment as he does to any other. He will learn how to do it right and in the least amount of time. The technical managers I have selected this way have proven to be the most eager to pick up management literature and to ask for management development training. They research how to prepare for an assignment, and how to solve problems, as they have always done before.

Many "people managers" don't know a thing about managing people. They have never read *First Break All the Rules, Peopleware, The 21 Irrefutable Laws of Leadership,* or any of those other great works. They prefer talking, meeting, documenting, and socializing, and they think they already know everything. But to know everything, one has to micromanage everything.

I never wanted to be a manager. I prefer building stuff. And when someone stops at my desk to talk about a problem, I still sometimes think, "My God, why bother me now?" But I *did* read the books. And I'm still learning (actively and painfully) what it takes to be a manager. So now, I take off my headphones and my wizard's hat, I smile at them, I give them a few pointers in some direction (praying it's a good one), and I might tell them that they should solve the rest of the problem themselves. And after getting rid of them, I put my headphones and wizard's hat back on, and I remind myself to do a follow-up later that day to see if all is going well.

Empowerment versus Delegation

The word *empowerment* is often used together with *delegation*, but there's a difference. Delegation is the act of handing over responsibilities for something to someone else (usually while remaining accountable for that person's performance). Empowerment is more than just delegation. It includes the support of risk taking, personal growth, and cultural change [Quinn, Spreitzer 1997]. Some say empowerment is not only granting employees authority, but also acknowledging how powerful they already are [Fox 1998].

> The leader is best when people are hardly aware of his existence […]. When his work is done, his aim fulfilled, the people say, 'We did it ourselves.' (Laozi)

Researchers found that managers have multiple reasons for empowering people. It usually improves worker satisfaction and the quality of life at work. Productivity and quality of service are also improved in a majority of organizations. And half of the companies investigated report that profitability and competitiveness have improved because of empowerment initiatives [Bowen, Lawler 1995:75]. Last but not least, customer satisfaction and employee retention are often named as a direct result of empowerment. Still, I can forgive you if you are a bit like me: stubborn, unreasonable, and willfully ignorant of empirical data.

However, I *cannot* forgive you if you ignore science. From the perspective of social complexity, even without all the benefits I just listed, an organization could (theoretically) still work. The *real* reason for empowerment is the *manageability* of the complex system itself. Smart managers don't just empower people to enjoy the radiant faces of employees. They empower people to prevent the whole system from breaking down.

Without bottom-up distributed control, a complex system like an Agile organization just doesn't *work*. The Soviet system didn't break down because of unhappy customers or miserable employees. It broke down because it was unsustainable. Therefore, even if you prefer to be the 21st-century version of a corporate dictator like Henry Ford, you *will* empower your people, just to keep your business running.

But as always, things are easier said than done. Although empowerment might be second nature for some organizations, in many other organizations (and other cultures) empowering employees requires a total culture change. A big transformation may have to be undertaken in many small steps. Empowerment programs often don't provide immediate results, meaning that organizations run the risk of aborting such a program prematurely [Caudron 1995:28]. In the remaining sections, we see what you can do about that.

Reduce Your Fear, Increase Your Status

Some managers don't like the idea of empowering people. They fear a loss of authority, power, and control. They also fear competition when subordinates become more knowledgeable than their own managers. And finally, after empowering their subordinates, managers fear there is nothing left for them to do, which makes them feel redundant. (This is particularly a problem in an economical downturn when organizations need to cut jobs, and top management is looking for dispensable people.) When managers feel insecure about their jobs, they hang on harder to their power and position, reluctant to share it with (what they perceive as) competitors.

Here's an important message for these managers:

> Giving power to your people does *not* diminish your own
> status. Quite the reverse. It is more likely to *increase* it.

The status you have in an organization is a function of the power of the people you are leading. Consider this: What sounds more interesting to you? Leading a team of industry veterans who are building a high-quality system that knocks people off their feet? Or leading a group of interns, fresh from school and wet behind the ears, building a system so bad it knocks your brain out? I'm quite sure that being the manager of the celebrity team means you have a much higher status in the eyes of many. The better your team, the bigger your power. And to make your team better, you empower them.

Management guru John Maxwell wrote that to make yourself indispensable, you better make yourself dispensable [Maxwell 1998:126]. Of course, this is a hyperbole, and much depends on the worldly views of your own manager. But speaking from personal experience, I noticed that the CEO's perception of my value to the organization correlated heavily with the way I allowed people to do what I wanted without doing any of it myself.

A complex system is not a zero sum game. Making poor countries wealthier does not diminish the wealth in rich countries. European settlers in the America's did not steal jobs from Native Americans. (Though they stole plenty of other things, I'm afraid.) And my "social capital" on Twitter and LinkedIn does not decrease when I compliment or recommend any of my friends or contacts. On the contrary, my online social standing *depends* on my support for others.

If you find yourself in a position in which you fear for the loss of power, control, and maybe even your job, consider this: I *invest* in other people's social capital *because* it increases my own. And I believe in *migration of work* to poor countries because it creates other and better jobs at home. And I believe you *must* empower people because it will increase your own status in the organization. Don't forget, we call them complex systems because situations are never as simple as people think, and often quite paradoxical.

From personal experience, I can tell you that top management usually doesn't fire managers of empowered teams. They are more likely to fire the ones responsible for unmanageable systems.

Choose the Right Maturity Level

Being an empowered employee is a skill. It must be learned, and it takes discipline to maintain it. As with most skills that people learn, it is best to start with the tasks that are easy, with little chance of things going wrong. My suggestion is to put all empowerment initiatives in one of three categories: low, moderate, and high. The *intention* is to get everyone to the higher level. But they can only achieve this by passing the previous ones first. After all, no apprentice doctor starts the first day of his career with an open heart surgery. (I hope.)

Low Empowerment

The "low" category of empowerment contains activities that have no far-reaching consequences for the company. In this category, we find developing internal workshops, establishing coding guidelines, and decorating the company's (or department's) Christmas tree. This category of empowerment should be a no-brainer for most organizations. In a dictatorial environment, this is where I would start with my empowerment program. It is like picking the low hanging fruit first.

But don't be fooled by harmless appearances. Things that are easy to set up can also be easy to mess up. When management gets to choose which workshops are developed, it will only confirm that empowerment is a farce. When the team gets into a nasty fight about the coding guidelines, and a manager steps in to set things right, it confirms that management is needed to resolve disagreements. And, needless to say, the Christmas tree should not be placed in the board room.

There is also the risk of aiming too low with your empowerment program. If the levels of self-reliance and self-efficacy of the people in your organization are high enough, you shouldn't just reach for things in the low category. Honestly, if you were my manager, and you tried to empower me this way, you would end up wearing the Christmas ornaments on your head.

Moderate Empowerment

In the "moderate" category of empowerment, we find things like interviewing job candidates by team members, self-education of employees, self-organizing project teams, freedom of working hours, and freedom of tool selection. Maybe even a contribution to the development of new business models. (A Christmas tree decoration service perhaps?)

This category of employee empowerment is hard enough for most organizations, and for some, it may already be a step too far. Nevertheless, I firmly believe the "moderate" category of empowerment is the level that ultimately *must* be achieved by the majority of organizations (at the least). And if you're doing Agile software development, you have no choice.

Do *not* yet consider this category of empowerment when you're unsure whether people have mastered the low level. During my driving lessons, my instructor gave me control over the brake only *after* I had shown I could control the steering wheel. And while I was struggling with my power over the steering wheel, the instructor exerted his power over the brake. Frequently.

On the other hand, for the most determined of employees, this category might still not be enough. We have one last category to go.

High Empowerment

In the high category of empowerment, we find organizations where people determine their salaries together, where people are allowed to work only on the projects that they want, where there is no distinction of job titles and everyone is called "associate," and where people can work at home or from the Bahamas if they so desire.

Changing an organizational culture to match the high category is so hard that it might be practically impossible to achieve for most businesses.

The few that do find themselves in this category were usually created that way. It is easier to build a fast and agile ship from scratch, than trying to convert the Queen Mary 2 from a cruiser to a yacht halfway between Grenada and Barbados. Likewise, it is easier to aggressively select empowered people at a startup company than it is to change the mindset of many existing employees in a big company. If you find yourself in the enviable position of starting a new company or a new business unit, you might want to aim for empowerment initiatives in the high category right from the start. Just make sure to hire people with a profile matching this kind of empowerment.

Like continuous improvement (see Chapter 15, "How to Improve Everything"), empowerment is a never-ending process [Fox 1998]. You can always strive for more, better, and higher, but you have to make sure that you understand the position from where you're starting. People should be allowed to *earn* the higher levels of empowerment by proving they've mastered the lower levels. Getting people to vote on each other's salaries might be several steps too far when they're still fighting over the colors of the Christmas lights.

Pick the Right Authority Level

Empowerment is often incorrectly perceived as a binary choice. Either you empower someone, or you don't. In reality, your options are more varied than that. We can distinguish between different levels of authority.

In your first driving lesson, your driving instructor may have given you the steering wheel, but I'm sure he told you exactly when to go left and when to go right. After a number of lessons, when you had gained some experience, he might have said, "Let's drive to the shopping center where you almost rammed a phone booth last week," and it would have been your job to find a way to get there. And with an experienced driver, the instructor might have said, "Why don't you drive around a bit while I take a nap?"

For each individual activity, we can distinguish seven levels of authority:

- **Level 1: Tell**: You make decisions and announce them to your people. (This is actually not empowerment at all.)
- **Level 2: Sell**: You make decisions, but you attempt to gain commitment from workers by "selling" your idea to them.

- **Level 3: Consult**: You invite and weigh input from workers before coming to a decision. But you make it clear that it's you who is making the decisions.

- **Level 4: Agree**: You invite workers to join in a discussion and to reach consensus as a group. Your voice is equal to the others.

- **Level 5: Advise**: You attempt to influence workers by telling them what your opinion is, but ultimately you leave it up to them to decide.

- **Level 6: Inquire**: You let the team decide first, with the suggestion that it would be nice, though not strictly necessary, if they can convince you afterward.

- **Level 7: Delegate**: You leave it entirely up to the team to deal with the matter while you go out and have a good time (or use that time to manage the system).

Levels 1, 2, 4, and 5 correspond to the four "leadership styles" discussed in **Situational Leadership Theory**.[1] But I think this extended version with seven levels is more complete, and more useful, because it doesn't stop after level 5.

You can vary the seven levels of authority depending on the topic. For example, in my most recent job…

- I **told** our people that I would be starting a new business unit in our organization. (There was no reason for selling this to our employees because the one I had to sell it to was our CEO.)

- I did **sell** the business model, and what type of customers we were after, to the people that I selected to join me in my effort.

- For the name of our business unit I decided to **consult** all team members, asking them for their ideas.

- When it was time to select a logo, I invited all team members to discuss the different designs and to **agree** together on the best one.

- The technical design of our product was ultimately a team responsibility, although I did **advise** them concerning some architectural issues.

- I didn't really care who was doing what in the team, but I did **inquire** sometimes to confirm that they made the right choices.

---

1 http://www.mgt30.com/slt/.

- Finally, I chose to **delegate** all the hard work. I was involved in coding for a while, but none of my code survived the team's refactoring efforts, so I deduced that I was better at adding value in other areas.

Every topic requires its own level of authority, and the further you go the better it is. But in some cases, it is best to start by *telling* or *selling* and then gradually increase the authority of team members as their experience grows.

HOW DO I SELECT AN AUTHORIZATION LEVEL?

If there were an easy answer to this question, we would automate empowerment and leave team management to a machine.

The real answer is that it's precisely the human factor that you need to deal with yourself. For every responsibility, and every person, you will wonder, "Can I leave this up to them?" And sometimes you will fail in selecting the right authorization level; sometimes you will succeed. But at the very least you will learn!

The levels of authority are not the same as the maturity levels mentioned in the previous section. A team could easily have a level 7 authority (full delegation) for setting up coding guidelines together because this doesn't require much skill or discipline. There could be a level 5 authority (advice from the manager) for tool selection because it requires a moderate amount of experience as an empowered employee. And determining salaries, which requires a high level of empowerment, might still be at authority level 3. This means that you value people's input, but the decision is still yours. Figure 7.1 depicts how the different levels of authority can be used for the three maturity levels.

You develop employees by gradually building up empowerment, giving them more and more challenging tasks. Confidence in their skills will grow with their successes so that they will be ready to take on further challenges.

FIGURE 7.1

Three maturity levels versus seven authority levels.

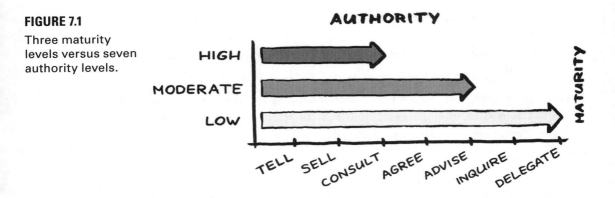

WHAT IF COMPETENCE LEVELS DIFFER?

What is the best way to deal with a situation in which different people on a team, or different teams in an organization, need different approaches to empowerment?

This is a delicate issue. My immediate response is not to lie to anyone. My second response is to treat everyone in a fair way. This means if Sam is granted a responsibility without needing to prove herself first, the same should apply to Max.

However, if you trust Sam's capability to do a job well, and you don't trust Max's capabilities to a similar extent (yet), it is only fair that you can explain why. Maybe Max hasn't performed a similar number of projects yet, or Max's work had a lot of problems last time. You must be fair, and you must be honest. You must make it clear to Max what he has to do to gain the same rights as Sam.

As much as possible, you should grant people the same rights. But I prefer not to grant people (or teams) the same authority levels when there's a clear difference in their capabilities because this is too easily interpreted as unfair by the ones that are most capable. Political correctness is a disservice to both novices and experts [Hunt 2008:26]. And if I have to choose between two evils, I'd rather be loyal to the most competent people.

Assign Teams or Individuals

We've seen two dimensions of empowering people: You can choose the necessary maturity level for empowerment, and you can choose the level of authority per task. A third dimension is the number of people you are going to involve for each task.

I recently had a team member with some experience in layout and design. I could have chosen him to handle the process of selecting the logo for our business unit. Instead, I chose to make it a team effort based on consensus (level 4 authority) because I wanted everyone to feel connected to the corporate goal.

On the other hand, although I knew that all team members were capable of thinking up new features for the product that we were building, only one person besides me had the power to actually add new items to our product backlog. Naturally, I welcomed any input the team could give us (level 3 authority). But, as the Product Owner(s) of the tool, it was me and my colleague who were making the final decisions together (level 4 authority).

You can see a variety of options for empowerment surfacing here:

- I can authorize one specific person at another (higher) level than the other persons in a team.
- For the people authorized at the same level, I can express the requirement that they must agree with each other.
- Alternatively, I can tell the people authorized at the same level that they are allowed to act on their own.
- Finally, I can tell the team that someone should be assigned to do something, but that the team can choose the person.

The situation I described earlier with me sharing Product Ownership with one other person in the team was an example of the first option.

An example of the second option would be that I wanted everyone to agree on the architecture of our product. Nobody was allowed to introduce new technologies or important design decisions all by themselves without involving the others.

An example of the third option would be that in our cross-functional team, each person was allowed to build any feature. There could be some favoritism, such as certain team members preferring front-end development over database stuff, or vice versa, but they didn't have to ask each other's permission to start working on a user story.

And finally, an example of the fourth option would be that I asked our team to make one person responsible for deployments to the production environment. And I didn't care who it was.

Having team members share responsibilities can be a good strategy for risk reduction. It is easier for one person to make a mistake than it is for an entire team to make that same mistake. On the other hand, in some situations it can be easier, or safer, to have just one person take responsibility for one important task. Like rewriting all the code the manager left behind.

As always, it depends.

The Delegation Checklist

In their book *Behind Closed Doors* Johanna Rothman and Esther Derby published a handy checklist that you can use for the delegation of tasks. I have augmented their list with a few questions of my own to cover the maturity level, level of authority, and individuality:

1. Is the risk factor of delegating this work adequately addressed?
2. Do the people have the right empowerment skills and discipline?
3. Have you considered and selected the right level of authority?
4. Have you considered the question of delegating to individuals or to teams?
5. Is what you are delegating a discrete chunk of work?
6. Do the people have the skills to do this particular kind of work?
7. Do the people have the right format for the work products to use?
8. Do the people have the tools necessary to be successful?
9. Do the people know what the results should look like?
10. Did you set the boundary conditions for the work (for example, budget, time, resources, and quality)?
11. Do the people know when the work is due?
12. Do the people know what progress looks like?
13. Do the people know how often to report to you on progress (adhering to interim milestones)?

14. Is someone available (you or another person) to coach or mentor the people in case they need help?

Source: Rothman, Johanna and Esther Derby. Behind Closed Doors. Raleigh: Pragmatic Bookshelf, 2005, page 124. http://pragprog.com. Used with permission. [Rothman, Derby 2005:124]

Every time you delegate work to other people, you should be able to answer "Yes" (or "N/A") to every question. If you have to answer "No" to any of the questions and you still need to delegate the work, openly discuss this dilemma with your people and agree on a compromise. Maybe the right tools have not arrived yet, or the deadline is unknown, or you still have to solve the coaching issue. As long as you talk openly about it, both you and the people you're delegating the work to can agree on intentions and commit to solutions and results. Even when circumstances are less than ideal.

If You Want Something Done, Practice Your Patience

In the science fiction movie The Fifth Element, the character Zorg is a devious and ruthless industrialist ruler who is time and time again confronted with the incompetence of his assistants. Near the end of the movie, frustrated after yet another of their failures, Zorg picks up the guns and utters the words, "If you want something done, do it yourself." It was one of my favorite lines in the movie, being so recognizable. I have probably said the same words dozens of times throughout my career.

Professor and researcher Kenneth W. Thomas would have recognized that Zorg had fallen into the "Micromanagement Trap":

> You would like to delegate more authority to workers, and decide that you will do this as soon as the workers show they can handle it. In the meantime, you feel the need to closely monitor and control events, making most of the operational decisions. What you are less aware of is that this micromanagement—even if you intend it to be temporary—often prevents the workers from being able to self-manage or otherwise show that they could handle more authority. So workers continue to act in a

dependent way and you are trapped into an exhausting attempt to make all the decisions, while wondering why workers aren't as responsible as you are.[2]

The *workers-are-not-ready-for-this* idea is one of the biggest obstacles to empowerment in organizations. The problem is, managers are usually right! Workers are often *not* fully ready for things that should be delegated. If they were they would probably already be doing those things! But the *if-you-want-something-done-do-it-yourself* solution is not the best way to get yourself out of such a situation.

You must treat delegation of authority as an *investment* [Rothman, Derby 2005:97]. It takes a while to get a return on your investment, and until that time delegation will just cost you time, energy, money, and possibly some frustration. Taking work back to do it yourself before workers are able to do that work without your supervision is like taking your money out of the bank before being paid interest. The useless effort of giving something away and then taking it back will only leave you with a net loss. In other words, the solution is *if-you-want-something-done-practice-your-patience*.

After you delegate something to an employee, when things go wrong, a good response would be, "What did *I* do wrong?" Maybe your explanation of the goal wasn't clear enough. Maybe you didn't properly define the constraints. Perhaps there was nobody coaching the worker. Maybe you should have selected a different level of authority. Or you should have delegated the work to a team instead of just one person. When something bad happens after you delegate a task to a worker, do not take (back) responsibility for the task. Instead, take responsibility for the way you've delegated it. Your business may require you to be as devious and ruthless as Zorg. But do *not* pick up the guns yourself.

Resist Your Manager's Resistance

I once had a CEO whose views on people management were different than mine. When someone down the line made a mistake, he automatically assumed that I had not properly constrained people's freedoms. And he thought I had too much confidence in people's abilities to do the work

---

2   Reprinted with permission of the publisher. From Intrinsic Motivation at Work, copyright © 2000 by Kenneth Wayne Thomas, Berrett-Koehler Publishers, Inc., San Francisco, CA. All rights reserved. http://www.bkconnection.com. [Thomas 2000:66].

I had empowered them to do and to learn from their mistakes as they went. (And I'm afraid some people needed plenty of learning.)

The CEO was both right and wrong. Looking back at some major financial or technical disasters, like free television sets being given away on a website, or emails with a hyperlink to a competitor being sent over a customer's mailing list, I would have been able to identify a number of issues on the Delegation Checklist that I had not properly addressed. Sometimes a job was too risky to be delegated to one person and should have been delegated to a team instead. Sometimes I should have opted for consensus together with the team, instead of full delegation. Sometimes I had not properly checked a person's skill set, or I had not given a clear description of the intended end results. And sometimes there simply was no coach around to assist a person with the work. In every case the CEO was wrong in telling me that I shouldn't have delegated the work. But he was right in claiming that I was in charge, and that I must try and prevent such problems from occurring. In short, I had not been stupid, but careless. (Or maybe naïve. I can't decide what sounds worse.)

If I tried to delegate my bookkeeping to a Nobel Prize winner, with just a five-minute explanation, he or she would probably still make a mess of things. It wouldn't mean that Nobel Prize winners are incapable of keeping my books. It would just mean that five minutes is not sufficient for delegating that work. (I know some people who would probably need five *weeks* to delegate their bookkeeping.)

When there is pressure from top management to get a situation back under control, always try and resist the temptation to do the work yourself. What you need to get under control is your method of delegation. Print the Delegation Checklist, check each item on the list, and show the results to upper management. When your manager tells you to take control over a situation, it is almost never intended as an instruction to do all the work yourself. You are simply expected to prove that you can lead a group of people in delivering quality results. Your manager doesn't care how things get done. He cares about results. It is you who gets to choose how things are done. (And how entails *not by you!*)

It also means you must resist the pressure from above to be on top of everything. Your manager should not expect you to know every detail of what's going on with the people you're managing, and he should not expect you to make every decision yourself. Again, tell your manager why you've delegated the work and decision making, and show him the checklist. Just telling him "I empowered someone else to do that," makes it easy for your manager to disagree with you and to think you've lost control. Instead, you must tell him "Look at my checklist. This is how I manage people to do work for me." It is hard for anyone to disagree with a professional approach to delegation. (And if the checklist doesn't settle it, just tell him it is all my fault.)

Address People's Ten Intrinsic Desires

Sometimes, empowerment fails because people cannot overcome the fear of acting without approval. Or they simply don't want any more responsibilities than they already have. I've also heard that, with team members watching each other to monitor shared responsibilities, some people feel like having multiple bosses.

The best way to approach this problem is to tie empowerment to people's intrinsic desires. First, you try to find out what it is that makes people's motivation tick (see the ten basic desires of Chapter 5, "How to Energize People"). For example, if one of the primary intrinsic drivers of a person is *order* (the need for a stable environment), you can choose to delegate the kind of work that most closely matches this desire, like asking her to maintain the wiki pages that document the team's preferred processes. Another person might have a passion for certain *ideals* (the need for social justice). In that case, you could offer to donate a small amount to his favorite cause, *if* he can keep the budget under control, which is a prerequisite for making the donation possible.

By allowing people to achieve what they desire, you increase their motivation. And increased motivation results in more readiness to take on other work. As you can see, the success of empowerment can depend on the individual and the approach and order of the work being delegated. Of course, you will have less problem delegating work to someone whose primary intrinsic driver is *status* (the need for social standing). Or at least the problems will be *different*.

Gently Massage the Environment

Last year, every time I changed my password on the corporate network, I also had to change it on my mobile phone, my chat client, my VPN connection, and various intranet applications. And not only that, but the password change, for some reason, messed up my roaming profile and the settings of several applications. Imagine my unpleasant surprise when system administrators revoked my freedom to manage my own password and imposed a corporate policy that required everyone to change his password *every two months*. To me, that was like being told to go to the dentist every week.

Besides top management and the workers, the third party putting up resistance to empowerment is the environment, which includes system administrators, staff, human resources, accounting departments, and so on. This resistance is usually the result of an (understandable) desire to prevent problems. But they often don't see or realize the significant costs (effort, demotivation) of the measures being taken. It is *your* job to make sure that the environment is supportive.

When people are faced with a department obstructing people's ability to do their jobs, step in immediately and rectify the situation. It could lead to some wheeling and dealing with another manager, who has different goals than you have.

The best thing you can do in such circumstances is to sit together and make an objective list of costs, benefits, risks, and opportunities. For example, the system administrators may have a policy not to allow access to software developers on live production servers. Talk about the costs of your people not having access to those servers (the amount of time lost per year of having to go through the system administrators). Discuss what the risks are, and talk about the impact of any harm done by software developers to the production servers. Also discuss the benefits of having system administrators delegate work to software developers (less mundane work for the administrators) and the opportunities, such as learning new techniques and technologies for remote and restricted access. Finally, you might want to practice your massage skills.

The balance of costs, benefits, risks, and opportunities will usually end up somewhere in the middle, so the least you should come up with is some form of compromise. A compromise is better than nothing, and your team members will be grateful.

So far, this chapter has been all about the practical side of empowerment and delegation. But all you've read so far will have been for nothing if you have not addressed the two basic virtues that make empowerment work: *trust* and *respect,* which are discussed next.

Trust

In management and leadership literature, one of the topics most often referred to is *trust*. Trust between two people operates in two directions. I can choose to trust you, and you can choose to trust me, but neither requires the other. In the situation of a manager and several team members, we can identify four types of trust relationships (see Figure 7.2): (1) trusting the team, (2) gaining trust from team members, (3) getting team members to trust each other, and (4) trusting yourself. Each relationship is described in the following section.

FIGURE 7.2
Four types of trust.

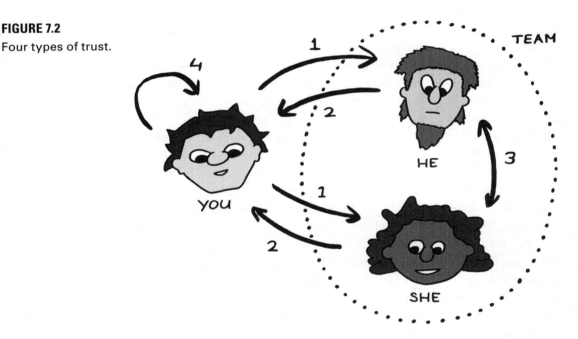

Trust Your Team

When you empower people, you should (occasionally) sit back and enjoy the peace of your workspace—and the contents of your cookie jar. Other people are doing the work. Not you. That's great. But try and keep it that way.

When an empowered team walks into your office and asks you to decide on an issue, find a way to have them solve the problem themselves. I once heard of a manager who tossed a coin for every decision his team asked him to make. This quickly motivated the team to make their own decisions because they balked at being ruled by a penny. I know some coaches use a mirror as a metaphor. As a manager (or coach) you can act as a mirror to the team. You can help them with their own thinking processes. If they look at you for guidance, you hold up the mirror and help them to find guidance in themselves.

When a team member walks into your office and asks you to do something for which you had delegated responsibility to someone else, make it clear to her that this is now the job of that other person. Tell her that trust is meant to be a transitive relation. If employee A trusts manager M to make a decision, and manager M trusts empowered employee B to make such decisions, then by agreement employee A should also trust employee B. *Never* betray your trust in employee B by making decisions for him, and certainly not behind his back!

And finally, when *nobody* walks into your office, don't criticize them for not consulting you about their decisions, even if they turn out to be terrible. If you want to be consulted in advance you must clearly communicate those expectations. Of course, if you *have* communicated such a requirement, and the team hasn't lived up to it, they have broken the trust, and need to repair it. A contribution to the cookie jar will do nicely, I think.

Earn Trust from Your People

Note that the heading of this section is not "People Must Trust Their Manager." Trust must be *earned*. And you can earn it by always delivering on your promises [Anderson 2004:41].

When I tell someone that I will get back to her about some problem, I *will* get back to her to talk about the problem. When I promise to email a document, I *will* send that document. And when I tell someone that he has full responsibility for a job, I will refrain from interfering and mind my own business, until my input is *explicitly* requested.

My spouse recently invited one of his colleagues to stay for the weekend in our house in Brussels. On the morning of her arrival, we were waiting for her call to tell us what time to pick her up from the railway station. But no call arrived. When we finally called her, she said she wasn't coming, for some vague and unconvincing reason. Any trust that I had in this person evaporated on the spot. Why someone would commit to a visit and then not even bother calling it off is beyond my understanding.

You build trust simply by doing what you have committed to. Trust means that people know they can rely on you. It is easy to build, but even easier to break. People destroy it when their behavior is unpredictably unpleasant. But trust also suffers when people are either predictably unpleasant (someone always doing precisely the things you don't want him to do) or unpredictably pleasant (someone doing the things you want only when you least expect it).

Make sure that your behavior as a manager is *predictably pleasant*, and I'm sure you will have no trouble earning trust from your people.

Help People Trust Each Other

Even when you trust people, and they trust you, the situation will still need some work when the team members are reluctant to trust each other. This is particularly true for newly formed teams, teams spread over multiple locations, and team members with different job titles, such as programmers versus testers.

When trust among team members is low (for whatever reason), you should concern yourself with *communication* and *commitment*.

First, you make sure that communication among team members is improved by increasing the bandwidth and quality of their communication. Daily (stand-up) meetings, colocation, pair programming, team dinners, and brainstorm sessions, are just a few of the many things that you and the team can do to get to know (and trust) each other.

Second, you see to it that commitment for activities in the team is being negotiated and respected. People new to Agile software development may need a little help in this area. Assist individual team members in doing what they promised to do so that their fellow team members can trust them. When it turns out they cannot keep their commitment, help them in communicating this early and honestly.

Your involvement may not be necessary with an experienced team that has been doing projects together for a long time. But when there's a small change in team membership, you might want to watch carefully that the new team members are participating fully in communication and commitment, and earning trust in their new team.

Trust Yourself

Every time I'm on a plane, I get to see the safety instructions, reminding me that I have to put on the oxygen mask on myself first, *before* helping any obnoxiously screaming little brats. You can only save others if you save yourself first. Another version of this principle says that you can only love others when you love yourself first.

This gave me the idea to suggest the following alternative:

You can only trust others if you trust yourself first.

In *Making Things Happen,* Scott Berkun describes why *self-reliance* is so important [Berkun 2008:256]. You must believe in yourself and stay true to your own reason and common sense, even when others disagree with you. You should only change your mind when new insights have convinced you, not when other people have pressured you to reconsider. Because doing something that you don't believe in is an act against the trust in yourself. A self-reliant person has confidence in herself, while still allowing new information to change her mind.

Respect

Trust and respect are the crucial virtues to make empowerment and delegation work. We have discussed the four types of trust, and in a similar way, we could elaborate on the four types of respect. However, for the sake of brevity, I will just highlight what I think is most important.

Respect People, Ask for Feedback

Disrespect for employees is perhaps the most common organizational disease in the world. Common because, when nothing is done about it, disrespectful behavior is the default state that organizations end up in.

In almost every organization, people associate the idea of "importance" with delegation. The one who delegates work is "more important" than the one to whom work is delegated. This idea propagates "down the line" to the "lowest" workers in the organization. Such a concept of importance automatically breeds feelings of superiority. And when a person feels superior to someone else, chances are high she will not treat that person respectfully. And research shows that disrespect for employees is the highest contributor to turnover in organizations.

Another study reported that after 20 years of research and 60,000 exit interviews, 80 percent of turnover can be related to unsatisfactory relationships with the boss.[3]

---

3   Reprinted with permission of the publisher. From *Love 'em or Lose 'em,* copyright © 2008 by Beverly Kaye and Sharon Jordan-Evans, Berrett-Koehler Publishers, Inc., San Francisco, CA. All rights reserved. http://www.bkconnection.com. [Kaye, Jordan-Evans 2008:96].

Like password policies and performance appraisals, disrespectful behavior is an almost inevitable result of hierarchical organizations. In complexity science we would call this an **attractor**. The system invariably ends up in that state (or collection of states) unless we do something about it. (We discuss attractors in more detail in Chapter 14, "The Landscape of Change.")

Managers must do everything they can to eliminate disrespectful, condescending, and rude behavior in their organization [Stallard 2007:65]. In setting a good example, a good manager does not intimidate, condescend, demean, act arrogant, withhold praise, slam doors, pound tables, swear, behave rudely, belittle people in front of others, give mostly negative feedback, yell at people, tell lies or "half-truths," act above the rules, enjoy making people sweat, act superior to or smarter than everyone else, act sexist, act bigoted, withhold critical information, use inappropriate humor, blow up in meetings, steal credit or the spotlight from others, block career moves, show favoritism, humiliate or embarrass others, overuse sarcasm, deliberately ignore or isolate people, set impossible goals or deadlines, let others take blame for their mistakes, undermine authority, show lack of caring for people, betray confidence, gossip or spread rumors, act as if others are stupid, use fear as a motivator, show revenge, interrupt constantly, fail to listen, demand perfection, or break promises. And these are, of course, just a few examples of things you should not do [Kaye, Jordan-Evans 2008:97-99].

The problem is, this list is probably not going to change you. Managers displaying disrespectful behavior often don't realize what they're doing and how their behavior is affecting other people. That's why I suggest that you simply ignore me. Except for this: Ask feedback from people.

Bad relationships of people with their bosses lead to loss of motivation, loss of creativity, and increased turnover. Disrespect for people is the single most expensive damage that you, as a manager, can inflict upon your organization. The goal of respecting people is not to make them happy. The goal is to increase productivity, creativity, and innovation. Happiness is a by-product and a welcome side-effect.

As a good manager, you must know how people think about you. You have no choice. You have to find out what parts of your behavior you need to change. And you probably won't know unless you ask people. It's really simple. All you have to do is ask the following questions:

- What is it that I should stop doing?
- What is it that I should start doing?
- What is it that I should continue doing?

Feedback can be scary, I know. You could be surprised at what people say about the way you assaulted an intern with a rubber chicken. But knowing is better than not knowing. No matter how painful.

But by far the best thing you can do is to stop associating delegation with importance. Asking someone to do work for you does *not* make you more important. If you succeed in getting this perverse idea of importance out of people's heads, you probably won't even need to struggle with disrespectful behavior. Respecting people, and retaining them, should then come naturally to everyone.

Be Respected, Give Feedback

Deliberately asking for feedback can help you in gaining respect from people. Anyone who *asks* to be criticized, anonymously, by his co-workers, is either crazy or cool. And I'm sure many people will give you the benefit of the doubt here. (I would.)

But that's not all you can do. Another step is to really understand the jobs of your team members and to give valuable feedback, *especially* in the case of IT professionals. Because what software developers and other IT professionals want to see in managers are people who understand their job and what it is they are trying to accomplish. It doesn't mean you have to understand the intricacies of jQuery syntax or how to configure load-balanced servers. But it does mean that you have to understand what's important for your team to build great software, and you must be able to talk about it.

Technical people are logical-thinking people. A manager who is somewhat challenged in the social areas but who understands what needs to be done is often preferred over a person who is doing his very best to be respected but who is unable to contribute to a technical discussion in a meaningful way. They can forgive you for writing the crappiest code on the planet. But if you mistake an architectural diagram for a metro map, you're screwed.

This concludes the two chapters on the empowerment of teams. Now it is time to investigate the other side of the golden medal of social complexity. Because there is no empowerment without alignment. No self-organization without boundaries. We will see that the second view of the Management 3.0 model is in an eternal struggle with the third one.

Summary

Managers should not boss team members around or try to discuss everything team members do. The best managers are like wizards in fantasy stories: They help heroes overcoming tough challenges, but they never do the work for them.

An empowered team will increase a manager's status because his team will (ultimately) perform better than other teams, which reflects on the manager. The manager can refer to three maturity levels and seven authority levels to determine how to delegate work to his team.

In any case, a manager must remember that empowerment is an investment in the team. It takes some time to get a return on that investment. In the meantime the manager must work with top managers and departments that might not be accustomed to self-organizing teams.

Between the manager and his team members, we can recognize that four types of trust and mutual respect all need to be in place. Or else self-organization might not work as intended.

Reflection and Action

Let's see if you can apply some ideas from this chapter to your organization:

- Estimate the time you spend per week with your team. Do you measure it in minutes, hours, or days? Is it too much or too little? Are they sufficiently empowered or not?

- Evaluate any managers reporting to you. Would you rate them as politicians or wizards?

- Imagine that you could delegate all your responsibilities to your team. Does that thought make you feel uncomfortable because there is nothing left for to you do? Or do you find the idea appealing because you will then have time for more interesting work?

- Evaluate every person in your team. How would you rate their empowerment maturity levels? Low, moderate, or high? What can you do to increase it?

- Think back to a disagreement or decision problem you had with your team. What was the proper authorization level for that decision? Did people know? Did they respect it?

- Think about the people on your team. Are there some who are perfectly able to handle the work you've delegated to them? If so, can they handle more? Are there any who are not doing well (yet)? If so, how long have you been investing in them, and when do you expect a return on that?

- Think about top management and other departments in your organization. Are they all supportive in your approach to empowerment? If not, what do you need to do about it?

- Consider the four types of trust. Are all the trust arrows between people in place? Or are there some who don't fully trust each other? What can you do about that?

- Ask your team the following questions every now and then: What should I stop doing? What should I start doing? What should I continue doing?

Chapter 8

Leading and Ruling on Purpose

Nature is not cruel, pitiless. This is one of the hardest lessons for humans to learn. We cannot admit that things might be neither good nor evil, neither cruel nor kind, but simply callous—indifferent to all suffering, lacking all purpose.

—Richard Dawkins, biological theorist, science author (1941–)

The previous chapters dealt with *Empower Teams*, the second view of the Management 3.0 model. We've seen that handing over work to other people is, in general, a good thing. But that doesn't mean you can just hand over anything and leave your organization to go enjoy a sabbatical on Tuvalu. There are some responsibilities that you should keep for yourself.

The third view of the Management 3.0 model is called *Align Constraints*, and the theory behind it is described here. The first part of this chapter deals with three responsibilities that are all related to defining *boundaries* and *direction*: developing a self-organizing system, protecting its people and its resources, and directing the group toward a purpose. (I discuss other responsibilities in subsequent chapters.) The second part of this chapter explains the difference between management and leadership and the importance of purpose.

Game of Life

Our investigation of constraints starts with the **Game of Life**, a simple zero-player game invented in 1970 by the British mathematician John Conway. It is "played" on a grid of cells, where each cell has eight neighbors, one in each direction, including the diagonals. The cells can be born and stay alive or die using the following three rules:

1. A cell becomes "alive" when exactly three of its neighbors are alive, which reflects the cell being "born," due to the availability of sufficient resources.

2. A cell remains alive when either two or three of its neighbors are alive, which means there are sufficient resources for the cell to "survive."

3. A cell dies, or remains dead, in all other cases, which corresponds to "overcrowding" (too many neighbors) or "insufficient resources" (too few neighbors).

The rules are applied repeatedly and to all cells at the same time. This results in a sequence of generations of the system, and fun and surprise on the part of the "player," who can actually do little more than watch how the most amazing patterns unfold. I like the game, because it is the only one where I always win.

Conway tried many different sets of rules. Some of these resulted in a grid always overgrowing with living cells. Others resulted in collapse and extinction of every initial configuration. The set of rules that Conway finally settled on is one that lets patterns grow toward stable systems, an example of which can be seen in Figure 8.1, where the initial configuration grows toward a stable one in just three steps.

FIGURE 8.1

A stable system after just three generations.[1]

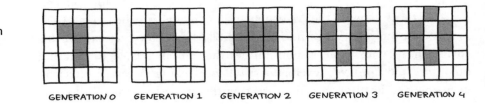

GENERATION 0   GENERATION 1   GENERATION 2   GENERATION 3   GENERATION 4

Such a stable situation (which can sometimes take hundreds or thousands of generations to take hold) consists of unchanging stationary objects (still lifes), objects that keep switching forms in endless cycles (oscillators) or gliders that move across the grid.

The Game of Life is an example of a **cellular automaton**, a mathematical system in which cells are influenced by other cells, according to some set of predefined rules. The Game of Life is particularly interesting because it is a fine example of a system with a small set of simple rules, having complex behavior and ordering itself.

The game also shows us that, whatever the initial situation is, the system will eventually always stabilize. But there's one catch: *The set of*

---

1 You can play with the Game of Life here: http://www.mgt30.com/gameoflife/.

rules has to be chosen carefully. Can we thus conclude that a stabilizing system needs a designer? Are managers needed to tweak the rules? For a manager that sounds compelling, doesn't it?

Universality Classes

The observation that rules must be tuned for a system to be both stabilizing and lively is important. A different set of rules leads to a different system with different behavior. The Game of Life is just one out of billions of possible cellular automata, many of them being dead, boring, or chaotic.

In an influential paper, Stephen Wolfram, founder of the first journal on complex systems and known for his work on Wolfram Alpha (a "computational knowledge engine"), once proposed a classification scheme that divided cellular automata into four categories, named **universality classes** [Wolfram 1984] [Waldrop 1992:225-226]:

- **Class I**: These are the systems with "doomsday rules." No matter what pattern of living and dead cells you start out with, everything just dies within a few generations.

- **Class II**: These systems are a bit livelier, but not much. Each initial pattern quickly collapses to a set of very boring static configurations.

- **Class III**: These systems are at the opposite extreme: They are too lively. Each initial pattern in the system results in total chaos with no configuration stabilizing and nothing being predictable.

- **Class IV**: These are the systems with a set of rules not leading to dead, static, or chaotic configurations. Emerging patterns in this category are lively, creative, often surprising, but also stabilizing.

It should not surprise you that, in dynamical systems, class I and II correspond to *order*, class III corresponds to *chaos*, and class IV (of which the Game of Life is a famous example) corresponds to *complexity*. Given that complexity is usually explained as the region *between* order and chaos, this means that class IV finds itself between II and III (see Figure 8.2). (This strange way of using numbers makes Wolfram's computational knowledge engine all the more surprising.)

FIGURE 8.2
Ordered versus complex versus chaotic.

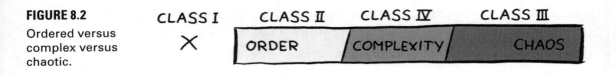

False Metaphor

The same universality classification can be used (or should I say *abused*?) as a metaphor when distinguishing complex systems themselves. Take the human brain, for example. A class I brain would be dead: Nothing happens in the brain. A class II brain could be comatose or catatonic: a state of silence or predictable repetitiveness. A class III brain could be insane or epileptic: displaying unpredictable and uncontrollable behavior. And finally, a class IV brain would be the only one considered lively and healthy. To prevent scientists from classifying *my* brain as a class III specimen, I must stress that I use this categorization only in a metaphorical way.

When classifying organizations we can make a similar metaphorical distinction between *ordered, chaotic,* and *complex* organizations. (I assume you will forgive me for ignoring the *dead* organizations for now.)

- In *ordered organizations* no creativity and innovation are taking place. Nobody is empowered to make his own decisions. Bureaucracy dictates how all work is to be carried out, and organizational behavior is regular and predictable (which usually means: regularly failing and predictably bad).

- In *chaotic organizations* there may be plenty of creativity, but not in a structured and predictable way. There is no emerging order in the organization, meaning that people simply empower themselves in getting things done. And everyone does as he or she pleases.

- *Complex organizations* find themselves right in between. In a complex organization, employees often don't empower themselves. (They don't select their own suppliers, hire their own families, or pay their own salaries.) They are empowered by managers, who are faced with the challenge of finding a balance between directives and delegation, between "benevolent" control and letting things go.

This classification of organizations is *not* scientific, but only a deceptively useful *metaphor*. I call it deceptive because the metaphor has led some managers (including me) to conclude that *they* are responsible for finding the right balance between order and control. But as we shall see, this conclusion is as wrong as it is common.

You're Not a Game Designer

We saw earlier that the set of rules of a cellular automaton determines what class of system it is. In designing the Game of Life, John Conway found that some sets of rules were too ordered, whereas other sets were too chaotic. It took him a while to find a set of rules that was nicely balanced, resulting in systems with complex behavior. Not too ordered, and not too chaotic.

Klaus Teuber took a similar approach when he was designing The Settlers of Catan, one of the most popular board games of all time. Teuber continuously played the game with his family, reconfiguring it again and again, changing the rules, the cards, and the pieces. It took him four years to find a set of rules that was nicely balanced and that enabled complex game play and heated family competition [Curry 2009].

What sets (most) games apart from living systems is their lack of the "adaptive" part. Traditional games do not change their own rules while they are in progress. But living systems do. Complex *adaptive* systems are systems that can find their own way toward that sweet spot of complexity, right between order and chaos, where life blooms and creativity thrives. Scientists call it the *edge of chaos*. But they also could have called it the edge of order because it is at the region between chaos and order where we find complexity. (Never expect a scientist to come up with a name that actually makes sense.)

The question is then *who* or *what* is tuning the rules in an organization so that the organization moves toward (and stays at) the edge of chaos, being neither too ordered nor too chaotic? A common misconception (and looking back at my earlier writings I have to plead guilty here) is that managers are somehow responsible for this.

But managers are not at all responsible for self-organization because this negates the concept of self-organization. And neither can managers choose the architecture of whatever emerges from a self-organizing team because then it is not emergence [Stacey 2000a:145].

It is tempting to think of managers as game designers, like John Conway and Klaus Teuber. When the manager chooses the wrong set of rules for the organization, it is either a class II system (too bureaucratic) or a class III system (too chaotic). And if they're really screwing up it will be a class I system (dead). Metaphorically this view is interesting, but scientifically it is hogwash. It loses the concept of a self-organizing system that evolves to produce its own novel strategies [Stacey 2000a:146].

Every organization is a complex adaptive system. It's like a game in which the rules are changed on-the-fly and where the job of designing the game is delegated to the participants themselves. Your job as a manager is not to create the right amount of rules in the organization. *Your job is to make sure that the people can create their own rules together.* And it's *their* collaborative effort that allows the system to find its own way to the edge of chaos. (Or the edge of order, if you prefer.)

Self-organization takes care of the edge of chaos when certain parameters fall within a critical range. The manager is not a game designer. He does not need to concern himself with the low-level rules of the game. He configures the high-level parameters, like diversity of team members, information flow between people, and connectivity between teams.

When setting up constraints in an organization, *one responsibility of a manager is the development of a self-organizing system.* Don't try to be John Conway or Klaus Teuber. You may define the boundaries of the board but not the rules of the game. When you take rule-making into your own hands, you will significantly influence and frustrate self-organization, and then creativity, innovation, and adaptability in the system will suffer.

But…Self-Organization Is Not Enough

I once saw the movie Gomorrah, based on the best-selling book by Roberto Saviano [Saviano, Jewiss 2008]. It tells the raw and harsh story of people living their lives inside and alongside the mafia. The movie makes it painfully clear what happens when government fails to guarantee people's freedoms and safety.

In an anarchistic society, freedom and safety are things you can acquire, like cars, iPods, and Che Guevara T-shirts. You buy them, sell them, or lose them. And when you are robbed of them, nobody will be responsible for protecting you, unless you have the means to pay for protection.

Self-organization is fundamental for every complex system. But in a human social system, self-organization alone is not enough. The mafia is self-organized. Self-organization is not necessarily a "good" thing. Or as Richard Dawkins put it, "Things might be neither good nor evil, neither cruel nor kind, but simply callous—indifferent to all suffering."

As a libertarian I hate to say this…but that's the point of having a government. Good government should bring freedom and safety to an entire society. Not just the ones who can pay for it.

So, what has this to do with management…? Everything! Project management expert Glen Alleman described the need for management as follows:

> *There is a difference between self-organizing and self-directing.* This is the role of management. This is not "directing" in the Command and Control sense. It is directing in the "required business value" sense. […] If self-organizing teams serve their customers, who "manages" the customer, when the customer is not prepared to behave in a "well-mannered" way? If there is more than one self-organizing team working on the same project, who co-ordinates the activities between these teams? When there are conflicts in resources, funding, requirements, who coordinates the resolution?[2]

Sometimes, people try to see self-organization as something different than anarchy. But, as I wrote earlier, I disagree with that point of view. My view is that self-organization is anarchy (which can be either complex or chaotic). An anarchist team may produce fantastic results, but they may not be the results that *you* think are valuable. Therefore, self-organization alone is not enough. At least a little management is needed to steer self-organization in a direction that is valuable for everyone in the system. Sanjiv Augustine calls it "light-touch leadership" [Augustine 2005]. I call it *alignment of constraints*. (I refer to aligning constraints, and not aligning people, because it is only the constraints that we control. And the people, we can only hope, will heed our constraints.)

When setting up constraints in an organization, *a second responsibility of a manager is the protection of the system*. As a manager, you put the basic controls in place to make it a good and safe organization to work for, and

---

2   Alleman, Glen B. "Self Organized Does Not Mean Self Directed." http://www.mgt30.com/self-directed/. Herding Cats. December 24, 2008. Reprinted by permission of Glen Alleman. [Alleman 2008].

then you protect its people and its shared resources, by making sure they are treated fairly. Because if you don't, your office manager's big Italian boyfriend might....

Manage the System, Not the People

Nobel Prize-winner Ilya Prigogine discovered that a complex system can self-organize only when there's a boundary around it. Such a boundary defines the "self" that will be developed through self-organization [Eoyang, Conway 1999].

A football team self-organizes within the boundaries of the playing field and the rules as they are laid down by the football association. A herd of wildebeest self-organizes within the boundaries imposed on it by the South-African ecosystem in which it lives. And criminal organizations self-organize according to what's forbidden and what's not. Without a boundary a system lacks the drive and constraints to organize itself.

The need for boundaries does *not* imply the need for management. It is a common misconception that a system without governance has no boundaries. There are *always* boundaries. I should know. I'm sitting here, trying to write a book within the boundaries imposed on me by my publisher, my employer, my spouse, my intellect, and (worst of all) my computer. And yet, as a freelance writer, I have no manager.

The universe itself is a boundary. Our planet forms a boundary. Natural resources form boundaries. And cultural constraints in a group of people also form a boundary. What we can learn from this is that there's always plenty of opportunity for self-organization to take place, and quite often at least *something* will emerge from that. But now that you're a manager, having defined the system in the first place, and governing the system to protect it, you must take the opportunity to make sure that what emerges has *value* to you and the environment. Because complexity science doesn't tell you to simply wait for the right solutions to emerge. The way managers define boundaries and constraints strongly influences what emerges from a self-organizing team [Lewin, Regine 2001]. You don't manage the people. You manage the system.

In biology, this is called *directed evolution* [Kelly 1994:301-302]. Biotech companies exploit the power of evolution to design drugs. They take charge of selective pressure and then allow nature to self-organize and do the rest. Directing evolution is a matter of changing boundaries so that nature produces molecules that are *valuable*. Directed self-organization in businesses is a matter of manipulating the constraints so that a group of people produces results that are valuable to the organization as a whole.

When aligning constraints for a group of people, *a third responsibility of a manager is defining the direction of the self-organizing system.* So yes, it's true. Managers *are* manipulators. But they are manipulators of the system, not the people.

And so we have identified three responsibilities for a manager when setting up constraints in an organization: 1) developing the system; 2) protecting the system; and 3) directing the system (see Figure 8.3).

DEVELOPING   PROTECTING   DIRECTING

FIGURE 8.3
Three responsibilities in setting up constraints.

BUT HOW DO I INITIATE A SELF-ORGANIZING TEAM?

There is nothing you have to do to get a self-organizing team started. Every group of people with a boundary and a purpose will self-organize. Just put a group of people together, set the restrictions, give them a goal, and watch. You'll see.

In Chapter 9, "How to Align Constraints," we discuss these responsibilities from a practical point of view. But first, in the second half of this chapter, we need to discuss the difference between management and leadership, and the meaning of purpose.

Managers or Leaders?

Management books often make a distinction between managers and leaders, depicting leadership as if it is more about heroics than management. Leaders are supposed to "define direction," whereas managers are just there to "maintain direction" [Maxwell 1998]. Managers are then advised to transform themselves to leaders, turning employees into willing followers, instead of herding them like sheep. One example is the book *Good to Great* in which Jim Collins lists a five-level hierarchy, which has managers positioned at lower levels than leaders [Collins 2001:20]. Such a hierarchy falsely suggests a linear progression, where being a leader is "more advanced" than being a manager.

Bah, nonsense!

Separating leadership from management is like comparing women to humans. It doesn't make sense. (Unless women understand something that I don't?) Comparing women to men seems more logical to me (but I'm just a man). Likewise, I think it makes more sense to compare *leaders* to *rulers*. Both are responsibilities, or behavioral styles, within the *job* that we call management.

Right Distinction: Leadership versus Governance

Seth Godin wrote that never in history has it been so easy for anyone to be a *leader* [Godin 2008]. These days, particularly since the explosive growth of the Internet and social media, each of us can attract our own followers. Godin explains that a crowd becomes a tribe when it has a leader, and that the people are following the leader out of their own free will. This is also called **adaptive leadership** [Marion, Uhl–Bien 2007:151] or **emergent leadership**. This kind of leadership *emerges* when a social system adapts. The interesting thing is, Godin writes, that people can follow different leaders for different causes.

In software projects, it is the same. Some people can take the lead on an architectural level, whereas some have the lead on a functional level. Others may be the first that people turn to when they need advice about tools or processes. A complex system does not need a single leader. In fact, a cross-functional team may even function better when it has multiple leaders, each with their own area(s) of interest.

In social systems, the *rulers* are of a different breed. Although leaders use the *power of attraction* to *convince* people what to do, rulers use the *power of authority* to *tell* people what to do. Ruling other people is the purpose of the ruler. And ruling includes law-making, enforcement, and sanctioning (also called the **trias politica**: legislature, executive, and judiciary).

Unfortunately, rulers have earned a bad reputation over the centuries. (Much of it deserved, by the way.) But ruling isn't all that bad. Laws, enforcement, and sanctions are necessary evils, and in many social systems rulers coexist peacefully, or sometimes stressfully, with leaders. For example: in any football match you will find leaders (one or more in each team) and rulers (the referees or arbiters). They all play their parts in making the game work for everyone.

It is obvious that managers are not only leaders but also rulers. They are the only ones with the authority to hire and fire people, and to place them in (or remove them from) teams or departments. This is also called **governance** or **administrative leadership** [Marion, Uhl-Bien 2007:153]. It is about telling people what projects to work on, what kind of clothes to wear, how much they are going to earn, and how much they must pay for a place at the parking lot.

To become a leader is *not* the highest purpose of a manager. Instead it is his job to decide how much to rule and how much to lead. Some managers lean toward ruling, others toward leading, but they all do at least a bit of both. Acting as a ruler corresponds to authority levels 1 (tell), 2 (sell), and 3 (consult), whereas acting as a leader corresponds to authority levels 4 (agree), 5 (advise), and 6 (inquire). (See Chapter 7," How to Empower Teams," for an explanation of these levels.) It is true that empowerment of people (changing the authority level) may turn you from someone who is predominantly ruling into a person who is primarily leading. But the authority level differs per activity. And with authority level 7 (full delegation) you're not even involved as a leader anymore.

Management gurus tend to misrepresent two things. First, the balancing act of leading versus ruling can take place at every level in the management chain. It is blatantly false to suggest that the top layer should be leading, whereas the bottom layer is primarily ruling. I am used to working with both rulers and leaders on every management layer. Some managers are good at ruling; some are better at leading. (I'm not good at either, but I am unbeatable at pretending.)

Second, a manager doesn't need to be both a ruler and a leader. Acting as a good ruler is hard enough already. If you want to be a great leader as well, you're just making it hard for yourself. Referees contribute to great football games by being good rulers. They don't attempt to lead. It's not their job. They are in charge, but they refrain from being the ones with the biggest egos. This is also called **enabling leadership** [Marion, Uhl-Bien 2007:152]. It is about empowering other people so that *they* can lead.

In his presentation *Step Back from Chaos*[3] Jonathan Whitty shows that managers are often not the hubs in a group's social network. The emerging leaders in a network are the ones through whom most of the communication flows (emergent leadership). It can be the manager's job to make sure such leadership is cultivated (with enabling leadership) and that the emerging leaders are following the rules (defined by administrative leadership, or...governance) (see Table 8.1).

TABLE 8.1

Three Types of Leadership

Type of Leadership	Description	Applied By
Administrative (governance)	Power of authority: ruling people	Managers
Emerging	Power of attraction: leading people	Anyone
Enabling	Allowing nonmanagers to lead	Managers

Meaning of Life

Now we know about the responsibilities of managers while defining constraints for self-organization, and we know about leadership versus governance. This would have been the end of this chapter, if it weren't that we also need to have a good understanding of the foundation for goal setting *before* we continue discussing any practical consequences. This foundation is about the concept of *purpose*, and it is the final topic of this chapter. Why are we here? Why are we doing this? And why are my sticky notes floating in the water cooler?

The "why" of things has been debated endlessly among philosophers, and it is usually denoted as **teleology**, the philosophical study of design and purpose. Many scientists want nothing to do with purpose. They say

---

3 http://www.mgt30.com/step-back/.

that purpose has no place in the hard sciences, like astronomy, physics, and chemistry [Corning 2003:172].

However, purpose is an important topic for socially complex systems (the study of which is definitely not a hard science) for two reasons. First, purpose can be seen as an emergent property of living systems.

> If we look we may find that direction and goals can emerge in biological evolution from a mob of direction-less and goal-less parts, without invoking vitalistic or supernatural explanations. Experiments in computational evolution conform this inherent teleogism, this self-produced "trend." [...] For those with an ear that burns at the combined sound of "goal" and "evolution," it helps to consider this trait less as a conscious goal, plan, or willful purpose, and more as an "urge" or "tendency."[4]

Replication can be seen as the "purpose" of genes, and survival might be the "purpose" of a species. This is not because some designer or owner imposes the purpose on these systems. It's only because the systems have an internal urge or tendency in that direction, or otherwise they cease to exist. Richard Dawkins calls it the **intrinsic purpose** that comes naturally to a system, in contrast to the **extrinsic purpose** given to a system by its owner (like the owner of a sheep dog assigning a purpose to his dog) [Dawkins 2009]. Other people seem to prefer using the terms **teleonomy** versus **teleology**. (I prefer to use all terms because my purpose is to look smart.)

> These days, the term that is most often used by biologists to characterize the internal teleology of living organisms is "teleonomy." ...the term connotes that the purposefulness found in nature is a product of evolution and not of a grand design. [...] Teleonomy in living systems is today accepted without question....[5]

The added social dimension in social complex systems is the second reason why purpose is important. It is inappropriate to discard the notion of purpose because human action is purposeful [Stacey 2000a:14].

---

4 Kelly, Kevin. Out of Control. Boston: Addison-Wesley, 1994. Used with permission. [Kelly 1994:411].
5 Corning, Peter. Nature's Magic. Cambridge: Cambridge University Press, 2003. [Corning 2003:172].

Assuming for the moment that human consciousness and free will are more than just illusions, they do indeed add a layer of meaning to social systems. Humans have goals. The need for **autonomous purpose** (or meaning of life) is one of our basic intrinsic desires. It ties back to our linear minds and our deterministic way of thinking.

> There is a great deal of evidence that people are hard-wired to care about purposes. We seem to need to see ourselves as going somewhere—as being on a journey in pursuit of a significant purpose.[6]

It appears that we've identified three kinds of purpose in living systems (and yes, organizations belong to the group of living systems [De Geus 1997]):

- Every living system (including genes, organisms, people, and organizations) has an **intrinsic purpose**.
- Every living system can have an **extrinsic purpose** *assigned* to it by an "owner" or "guardian."
- Every living system can have an **autonomous purpose** *assumed* by itself.

We all share the need for goals, but our goals are different from person to person, and also different from the intrinsic and extrinsic purposes of the social systems that we take part in. Assuming that all software project teams are social complex systems, and that we want those teams to have goals, I therefore think it is an important goal for this chapter to get to the bottom of this thing called purpose.

Purpose of a Team

What is your goal as a person? Is your goal to find happiness? Is your goal to be rich and famous? Is your goal to build the world's biggest collection of harmonicas? My goal is to rule the world. What's yours? Whatever your answer is, I bet that copying your genes to a younger generation is probably *not* your highest priority.

Dawkins wrote that it is the "goal" of our genes to be copied around [Dawkins 1989]. Our "selfish" genes have programmed us to act as vehicles

---

6 Reprinted with permission of the publisher. *From Intrinsic Motivation at Work*, copyright © 2000 by Kenneth Wayne Thomas, Berrett-Koehler Publishers, Inc., San Francisco, CA. All rights reserved. http://www.bkconnection.com.. [Thomas 2000:22].

for gene-transmission. But that doesn't mean that for us, as human beings, reproduction is our goal. Humanity is an emergent property of the human gene pool. We can appreciate that our genes have conceived us, but now that we're here we prefer to draw our own plans, thank-you-very-much.

The purpose of something that emerges from interacting parts is not determined by the purposes of those parts, but rather by the complex interaction between those parts.

- The goal of a brain is not a result of the goals of its neurons but of the interaction between the neurons.

- The goal of a city is not a result of the goals of its residents but of the interaction between the residents.

- The goal of a team is not a result of the goals of its team members but of the interaction between the team members.

The human mind has an "overdeveloped sense of cause and effect which primes us to see purpose and design everywhere, even where there is none" [Brooks 2009]. Or as Richard Dawkins put it:

> We humans are obsessed with purpose. [...] The question of purpose, which doesn't necessarily have to have an answer, is one that leaps to the front of the human mind, whether it is appropriate or not.[7]

So, is it appropriate to ask what the purpose is of an organization?

In 1970, Milton Friedman, a Nobel Prize-winner, and one of the most celebrated economists of the 20th century, wrote a famous article called "The Social Responsibility of Business Is to Increase Its Profits" [Friedman 1970]. Friedman denied that companies have nonfinancial or social responsibilities. In the 80s this view was implemented through *shareholder value*, the idea that the only goal of a business is to enrich its shareholders. This concept quickly found its way into many company mission statements. Jack Welch, the former CEO of General Electric, has been regarded by many as the father of the shareholder value movement. But the recent economic crisis proved that the shareholder value idea has its shortcomings. (And many of those companies were coming up very short indeed.)

> Shareholder value is an antisocial dogma that has no place in a democratic society. Period. It breeds a society of exploitation—of people as well as of institutions. It is bad

---

7   Dawkins, Richard "The Purpose of Purpose" http://www.mgt30.com/purpose/, June 18, 2009. [Dawkins 2009].

for business because it undermines its respect and credibility. Look at the Enrons, the Andersons, and all that followed.[8]

The major problem is that great economists and businessmen have been confusing the different kinds of purpose. An organization is an emergent phenomenon. It is the result of the interaction between shareholders, managers, employees, customers, and suppliers. All these stakeholders have their own individual goals, but none of them can claim that his goals are also those of the entire emergent system.

Now here comes (for some people) the hardest part. Brace yourself....

Shareholders are *not* the owners of everything in an organization. They are only owners of the *assets* in an organization. Shareholders do not own people, or their thoughts, or their mutual relationships. And the cliché "our people are our greatest asset" is a terrible use of terminology. People are not listed on balance sheets—and for good reasons.

Managers and employees have different individual goals and so do customers and suppliers. An organization is a social structure of various stakeholders who all want to satisfy their own goals through interaction. Therefore, the logical conclusion is that shareholder value is *not* the goal of an organization. It is the individual goal of the shareholders. And though shareholders can assign extrinsic purpose to anything they own, they can assign that purpose only to the assets of their organization. They cannot assign that same purpose to employees because they do not own the employees. Shareholders are not herding sheep.

Milton Friedman was right when he thought that the goal of businessmen is to make money. But complexity theory barely existed when Friedman wrote his famous article. In his time, companies were still mostly seen as machines, and shareholders were seen as the owners of the machines. Friedman would have been right about shareholder value if an organization is indeed a machine. But it isn't. It's a living system. In the words of Jack Welch, whose view on shareholder value turned out to have become more nuanced 30 years later, "Shareholder value is an outcome—not a strategy" [BusinessWeek 2009].

I once asked people what they thought of the goal of software project teams. These were some of the answers that I got:

---

8 Reprinted with permission of the publisher. From Managers Not Mbas, copyright © 2005 by Mintzberg, Henry, Berrett-Koehler Publishers, Inc., San Francisco, CA. All rights reserved. http://www.bkconnection.com. [Mintzberg 2005].

innovation, happy customers, working software, on-budget and on-time, great software, repeat customers, delighted users, happy developers, making money, more efficient users, solving business problems, adding business value, flexible process and product changes, cost savings, higher profits, automation, knowledge sharing, learning experiences, long term commercial success, creating something new...

Of course, it was just a trick question. The intrinsic purpose of a software project team is to produce software. That is the only native "trend" or "urge" in every software project that I can think of. When the team stops producing software (or intermediate products for software), it stops being a software project team. But more interesting is the idea that a team, because it is a living system, can define its own autonomous purpose.

A project team is a social system of various stakeholders. The goals I received from people via Twitter are all examples of goals for individual stakeholders. Neither customers nor team members nor managers can automatically promote their own goal as the goal of the entire project team. The team does not exist exclusively to satisfy the ProductOwner. And they do not exist exclusively to satisfy you. If you attempt such a thing, you're making the same mistake as Milton Friedman, treating the project like a machine instead of a living system. But Friedman was a Nobel Prize-winner. There might be worse things than being in the same league as him.

Assigning an Extrinsic Purpose

If not (exclusively) to satisfy the ProductOwner, or the manager, then what *is* the purpose of a software team?

Software projects might be compared to military operations because they need the same kind of directives. A commander needs to take care of the movements of his troops, or else his soldiers will be marching and crawling all over the place. The whole point of defining an extrinsic goal for military troops is to give self-organization a proper direction. (Remember, self-organization is not the same as self-direction. Management can define a direction, and self-organizing teams then find their own way toward it.)

A commander specifies an extrinsic purpose, and he allows self-organization to take over because the troops will be smart enough to figure out for themselves how to get there. Or else they're dead. (In Chapter 7 we discussed *why* people have to figure things out for themselves, and in Chapter 11, "How to Develop Competence," you see *how* they are supposed to do that.)

By comparison, the intrinsic goal of a software project team seems a bit boring. Its sole purpose is just to exist and to produce software. You will not win a war with a purpose like that.

That's why you specify a new extrinsic goal for your team. It doesn't invalidate the intrinsic goal. But it does help in defining boundaries, setting constraints, and allowing self-organization to take place in the right direction. Your team will be smart enough to figure out how to get there. Or else it's dead. (Well, sort of.)

Why is the manager allowed to assign an extrinsic purpose to an entire software project team? Because he is the only one who is responsible for the whole system. None of the other stakeholders are.

This chapter of the book also had a purpose. Its purpose was to describe the third view of the Management 3.0 model, explaining that a manager must develop, protect, and direct a team while defining constraints for self-organization; that leadership and governance are both part of management; and that we can recognize three kinds of purpose for teams. But we haven't finished with these topics yet. This chapter marks the end of the theoretical part of *Align Constraints*. Chapter 9 picks up where we left by looking at things from the practical side.

Summary

Self-organizing systems are able to create their own rules. All is needed for such a system to work is a set of simple constraints, sometimes called a boundary. It is important for managers to tune these constraints, and not to try and design all the rules. This means the job of a manager is to manage the system, and not the people in it.

People sometimes use a metaphor distinguishing between ordered, complex, and chaotic organizations. Strictly speaking, this metaphor is false, because all organizations are complex. But it can be useful nonetheless.

Another incorrect use of terminology is the distinction of managers versus leaders. Managers and leaders are not different people. Leadership and governance are two sides of the same coin, and both roles are part of the job of a manager.

Last but not least, there can be three types of purpose in a self-organizing team: The intrinsic purpose is innate to the team; the extrinsic purpose is assigned by the manager; and the autonomous purpose is assumed by the team itself.

Reflection and Action

Let's see if you can apply some ideas from this chapter to your organization:

- Imagine that your team is completely self-directed, with no interference or directions from you. Which outcomes would you fear? What boundaries would you want to keep in place to prevent bad things from happening?

- Think about your own management capabilities. What are you good at? Leading or ruling? Do you want to emphasize one or the other? How?

- Think about yourself, as a person. What is your purpose in your job? How is this purpose different from other people?

Chapter 9

How to Align Constraints

My life has no purpose, no direction, no aim, no meaning, and yet I'm happy.
I can't figure it out. What am I doing right?

—Charles M. Schulz, cartoonist (1922–2000)

Much has been written about vision, mission, and goal setting, but few experts seem to agree on what the words really *mean*. Dictionaries don't agree with encyclopedias, and process frameworks don't agree with leading consultants. Or the other way around.

This chapter continues where the previous one stopped. It is about purpose, vision, mission, and goals, and the practical side of *Align Constraints*. My own use of these terms could match existing definitions (by sheer luck), although it is most likely that they differ somewhat. At the least, I try to be consistent with my own writing. But most important, this chapter gives you *useful* recipes for developing, protecting, and directing your teams with proper constraints.

Again, this chapter consists of two parts. The first part is about goal setting. You can be forgiven for thinking that goal setting deals exclusively with directing a self-organizing team, but that is not correct. We can easily define goals for the development and protection of a team. Goals don't have to be just about setting a course in a certain direction for the work people do every day. However, it is common for managers to think in such ways; therefore, I've dedicated the second part of this chapter to a few suggestions that deal exclusively with the development and protection of a self-organizing team.

Give People a Shared Goal

In Chapter 8, "Leading and Ruling on Purpose," I used the terms goal, meaning, and purpose interchangeably. However, I have developed a personal preference for using the term "goal" only in the case of an *extrinsic* or *autonomous* purpose, and the term "meaning" only when talking about an *intrinsic* purpose. My goal as a living being can change regularly, depending on whatever happens in my environment; but the meaning of my life is rather static. (So far, the answer has always been 42.)

Management literature is virtually unanimous about the value of goal setting, although implementations of it are often quite terrible. Goals are necessary for expressing directives. But they also significantly help to improve morale among team members. That's two for the price of one!

Leadership researchers found that among the strongest needs of teams were a vision from their leaders [Thomas 2000:57]. Defining a purpose for a team enables a manager to unite and motivate people [Stallard 2007:17] by giving them a shared and realizable dream [Thomas 2000:56–57]. And perhaps most important, a goal gives a group of people an "awareness of their context" [Fox 1998]. (For the moment, let's consider vision, mission, goal, objectives, and purpose as equivalents.)

The lack of an explicit organizational goal may result in managers thinking only about their own individual goals, meaning they are acting like any other stakeholder in the system. They tend to optimize their own jobs at the expense of the whole organization [Lencioni 2002].

The message is clear: A manager is responsible for defining a shared goal across a group. In the past, this has been called **management by objectives (MBO)**.[1] But MBO has earned itself a bad name among Agile experts because many managers have been implementing it so badly throughout the years. What usually happens with goal setting is that top management defines an annual "shared" goal and hands out bonuses at the end of the year when this goal is achieved. Let me make it clear: This is *not* Agile!

A shared objective (extrinsic purpose) *transcends* any goals of individuals or (sub)teams within the group for which the manager is responsible, and therefore the corporate goal should also *transcend* the goal of the CEO. It is, literally, a "higher purpose" that the manager assigns to a whole group, intending it both as a directive *and* as a way to improve employee satisfaction.

The shared goal is *not* the same as the goal of the customer (who is just a stakeholder); it is *not* the same as the goal of the project manager (who is just a stakeholder); it is *not* the same as the goal of the shareholder (who is just a stakeholder); and it is *not* the same as the goal of the manager

---

1 http://www.mgt30.com/mbo/

himself (who is…well, I'm sure you get my point). Elevating any of these stakeholders' goals to the group level would lead to suboptimization and dysfunctional measurements (see Figure 9.1).

STAKEHOLDERS   MANAGER

FIGURE 9.1

Goals per stakeholder and a shared goal from the manager.

I have compiled a small list of examples of shared goals that can help you define your own:

- Our goal is to be a profitable provider of backup services, considered by many as the best in our country, in terms of reliability and customer service.

- By October 31, the first version of our product will have been released to customers, and the amount of positive feedback we get from users in the last quarter of the year should be higher than the amount of negative feedback we got in the preceding quarter.

- By the end of next year, the public will recognize that we have beaten the iPhone.

- All team members will pass professional exams next year.

- MyBigCalc.com will be the most visited site on the Internet for online calculations of tax deductions.

- Next year, we are going to win the Best Product award for our industry.

- FlimsyTool 3.5 will solve all reported user problems without incurring any negative consequences for performance and security.

Note that a shared goal does not have to be an exact scientifically measurable objective. We're talking about pointing people in a general direction, not teleporting them to a space ship in FTL flight.

Checklist for Agile Goals

Should you define just one goal, or can you have multiple goals? Scott Berkun suggests that you can create an ordered list of goals [Berkun 2008:262]. Ken Blanchard also suggests multiple goals and writing each one on a separate page in less than 250 words [Blanchard, Johnson 1982:34]. I would suggest that, in theory, having one goal is best. But theory often takes a lot of practice, so you might end up with a couple of extra goals.

When you've defined a set of goals, you could run each of them against the following ridiculously long checklist. I created it by combining various sources, including the famous S.M.A.R.T. criteria[2] (that I disagree with) and various wisdom tiles from my grandmother's bathroom:

- Is the goal **specific** and **understandable** enough so that people know what you mean?
- Is the goal **simple** and **concise** enough so that it fits on a small card or sticky note?
- Is the goal **manageable** and **measurable** so that success can be determined?
- Is the goal **memorable** and **reproducible** so that people can easily communicate it to others?
- Is the goal **attainable** and **realistic** so that people have a chance of actually achieving it?
- Is the goal **ambitious** and **stimulating** enough so that it isn't (too) easy to achieve?
- Is the goal **actionable** and **assignable** so that it can be turned into specific actions?
- Is the goal **agreed-upon** and **committable** so that people actually feel responsibility for it?
- Is the goal **relevant** and **useful** enough for people so that they really care about it?

---

2 http://www.mgt30.com/smart/

- Is the goal **time-bound** and **time-specific** so that people know when to do it?

- Is the goal **tangible** and **real** so that people can see the effects of achieving it?

- Is the goal **excitable** and **igniting** so that it motivates people to do their best?

- Is the goal **inspiring** and **visionary** so that it helps people to see a bigger picture?

- Is the goal **value-based** and **fundamental** so that it builds on top of company values, team values, or personal values?

- Is the goal **revisitable** and **assessable** so that you can reassess its applicability later?

A crucial difference between old-style goal setting associated with MBO and new-style Agile goal setting as an Agile manager is that the criteria for goals must depend on the context. For example: It is too simplistic to suggest that all goals should be SMART (specific, measurable, attainable, relevant, and time-bound). If your goal is to enjoy a vacation in Norway, how are you going to measure that? Will you track the number of thrilling experiences or the average number of laughs per day? Does it matter for the decisions that you need to make now? And if your goal is to beat your competitors next year, are you going to measure this by revenue, profits, market share, employees, or customers? And does that actually matter for inspiring people right *now*?

A goal that satisfies all previously listed criteria is impossible to define. You simply have to pick a few criteria that you find important to your *current* situation. Some goals must be simple, whereas others must be actionable. Some should be measurable, whereas others need to be inspiring. What matters is that goals help people with the decisions they need to make right now.

There are also a few things that you should stay away from when you're setting goals. Susan M. Heathfield described five possible dangers [Heathfield 2010a]:

- Goals should *not* be created to intimidate people and to threaten them with loss of their jobs if they're unable to achieve them.

- Goals should *not* be defined merely to impress shareholders or people watching the organization from the sideline.

- Goals should *not* favor short-term wins over long-term losses.

- Goals should *not* distract people from a desired outcome by focusing only on an action plan.

- And you should aim not to have too many goals. Which sounds like a fine goal to me.

But by far, the biggest danger with goals is when managers connect them to rewards. In Chapter 5, "How to Energize People," we discussed the consequences of extrinsic motivation, which are more often bad than good. You should *not* introduce unpredictable nonlinear dynamics when trying to set a course for your teams. Always connect goals to people's intrinsic desires. Enjoying your vacation *is* the reward. The reward is *not* some financial bonus connected to a certain number of laughs per day.

To summarize how goal setting in Agile management is different from old-style goal setting:

- An Agile goal is a "higher purpose," which transcends the goals of all individuals. It is a goal for the entire living system, not a goal just for the CEO or the shareholders.

- Agile goals are not required to conform to a whole range of criteria, like specific, measurable, and so on. A goal depends on its context. Sometimes it should be inspiring; sometimes it should be measurable.

- An Agile goal should not be connected to rewards or incentives. Extrinsic motivation distorts the system and has nonlinear consequences, which often defeat the purpose of the goal itself. Instead a goal should address people's intrinsic desires.

- Goals are allowed to change more than once per year. They are not created to please shareholders but to give employees a sense of direction.

Communicate Your Goal

In a board meeting, I once heard someone ask: "What was our corporate shared value of this year again?" And the COO answered that it was "courage." I didn't even know there was a corporate value of the year. And it was almost Christmas. Perhaps the year-end results of the business would have been a little better if a few more people in the organization had actually known that courage was valued and supported. Who knows? Who knew?

Let me share with you my secret technique that occasionally helps me in achieving my goals…I tell everyone!

I tell my friends about the goals I have. When people know what my goals are, it tends to strengthen my own resolve to actually achieve them. I regularly get questions like "When is your book coming out?" "How is that new business of yours? Any customers yet?" and "How far are you from becoming a billionaire?" These questions remind me about the goals that I set earlier. By communicating goals to friends and colleagues, I make sure that the environment gently pushes me and keeps tab on my progress. It's like handing over management of myself to the environment. I do *not* want to hear someone say, "I knew it. I always thought you wouldn't achieve it." But keeping a goal to yourself is the easy way to failure. Because if you fail, cognitive dissonance kicks in, and you simply convince yourself that your goal was never serious in the first place. So you tell people about your goal because you don't want to fail. And *that* takes courage.

ACTUALLY, THIS DOESN'T ALWAYS APPLY

Some reviewers pointed out that, according to research, many people actually perform *better* when they keep their goals to themselves. Apparently, when you communicate your personal goals to others, it satisfies your self-identity just enough that you're then less motivated to do the real work needed to achieve the goal [Sivers 2009].

So perhaps my analogy falls flat on its face. But my goal is to convince you that you need to communicate corporate goals to people to give them a sense of direction. I just hope I succeeded at that.

Someone once said to me that, according to research, documented goals had no measurable effect on the success of software projects (source unknown). But what matters is not the act of writing goals on paper. I can write anything I like on a piece of paper, and I'm sure that it will have no effect whatsoever on my project. Goal setting is about making sure that everyone in the organization acts in accordance with your boundaries and directives. Every day. All the time. As steering wheels, maintaining direction in an organization, your paper, plaques, and posters are totally inadequate. People must not just read about your goal. They also must *feel* it in everything they do, weighing every action against it.

How?

By *talking with people* about your goal and reviewing their actions. Also by *asking questions*, like "Do you still know what your goal is?" and "How is this action going to help us in achieving our goal?" A goal works only when the people in the system *use* it to evaluate their actions. It is a goal when *they* can recite it. It's not a goal when only you can, at the end of the year before Christmas.

Therefore, when people are unable to answer such questions, take it as a hint that your approach to goal setting needs a little rework. And maybe some courage, too.

AND THEN WE CAN CONNECT GOALS TO BONUSES, RIGHT?

NOOOOoooooooooooo! Don't even think about it!

Vision versus Mission

In their book Made to Stick, Chip Heath and Dan Heath talk about the concept of Commander's Intent:

> CI [Commander's Intent] is a crisp, plain-talk statement that appears at the top of every order, specifying the plan's goal, the desired end-state of an operation. [...] Commander's Intent manages to align the behavior of soldiers at all levels without requiring play-by-play instructions from their leaders.[3]

The equivalent of Commander's Intent in organizations might be the vision statement and the mission statement. Vision and mission are two different but closely related ways of specifying goals. These are the definitions on Wikipedia[4]:

---

3 Heath, Chip and Dan Heath. Made to Stick. New York: Random House, 2007. Used with permission. [Heath 2007]
4 http://www.mgt30.com/mission/

A **vision statement** outlines what the organization wants to be. It concentrates on the future. It is a source of inspiration. It provides clear decision-making criteria.[5]

A **mission statement** tells you the fundamental purpose of the organization. It concentrates on the present. It defines the customer and the critical processes. It informs you of the desired level of performance.[6]

My interpretation is that vision statements are usually created for businesses, projects, and products. They are outward facing, dealing with the place a system has in the world and the change it will bring to its environment. Whereas mission statements are more commonly used for groups and teams. They are inward facing, steering the internal dynamics of a system. The vision is about a desired end state, and the mission is about the way to get there. Peace on earth is a vision. Eradicating terrorism is a mission. A keynote speech at a conference as a famous author is my vision. Finishing this book is my mission.

When reviewing actual vision and mission statements from various organizations, I noticed that most of them have either a vision statement or a mission statement, but not both. And in some cases the two terms are even used interchangeably, for one and the same statement. This is understandable because handing out separate vision statements and mission statements doesn't help anyone. Commander's Intent does not distinguish between mission and vision, either. The mission is to beat the crap out of the enemy, and the vision is to get people safely back to their home DVD collections. And their families, of course. A commander doesn't need two separate statements for that.

To make matters clearer (or more confusing), I advise team managers not to use the term "vision statement" for a team. You see, a vision statement is sometimes already written by one of the stakeholders. Some Scrum experts suggest that this is a responsibility of the Product Owner [Sterling 2010].

But what about the other stakeholders? Are they also allowed to come forward with their own vision statements? In my view they are. Every stakeholder has a goal, and they can plaster their vision statements all over the office, as far as I'm concerned (assuming they have permission from

---

5 Reprinted under the Creative Commons License.
Please visit http://creativecommons.org/
6 Reprinted under the Creative Commons License.
Please visit http://creativecommons.org/

their office managers). But it does not mean that the Product Owner (or any other stakeholder) gets to say what the purpose of the whole team is. A team is more than just the sum of its stakeholders. The mistake would be similar to the misdirected idea of shareholders imposing their "shareholder value" concept on entire organizations.

Summarizing, my advice would be to define vision statements for your products and projects. Such statements can paint a happy picture of delighted users, market domination, and world peace. Define mission statements for your organization and your teams. These statements can talk about technical excellence, innovative achievements, and defeating the competition, whoever that may be. (I hope it's not me.)

Examples of Organizational Goals

When defining goals (either visions or missions), people sometimes get carried away. Let's review some interesting examples of company mission statements. (The names and details have been changed, to protect the innocent....)

> ParcelExpress is committed to providing great customer experience, to being a fantastic place to work, a mindful steward of the environment, and a useful contributor to the communities where we work and live. At Parcel-Express, we care about connecting people and places, in sustainable ways, and improving the quality of people's lives around the globe.
>
> As a software business, and as employees, we value integrity, openness, honesty, constructive self-criticism, mutual respect, continual self-improvement, and personal excellence. We care about our customers and partners and we are committed to delivering great technologies. We take on challenging projects, and we make sure to see them through. We feel responsible for our customers, partners, shareholders, and employees by delivering results, and striving for the highest possible quality.

Uhm....

Are these goals concise? Inspiring? Useful? Measurable? Motivational? I'm afraid not. What about memorable? If people cannot memorize a mission statement, how is this goal going to direct them in their everyday decisions? Think of an employee who has to make a quick decision between either releasing something useless on time, versus releasing something useful too late. What can she do? Her product is out of date before she has finished digging up and reading a mission statement like the preceding one.

Here is an interesting example of a company mission statement:

> Google's mission is to organize the world's information and make it universally accessible and useful.[7]

Exactly!

Imagine a person working for Google who is facing the same dilemma. What does he do? Well, releasing something that is useless is definitely not going to help anyone organize the world's information. Google's mission statement is understandable, concise, memorable, ambitious, actionable, useful, plain, tangible, excitable, and inspiring. It seems to fulfill about half of the criteria for goals, which is a good score. And it allows for much quicker decisions. Sure, it doesn't answer all questions, and it's not supposed to. But it gives people a direction, so they can answer their own questions in many cases.

Allow Your Team an Autonomous Goal

We discussed giving teams a goal, but what about self-organizing teams that come up with their own goal?

It takes a talented group of people to come up with a goal of their own, which transcends the goals of all participants. But never disregard the possibility that a self-organizing system may have devised a goal (or "purpose") for itself. The goal an employee has for herself is real, and it's probably different from the corporate goal. Likewise, the goal a team has for itself is real, and also likely to be different from any goals that you have in store for them.

Most teams do not formulate their own goals. And if they do have a shared goal they all agree upon, it has usually formed in an implicit and informal manner, such as "We are THE high-productivity team of the organization," or "Whatever happens, we want it to be fun," or "We are professionals. We don't do copy/paste here." However, some professional

---

7   Taken from Google's corporate website: http://www.mgt30.com/google/

teams do have the ability to sit together and talk about a more elaborate or nuanced shared goal, to which all team members commit themselves explicitly.

If your team has defined its own goal, whether implicitly or explicitly, let them be. Allow them that freedom. Don't frustrate your team by over-ruling a goal they are happy with. Instead, pride yourself on having a self-organizing team. Many other managers, including me, would envy you.

And if they don't have a goal for themselves, it couldn't hurt to ask them about it. It might just give them an interesting idea. But *never tell them* to create their own goal. That would hardly count as self-organization, would it?

Compromise on Your Goal and Your Team's Goal

When you ask your spouse to find a travel guide for Chile, two important things happen: First, she will make all kinds of assumptions about what you really mean. This means you need to make explicit any constraints that you have concerning the travel guide. (In other words, use the Del-egation Checklist in Chapter 7, "How to Energize People.") Because she might return with a 20-page booklet containing only pictures and no text. Second, your spouse has goals of her own. Her goal might be to spend her entire weekend shopping for clothes, leaving her little room for a detailed comparison of Rough Guide versus Lonely Planet.

When you delegate work there can be a conflict of goals. It happens when (sub)goals of the organization (or of a project) are to be achieved by a team and this team happens to have self-organized and created its own shared team goal. A similar situation occurs when organizational or team-level (sub)goals are delegated to the level of an individual employee.

The usual advice from consultants and management gurus is to simply align people and teams to the goals of the projects they work on, or the organization they work for. But this advice doesn't acknowledge that a living system can define its own autonomous purpose.

My conclusion is therefore, in the case of a conflict between the ex-trinsic purpose imposed by a manager and the autonomous purpose de-fined by the system itself, there has to be a *compromise*. The subgoal that you have in store for a team (for example: "delivery on the deadline") and the goal that they have defined for themselves (for example, "we don't do copy/paste here") need to be *adapted* to each other. It is hard for some managers to accept that one doesn't overrule the other.

My personal goals do not overrule the goals of my spouse or my children. When I need them to do something for me, and it conflicts with the needs they have for themselves, we will just have to work it out. Together. Likewise, you will have to work out any conflicting goals with your team. Overruling the team will only make matters worse, as you will incur a significant motivational debt that is very hard to pay back.

Create a Boundary List of Authority

The first part of this chapter was all about goal setting, which is not only important for setting the direction of teams, but also for their development and protection. But, acknowledging that goals are most often used by managers for setting a team's direction, we will use the second part of this chapter to focus specifically on developing and protecting self-organizing teams.

Often, when managers "empower" people, they don't give them clear boundaries of their authority. This means people usually have to find out by trial and error, incurring some emotional damage along the way. Donald Reinertsen calls it the "discovery of invisible electric fences" [Reinertsen 1997:107-108]. It is a waste of time and resources. Worse, repeatedly running into invisible electric fences tends to kill people's motivation. They have no idea what other invisible fences surround them, and then they prefer not to move around anymore.

To solve this problem Reinertsen has offered a list of *Key Decision Areas* [Reinertsen 1997:107]. When combined with the seven authority levels (see Chapter 7), and the choice of authorizing individual or teams, this gives you a powerful tool for defining the boundaries of authority (see Table 9.1).

Key Decision Area	How (Authority Level)	Who (Team/Individual)
Define features	...	...
Define budget	...	...
Select team	...	...
Select location	...	...
Etc.	...	...

TABLE 9.1

Boundary List of Authority

As previously mentioned, authority levels 1, 2, and 3 will make you more of a ruler than a leader, because it is you who will be making the final decisions. In the Who (Team/Individual) column you can name the individuals or teams you want to involve in your decisions. With levels 4, 5, and 6, you intend to act as a leader, suggesting directions but leaving the decisions to others. In this case, in the last column, you name the teams or individuals to whom you've delegated final decision making.

Creating a boundary list of authority can help people to avoid running into any electrical fences, which keeps them motivated and productive.

Choose the Proper Management Angle

The metaphor of ordered versus chaotic organizations (see Chapter 8) is useful when considering the right approach to management. Are people in the organization confronted with many rules? Or aren't they even aware that there are some rules? Are they complaining about bureaucracy? Or are they complaining about projects blowing up around them? Do people fear breaking the rules? Or are they begging for more? Are they unwilling to commit to anything because the organization doesn't allow them to do things "their way"? Or are they doing things "their way," while in the meantime annoying your customers and destroying the business?

Some organizations are too rigid in their approach to management, whereas others are too lax. Pilots shouldn't be treated like monkeys, but neither should you let monkeys fly a plane. With airplanes it is relatively easy to notice a difference in the skill of handling them. With computers it is a bit harder. (I recently read about an orangutan taking pictures and putting them on Facebook. Go figure.)

You solve this problem by going through the key decision areas and comparing your actual versus your preferred level of authority. In ordered organizations the level is often set too high. In chaotic organizations it is too low.

For example, consider the key decision area "Determine test procedures." When teams are complaining about bureaucratic test procedures, it could be an indication that the authority level is too high, and that people should be empowered to define their own (more Agile) procedures together. Provided, of course, that they commit to certain quality constraints for the products they deliver. On the other hand, when products are of terrible quality, and nobody knows about any test procedures, it is probably time to increase the authority level, disempowering people and placing authority in the hands of someone capable of reorganizing quality assurance and testing.

You will find that the best management angle differs between key decision areas. For example, I find that the approach to recruitment and human resources in many organizations is (too) rigid, whereas their adoption of decent software engineering principles is usually too lax. Claiming that a whole company is either ordered or chaotic is too easy. On one side it may be too ordered, on the other it may be too chaotic. Which makes the risk of falling over too big. (Or am I stretching the metaphor too far?)

Authority needs to be set to the *lowest possible level* that is just enough to get good results from people. It follows the principle that rule-making should, preferably, be done by the people in the organization and not by the manager. If you're in a bureaucratic organization, you *lower* the authority level to a point where rule-making (and adherence to rules) still takes place. But any lower than that and people's rule-making capabilities (and thereby creativity and productivity) dissolve into thin air. On the other hand, if you're in a chaotic organization, you *increase* the authority level to the point where rule-making starts having an effect, but not higher. In either case, it's like driving your car and keeping the gas pedal pushed down as far as possible, but keeping it right at the threshold where you're still safe from traffic control cameras and uncomfortable discussions with the police. If you succeed you have, almost literally, brought your business to the edge of order, and the edge of chaos. And that's where all the creative, productive, and fearless businesses are.

Protect People

So far, I have primarily discussed the development of self-organizing teams and the direction of teams toward a purpose. But let's not forget about protection of people and resources....

The first three years in high school were the worst of my life. Some guys in my class had chosen me as the center of attention in their need for bullying and harassment. I was regularly the victim of vicious jokes, bad treatment, name calling, destruction of stuff I owned, and my schoolbag flying over my head across the room. I was unable to stand up for myself because, at that time, I didn't know how.

A classroom full of kids is a fine example of a self-organizing system. True, the teachers have some constraints concerning children's presence, homework, and tests, but despite plenty of school rules and directives, whatever else happens in and around school is left to the kids themselves to handle. And there are always a few that suffer from this.

Self-organization is not necessarily a good thing. A group of thugs mistreating a timid kid is an effect of self-organization that needs eradication. Self-organization implicitly assumes that people take care of themselves, which is something not everyone is capable of.

Management literature has plenty of examples of people being mistreated by their colleagues at work. They too can be the victims of vicious jokes, bad treatment, name calling, destruction of stuff they own, or their lunch boxes flying over their head across the room.

As a manager, you are responsible for both promoting self-organization *and* protecting people, like my school was responsible for allowing kids to play *and* protecting them at the same time. (They didn't do a spectacular job, I must add.)

But how do you find out if someone is being mistreated?

Honestly, I'm no psychologist. But from personal experience, I can tell you that it probably won't help asking someone "Are you being treated well?" Because everyone, including the kid with the black eye, will say, "Yeah, sure." Some organizations have a counselor to whom employees can turn with their personal problems. But my school had a counselor, too. Of course, I never went there. What did they expect? That I would enter his office saying, "Hi, I just came by to report how sad I feel that the others caused a carton of chocolate milk to burst in my schoolbag?"

I think there are two other approaches that *might* work. The first is asking someone, "Who are your friends here?" At school, I wouldn't have been able to answer that question (if educators had bothered to ask) because, the truth is, I didn't have any. Note carefully whether the interviewed person can produce a couple of friends' names at the blink of an eye, without sweating and swallowing heavily. Of course, a lack of friends at work doesn't necessarily indicate that something bad is happening. But you might start by showing genuine interest in the person, like "Well, that doesn't have to be a terrible thing, but why don't you and I have lunch together and talk about work and stuff?" It could make a big difference to someone. I know for certain my defenses would have crumbled quickly in front of a friendly face.

The second approach could be to ask the other people. Sure, I could have kept my defenses up and named a few neutral classmates as my "friends." But my teachers could have asked them, "Are the other kids in class being treated equally well?," or "Which of the kids in class are having a hard time?" Plenty of other kids knew about my unfortunate position in the pecking order. But nobody ever asked them. And I spent my time in the boys' locker room, using my T-shirt to wipe the chocolate milk from the pages of my school books.

But you still have a choice. You can ask.

By the way, there's no need to feel concerned about me now. I have learned to bite back so hard that my teeth needed renovation.

Protect Shared Resources

When I wrote this, I was working at ISM eCompany in a big open office space in the Van Nelle Factory in Rotterdam (see Figure 9.2). About 100 people work in an office that was the first of its kind in Europe when it was built in 1929. And more than 80 years later, architecture lovers from all over the world still come to admire it, take pictures, and make drawings. I sometimes waved at them.

FIGURE 9.2
ISM eCompany, Van Nelle office.[8]

A big open office space has advantages and disadvantages. Advantages are flexibility and easy communication. The main disadvantage is that it is a shared resource for all who work there. Climate, sound, and light are hard to manage in a space like that, and the optimal configuration for the

8 Reprinted by permission of Stephan Meijer - NoPicsPlease.com

whole is never optimal for all. But our office manager did the best she could in trying to maximize pleasant working conditions, while maintaining tight rules to keep things under control. A shared open office is not the ideal environment to give people full responsibility over their own working space.

When shared resources are not managed by a central authority, self-organization often results in the **Tragedy of the Commons**.[9] The name refers to a situation in which multiple self-organizing systems, all acting in their own self-interest, overexploit a shared limited resource, even when they all know it is not in anyone's interest for this to happen. The impact that humanity has on CO_2 levels in the air, trees in the forests, and fish in the sea is right now the most debated and intensively researched case of the Tragedy of the Commons.

Organizations also have shared resources, such as budgets, office space, and system administrators. We could see them as the business-equivalent of the air we breathe, the landscape we change, and the fish we eat.

Research indicates that four ingredients (called the four I's) are needed for sustainability of shared resources [Van Vugt 2009:42]:

- **Institutions** [managers] who work on building trusting relationships between competing systems [teams] in order to increase acceptance of common rules.

- **Information** that increases understanding of the physical and social environment, in order to reduce uncertainty (because uncertainty results in bias towards self-interest).

- **Identity**, or a need for a social "belonging" that encompasses all participants, to improve and broaden one's sense of community and reduce competition.

- **Incentives** that address the need to improve oneself, while punishing overuse and rewarding responsible use.

Research shows that it is imperative that there is some form of management to protect these shared resources by working on the four I's. (I realize that most modern day governments are not setting a good example of how to do that.) In the case of shared resources, whether it concerns money, space, or system administrators, someone outside of the development teams must keep an eye on long-term sustainability instead of short-term individual gains.

---

9 http://www.mgt30.com/tragedy/

Constrain Quality

I am not a saint. There have been some awful quality problems in the products that I was directly or indirectly responsible for. No, I was not responsible for accidentally sending that email to 1,000,000 people instead of just 10,000 registered users. And it was not me who messed up the home addresses of a few thousand online buyers so that their products could not be delivered. And I had nothing to do with the bug that allowed 9 out of 10 players in a lottery to win the main prize. But I will eagerly tell you about my own programming errors. If you show me yours, I'll show you mine.

The problem with quality is that it is often simply assumed by everyone. This is exemplified by the well-known triangle of constraints, or **project management triangle**,[10] which lists three important constraints (scope, cost, and schedule), but not quality. Customers just assume they will get quality products, and managers assume that employees know how to build them. And, unfortunately, 80% of people actually *believe* that the quality of their work is above average. Obviously it isn't.

Self-organization can solve many quality problems, as long as you put the right constraints in place. It is sometimes said that managers get what they measure. If you make it a point that products must be delivered to customers before their deadlines, self-organizing teams will do exactly that. They will push (sometimes crappy) products out the door on the day of the deadline. If you make it a point that products have to be reliable, scalable, well-performing, and secure, self-organizing teams will build exactly that. They will deliver high-quality products many months after the customer gave up waiting for them and went elsewhere. And if you manage your constraints to have products delivered on time *and* of high quality, again you get exactly what you want. But the products will contain less than half of the features the customer asked for.

I prefer to depict these choices in my favorite adaptation of the iron triangle, where quality is added to turn the triangle into a square (see Figure 9.3). The idea of the square is that changing one corner in one direction has a similar effect on either of the two adjacent corners, or else a reversed effect on the opposite corner. For example: Increased functionality means more resources or an increased time schedule, or else a *lower* quality. And loss of resources leads to less functionality or decreased quality, or else an *increased* schedule.

---

10 http://www.mgt30.com/triangle/

FIGURE 9.3
Iron Square of
Constraints.

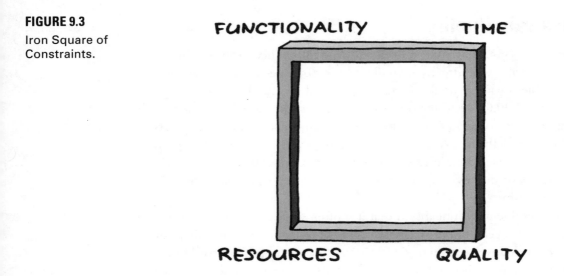

As a manager, part of your job is to really think about the kind of constraints you place on self-organizing teams. You not only get what you ask for, but you also *don't* get what you *don't* ask for. Too often, managers forget to define clear constraints for quality in their products. And if you don't define it, you are not going to get it. (We revisit this topic in Chapter 11, "How to Develop Competence," when we discuss the various ways of achieving competence.)

Create a Social Contract

You have come to the end of this chapter, and by now, you have learned to define goals, rules, and boundaries for the people in your organization, and you sent the team on a great and inspiring mission.

But what do they get in return? Why should people subscribe to your vision? What's in it for them? Only a salary?

Israel Gat described how he used the idea of a **social contract** to define the obligations that the manager feels he has toward his employees.

> Team, my overarching organizational objective is to preserve our team and its institutional knowledge for our corporation and its customers for years to come. We will achieve this goal by enhancing our software engineering

prowess to the level that the resultant benefits will outweigh the repercussions of the current financial crisis.
[...] Whether you will or will not be with the company
in the future, I acknowledge your need to develop professionally as Agile practitioners and commit to invest in
your education/training.[11]

In this social contract, Israel Gat described not only (part of) a mission,
but also what he acknowledged to be his own responsibilities toward the
team members. In this case, it was investing in education to address their
need to further develop themselves professionally.

Social contract theory[12] is a philosophical concept describing how
groups of people maintain social order by giving up some of their freedoms to an authority. It is an agreement by the governed on a set of rules
by which they should be governed, and it usually applies to societies and
their governments. But the idea translates quite well to organizations,
even though the "governed" do not have the right to elect their "gov-
ernors." What is similar is that the contract lists the obligations of the
authorities toward the people, and that everyone is automatically assumed
to agree on the contract, or else they are free to leave. (Which, I am sad to
add, can be a bit troublesome in the case of some countries.)

A social contract should address the basic necessities of people. In a society, they are not only things like food, shelter, and safety, but also freedom of speech, basic education, equality, and (if you're fortunate enough
to be born in a modern country) healthcare. In an organizational context,
we're talking about similar things, such as the freedom to voice your
opinion, professional development, nondiscrimination, and a little help
when you're not feeling well.

This brings us to the end of the *Align Constraints* topic of Management
3.0 and back to the earlier part of the book, where we discussed that management is all about people, and that it needs to acknowledge their basic
intrinsic desires. Chapter 10, "The Craft of Rulemaking," and Chapter
11, "How to Grow Competence," also deal with an intrinsic desire: The
need for people to feel competent at what they do, and the need for managers to know they are working with competent people.

---

11 Gat, Israel. "A Social Contract for Agile" http://www.mgt30.com/contract-agile/
The Agile Executive. February 3, 2009. Used with permission. [Gat 2009]
12 http://www.mgt30.com/contract/

Summary

A self-organizing team must have a shared goal, which can be assigned by their manager. The way this goal is best defined (for example: simple, measurable, attainable, and so on) depends on the context.

Most important is that the goal is not connected to rewards (and certainly not financial ones) and that it is communicated well so that it guides team members in their work.

It is wise to also allow a team to define its own autonomous goal. If it does, it is important to try and compromise on your assigned goal and its autonomous goal.

Self-organizing teams benefit from having a clear boundary list. This list defines what teams can do by themselves and at what level they are authorized to perform those activities.

Self-organizing teams don't automatically protect either their own team members or their environment against the team. That's why managers have a responsibility to watch over individuals and any shared resources.

Reflection and Action

Let's see if you can apply some ideas from this chapter to your organization:

- Define an extrinsic goal for your team that transcends the goals of all individuals, including your own.

- Make sure everyone understands the goal. Check regularly with team members to see if they use the goal in their everyday decision making.

- Ask your team what its autonomous goal is. If the team doesn't have one, don't tell it to define one. Just let the team wonder about your question.

- Compare your extrinsic goal with the autonomous goal of the team. Can the two goals lead to conflicts? Discuss with the team how any conflicts will be resolved.

- Create a boundary list of authority. Make it clear not only who can make which decisions, but also which authority level is applied in which case.

- Make it your own goal to understand how people on your team really feel—about their own position and about each other.

- Think about the shared resources in your organization. Which ones are there? Are they all properly managed? What can you do to prevent that they are exploited by multiple teams?

- Discuss how to constrain the quality levels that the products of your self-organizing team should adhere to. What is needed to make that work?

- Consider a social contract with your team. There are things you expect from the team. But what can it expect from you? Are you prepared to put that in writing?

Chapter **10**

The Craft of Rulemaking

Criticism comes easier than craftsmanship.

> —Zeuxis, painter (5th century BC)

People often attempt to prevent future problems by introducing rules in an organization in the form of *"When situation X occurs, people must do Y."* I readily admit that I have been guilty of such attempts; although I am now convinced that rulemaking by managers is not the best approach to organizational stability.

In previous chapters, we have seen that a business can best organize itself and move to the edge of chaos when rule-discovery and rulemaking are delegated to team members, whereas managers concern themselves primarily with defining direction and imposing the right constraints. But many teams cannot succeed if there is not a sufficient level of competence among team members.

This chapter represents the first half of *Develop Competence*, the fourth view in the Management 3.0 model. It takes a deeper look at the rulemaking process. We can see that it is not as straightforward as linear-thinking people would expect. And this is, of course, exactly what we, as complex-thinking people, already assumed.

Learning Systems

In his book *Hidden Order: How Adaptation Builds Complexity*, Computer Scientist and Psychologist John Holland describes the idea of **learning classifier systems (LCS)**[1]: a generic pattern for learning capabilities in complex adaptive systems [Holland 1995:42–80].

---

1 http://www.mgt30.com/lcs/.

Performance System

The first part of an LCS is what Holland calls a **performance system**. It consists of a potentially large number of **stimulus–response rules**, where the rules are meant to act upon messages received from the environment (or from other rules). The result of applying those rules is that a number of new messages are emitted, either to follow-up rules or to the external environment.

Being a software developer my mind is filled with plenty of rules for building software. The input that I receive from the environment consists of the things my colleagues are doing (or the things they are only saying they're doing), the code that I am working on, the requirements from the customer, the features and restrictions of the development environment, and so on. The many messages from the environment are evaluated, in parallel, using hundreds if not thousands of rules in my mind, both consciously and unconsciously, which results in one or more new actions, such as code to be written, changes to existing code, conversations with my colleagues, or discussions with the customer.

I know this all sounds obvious. But the key concept is that the performance system consists of many *potentially conflicting* rules, in which different rules are triggered under different circumstances, given different messages from the environment. It is as if the performance system is an ecosystem of rules, in which rules are both competing and collaborating with each other, and the "fittest" rules are the ones contributing most effectively to the whole complex adaptive system.

Credit Assignment

The second part of an LCS is called **credit assignment**. Rules that appear to lead to improved performance of the entire system are credited, which increases their strength within the performance system. Rules that were triggered and subsequently failed to deliver beneficial effects, or even appeared to hurt the total system, will see their strength reduced. The strength of each rule determines the chance of being triggered the next time, for similar input messages.

Credit assignment ensures that *experience* is built up in the system by strengthening some rules and weakening others. The rules together form an **internal model** of what the world outside looks like and how the system needs to respond to it. And when the environment changes, strong rules start failing and weak ones could succeed more often than before. This enables the performance system to adapt to new situations and to continuously correct and tune its internal model.

Rule Discovery

The last part of an LCS deals with **rule discovery**: Where do the agents in a complex system get their rules from? Holland describes how new rules can be constructed from existing rules by recombination of building blocks. This is essentially how DNA works: by recombination of existing genes and their alleles.

Holland was one of the first to create evolutionary models for rule-based decision making in complex adaptive systems, which earned him a reputation as the father of genetic algorithms. Not only did he convincingly describe how these performance systems are an interesting model for learning and developing knowledge in complex adaptive systems, but he also showed that they can be implemented easily to create evolutionary algorithms with powerful problem-solving capabilities.

Rules versus Constraints

Computer graphics expert Craig Reynolds discovered that the flocking of birds can easily be modeled on a computer [Reynolds 1987]. This type of behavior, also apparent in many other kinds of animals, emerges through the application of a few simple constraints (see Figure 10.1):

- Fly in the same direction *(alignment)*.
- Don't bump into each other *(separation)*.
- Stay with the group *(cohesion)*.

Specific implementations of these constraints are often used in the movie industry to create computer animated birds, bats, fish, and penguins.[2]

Though we usually don't speak of flocking when it concerns the human species (except for some behaviors related to Twitter), a team of humans and a flock of birds do seem to have a number of similarities. For software developers, the concept of flocking might roughly translate to the following principles:

---

2   An example of a model for flocking behavior is available via http://www.mgt30.com/boids/.

- Agree on the team's direction; don't go at it yourself *(alignment)*.

- Don't collide with team members, and prevent problems *(separation)*.

- Work together with the team; don't single yourself out *(cohesion)*.

FIGURE 10.1

Flocking of birds (can you spot the three errors?)

Flocking behavior is often presented as an example of how a system can develop complex behavior with only a few simple rules. However, I believe the term *rules* here is imprecise and maybe even misleading.

We saw that rules in complex systems form the backbone of **stimulus–response mechanisms**. An agent receives some input (possibly from other agents), processes it using a number of its internal rules, and then responds by emitting some output. The rules that the agent uses can (more or less) be described as a collection of If-Then–Else constructs.

Now, I don't know much about modeling computer-generated animals, but I'm sure that the three "rules" listed are not enough to get the job done. A lot more code is needed to get the virtual birds, bats, fish, and penguins to behave as expected. The actual rules, written in some programming language, might look like this:

1. Calculate the average *position* of the birds that I can see.

2. Calculate the average *direction* of the birds that I can see.

3. If my distance from the average position > constant A, then adjust my direction toward the average by X degrees.

4. If the distance between me and some other bird < constant B, then move away from it by Y degrees.

5. If my direction deviates more than C degrees from the average direction, then adjust my direction by Z degrees towards the average.

6. And so on....

7. Repeat until somebody quacks to say we're landing.

Such rules are a better reflection of what each agent in the group actually does. The result is that each individual bird doesn't go astray, avoids collisions, and keeps up with the group. And this is exactly what evolution required them to do. (The alternative would have been an expensive flight control center.) The actual rulemaking process, carried out by each individual, is the result of their various performance systems with credit assignment and rule discovery mechanisms.

The mistake naïve managers make is that they directly try to "program" team members by giving them rules to follow. "IF you receive this type of document, THEN you must perform that activity," and "IF the customer reports a bug, THEN you must start this-or-that procedure." But the power of complex adaptive systems is that agents can manage their own rulemaking process. Managers restrict themselves to setting constraints, and they allow the performance systems in their team members to kick in and use their innate problem-solving potential. And besides, rules from management usually don't get the job done anyway. After all, a reliable way to bring an organization to its knees is for people to do exactly what the rules tell them to do and nothing else [Stacey 2000a:59].

Apparently, organizations work well when people work *with and around* the rules, not just *following* the rules. And by this I mean the formal systems of rules imposed by management, not the informal, day-to-day, cooperative rules that people mutually agree upon while they are working together. The latter is exactly how knowledge workers prefer to do their jobs.

> Creativity requires doing things differently from the way they are usually done, or even defying the norms of society [...] In a certain sense, creative people defy the rules, even those who do not call attention to themselves

through antisocial behavior. Thus, creativity can be seen as a "failure" to conform to the norms of society.[3]

Agile software development is the natural approach to managing software projects and working with creative people. It sets constraints like "collaborate with the customer," "allow frequent changes," and "only deliver stuff that works." And then it is up to the team to select and implement rules like "IF a snow storm makes traveling difficult, THEN we do our weekly demo using Skype," or "IF there is a change request, THEN we create a new branch in source control," and "IF someone breaks the build, THEN he must wear the funny rabbit ears."

Agile software development is *not* in the first place about pair programming, TDD, or user stories. (The Agile Manifesto doesn't even mention any of these!) Sure, well-known practices are important as an invaluable source of knowledge and experience. But the more you're imposing them as fixed rules, the more you are constraining the innate rule-making capabilities of your team members.

And then they have lost the ability to be really Agile.

The Agile Blind Spot

I believe a "weakness" of the Agile Manifesto is that it doesn't (explicitly) recognize that all software projects need people being smart, disciplined, and attentive. The "people over process" paradigm is great, until you find out that your team consists of two trolls, a parrot, and a hairdresser, and a relatively bright project manager, who happens to be deaf, blind, and mute. No amount of coaching can help a team like that to magically self-organize and to deliver a successful product. I call this the Agile "blind spot." Agile (as promoted by the manifesto) is great only when the team is great (or at least good enough). To be fair, the need for great teams is probably even twice as important in non–Agile environments, but the Agile Manifesto too leaves the competence issue unresolved.

To address this problem, I usually compare Agile management with traffic management. Traffic management is the art of reducing the number of casualties in traffic, despite most drivers being either dummies, lunatics, or flatliners.

---

3   This text was published in the Encyclopedia of Creativity, Arthur Cropley, Definitions of Creativity, page 518, Copyright Academic Press 1999. Used with permission. [Cropley 1999:518].

Wikipedia claims that my home country, The Netherlands, has the lowest traffic-related death rate in the world.[4] Yet we live with 17 million people, and 136,000 km of roads, crammed together in an area smaller than West Virginia. And I know for certain that the drivers around me are not a hair smarter than elsewhere in the world. (To be honest, San Marino, the Marshall Islands and some other islands have an even better score. But it's hard to compete with a hill in Italy and some rocks in the Atlantic.)

The Dutch use no less than seven complementary approaches to achieve such a low casualty rate. The principles behind these methods could be used by Agile managers who want to lower the fatality rates among their own projects:

- **Culture**: I've been told by a good friend of mine, an expert in traffic management, that the Dutch culture is one of the most important contributors to the (relative) safety on our roads. Dutch people *care*. About their car, their money, and other's people's lives. (And in that order, I think.) *Translation*: No matter what other methods you apply to achieve competence in a social system, in the end it all depends on whether people actually care.

- **Instructors**: In the Netherlands, you can only learn to drive with the help of an instructor. Putting a "learning" sign on the roof of your own car, or getting help from your dad, is simply not allowed. For at least 20 or 30 lessons, you are instructed by someone who is driven around the city all day by pupils, and who asks big piles of cash for this privilege. (I would demand a similar amount of money if I had to watch the same scenery 40 times a week.) *Translation*: Teach people how to do their jobs properly. Again, and again, and again.

- **Driver's license**: You must take a test and prove that you are capable of participating in (Dutch) traffic, or else you won't be allowed to go out on the roads by yourself. *Translation*: Require that people are properly tested before allowing them to participate in (challenging) projects.

- **Traffic signs**: I think we are the country with the most traffic signs in the world. There's not a square kilometer left that doesn't have some neatly positioned signs, road markings, traffic

4   http://www.mgt30.com/traffic/.

lights, cameras, or other regulatory stuff on it. (And when it's raining, even our cows are aligned in the same direction.) *Translation*: Decrease the chance of problems in your teams by using smart and proactive tools, checklists, alerts, notifications, and other regulatory stuff.

- **Traffic police**: Yes, we all hate them. Me, too. I paid many hundreds of Euros for speeding tickets last year. (I prefer calling it the "speed tax.") *Translation*: Have a process manager walking around whose job it is to take samples of the results in your projects and check whether quality output is produced. And if not, well...you decide.

- **Car horn**: This is a favorite part of my car. Letting other people know that they are endangering either you or someone else is crucial in keeping the number of casualties down to a minimum. *Translation*: Make sure your team members have the guts to tell each other how to improve their daily work. Let them honk their horns, or give each other a finger. Figuratively speaking, of course.

- **Government**: When everything else fails, the government will step in. They investigate what went wrong; they make new rules or constraints; and they decide who's right and who's wrong. *Translation*: Management will need to clean up the mess.

Smart, disciplined, and attentive people don't need a driver's license, or traffic signs. They don't need to be taken off the road by the police, and others don't need to scold them about their dangerous behavior. They simply do their jobs well. And that's what most Agile development methods assume. It is their blind spot. But the world isn't perfect, and neither are most drivers, sorry, employees. Therefore management has to figure out how to address the blind spot and how to drive safely.

What's Important: Craftsmanship

You may have noticed that I love talking about driving. It's a male thing, I suppose. It's somewhere in my Y chromosome. I embrace every opportunity I can find to hop in my car and start driving. And (like every male on the planet) I think I'm a good driver, unlike the other drivers around me, who are all numskulls.

You see, I *always* watch the other cars around me on the road. When changing lanes, I check all sides and mirrors. My distance to the cars in front of me is enough to allow for the occasional extreme speed reduction. I match my speed with weather conditions. I play music in my car (loudly) but I don't wear headphones. I don't use my mobile phone while driving. And, as far as I can tell, I am *the only person in the world* who is able to *not* cross the lines that mark my lane while taking a curve to the left or the right.

I have adopted this behavior myself. Though I might have copied some ideas from other people, it was my choice to learn these rules and use them.

In software development, it is the same. We learn practices from colleagues, books, seminars, webcasts, or other sources. But it is our personal choice to seek them out and to apply them. It is not the number of official rules in an organization that makes the difference. What really counts are the rules that people are willing to learn and use.

In "Six years later: What the Agile Manifesto left out," Brian Marick, one of the original signatories of the Agile Manifesto, wrote that **skill** and **discipline** were, regrettably, never explicitly mentioned [Marick 2007]. (Though it has to be said that the manifesto mentions "continuous attention to technical excellence" on the second page, among the twelve principles.)

Consequently, the lack of explicitly *mentioning* skill and discipline introduced the problem of many people incorrectly *interpreting* Agile as being "undisciplined," which is untrue, or *forgetting* about having to work on the skilled and disciplined qualities of software teams. Scott Ambler wrote about this in his article "The Discipline of Agile" [Ambler 2007]. The truth is that discipline is *essential* to software development (and many other professions as well). Many professional software developers came to a similar conclusion, and so we now have a *Manifesto for Software Craftsmanship*, which explicitly mentions "well-crafted software" and a "community of professionals."

Unfortunately, although many people *think* they are good drivers, not many people actively *learn* to be good drivers. In one of my presentations I put it like this:

> Agilists *assume* craftsmanship.

> Few people *pursue* craftsmanship.

When we go to a doctor, we *expect* the doctor to be skilled. When I step in someone else's car, I *expect* the driver to be disciplined. (Except when I'm in a taxi in Romania.) And when someone hires a software developer, she *expects* him to know his craft. (And she should *verify* this, too!)

Craftsmanship is something Agile doesn't introduce by itself. And just thinking and talking about it doesn't give you successful projects. Managers who want better results must acknowledge that they have to actively change the attitudes and behavior of their people. They must stimulate craftsmanship and discipline. Or else….accidents *will* happen.

Positive Feedback Loops

Talking about fatal accidents…. While writing this chapter I heard a news item on the radio about three employees of a retirement home who had been suspended because they accidentally injected one of its residents with a wrong medicine, after which the unfortunate person died. Was this a case of lack of discipline? A lack of skill?

From other news items, I have learned that jobs in Dutch retirement homes are hard and stressful due to a severe lack of resources. Lethal errors in the treatment of elderly people seem to be a problem of the system, not a problem of the employees. Suspending three employees will probably mean *more* work for the remaining colleagues—and an increased risk of suffering from more errors.

Feedback is the term scientists use for the influence a system exerts on itself. **Positive feedback** means that the system is *reinforcing* the change in one of its variables, resulting in an increased change of that variable in the same direction. The variable is influencing the whole, and the whole is influencing the variable, and thus the effect increases itself. In layman's terms, we're talking about a **vicious cycle** (see Figure 10.2).

FIGURE 10.2

Reinforcing feedback: An increase results in further increase, and vice versa.

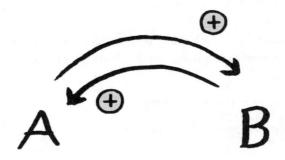

The sound of a loudspeaker, when picked up and fed back by a microphone, rapidly increases to unbearable shriek [Gleick 1988:61]. High-tech companies have scrambled to locate in the Silicon Valley area, simply because a lot of older high-tech companies were already there [Waldrop 1992:17]. A development team sticks to the programming environment that it knows, only because it allows the team to produce code fast, leading to even more experience with the same programming environment [Weinberg 1992:11]. Employee morale drops when the best people leave an organization, leading to higher pressure on the ones left behind, which further breaks down their morale [Yourdon 2004:154]. But reinforcing feedback cycles are not all that bad. For example, quality in a product pays back for itself when it leads to cost reduction and improved productivity, which in turn enables a further increase of quality [DeMarco, Lister 1999:22].

The "positive" part of positive feedback is just a mathematical qualifier. The effects can be valued as either positive or negative by the people involved. Vicious cycles can be virtuous, too. In fact, reinforcing feedback loops are the backbone of self-organization [Waldrop 1992:34].

Reinforcing feedback loops are the cause for both instability and power, for **lock-in effects** and **snowball effects**. They are the mechanism that support what economists call **increasing returns**, or "them that has, get more" or "success breeds success." Kevin Kelly called the positive feedback loop the "third law of God" [Kelly 1994:469]. It has enabled both life and misery.

Knowing how to recognize positive feedback loops is important because it enables you to understand why an organization can get stuck in a certain kind of behavior and to do something about it. Recognizing (and influencing) feedback loops is one of the core ideas of systems thinking (see Chapter 3, "Complex Systems Theory"). But recognizing *negative* feedback loops can be just as important, because that enables you to understand why changing a system can sometimes be so difficult.

Negative Feedback Loops

Negative feedback works the other way around. Negative feedback is the *opposing* effect a system has on one of its internal variables. As soon as the variable starts changing in one direction, the system counteracts, slowing down the change (see Figure 10.3).

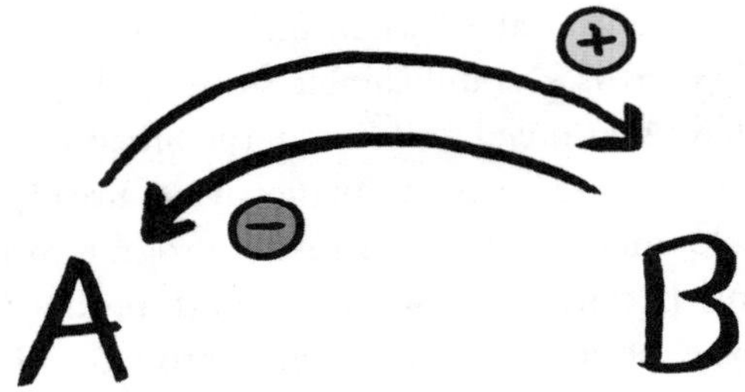

FIGURE 10.3

Opposing feedback: An increase results in a decrease, and vice versa.

An *increased* level of CO2 in the blood results in stimulation of lung movements and increased respiratory rate, which *decreases* the level of CO2 [Solé 2000:90]. When a beehive gets too cold, the bees huddle together, buzz their wings, and heat it back up [Miller, Page 2007:15]. **The Law of Diminishing Returns**[5] says that increased availability of a product will lower its price on the market, and a moment comes when it's not worth the effort of further increasing production [Waldrop 1992:34]. When an organization grows, the amount of overhead increases with the square of its size, whereas the horsepower of the organization grows only linearly, diminishing the returns on its production [Coplien, Harrison 2005:104]. When a member of a team violates the group's norms, team members may consult and agree on corrective action [Arrow 2000:202]. And in a runaway project technical reviews can introduce opposing feedback loops that help getting things back under control [Weinberg 1992:95].

The purpose of negative feedback loops is often to bring **stability** to a system, also called **homeostasis**, to ensure that the effects of positive feedback loops, although often valuable, don't get out of hand. In fact, complexity scientist Peter Corning argues that "feedback" is only feedback when there is such a purpose behind it:

> The classic example is the household thermostat, which senses room temperatures and turns the furnace on or off accordingly. To use the system scientist William T. Power's classic formulation, feedback "signals" are compared to the internal "reference signals," and it is the relationship between the two signals that determines what the behavior of the system will be. Any usage of the term "feedback" that departs from this goal-oriented, information-driven model is at best metaphorical and at worst misleading.[6]

---

5   http://www.mgt30.com/returns/.

6   Corning, Peter. *Nature's Magic.* Cambridge: Cambridge University Press, 2003. [Corning 2003:180].

One thing scientists have noted about these *intentional* negative feedback loops is that short cycles are often better than long ones. Restoring the oxygen level in the blood must be done as soon as possible. Measuring and tuning the temperature in your house has to be done by the minute, not by the hour. And evaluating and correcting a project once per day is better than once per month.

Interestingly enough, opposing feedback itself is also subject to a negative feedback loop. Shorter cycles are usually also costlier, meaning that there is a point at which it makes no sense anymore to further reduce the length of the feedback cycle. It may be great to reduce the Scrum sprint length from four weeks to one. But reducing it to one day might not be worth the trouble. At some point performance improvement levels off and does not outweigh the added costs of increased overhead and measurements—unless you decouple cycles from overhead, like Kanban does. But that is a story for another day. (Because this negative feedback cycle is not intentional, Peter Corning would claim this to be negative feedback only in a metaphorical sense.)

Social systems are complex because there are numerous interactions among the participants in the system, many of them giving rise to both reinforcing and opposing feedback loops, sometimes intentional, sometimes not. Positive feedback loops are destabilizing, accelerating systems *away* from equilibrium, away from death, and toward life. Negative feedback loops are stabilizing, bringing systems toward equilibrium, keeping them away from chaos. A multitude of positive and negative feedback loops is often the reason why changing a single variable in a system can have so many consequences, many of them contradictory, making it impossible to predict what will happen in the system. In these cases you're left with just one option: Give it a try to see what happens.

ISN'T POSITIVE FEEDBACK BETTER THAN NEGATIVE FEEDBACK?

Good and bad feedback is not the kind of feedback that I refer to in these paragraphs. We're now discussing reinforcing (positive) feedback and opposing (negative) feedback in a mathematical sense.

Do not confuse this with "positive" and "negative" feedback in the sense of saying positive things to a person to support some kind of behavior, or negative things to criticize something. That is a completely different topic, not addressed here.

Discipline * Skill = Competence

I'm sure you recognize this problem. You are in a hurry, and you skip the routine of checking whether you have all your belongings with you when you leave your house. Half an hour later you're driving back to the house, snarling and cursing because you forgot your wallet, and now you're even more in a hurry than you were before.

I believe **discipline** is one of the two crucial dimensions of competence. How would you rate a pilot who regularly forgets to check the engines? Or a surgeon who sometimes doesn't take the time to wash his hands? Or an actor on stage who sometimes doesn't know his lines? As a consumer, or a patient, would you accept the excuse "Sorry, I was in a hurry?"

The importance of discipline in any craft is evident. Gerald Weinberg wrote about the Boomerang Effect of people not following procedures: Some part of quality assurance is skipped, which leads to an increased number of problems in a shipped product, which leads to an increased number of problems reported by customers, which leads to more emergency interruptions, which leads to bigger time pressure on the development team, which leads to more procedures being skipped [Weinberg 1992:278-282]. We all know from personal experience that, ultimately, skipping discipline makes you go slower, not faster. It is a vicious cycle indeed.

In the same vein, Mary and Tom Poppendieck described that a software development team cannot go fast without building quality into their product [Poppendieck 2007:190]. Skipping checklists and procedures only *seems* to make you go faster, at first. But soon, the lack of quality (or **technical debt**[7]) in your product will wear you down.

Weinberg described six maturity levels for following processes [Weinberg 1992:23]:

- **Oblivious**: "We don't even know that we're performing a process."
- **Variable**: "We do whatever we feel like at the moment."
- **Routine**: "We follow our routines (except when we panic)."
- **Steering**: "We choose among our routines by the results they produce."
- **Anticipating**: "We establish routines based on our past experience with them."

---

7 http://www.mgt30.com/debt/.

- **Congruent**: "Everyone is involved in improving everything all the time."[8]

Weinberg used these six levels to classify organizations, but I prefer to classify only individual people for specific activities. Whatever happens to an organization is an emergent result of the interaction between people, many of them having different levels of discipline for different activities. I am sometimes complimented for my discipline at book writing, which may be at level 5 (anticipating) or even level 6 (congruent). But at the same time, if you hear someone cursing and yelling, it could be me going back for my wallet, an activity that is apparently still at level 1 (oblivious). (Or it could be my spouse. Amazingly, while I was rewriting this paragraph, he returned to retrieve his wallet, after having left the house ten minutes earlier....)

A similar arrangement of six levels was introduced by Ross Pettit, who named his levels Regressive, Neutral, Collaborative, Operating, Adaptive, and Innovating.[9] The meaning of Pettit's six levels is somewhat different, but, like Weinberg, he seems to be indicating levels of maturity in selecting and applying processes.

The second crucial part of competence is **skill**. A skilled software developer can still be undisciplined, whereas a disciplined developer is not necessarily skilled. Therefore it seems to me that a person's skill level is another dimension in which we can rank maturity.

Two similar approaches indicate the skill level of craftsmen and craftswomen. The **guild system**, which stems from medieval Europe, lists three ranks for people practicing a particular craft: *apprentice, journeyman,* and *master*.[10] This system is practically the same as the Japanese **Shuhari** variant which describes the three stages of practicing a martial art: *Shu, Ha,* and *Ri*.[11] In both systems, people ranked at the first level are learning fundamental techniques; people ranked at the second level focus on exceptions and reflections; whereas no hard thinking is needed, and everything just comes naturally, for the people at the third level.

Another well-known model is the **Dreyfus model** of skill acquisition,[12] which consists of not three but five stages of increasing skill:

---

8   Weinberg, Gerald. Quality Software Management. New York: Dorset House Pub, 1992. [Weinberg 1992:23].

9   From the presentation "Agile Made Us Better, But we Signed Up for Great," available at http://www.mgt30.com/better/. [Pettit 2008].

10 http://www.mgt30.com/master/.

11 http://www.mgt30.com/shuhari/.

12 http://www.mgt30.com/dreyfus/.

novice, advanced beginner, competent, proficient, and *expert.* But whether skill can be measured in three, four, five, or seventeen stages is, in my opinion, not the most interesting discussion. More relevant is that skill differs from discipline, and therefore they must be developed separately.

When we draw the two dimensions of discipline and skill, we arrive at the Discipline-Skill Grid (see Figure 10.4). It nicely depicts that maturity can be measured in two directions. One can lose his skills through old age, physical injury, or technological advancements, and one can lose her discipline through demotivation or distractions. Competence requires both, and therefore managers need to take care of both dimensions.

FIGURE 10.4

Discipline-Skill Grid.

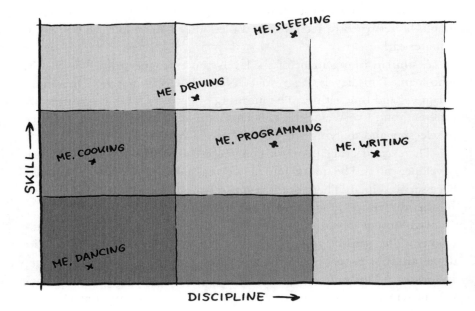

Diversity of Rules

The behavior of a team is guided by rules. Rules on how to document requirements, how to estimate work, how to commit source code, how to write test code, how to deploy solutions, and so on. And each team member maintains his own set of rules. One developer commits test code to a branch in source control before writing production code, whereas another prefers to shelve all her code, committing it to the trunk only after she knows that everything runs flawlessly. One designer makes interaction designs with Visio wireframes, whereas another claims that nothing beats slate and crayon markers. One tester documents acceptance tests together with requirements in a custom collaboration tool, whereas another prefers a simple spreadsheet in Google Docs. And I am in favor of sparse source code comments, whereas other people prefer source headers with a size comparable to the United States trade deficit.

Is it bad when people follow their own rules?

Well, no. Yes. Maybe. It depends....

For a Scrum Master, it is inconvenient when each team member adopts a different way of estimating user stories. The entire team has to agree on story points versus ideal hours, or it would be impossible to calculate the team's velocity. Likewise, there must be agreement on dates and times for meetings, the length of sprints, and so on.

On the other hand, there is often no need to fully synchronize source code practices. As a team member, as long as the code on the trunk is fully tested, I could live with people's different preferences for shelving, branching, commenting, and such. And I don't care about the medium used for interaction designs. I care more about the team members being motivated. And I care about myself being motivated, which means I'm not going to pair with others when I'm not in the mood for it (which is quite often). I want to be judged for the *value* of my output, not the *manner* in which I created it. If I can produce the best-quality source code while sitting naked in a conference room wearing my boxer shorts on my head, then who is to complain? (This is just an example, of course. I tried, but it didn't work.)

Managers must be wary of senseless synchronization of rules in a team. People should be allowed to do things their own way. This freedom helps to keep them motivated. Team members can choose to copy each other's rules when the output of others turns out to be better than their own. (If the code I wrote in that conference room had been awesome, I'm sure other people would have followed my example.)

Last but not least, competing rules in a team can actually strengthen the whole. Problems with source code might go undetected when all team members handle code in the same way, using the same rules. From Chapter 4, "The Information-Innovation System," we know that diversity increases a team's flexibility and resilience. This doesn't just apply to people, but also to the practices they follow.

> **DO TEAMS NOT TYPICALLY AGREE ON THEIR RULES?**
>
> Yes, it is a natural part of self-organization that rules in a team are adopted by all team members. But there is still plenty of diversity and variation in every team. It is impossible (and unnecessary) to regulate and formalize every possible action people can take in a team.

That's one other reason to keep inventing and experimenting with *new* practices. You will not only improve yourself, but the quality of the team as well. Next time, I'm going to try coding in the board room, and I might swap the boxer shorts for swimming trunks.

Subsidiarity Principle

Allowing people to follow different practices can be a good thing, whereas at other times it is necessary for people to do things in the same way. But how do you determine which rules should be followed by which people? There is an answer to this problem in the **Subsidiarity Principle:**[13]

> Subsidiarity is an organizing principle that matters ought to be handled by the smallest, lowest or least centralized competent authority. The Oxford English Dictionary defines subsidiarity as the idea that a central authority should have a subsidiary function, performing only those tasks which cannot be performed effectively at a more immediate or local level. The concept is applicable in the fields of government, political science, cybernetics, and management.

Rules are the responsibility of individual workers, *unless* they cannot perform their tasks effectively, in which case rules need to be established at the next higher level in the hierarchy. This means that I can follow my own rules for writing unit tests, *unless* the team can prove that it is *more effective* to establish centralized rules for this at the team level. At the same time it is obvious that sprint planning meetings cannot be done effectively by me at the individual level, which automatically makes it a responsibility for the team. And then the pattern repeats itself. The team can follow

---

13 http://www.mgt30.com/subsidiarity/. Reprinted under the Creative Commons License. Please visit http://creativecommons.org/.

its own rules for sprint planning meetings, *unless* the next level (middle management) can prove that it is more effective to establish centralized rules for planning meetings at the department level.

Again and again, we arrive at the same conclusion, and I apologize for sounding repetitive. In previous chapters, it was through concepts like the Darkness Principle and the Conant-Ashby Theorem. This time it is the Subsidiarity Principle telling us the same thing: People can make rules on their own. They don't need managers for that.

It's OK for individual workers and teams to copy each other's ideas and synchronize rules without direction from a manager. But it's *also* OK for people to deviate from the norm and to experiment with new practices. And when a higher level authority steps in to say, "You are not allowed to do it that way," the best answer would be:

> Please explain why your higher-level rules are more effective than my individual rules.

When used this way, the Subsidiarity Principle enables a free flow of ideas and practices within the boundaries of effectiveness. People can follow their own rules until their manager can prove that, to achieve some goals, it is more effective to synchronize the way they work.

So, the next time you tell people which rules to follow, a reasonable answer for them is, *"Please explain how that is more effective."* They are not required to slavishly do what you've told them to. It is fair to be given a decent explanation, so that they know *how* their work fits into the bigger picture.

Risk Perception and False Security

It struck me several times that the flow of traffic at the Hofplein in Rotterdam, one of the busiest roundabouts in my city, is better when the traffic lights are turned off. Despite the anarchy that such a situation brings to the streets, people get to the other side of the roundabout faster than when the lights are operational. And this not only applies to motorists but to pedestrians and cyclists as well.

In a Dutch article, *"Traffic is safer without rules,"* traffic expert Hans Monderman explained that the flow of traffic at an intersection can *increase*, while at the same time casualty rates *decrease*, when all traffic lights and road signs are removed [Sprangers 2007]. The reason is that, in a situation without rules or guidance, people feel compelled to take responsibility and to judge for themselves how to reach the other side safely and in one piece.

The cause of this paradox can be found in **risk perception** and **false security**. Remove the green traffic light (false security) and car drivers will not blindly go full throttle on the assumption that they have priority over everybody else. Wipe away the crosswalk, and pedestrians will watch out for any dangerous vehicles (increased risk perception). This psychological phenomenon is also called **risk compensation**.[14] Monderman claimed that the number of accidents diminished, and traffic throughput increased, in all situations where this concept was introduced. The idea is called **shared space**, which entails that all participants in traffic are equal, and that they all have to watch out for each other. Nobody should assume priority over others.

I dare claim that the shared space principle also applies to software development practices. Rules on how code should be developed, how it should be tested, and how new versions are to be built and deployed, may not automatically lead to higher quality products. On the contrary, a documented test procedure that doesn't take specific project characteristics into account can lead to false security among team members. And an official requirements specification process that is deliberately ignored by team members may actually help them to increase their risk perception, seeing problems more clearly because they know they have to watch out.

In most projects, existing rules have to be treated not as laws but as *rules of thumb*. They point people in a direction that is often a smart solution to a problem, but not always. Sometimes it is necessary to abolish rules precisely to prevent people from blindly following them. In some of the most successful projects I participated in, we ignored rules and made better decisions on the spot. By going around road blocks and ignoring traffic lights, we reached the other side of our time boxes timely and safely.

I am usually a bit reserved when an unpleasant incident has occurred in a project and someone is calling out that new rules are necessary to prevent similar problems in the future. When I would do as they asked, I would be no different than the average bureaucrat planting new road signs at intersections for every potential danger that somebody has encountered earlier. Some call this approach the **Precautionary Principle**,[15] and it is an official policy in many governments, including the European Union. Basically it says that, when something *might* go wrong someday, simply

---

14 http://www.mgt30.com/risk/.
15 http://www.mgt30.com/precaution/.

make a new law to prevent it from happening, just in case. And I really don't like that approach.

Some methodologies and frameworks seem to be based on the Precautionary Principle. They suggest adding process descriptions for all kinds of potential problems. Unfortunately, I never saw them suggesting that some processes may have to be *removed* to make things run better. This is quite understandable, of course: It is unlikely that you will hear politicians and traffic controllers admit that their rulemaking efforts are often in vain, and sometimes even counterproductive.

Fortunately, software development experts seem to be smarter nowadays. They are increasingly aware that no single methodology is appropriate. Ivar Jacobson, one of the founding fathers of the Unified Process, has admitted the same in a three-part article titled *"Enough of Processes: Let's do Practices"* [Jacobson 2007]. No one should rely on rules devised by others who know nothing of the situation that you find yourself faced with in your own project. In general, you achieve the best results if you create your own rules on the spot, appropriate to the situation of the day. Three researchers who have studied Agile software methods came to the same conclusion, claiming that the best way to implement Agile processes is to do it your own way. [Wailgum 2007].

I have participated in Dutch traffic for almost 20 years, and I've never been involved in an accident with other people. That's because I constantly watch all vehicles, cyclists, and pedestrians around me, preferring my own judgment over what the traffic signals are saying. My spouse, on the other hand, failed his first driving test when he trusted a green traffic light and almost drove into a pedestrian who crossed the street while ignoring a red light. Since then he has learned to trust his own senses first, and the official rules second (if time permits).

Memetics

I am writing this right after Christmas, which is one of the most successful examples of mass delusion. It is a time of the year I always look forward to, and not only because of the food. I admit that I enjoy participating in the silly behavior of putting up a Christmas tree, lighting candles, buying presents, watching movies, and singing Christmas songs, as much as anybody else.

Ideas, concepts, beliefs, theories, ideologies, fads, and fashions are often called **memes** [Dawkins 1989]. People copy these *units of information* from each other through mimicry, interaction, correlation, teaching, and learning [Stacey 2000a:168]. Santa Claus is a meme; the Christmas tree is a meme; putting presents in stockings (or in shoes as we do here in Holland) is a meme; Rudolf the Red-Nosed Reindeer is a meme; the birth of Jesus Christ is a meme; and angels and elves are memes.

It is the same with rules, procedures, and practices for software development. They are ideas, concepts, and beliefs that people copy from each other through mimicry, interaction, and learning. Stand-up meetings are a meme; pair programming is a meme; refactoring is a meme; iterative development is a meme; and user stories are a meme. **Memetics** is the study of evolutionary models of information transfer, often in a cultural context.

We refer to a collection of interdependent memes as a **memeplex** (see Figure 10.5). Christmas is a typical memeplex. And so is Agile software development. **Universal Darwinism**[16] shows us that memes group together in a memeplex because they will copy themselves more successfully when they are "teamed up." (Genes do the same thing, in which case they are called **gene complexes**.) Christmas is a successful memeplex in that all the different memes, despite having many different origins, now reinforce each other, rendering them virtually indestructible. Rudolph the Red-Nosed Reindeer probably wouldn't have survived on his own. But the meme has, quite literally, teamed up with Santa Claus and now seems to have reached an immortal status.

Likewise, the practices in Agile software development also tend to reinforce each other. Refactoring suggests test-driven development, weekly iterations suggest working with user stories, and stand-up meetings work better with a task board. Most of the Agile practices already existed long before Agile software development, an argument often heard from Agile skeptics. But that's beside the point. The important thing is that the rise of the Agile memeplex has catalyzed a copying frenzy of the many Agile practices to a level that they might never have reached on their own [Kruchten 2007].

---

16 http://www.mgt30.com/darwinism/.

FIGURE 10.5
Christmas:
a memeplex.

The fact that an Agile memeplex is much stronger than the individual memes is something I have experienced myself. My early attempts at introducing time boxes and high-level requirements in my last job were total failures because I selected individual practices that (I thought) would be beneficial. They failed to catch on, and not because of lack of effort on my part. It was like trying to get everyone to sing to the tune of Rudolph the Red-Nosed Reindeer in the summer. It just didn't work. The memes by themselves weren't strong enough. However, at some point I realized that it was better just to try Scrum. By the book. Scrum was more specific, more extensive, and far more successful than any of my own attempts at process improvement. Scrum is a memeplex. The memes reinforce and help each other to be copied around in the minds of the people. This makes it easier to implement Scrum-by-the-book than it is to implement only time boxes and high-level requirements.

DOES THAT IMPLY A BIG TOP-DOWN REVOLUTION?

Not at all. Organizational change can be achieved both top-down and bottom up. (Though many would claim that bottom-up works best.) Both managers (top-down) and team members (bottom-up) can benefit from adopting whole memeplexes in their change efforts.

And it doesn't mean you should adopt all practices at the same time as part of one big revolution. After all, it takes some people *months* to prepare for Christmas.

We can make a few interesting observations when looking at Agile practices as memes:

- It can be easier to get people to adopt multiple ideas, concepts, or practices simultaneously than it is to have them adopt just one. (For example: teaching them to apply Extreme Programming instead of only unit testing, and then immediately start adapting XP to the context of the organization).

- In a memeplex, not all ideas, concepts, and practices need to be beneficial. Some of them can be harmful. But because they are all part of the same memeplex, the bad ideas help the good ideas to be copied around as well, which neutralizes the bad effects. (An example which might be on dangerous ground: I have seen no conclusive evidence of the value of collective code ownership, but this practice seems to reinforce the other Agile practices, so it won't hurt copying it along as well.)

- Removal of individual memes from the memeplex may weaken, or even destroy, the strength of the memeplex. (Example: Removal of collective code ownership might lead to an Agile adoption breaking down completely.)

- There may be multiple competing memeplexes that reinforce and need each other because their competition draws attention away from alternatives. (Example: Competition between XP, Scrum, and Kanban within the Agile world draws attention to the Agile brands in general.)

- Memes may have different origins and can even be exchanged and shared across multiple memeplexes. (Example: User stories started as a meme within XP, but are now firmly locked into the Scrum memeplex as well.)

I think it is useful to think of Agile brands and methodologies as memeplexes. Their sole purpose and value is to catalyze the copying of the individual Agile practices. Anyone claiming that Agile didn't bring much to the software development profession that wasn't already there, completely misses the point from an evolutionary perspective.

The moment when self-replicating molecules started teaming up in gene complexes to help each other being copied around was pivotal for evolutionary biology. Similarly, from the perspective of cultural anthropology, there wouldn't have been cultures, religions, and sciences when humans had not invented the concept of grouping ideas and copying them under one name. I therefore believe that we will look back at the rise of the Agile brands being nothing more and nothing less than named collections of good practices as a crucial step in the evolution of software development.

Broken Windows

My home desk is a mess. When I look around, I see books, magazines, invoices, glasses, a hideous little Christmas tree, speakers, external hard drives, two calculators, a scanner, a printer, Post-It notes, medicines, business cards, pencils, pens, color markers, a ruler, batteries, and there's even an acorn (from Kiev) and a chestnut (from Helsinki). The messier my desk is, the messier it gets. After all, with a loaded desktop, nobody will notice when I throw another pinecone on it.

The concept of problems getting worse over time was popularized through the **Broken Windows theory**, which says that signs of disorderly and petty criminal behavior trigger more disorderly and criminal behavior, thus causing the behavior to spread. By addressing all the little ways in which people make a mess of their environment, and cleaning things up frequently, it is believed that more serious crimes can be prevented [Wilson, Kelling 1982:2-3].

A number of scholars have criticized the Broken Windows theory. They have found issues with correlation and causality, which may have led to fallacies in several case studies, including the famous New York City crime rate example described in *The Tipping Point* [Gladwell 2002]. However, there is sufficient evidence that at least the principle behind the Broken Windows theory is sound [Keizer 2008]. The theory is also a logical extension of a more generic idea called **Lewin's Equation**:

$$B = f(P,E)$$

This equation, developed by psychologist Kurt Lewin, states that behavior is a function of the person and his or her environment. It is not a scientific equation but merely an idea derived from experience. It suggests that people tend to adapt their behavior to the environment that they live in.

Given that people also copy each other's norms and behaviors (memetics), and that therefore bad behavior is likely to lead to more bad behavior (positive feedback loop), it is easy to see how combining all these concepts automatically leads to the Broken Windows theory.

But what can we learn from this? In my opinion, two things:

- Big problems often start as small problems that weren't nipped in the bud when they were still manageable.

- If a problem is too big to handle, target another related but smaller problem.

We discuss such ideas in more detail in the next chapter, where we look at the practical side of Develop Competence. In the meantime, to prevent my entire house from becoming as disorganized and messy as my desk, I will try to keep my desk clean!

Summary

Learning systems can be modeled as complex systems consisting of competing rules. These rules may be diverse and are not necessarily synchronized across an entire team.

The development of rules in a team is a matter of competence. The Agile Manifesto never explicitly mentioned competence, which might be its blind spot, and one of the reasons for the growth of the craftsmanship movement. The development of competence takes place in two dimensions: discipline and skill.

The subsidiarity principle suggests that rules should be created at the level of the lowest competent authority, which means that rulemaking must be delegated to the (competent) team.

However, sometimes rules should not be created but discarded. Having too many rules in a team invites feelings of false security and a tendency for risk compensation.

We can refer to the study of memetics and the broken windows theory to learn how behavior propagates among groups of people and to understand how to approach the introduction of good practices in an organization.

Reflection and Action

Let's see if you can apply some ideas from this chapter to your organization:

- Draw a Discipline–Skill Grid for your team. Do you know where to place each person on the scales of discipline and skill? If not, why don't you know? If you do, is the result like you want it to be? If not, what will you do about it?

- Create a list of the important rules (or better: constraints) in your organization. Make sure people know them and that the list doesn't grow larger than 10. When an 11th rule or constraint is added, another should be removed. People aren't good at remembering dozens of things that are important, so keep the number small.

- Appoint one of your projects as a "Shared Space Project," where there are no predefined rules, which increases risk perception and decreases false security. There is only a shared space and a boundary. Allow all rules to emerge from the team, and evaluate the effects.

- Consider the approach to Agile software development in your organization. Does it have a recognizable name? Is the collection of practices easy to copy from one mind to another under one umbrella term? Or is it a fragmented approach that is hard to learn by new team members?

- Make a list of the small problems that bother you. How are you addressing them? Do you spend time only on solving big problems? Are you allowing the small ones to become big?

Chapter 11

How to Develop Competence

If a child shows himself to be incorrigible, he should be decently and quietly beheaded at the age of twelve, lest he grow to maturity, marry, and perpetuate his kind.

> —Don Marquis, American humorist, journalist and author
> (1878–1937)

In the previous chapter, you may have noticed that I discussed maturity without going into details about any **maturity models**, of which there are many dozens in the world of software development and in other business environments. That's because I find the concept of maturity models of little use, and perhaps even a bit offensive.

How would you rate the "maturity" of advertising agencies? Would you measure how well they perform tasks such as conversion of graphics files, ad placement negotiations, and search engine optimization? Or would you simply look at the repeated success of their advertisements? How would you rate the "maturity" of plumbers? Would you measure their competence at wielding pipes, pumps, gauges, and valves? Or would you just consider whether they are leaving behind happy housemen and housewives? Like some other managers and writers, I believe maturity models are too narrowly focused on processes.

AREN'T MATURITY MODELS ABOUT RESULTS?

Yes, maturity models claim to be process-agnostic, which is good. But their assumption is that the repeatability of a reliable quality level is in the implementation of processes (regardless of what they are). And what is measured is an organization's capability of learning and applying processes—not its capability of being innovative and adaptive in a complex environment.

> While well intentioned, many of these models are mechanistic and [...] invariably fail to recognize that the sole compelling reason for a firm to develop business process management practices at the enterprise level is to improve the performance of the organization in delivering value to customers and shareholders. Accordingly, many of these 'Process Maturity' models do not explicitly take into account the following two fundamental realities: 1) Organizations are both complex business and complex social systems; 2) Exemplary business process management performance demands that leaders work collaboratively and cross-functionally.[1]

Organizations are living systems. Assigning *one* rank (a maturity level) to an entire organization is just as useless, and potentially offensive, as assigning one single rating to me, Jurgen Appelo, for *everything* that I am, produce, and stand for. It flies in the face of complex thinking. (OK, I'll be fair: Some models do indeed offer different numbers, but many consultants and businesses prefer to work with just one rank.) Therefore I don't believe the way maturity models are used in business is the proper way to address and assess professionalism in organizations. Instead of classifying entire organizations, we should classify only specific activities performed by specific people.

In this chapter, I discuss my own views of maturity and professionalism, grounded in complexity. I see the "maturity" of an organization as an emergent property generated by the maturity of many activities performed by many people. And to steer clear of any associations with maturity models, I prefer the term **competence** over maturity.

> If it is performance that really counts, then we need to go beyond maturity to look at how an organization develops business process competence.[2]

To paraphrase Robert C. Martin, "Teens talk about their maturity, adults don't."

---

1   Spanyi, Andrew. "Beyond Process Maturity to Process Competence." BPTrends, June, 2004 http://www.mgt30.com/maturity/. Used with permission. [Spanyi 2004].
2   Spanyi, Andrew. "Beyond Process Maturity to Process Competence." BPTrends, June, 2004 http://www.mgt30.com/maturity/. Used with permission. [Spanyi 2004].

Seven Approaches to Competence Development

While preparing for various speaking engagements, I once contacted a person who specialized in representing professional speakers. I sent her an email describing myself, my talks at conferences in Europe and the United States, the book I was writing, and the opportunity for new business. I waited three weeks and got no reply. After sending her a reminder, I promptly received an apology and the promise that I would be called the very next day. Then I waited, and waited.... And after three days I reconsidered my idea of hiring her to handle my business emails and customer calls.

Chapter 10, "The Craft of Rulemaking," discussed seven approaches to discipline in traffic management. When we translate these to software development (and business in general) and broaden the concept of discipline to competence, we arrive at seven approaches to developing competence in an organization. The first approach is where it should all begin, and each subsequent approach can be seen as a "fall-back scenario" for the previous ones:

- **Self:** Self-discipline and self-development refer to one's own initiative to adopt particular patterns of behavior. Nobody needs to tell me that I should answer other people's calls and emails within a reasonable amount of time. It is part of the behavior I have adopted myself and that I intend to stick to.

- **Coach:** Coaching is the method of training a person with the aim to develop specific skills and behaviors. A coach might help someone in establishing proper email usage patterns, making sure that she doesn't leave other people's emails unattended.

- **Tests:** A test says (or *should* say) that some authority has verified that a person has shown the necessary skills, behaviors, and willingness to carry out certain tasks—like picking up a working phone and dialing a correct number.

- **Tools:** Signs and signals are a way to steer people's behavior by making sure that they know what they need to do. Just one hour before I wrote this paragraph, I ticked off "call back customer" from my own To-Do list. I configured the system to notify me in case I forget about such important items.

- **Peers:** Peer pressure refers to the influence exerted by peers in a group to encourage a person to change her behavior to conform to the norms of the group. The first time a person keeps me waiting, I gently and understandingly remind her when I am still waiting for a reply. The second time I make sure to communicate honest and heartfelt annoyance. The third time I bite her head off.

- **Supervisors:** Supervising is the act of making sure, on behalf of an organization's management, that people are doing their jobs properly. For example: in some organizations it might be a good idea to check occasionally whether people are handling their calls and emails properly and timely.

- **Manager:** Leading and governing are part of the manager's job. It is about setting good examples and about ruling and judging in case someone has acted against the interest of the organization—like damaging the corporate reputation by completely ignoring a potential customer.

Developing competence in an organization can be seen as a concern spanning seven approaches. Competence is, in the first place, a *personal responsibility*. When people aren't capable of developing competent behavior themselves, they may need to be *coached* into it. If that coach is unavailable, or incompetent himself, development of competence can possibly be achieved through some combination of *tests*, properly used *tools*, and the person's *peers*. Finally, when none of this works, and a *supervisor* is unavailable (or incompetent as well), then the *manager* is the one who (rightfully) gets the blame for any business lost.

WHAT IF THE MANAGER FAILS, TOO?

If competency problems fall through the entire competency stack, and the manager fails as well, then I suppose either customers or top management (or both) will suffer the consequences.

HOW DOES THIS RELATE TO SOFTWARE CRAFTSMANSHIP?

The Manifesto for Software Craftsmanship is an example of the realization that the Agile Manifesto alone is not enough to achieve competence in software development organizations.

> Craftsmanship among software developers is a lofty goal, and the craftsmanship movement primarily tries to address this with the top two approaches mentioned here (self-discipline and coaching). I therefore see craftsmanship as part of the complete picture of organizational competence.

Optimize the Whole: Multiple Levels

Chapter 4, "The Information–Innovation System," discussed the problem of measuring (and rewarding) the wrong things in a system, which leads to nasty side effects. Chapter 9, "How to Align Constraints," discussed the Tragedy of the Commons and the idea that true self-organization enables a system to optimize only for itself, which *requires* that the system and the direction it takes are somehow constrained by the environment. In systems theory, these concepts are known as the **Sub-optimization Principle**[3]:

> If each subsystem, regarded separately, is made to operate with maximum efficiency, the system as a whole will not operate with utmost efficiency.[4]

The answer to this problem, and one of the basic principles of Lean software development, is to always *optimize the whole* [Poppendieck 2007:38]. Peter Drucker once said: "*What gets measured gets managed,*" and an alternative saying is, "*What you measure is what you get (WYMIWYG).*" Logically it follows that to get an optimized whole, we have to measure the whole. What you measure (and constrain) has to cover everything, from start to finish, from top to bottom, or else the unmeasured and unconstrained parts in the system will self-organize toward suboptimal results.

Many times, I have struggled with the suboptimization principle. I have measured overrun on projects at the team level, and subsequently got complaints from some team members that *they* were not responsible for the overrun because *they* got involved only later in the project. I have measured individual skills and subsequently got complaints that *those* particular skills had nothing to do with getting *products* delivered to the

---

3   Taken from Principia Cybernetica Web: http://www.mgt30.com/suboptimize/.
4   Skyttner, L. General systems theory: Ideas and applications, River Edge, NJ: World Scientific. 2001. Used with permission. [Skyttner 2001:93].

customer. Sometimes it seemed my only reliable metric was the steady number of complaints from people about the metrics.

Agile experts strongly believe that team members have to self-organize to optimize the output of the whole team and not of the individual team members. I agree. But then many Agilists suggest measuring *only* teams, not individuals. That's where I am of a different opinion.

If this were a correct approach, then the same reasoning would apply to teams within a business unit, and business units within an organization. In every case, measurement of (only) the subsystem would lead to sub-optimization at the next higher level. Taken to its extreme there would be one and only one proper metric: "continued survival and success of the whole organization and its environment," which doesn't look like a particularly useful one to me. (Note: Even "profitability" is not a good metric at the organizational level, now that the credit crisis has proved that this metric alone also leads to suboptimization.)

Evidently, "optimize the whole" *cannot* mean that we need to move *all* metrics to higher organizational levels. After a few recursive steps, there wouldn't be a sensible metric left to use. A more logical approach is to ensure that the *combination* of our metrics leaves no gaps in our measurements and understanding of the entire system. A metric of individual performance is fine *if and only if* it is augmented with metrics at the team level. And metrics concerning individual teams are OK *if and only if* supplemented with metrics for entire business units and the organization as a whole.

We could even turn this into a fifth Agile value:

> Global metrics over local metrics.

While there is value in the item on the right, we value the item on the left more. But that doesn't mean that the item on the right is unimportant.

Optimize the Whole: Multiple Dimensions

Chapter 9 showed how the traditional **triangle of constraints** can be extended to a square so that we don't forget to constrain quality. But I find that both the triangle and the square still lack in power to convey the full dynamics of complex software projects. Reality sometimes seems more like an Escher cube of constraints: completely impossible (see Figure 11.1).

Let's try and adapt the triangle and the square to something more useful. We already made the first step in Chapter 9: separating scope into *features* and *qualities*, two sides of the same coin that often need to be managed quite differently. It emphasizes that qualities need to be considered separate from functionalities.

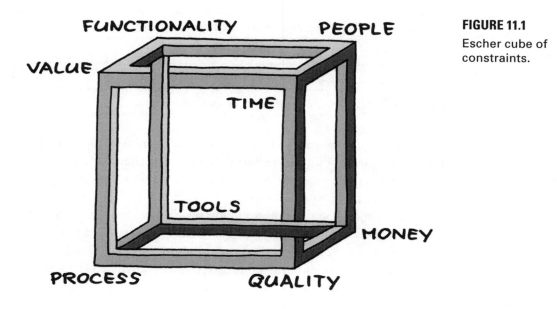

FIGURE 11.1

Escher cube of constraints.

But we can go even further in dissecting projects. What some people call "resources" is actually a combination of *people* and *tools*, which each require a very different management approach. Furthermore, Alistair Cockburn claimed that *process* is an additional dimension missing in the original triangle [Cockburn 2003]. And Jim Highsmith modified the triangle by adding *(business) value* as a new dimension (and rearranging the other constraints). [Highsmith 2009:21].

This brings us to at least seven measurable dimensions, or perspectives, in software projects (see Table 11.1). The table is not exhaustive. (In theoretical physics, M-theory is a theory in which no less than 11 dimensions are identified.[5] Three dimensions is *so* 20th century.) I am sure people can come up with a few more dimensions and some better examples of metrics than I am giving here.

_____

5 http://www.mgt30.com/m-theory/.

TABLE 11.1

Seven Project
Dimensions and
Examples of Some
Metrics

Dimension	Example of Measurement
Functionality	Story points completed (velocity)
Quality	Problems reported by testers
Tools	Costs per month
People	Impediments reported by team members
Time	Days remaining until live release
Process	Checklists completed
Value	Increase in usage in users per minute

The point of this exercise is that you must take care to measure multiple perspectives and not focus on either process or functionality alone. And as I discussed before, plenty of organizational models tend to favor process over all other project dimensions.

Measuring outcome is more important than measuring process. But measuring both is even more valuable. My actual weight is more important than measuring my daily intake of calories, heart rate, blood pressure, and the total of calories burned on my yet-to-be-purchased cross-trainer. But considering all these measurements together gives me a better idea of what's really going on in the system that I call "me."

The suboptimization principle tells us that, ideally, our metrics must cover the entire system or else we will suboptimize. A focus only on *working features delivered* (functionality) or *sprint demos accepted* (process) can lead to quality degradation, demotivation among team members, and reduced business value for the customer. The system will give you that which is measured. Therefore, try to have simple measures for all of the seven project dimensions. The system will then self-organize, and develop competency, to give you total system optimization.

Creating metrics in multiple perspectives to cover the entire system was famously presented as the **balanced scorecard**, by Robert Kaplan and David Norton, more than a decade ago [Kaplan, Norton 1996]. My own suggestion is simply for development managers to replace their original five perspectives (financial, customer, internal business, innovation, and learning) with the seven dimensions that I believe to be more useful for software development.

Tips for Performance Metrics

Performance metrics are important. At school, in sports, and in the arts, people want to know how well they are doing. They get grades for their knowledge of math, languages, and geography; rankings for their performances in football, basketball, and tennis; and ratings for their books, plays, or TV shows. If you don't know how you're doing, you cannot verify if you're doing better next time. That's why people want to know their score on a Microsoft certification exam. It's why they hook up their Nike shoes to their iPods, tracking their running achievements. And it's why I'm looking forward to your Amazon rating for this book.

One responsibility of a manager is to make sure that employees get to know and understand how well they are doing their jobs. And whether you are producing metrics for individuals or groups, there are a number of tips you may want to keep in mind when measuring their performance:

- **Distinguish skill from discipline:** In the previous chapter, we discussed two rankings for maturity: skill and discipline. You may want to evaluate people and teams separately for both. This helps skilled people (who may think that they're too good to fail) not to forget about discipline. It also helps to avoid overconfidence in disciplined people (who may think they're good just because they follow procedures). Some examples of measuring discipline: Task board is up-to-date, meetings start on time, code coverage always higher than 95%. Some examples of measuring skill: No build failures, few bugs reported, and customer demos always accepted.

- **Do not rate knowledge or experience:** I see knowledge and experience as prerequisites for skill and discipline, but I believe measuring people's knowledge and experience doesn't make much sense. Knowledge and experience are about *being*. Skill and discipline are about *delivering*. As a writer I don't get ratings for *being* a writer. I get ratings for *delivering* writings. Nobody in your organization should be earning ratings for knowledge and experience, while wasting their time playing Farmville.

- **Rate multiple activities**: Each of us has some things he is good at and some things he is not. You can accept the humiliation of a bad rating for one activity when there is another one on which you've scored well. Similarly, employees can accept criticism more easily when it is compensated with compliments in other areas. Having multiple ratings also makes it easier to be honest and fair to a person. Rate people for the quality of a software release *and* its timeliness, for customer satisfaction *and* cost effectiveness, for official standards adhered to *and* team flexibility.

- **Rate multiple performances:** One of my high school teachers had a system in which he organized at least ten test scores a year per person, and he promised not to count the lowest one because "we all have a bad day sometimes." People in general prefer to be rated multiple times for similar activities. They want a chance to do better next time. Have them rated for each project that they do and each new release that goes into production.

- **Use relative ratings where possible:** Compare the performance of a team against its previous performances over time ("you're now doing 15% better than last time"); against other teams in the organization ("you're doing 20% worse than the guys in project X"); or against external businesses ("we're doing 32% better than company B"). With relative metrics teams can strive to do better every time instead of trying to meet one target and then staying there. [Highsmith 2009:353].

- **Keep the feedback loop as short as possible:** There should be as little delay as possible between the time of an activity and feedback from the metrics. It is one of the reasons I started writing a blog before writing a book. I needed the immediate feedback from readers on my blog to know how to write better. Only one and a half years later, I felt confident enough to start writing a book, which has a much longer feedback cycle.

- **Use both leading and lagging indicators:** Leading indicators are metrics that, when they change, indicate that you *might* be on the right track in achieving your goal. (Example: Increased code coverage of unit tests *might* indicate higher quality in a product.) Lagging indicators are metrics that *verify* whether you have achieved a goal after completing the work. (Example: Reduced defects reported by customers *verifies* quality after the product's release.) In general it is advised to use both leading and lagging indicators [Cohn 2009:440].

- **Never create the ratings yourself:** The value of your opinion as a manager about the performance of a person or team is very, very, *very* small. Make sure that all ratings, whether qualitative or quantitative, are produced by the environment. Not by you. You may be the messenger sometimes, but not the assessor. Be the judge, not the prosecutor.

Talking about judges…. Yes, I plead guilty (again). Like many other naïve managers in the world, I have personally ranked and rated employees, once per year, using one single value on a 5-level scale. But I regret that now. I believe that people should be rated with *multiple ratings, multiple times, as soon as possible*. And *not by me*. Let the world know I'm sorry. It won't happen again.

So far, we have discussed the different ways of *measuring* competence in an organization. Let's now review the seven levels of *achieving* that competence.

Four Ingredients for Self-Development

I must write. Sometimes, I'm not in the mood to write. I would rather read my favorite novels.[6] But still, I write.

Why?

It is called **self-discipline**.

> *Self-discipline* refers to the training that one gives one's self to accomplish a certain task or to adopt a particular pattern of behavior, even though one would really rather be doing something else.[7]

Research shows that self-discipline is twice as important as IQ for final grades of students. It appears that to achieve competence, effort matters more than talent [Jensen 2006].

I have been wondering what enables people to keep discipline. This is what I came up with:

1. It starts with the realization that something is **important**. If you don't understand the value of something, you will never have

---

6 http://www.mgt30.com/malazan/.
7 http://www.mgt30.com/self-discipline/. Reprinted under the Creative Commons License. Please visit http://creativecommons.org/.

the discipline to start (and keep) doing it. (I know personal exercising, bookkeeping, and cooking are important, so no problems there.)

2. It requires basic **time management** skills. If you cannot fit something important into your busy weekly schedule, it will never happen. (I have trouble scheduling personal exercises. Reading and writing always seem more important to me.)

3. When understanding and time management are properly tackled, it is crucial **not to forget**. (I can easily fit bookkeeping into my schedule, but I often forget about it. And after a month it's a real pain figuring out where all my money went.)

4. Possibly the toughest one, people need to be motivated. No **motivation**, no discipline. (Fortunately, I never forget that I need to eat. But when I'm on my own, I'm just not motivated to cook for myself. I keep several carryout restaurants very profitable. And now I understand where all my money goes….)

These are the four ingredients for keeping discipline. And you can assist people with each of them:

1. Help people to understand the importance of things. Teach them that refactoring is important. That version control is important. That face-to-face communication is important. Teach people well and you can solve the first 20% of their disciplinary problems.

2. You can help by teaching people basic time management skills. Show them how to distinguish importance from urgency. Show them how to reserve time slots for regular activities and how to create schedules. If they can brush their teeth every day to get rid of germs, why shouldn't they brush their code every day to get rid of bugs? This can solve another 20% of your people's disciplinary problems.

3. You can help people by teaching them techniques so that they don't forget. Show them how to set reminders and how to set up daily routines that can turn a list of ordinary tasks into a good habit. Methods for personal organization, like David Allen's *Getting Things Done* [Allen 2003] and Jim Benson's *Personal Kanban*,[8] also assist people in getting their tasks and projects under

---

8 Jim Benson's website is available via http://www.mgt30.com/personal-kanban/.

control. That can solve yet another 20% of the self-discipline problem.

4.   Show people how to make their tasks more enjoyable. Chris Spagnuolo described that fun is a crucial part of motivation [Spagnuolo 2008]. It is also one of the themes in the best-selling book *Fish!* [Lundin 2000]. People will be better motivated when mundane tasks are made more enjoyable. That's another 20% you've earned yourself there.

OK, that was 80% when added up. What about the last 20%?

Even when people understand the importance, when they have the time, when they don't forget, and when they are motivated, they *still* might skip an activity, when they come to realize *that they're the only one doing it!*

Therefore, the last 20% is *you!* It is you who must lead by example. You must *show* self-discipline if you want people to follow with similar behavior. Never be late for a meeting, or else people will think that it's OK to be late. Don't deliver code that is neither refactored nor versioned, or other people will do the same. And never forget to answer an email message, or people will stop answering your messages (or a customer's messages).

And that's how I came to write this chapter, even though I also wanted to read my Steven Erikson books. A high-quality book chapter is *important* to me. I organize my other activities so that I have *time* to write. I have a checklist that guarantees that I *don't forget* to run the spell checker, to check notes and references, to add the copyright notice, and to create PDF versions. And by tweeting about my writing efforts, by making my own illustrations, and by formatting and publishing draft chapters in nice layouts, I *motivate* myself because it makes the whole process more fun.

Plus, hopefully, I have inspired one or two people to follow my *example.*

Managing versus Coaching versus Mentoring

In many organizations, people are used to the idea that functional managers are responsible for assisting people with their personal development. As managers, we care about our people's skills, their knowledge and experience, their training, and their discipline (or in some cases, lack thereof). For their good behavior we offer compliments, and for their bad behavior we give a scolding and maybe a shoulder to cry on.

As functional managers, it seems we are our people's personal **coaches**:

> Part of a manager's job is to coach his or her direct reports to increase their capability and effectiveness within the organization. Coaching can focus on either interpersonal skills or technical work that is relevant to the job. [...] You may coach someone who has decided to work on a performance issue, or you may coach to develop new skills and insights.[9]

But there are other options as well...

Managing people is different from coaching people. As a line manager, you might be responsible for interviewing job candidates, controlling budgets, negotiating salaries, checking daily reports, checking weekly reports, checking monthly reports, checking yearly reports, and reminding people how important it is that they give you those reports. So you can check them.

As a line manager, you must also make sure that people who need it have a personal coach. *But that doesn't have to be you!* You can delegate this responsibility and empower (senior) people to coach the (junior) colleagues to develop their skills and capabilities. In earlier centuries it was common for masters in a trade to delegate the coaching of apprentices to journeymen. The journeymen were often better at coaching than their masters [Snowden 2010a], and it is therefore sometimes advised to use coaches at a competence level close to the level of the trainee [Hunt 2008:31].

Every person in the organization has just one manager, but they have zero, one, or even multiple coaches for different areas of personal development. You don't even have to be a coach for the senior employees. You can delegate that by hiring an external consultant. While still acting as everyone's manager, you could save yourself a lot of time, while empowering people by giving them coaching responsibilities (if they are promising as coaches), all in a single stroke! And if your organization doesn't have good coaches, you should either hire them or develop them [Adkins 2010].

Coaching responsibilities of managers are a frequently recurring theme in management literature. I believe it is a fallacy that has grown from traditional hierarchical thinking, which assumes that managers have higher competency than their subordinates (often a primary reason to be moved up in the chain of command). From a complex systems perspective

---

9   Rothman, Johanna and Esther Derby. Behind Closed Doors. Raleigh: Pragmatic Bookshelf, 2005. http://pragprog.com. Used with permission. [Rothman, Derby 2005:124].

this is nonsense. Top managers cannot be superheroes. A manager is just as fallible as his subordinates. (Or even more so when the stakes are higher.) The only thing you need to be good at is figuring out which persons, inside or outside the organization, would be fine coaches to assist in the various competences your people need to develop. Mary and Tom Poppendieck call them **competency leaders**, responsible for setting standards and developing people:

> What do competency leaders actually do? First and foremost they are committed to developing excellent technology in their organization. They begin by framing good software development in terms of an enabling architecture, mistake-proofed processes, evolutionary development, and technical expertise. [...] They set standards, insist on code clarity, and make sure code reviews are focused on enhancing learning. [...] Probably the most important role of a competency leader is that of a teacher who guides the purposeful practice necessary to develop expertise. [...] Competency leaders are often line managers, but line managers are not always competency leaders.[10]

One last word of advice is appropriate here for people seeking **mentors**. A mentor is not a coach, though the words are often mixed up as if they are synonyms. A mentor deals with an employee's personal life or career, has no specific agenda, and has focus only on the individual. A coach deals with a person's tasks and responsibilities, has a specific agenda or development approach, and has a focus on a person's performance [Starcevich 2009]. As a manager you may *assign* the coach, but you have nothing to do with someone's mentor. Mentors are like lovers and mistresses. Whether someone has one is very interesting but nevertheless none of your business.

Consider Certification

Like many Agile software development evangelists, I am skeptical toward people taking pride in their certificates. In my experience, a certificate proves little about a person's capabilities, other than that she was *at some*

---

10 Poppendieck, *Leading Lean Software Development: Results Are Not The Point*, © 2009 Poppendieck LLC. Reproduced by permission of Pearson Education, Inc. [Poppendieck 2009:96–97].

point in the past in some measurable way *aware* of some information. That's it. Even "skill-based" certifications, which supposedly test for a person's skills instead of their knowledge, prove little more than the ability of a person to perform certain activities in a sandbox. They certainly don't test the skill in successfully completing a real project.

It *seems* that certificates have little effect on a person's competence. My friend Rudie, the expert in traffic management, believes that the Dutch driver's license has been the *least* important contributor to the Dutch top position as one of the safest countries in the world to drive around in your car. The main contributor to Dutch (relative) road safety, he said to me, has been one of culture, not certification.

In software development and project management, we have a similar issue.

> The Project Management Institute's PMP (Project Management Professional) certification seems to have quite rigorous requirements—they require their PMPs to take ongoing education classes, have a certain amount of experience, and so on. And I'm sorry to say that, although I've known good PMPs, it's also true that the worst project managers I've met were PMPs who should never have been put in charge of a project. They were also the ones most proud of their certification, and most unaware of their deficiencies. I don't know what the PMP means, but it does not mean "basic minimum of competence."[11]

This critique could apply to any certification, but I believe it could easily lead to the fallacy of Hasty Generalization.[12] You see, despite there being many certified people with terrible performances, this doesn't mean that certification has no effect on organizations. It could very well be (as I believe is the case) that certification is part of a bigger and complex approach to address the issue of competency. True, certification in itself may have little effect. And certificates may falsely lead people to believe that they have a formal degree of competence. A certificate by itself is useless. *But* it can have a positive effect when combined with other measures. Certificates (and the classes and self-teaching required to earn them) lay a foundation of awareness for what's out there and what's important.

---

11 Shore, James. "Why I Don't Provide Agile Certification." The Art of Agile, March 31, 2009. http://www.mgt30.com/certification/. Reprinted by permission of James Shore. [Shore 2009].
12 http://www.mgt30.com/hasty/.

Kevin Kelly wrote that knowledge is lumpy and uneven, with small areas of expertise separated by deserts of ignorance [Kelly 1994:454]. Certificates are a way to make those deserts in a person's mind fertile. When combined with a personal coach, social pressure, proper tools, some supervision, and capable management, a certificate could pay for itself a hundred times.

The Dutch know that a driver's license alone is not enough to minimize casualties in traffic. But when discipline, road marks, car horns, traffic police, and law making are in place, the effort of obtaining a driver's license could be the catalyst that makes all the other measures work a lot better.

Harness Social Pressure

When people mention **peer pressure** (or **social pressure**) they often refer to teens being involved in drugs, alcohol, gambling, smoking, or orgies. Parents usually assume peer pressure to be "negative," which correlates strongly to activities being fun and *pleasurable*. I wouldn't know from personal experience, because I was never really part of a social group as a teen, and therefore (regretfully) nobody tempted me.

Parents have given peer pressure a bad name, which has resulted in articles with titles like *"Dealing with Peer Pressure*[13]*,"* and *"Beating Peer Pressure*[14]*."* But not all peer pressure is about tempting teens with pleasure. It can also refer to social groups pushing themselves to work harder (which, for some reason, parents refer to as "positive" pressure). Examples are studying together for higher grades, training to be better at sports, achieving higher code coverage, and many other activities that deal with *performance* rather than pleasure.

Whether "positive" or "negative," performance-based or pleasure-based, from a systemic point of view, social pressure is an example of a positive feedback loop. The more members of a social group exhibit some kind of behavior, the more the remaining members will feel pressured into adopting that same behavior. And before you know it, the whole group is doing exactly the same thing. Whether it's TDD or LSD, suddenly they're all in it together.

Peer pressure can be valuable in software development. But there are a few things you must know to make it work properly:

---

13 Example article available at: http://www.mgt30.com/pressure1/.
14 Example article available at: http://www.mgt30.com/pressure2/.

1. Social pressure in a group works only when people want to belong to that group. This means that, as a manager, you must enable team building (or team growing). *Don't* create one big anonymous pool of software developers, but organize people in teams; *fight* people who try to break up those teams; *resist* those who want to force people to relocate to another team; *allow* team members to switch to other teams if they want; and *support* any initiatives that the teams have in adopting a distinct identity. Only when people *feel* that they are part of a unique team are they willing to change their behavior and conform to team rules.

2. Give social pressure a direction by *making the group responsible* for achieving a shared **goal**. Sports teams win or lose together. And so do development teams. Team responsibilities *are shared responsibilities*.

3. Take a step back. Let self-organization do its work, and wait for social pressure to change people's behavior. There's a good chance that the team will experience a transition after which everybody is performing the same activities and using the same procedures.

Of course, that's the theory. *Reality* sometimes requires some additional pushing and pulling, but this is the basic pattern to make peer pressure work: *Make teams, set goals, and step back.*

Don't forget that someone who doesn't feel part of a group cannot be influenced by peer pressure. My own teen years were devoid of group thinking, and it shows. I don't drink, I don't smoke, I don't do drugs, and I don't gamble. And I suspect that I missed out on some orgies.

WHAT IF PEOPLE DON'T LEARN?

If people don't address their own competence through self-development, coaching, certification, and social pressure, there are three things you should do:

Talk to them about it.

Talk to them about it one last time.

Get rid of them.

Use Adaptable Tools

There's a type of resource often neglected when we talk about self-organizing teams, and getting things done.

I am referring to **tools**.

We use *tools* to increase our productivity, quality, and efficiency. But for highly productive self-organizing teams, tools have to be more than that. The best tools are a bit like fellow team members pointing out your errors, notifying you of potential problems, and coaching you into delivering work of higher quality. They differ from your human teammates only because, with the exception of the task board, they are not required to attend the 15-minute daily stand-up meeting.

Tools can play an important role in increasing discipline in an organization. Practitioners of Lean software development talk about configuring tools in such a way that they make processes **mistake-proof** (also called "poka yoke"), meaning they make it hard for people to deliver faulty products [Poppendieck 2007:196]. Mistake-proofing can be seen as the technical variant of the human coach, who guides you in achieving higher levels of discipline.

In my last job, I was responsible for creating an internal application that alerted project managers on overrun levels; actively acquired project ratings from team members; required that all time registration data was verified by two stakeholders; notified people of any hours not adding up properly in a week; and proactively checked whether lists of teams and active projects were still up-to-date. Yes, some people found the application annoying. But even more colleagues complained when the proactive alert system was out of order.

People and processes are at the center of your business, and tools are no exception to that. This means that, just like people and processes, tools must be carefully selected and *adapted* to properly match your business needs. Never change your business to match your tools. As, Joel Spolsky once wrote:

> If it's a core business function—do it yourself, no matter what.[15]

I would almost suggest that we can extend this principle to tools:

> If the tool is a core business function—make it yourself, no matter what.

---

15 Spolsky, Joel. "In Defense of Not-Invented-Here Syndrome." Joel on Software, 14 Oct. 2001. http://www.mgt30.com/nihs/. [Spolsky 2001].

Don't get me wrong. I would never suggest that everybody should build their own Visual Studio or Eclipse. But you should select tools that have the same potential for adaptability as Visual Studio and Eclipse have. Don't select tools that are only *customizable*. Most often "customizable" means that you can change some standard list items, rearrange the menus, and select your favorite colors. But that is *not* what I mean with adaptability. Likewise, don't think that you're safe with tools that call themselves *Agile* tools. The term "Agile" usually reflects their marketing, not their architecture. I've seen "Agile" tools that were less agile than Kim Jong-il stuck in a glacier.

To have your tools work *with* you, and not *against* you, they must change along with your business and your people. They help you in making your processes mistake-proof, or *poka yoke*. They check for inconsistencies, block incorrect data, send alerts, proactively verify crucial information, and so on. If you don't make your tools yourself, then at least make sure that you can access your tool's database and its API, and that it can be scripted, extended with plug-ins, and augmented with your own notifications and reports. You want your tools not just customizable, but adaptable. (And your tools should delight people in using them because this stimulates effective learning.)

Consider a Supervisor

I once read that "managing is harder than programming, because making people do what you want is far more difficult than making computers do what you want." (Don't flame me if you don't agree. I'm quoting from an unknown source here.)

This quote kept running through my mind when I recently encountered a number of, well…. let's call them disciplinary challenges, like…

- *Not being at a meeting, without notice, despite having accepted the request*
- *Not keeping systems or task boards up-to-date with the latest task/story statuses*
- *Not actively checking if there's overrun on a budget*
- *Not responding to a show-stopper problem within promised response time*
- *Not storing project documents in the shared repository*

Is this a case of hanging out the dirty laundry? Not really. We're all people, employees, and managers alike. We're not computers, we all make mistakes. If you don't have some similar problems in your organization, I assume you work with robots, not with human beings.

Still, they are problems nonetheless. If my computer was this unreliable, I would throw it out the window. (Actually I might carry it all the way up to the 7th floor of an office building and *then* throw it out the window.) But we don't do that with employees anymore these days. Managers have discovered how to be humans themselves. They can understand the reasons for people's nondisciplined behavior, with excuses such as *I-Didn't-Know-This-Was-A-Rule, Sorry-I-Forgot, There-Was-Too-Much-On-My-Mind, I-Was-Kept-Busy-With-Some-Major-Problem, I-Was-Sick, My-Dog-Was-Sick, My-Dog-Ate-My-Agenda, My-Dog-Ran-Away*, and of course *My-Dog-Died*.

So, we understand being human. But what to do about the problems?

One solution that people often come up with is that some **supervisor** should be made responsible to *inspect* things. This seems to be Step One on The Road to Bureaucracy, and it is a direction that *Agile* and *Lean* people fervently argue against.

For example, Mary and Tom Poppendieck argue that inspection to find defects is waste, and they call for **zero-inspection**. They claim that resources should be spent on *preventing* problems instead of *fixing* them because it's cheaper. [Poppendieck 2007:7].

On the other hand: Tom and Kai Gilb, famous for their work on Software Inspection [Gilb 1993], teach people how to inspect documents to find and measure defects.[16] They even have certificates for inspection, like Inspection Leaders and Inspection Process Owners!

What's going on here? Can these different viewpoints be aligned? *Can I earn myself a certificate for doing zero inspections?* Or are we witnessing a clash between the two most celebrated family duos in software development?

My guess is that their viewpoints are simply two sides of one and the same coin. Yes, preventing problems is cheaper than fixing problems but only 98% of the times. It has been noted by others that zero defects is unattainable because preventing those last few problems is far too expensive.

---

16 Tom and Kai Gilb's resources on inspections are available at:
http://www.mgt30.com/inspection/.

The "Zero Defects" sloganeering is counterproductive, unhelpful, statistically impossible, and completely cost prohibitive. Statistically, zero defects means a defect level of infinity sigma, which is not possible. What most people mean, is an attitude toward process improvement, but the sloganeering gets in the way. The "Zero Defects" movement has an implicit assumption that all defects are equal. This is not true. In fact, for most firms and products, defects must be identified and prioritized, and attacked and treated from most important to least important. For the defects at the bottom of that prioritized list, it might even make sense to move on and not eliminate or reduce those.[17]

It seems that we can allow *some* problems to flow to the next phase in the process, where detecting and fixing them (or *not* fixing them) can be cheaper.

One typical form of inspection is the **assessment**. There are various Agile assessment tools available for organizations to check how well their Agile teams are performing [Cohn 2009:430–438]. By their very nature assessments are inspections because they inspect development teams *after* adopting Agile practices. There is no way to mistake-proof the adoption of Agile practices, which is unfortunate for software teams but good news for the growing industry of consultants, including both the Gilbs and the Poppendiecks.

Competence is achieved through self-discipline, coaching, certification, peer pressure, tools, and supervising. In that order. It is almost always cheaper to solve problems earlier in this chain. Supervising and inspecting is the final gate where problems can be detected and prevented from ending up at the manager's desk, or worse…at the customer's desk. The less we need to inspect, the better. But zero-inspection is like full code coverage. A *lofty goal* that, in practice, is unattainable because of its exponential costs. There will always be some work left for some supervisor to inspect, certified or not. *(And if you don't agree, I could refer you to the reviewers of this book, who might be interested to know how all their hard inspection work could have been prevented with mistake-proofing.)*

---

17 Abilla, Pete, "Zero Defects Is Wrong Approach"
http://www.mgt30.com/zero-defects/. shmula April 3, 2007. Reprinted by permission of Pete Abilla. [Abilla 2007].

Organize One-on-Ones

In the previous sections, I described the levels one to six of achieving competence in an organization. The seventh is about management. That would be your job, I suppose.

In *Behind Closed Doors,* Johanna Rothman and Esther Derby described how to organize one-on-ones with your team members [Rothman, Derby 11,150]. From a systemic point of view, regular face-to-face meetings with individual employees are a perfectly rational thing to do. It stimulates information flow and faster feedback in the system.

I don't find it necessary to repeat the great advice given by Rothman and Derby here. I suggest you pick up their book. But I do like to point out that I find that some managers, including myself, experience trouble keeping up the schedule of a biweekly face-to-face meeting with every reporting employee. As with any other important activity that is difficult to sustain, it seems there's only one thing to do to: Apply the four ingredients for self-discipline:

1. Realize that one-on-ones are *important*. Of course, that's why I'm giving it a section in this chapter, and why you are reading it.

2. Tackle the *time management* problem by giving these meetings a fixed time slot in your schedule, say half an hour per person. I noticed that it helped me to schedule them for all team members in the same afternoon, every two weeks. This made it easier to shield the meetings collectively from other urgent activities.

3. I found the *not forgetting* part not to be a problem because the employees themselves were quick to stand at my desk in the rare cases when that happened.

4. *Motivate* yourself by making one-on-ones more interesting (or even fun) to do. You can organize your one-on-ones while having lunch, while pair programming, or while secretly using a messaging system during an extremely boring meeting.

Every regular task can be turned into an interesting activity if you set your mind to it. But whatever you do, don't ignore your frequent private talks with your employees because they are the heartbeat of your system.

Organize 360-Degree Meetings

The Law of Requisite Variety, described in Chapter 4, "The Information-Innovation System," explains that simple metrics and controls can never properly evaluate a complex system. And the *Darkness Principle*, described in Chapter 6, "The Basics of Self-Organization," can explain why a manager can never accurately evaluate an employee. So, how do we evaluate people?

> Deming and the quality experts question objective performance appraisal from another perspective. They argue that it is impossible to define a subset of performance measures that can encompass the full set of behaviors that an organization wants from its employees. [...] Empirical research suggests that managers are not capable of reliably evaluating performance over time.[18]

My recent employer used the December month to produce performance appraisals of our employees. Managers burdened with this task are caught between a rock and a hard place because for a manager, employee appraisals are the easiest way to fail. When upper-level management and lower-level employees are involved, and fingers are pointing both ways, middle managers find themselves right in between. Evaluating employees is about as much fun as sitting on the Israeli-Palestinian border with a sign saying, "I'm not on either side. But can we talk?"

The annual performance appraisal process stinks on all sides, for various reasons:

- People should not be rated on a form with generic terms like "punctuality," "communication," and "enthusiasm." The very nature of a generic form is degrading, and it doesn't capture the inherent diversity of people and their jobs [Bobinski 2010].

- An annual review process is far too slow to be meaningful. People cannot remember what happened in 12 months. And the steering of people in an organization should happen much more frequently [Derby 2010].

- With annual reviews both employees and top management have their own hidden agendas, which make the reviews "dishonest and fraudulent" [Culbert 2010].

---

18 Dent, Eric B. "Complexity Science: a Worldview Shift" Emergence. Vol. 1, Issue 4, 1999. Used with permission. [Dent 1999:15].

- Finally, "it smacks of an old-fashioned, paternalistic, top-down, autocratic mode of management that treats employees as possessions of the company" [Heathfield 2010c].

Fortunately, there is a way to do performance reviews right. It starts by adopting the concept of **360-degree feedback**[19] [Heathfield 2010b]. It is based on the assumption that no single viewpoint can properly reflect an employee's performance. And therefore you need multiple views, from different people, to achieve a better picture of a person's contribution to the organization [Dent 1999:16].

Unfortunately, many 360-degree evaluations are abused by managers to support the old-fashioned, paternalistic, top-down, autocratic mode of management (see Figure 11.2). And that's not what the Agile manager wants.

FIGURE 11.2
360-degree feedback.

Here's a better alternative:

Invite the whole team for a meeting in an informal setting (like lunch or dinner in a safe and casual environment), and tell them in advance that the team will evaluate each team member's performance, face-to-face.

---

19 http://www.mgt30.com/360-degree/.

You, as a manager or team leader, can volunteer to be the first one to be evaluated. This shows courage and respect. And it helps to loosen up the atmosphere so that people know what to expect (and how to behave) when it's their turn to receive feedback. Plus, very important: You thank every person who gives you honest, valuable, and constructive feedback. Because sometimes it's not easy to be honest. And you need to reward it when people are.

Have one person ask everyone else questions (about your performance) and let him take notes (possibly using the official HR forms). When your evaluation is complete, continue with the next person at the table. And maybe then it's someone else's turn to take notes.

Why should you organize a 360-degree meeting? Why is this better than the traditional way of evaluating people?

- People can discuss an issue about somebody's performance so that it's immediately clear whether the majority of the team shares that particular concern. It makes no sense documenting "concerns" that nobody else is concerned about.

- When an issue is not clear, the person who is evaluated can ask to clarify the issue so that he understands what the real problem is. He can press for more concrete examples of criticism that sounds a bit too abstract. Or he can respond and explain circumstances that put the issue in a whole new light. Sometimes the real problem can turn out to be a very different one.

- People force themselves to be fair and more understanding in a face-to-face situation. It is (too) easy to criticize someone anonymously behind her back. It is nicer and more civilized to bring something to her attention when she's present at the table. Possibly fellow team members can help to carefully paint a proper picture that isn't distorted by spite or vengeance.

- There is a good chance that the team at the table will make sure everyone is evaluated in equal measures. Nobody is perfect, and everybody can learn more about themselves. It won't be considered fair by the team if one person gets to swallow far more feedback than another. And so the team will tend to balance the amount of criticism they provide.

- You can have these 360-degree meetings a few times per year so that people don't have to dig too deep in their long-term memory. And once per year you can ask the team members to finalize the official evaluation forms and to deliver them to you so you can sign them and send them off to the HR department. But they will be true 360-degree evaluations you will be signing, not just your own.

Naturally, I would advise you to have a 360-degree meeting only when you have a team of trusting, respectful, and caring team members. If team members are not capable of giving or receiving open, honest, and constructive feedback, you might have another problem to solve first.

The 360-degree meeting I had last time with my team was one of the most fulfilling evenings I had in months. They told me things about myself that I had never realized. And I was able to better formulate some people's issues with the help of fellow team members. We were all very pleased that we could have this conversation with each other. We all shared food, pain, fun, and drinks at the same time.

Grow Standards

Every time I'm in the United States, I waste time on physical and mental conversions of standards. I convert all transactions from dollars to euros, and vice versa. I convert miles to kilometers, gallons to liters, and a.m./p.m. to 24 hours. And by now, I have at least four adapter plugs to convert from European electrical sockets to U.S. sockets because I sometimes forget to pack them, despite that they *are* listed on my traveling checklist. (You must be wondering why you're reading *my* advice about competence....)

Despite the hassle that travelers worldwide have to put up with, I don't think it is a good idea to ask the United Nations to *enforce* global standards for sockets, currencies, and measurement systems. Different parts in a complex system will always try to optimize for themselves, and therefore local systems *will* switch to global standards when it is optimal for them to do so. This is exactly what happened in Europe: Sixteen European countries voluntarily switched to a new pan-European currency because they figured that the opportunities and long-term cost savings were higher than the one-time switching costs. Some other European countries have not (yet) taken this step because their perceived costs (financial, political, and cultural) are apparently still higher than the benefits.

Standardization is usually not something that needs to be enforced. No worldwide government was necessary to make billions of people around the world use the 24-hour clock,[20] the Gregorian calendar,[21] the English language,[22] or right-hand traffic.[23] True, there are plenty of deviations from the international standards. Positive feedback loops will only lead to adoption of standards when it pays to do so.

We monitor our performance by comparing our work to standards. In the past such standards were external and set by managers as fixed levels. But self-organizing teams can manage their own internal standards of competence. They are more dynamic because people can raise them themselves as they become more competent over time [Thomas 2000:31].

In software development, competency leaders work with people to discuss their own internal standards, not management-imposed standards. Like naming conventions, coding standards, user interaction conventions, file structures, configuration management practices, tools, error log standards, and security standards [Poppendieck 2007:193]. There is no need for management to make top-down standardization happen. Bottom-up standardization *will* happen when goals and metrics make it painfully clear for employees that it is more optimal for them to change.

Work the System, Not the Rules or the People

This chapter ends with some final words for managers who want to improve competency in their organization: Remember that your job is to improve the *system*, not the rules, nor the people. When you set the right constraints, rules and people will take care of themselves.

- Allow standards for competence to emerge through positive feedback loops. For example, Agilists know that locating people in the same room, and visibly publishing the results of metrics, encourages people to copy each other's (good) behavior.

- Introduce memeplexes instead of individual ideas to accelerate the adoption of good practices. For example, most ideas in David Allen's *Getting Things Done* method existed long before he wrote his book. But what's good about his approach is the total package, and the memorable brand, which make it easier for people to start applying the practices.

---

20 http://www.mgt30.com/clock/.
21 http://www.mgt30.com/calendar/.
22 http://www.mgt30.com/english/.
23 http://www.mgt30.com/right-hand/.

- Allow people to have "barely enough" competence levels in some areas so that they can focus on the things they are good at. The pay-off for the organization is higher when people can pursue the work they love to do, instead of aiming for "above expectations" in areas that they don't care about. It makes no sense to homogenize employees. Instead, it is far more effective to exploit people's different talents and to let them compensate for each other's weaknesses. For example: a person who is not so good at verbal communication and personal interaction may be a superhero when designing architectures. The time he spends on "improve your communicative skills" will not pay off as well as the time he spends on "learn how to make our product more scalable."

- Big problems start as small problems. Minor carelessness ultimately leads to total quality disasters. Don't spend your time only on big problems because you are allowing the small ones to become big as well. For example, set constraints on code quality to prevent the broken windows effect from turning an entire project into a Somalian battleground [Hunt, Thomas 2000:5].

A professional organization has a system that pushes people to become more competent at what they do. And developing competence is what the fourth view of the Management 3.0 model is all about. I believe that a self-organizing system of competence is the only maturity level you will ever need.

Summary

Many maturity models are available to assess competence in businesses, but most of them don't consider all dimensions of software development. And neither do they address that organizations are complex social systems.

To know how a business performs, we need to measure it, which requires measurements on multiple organizational levels and in multiple dimensions: people, tools, functionality, quality, time, process, and value.

From traffic management we can learn that there are seven approaches to competence development: self-development, coaching, certification, peer pressure, adaptable tools, supervision, and management. Though some of these are more important than others, they all have a role to play in the development of discipline and skills.

The management part of competence development consists of multiple responsibilities, like having one-on-one sessions, organizing 360-degree meetings, growing bottom-up standards, and working the system, not the people.

Reflection and Action

Let's see if you can apply some ideas from this chapter to your organization:

- Review the seven dimensions of software projects (functionality, quality, tools, people, time, process, value) and for each dimension try to come up with at least one metric that would be important for your organization. Implement these metrics.

- Consider your own approach to discipline. Are you leading people by example? Will they understand what it means to be disciplined just by watching you work?

- Address the need for coaches in your organization. Do the people who need to develop their competence have a coach? If not, why not?

- Address the option to have people certified. Which people need to learn a coherent foundation of knowledge that can catalyze the other approaches to competency development?

- Consider team formation in your organization. Is there a team identity that people can relate to so that the positive aspects of social pressure can do their work?

- Discuss the tools with your team. Are the primary tools needed for software projects all adaptable enough?

- Consider the need for supervision. Is competence in teams at a high enough level to do away with supervision? Or is there value in someone sampling and checking the results of teams?

- Organize one-on-ones with people. Schedule them as a recurring item in your calendar, with a reminder, so you won't forget.

- Organize 360-degree meetings a few times per year. Allow team members themselves to document the results, but put your own signature on it.

- Review the standards in your organization. Make sure that everyone knows them and uses them. Or else simply do away with them (the standards, not the people).

Chapter **12**

Communication on Structure

The speed of communications is wondrous to behold. It is also true that speed can multiply the distribution of information that we know to be untrue.

—Edward R. Murrow, journalist (1908–1965)

The first line in the Agile Manifesto tells us about the value of *interaction between individuals*. In my last job I noticed that the level of interaction with my own team members, who all had their desks around me, was quite different from my interaction with fellow managers and management team members, who were separated from me by glass, steel, concrete, computers, and (on lucky days) pastry. It appears that the structure of an organization has a huge effect on how people communicate with each other. This means that, no matter whether you are responsible for 5 or 500 people, you have to think about the *form* of your part of the organization. How do you give it a structure? How do you allow it to disseminate information? How do you influence the way people communicate and interact with each other? How do you make sure you know when cupcakes are being passed around?

Complex systems theory has a few things to say about system structures and information flows. In this chapter we review the most important findings and discuss various balancing acts carried out in complex systems. This enables us to evaluate different ways of growing organizational structures, which is exactly what the fifth view in the Management 3.0 model tells us to do.

And now that you have consumed two-thirds of this book, it is probably safe to assume that the scientific references are not putting you off (too much). Considering that we still have plenty of terrain to cover, I now gently increase our pace through the academic trenches. As before, this chapter is mainly theoretical, whereas the next one covers the practical side. Hold on to your hats—and your muffins.

Is It a Bug or a Feature?

Allow me to share with you a story about communication that involves one of my favorite possessions: my car.

When I bought my car a few years ago, I noticed that the knob on the gear stick was loose. I could rotate it 360 degrees. I assumed that it was not supposed to be delivered that way, but I didn't care. In fact, while driving my car for a year, I got used to this "problem," and it turned out that I actually liked it. The knob nicely rotated with the movement of my hand while shifting gears, and I thought that was cool. I also liked to fumble with it while waiting for traffic lights to turn green. (Which, in my country, amounts to a lot of fumbling.)

A year after I purchased the car, I turned it in for its first scheduled maintenance. Then, after I got it back, while driving home happily in my serviced car, I suddenly noticed something was wrong…. I was feeling resistance to my fumbling. I was unable to rotate the knob on the gear stick, and it appeared that the service guy had fastened it! A jolt of anger shot through my system: Oh my god, they fixed the bug. (You bastards!)

It was a classic example of the **False Consensus Effect**,[1] where someone projects his own way of thinking onto other people, assuming to understand what the other person wants [Arrow 2000:125]. But the "problem" that one person sees can be considered to be a "feature" by another.

I really liked the little problem in my car. The rotating knob on the gear stick was a benefit to me. I possibly had the only car in the world with that feature. But not anymore. Somebody assumed to understand what my problems and benefits are. There had been no communication, and no verification through feedback.

Communication and Feedback

Granted, most people probably would have wanted the gear stick in the car to be fixed. And some would call it a "fair assumption" that the mechanic thought I wanted it fixed as well. But that didn't change that it was an assumption. He didn't ask. And if the car service company had told me in advance, "We are going to fix anything that's loose," it wouldn't have made much difference because a one-way message still doesn't count

---

1   http://www.mgt30.com/consensus/.

as "communication." The customary way of thinking of communication as "the transmission of information from one person to another" is wrong, wrote Alistair Cockburn in *Agile Software Development* [Cockburn 2007:8–13].

To explain this, let's review what actually happens when you intend to "communicate" something to me (see Figure 12.1). Your thoughts result in a *translation* of what you actually mean, according to your own internal model of the world, to some physical actions on your part, like speaking words, modulating pitch, speed, and volume, gesturing with your hands, moving your facial muscles, typing text into a device, or writing something on a piece of paper. This first part of our communication already has plenty of opportunity to invite problems to creep in because your translation from thoughts to actions may be erratic, like confusing left with right (as I usually do). Or you may employ context- or culture-dependent assumptions, like nodding your head means "yes," and shaking it means "no," which is an assumption that will fail in various parts of the world [Adams 1986].

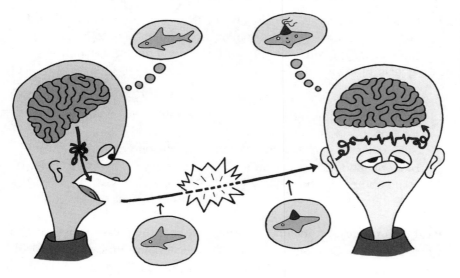

FIGURE 12.1

Problematic communication, from one mind to another.

Subsequently, your erroneous or ambiguous signals traverse some medium, such as the air, a computer network, or the post office. This means that noise and faulty mechanisms in the medium may further distort your message before it arrives at my sensory inputs (particularly when the medium at some point involves my own wireless network at home).

Then the unreliable signals arrive at my eyes and ears, which may not work fully as expected because of the weird stuff I drank last night. The part that gets through is then processed using pattern-matching, and I arrive at a conclusion of what you are trying to say to me. But the words you speak, or the way you move your face and hands, might be unfamiliar to me. And even when the information gets through correctly, I might still associate your signals with other meanings because the internal reference models I have in my head could be very different from yours. You keep talking about Scrum, and in my mind I see 16 big, dirty men wrestling over a ball in the grass….

So you see, many things can go wrong on the way from your brain to mine, and it is almost guaranteed that your meaning of what you intended to send is not the same as the meaning that I attach to what I received. This, as Cockburn indicates, is *not* communication. This is *mis*communication and often leads to confusion and conflict.

BUT SIGNALING AN SOS IS COMMUNICATION, TOO!

I don't think it is. When we accept that communication is "the process of transferring information from one person to another," there is still the requirement that the second person has properly received the *information*.

An SOS signal as seen by a 5-year-old child will not result in communication because the child has no idea what the signal means. Information implies meaning; otherwise it is just data. And an SOS is just a signal. It is only *communication* when a receiver properly understands it and acts accordingly. Otherwise, it is failed communication.

Real communication includes making sure that the meaning assigned to a message is the same on both sides. Technical communication protocols (such as the Internet's TCP/IP model and the HTTP protocol) contain various techniques for (trying to) make sure that what gets sent by one system is *properly* received by the other. With human communication we have the same requirement. It is only really communication when both parties agree that they have properly exchanged information and that both are assigning the same meaning to it. This is one reason why Scrum teams have face-to-face planning meetings with Product Owners, so they can verify each other's understanding.

> ## ISN'T IT IMPOSSIBLE TO FULLY AGREE ON MEANING?
>
> Indeed, it is. Until people can directly read each other's minds, their agreement on meaning will only be an approximation at best.
>
> Verbal verification of meaning is the next best thing after telepathy.

Miscommunication Is the Norm

Poor communication is so common that complexity researcher Ralph Stacey sees it as the norm in many organizations. People always complain about poor communication. And no matter how many new systems, procedures, and reports are introduced, the complaints remain the same. There is still poor communication. Stacey suggests that the "poor communication" complaint is simply a side effect of what is the most effective way of developing knowledge. [Stacey 2000a:5]

I think Stacey touches upon an interesting point here. Communication problems are the norm in all organizations, and there *seems* to be little we can do about it. Have you noticed that problems in software projects are (almost) always the result of bad **communication**?

Based on my observations, I see communication as a function of three phenomena: information, relationships, and feedback.

Communication = Information ★ Relationships ★ Feedback

Roger Lewin writes that abysmal relationships are the root of most organizational problems [Lewin 1999]. I think he has a good point, but it is only one part of the equation. Without the availability of good information, there wouldn't be anything valuable to communicate. Without good relationships between people, there wouldn't be a way to share that information. And without good feedback mechanisms, there would be no verification that the information has properly crossed the distance from one person to another.

> ## WHAT ABOUT COLLABORATION?
>
> In this chapter, I repeatedly refer to communication, and it seems as if I am forgetting about collaboration. But I believe it is hard to compare communication with collaboration. Various sources tell me that communication is a prerequisite for collaboration, and that collaboration also entails community, connections, decisions, actions, emotions, and so on. [Cockburn 2007:372].
>
> Therefore it seems that collaboration is a theme that pervades all dimensions of management, and all chapters of this book. In this chapter (and Chapter 13, "How to Grow Structure"), I focus on communication and structure.

Like Stacey, I believe there is never enough communication. But we also never have enough money, not enough resources, and not enough time. So yes, the complaints will always remain, but we can certainly try to do the best we can with what we have. And this requires that we understand the structure of systems, beginning with the recognition that every organization is a network.

Capabilities of Communicators

In mathematics and sociology, a **small-world network**[2] is a system in which every agent can be reached from every other agent with only a small number of steps through the network, despite most of them not being direct neighbors of each other. An organization is such a small-world network. Everyone knows everyone, either directly or indirectly, through one or two other people (quite often a secretary, office manager, or janitor). But interestingly enough, the whole population on Earth is also a small-world network. This has been argued using the famous concept of **six degrees of separation**,[3] which says that everyone on this planet is at most six social steps removed from each other [Gladwell 2002:47].

Social network analysis is a branch of network theory dealing with social networks and how information flows through them. Karen Stephenson, a corporate anthropologist, identifies three archetypes of communicators in a social network [Stephenson 2005]:

---

2   http://www.mgt30.com/small-world/.
3   http://www.mgt30.com/six-degrees/.

- **Hubs** are people who draw information to themselves and then broadcast it all around them.

- **Gatekeepers** are experts at carefully managing information flows, knowing what to say to whom, and what not [to say].

- **Pulsetakers** are great observers of people and trends, being excellent mentors and coaches.

Stephenson writes that "Hubs know the most people; Gatekeepers know the right people; and Pulsetakers know the most people who know the right people."

In his bestselling book *The Tipping Point,* Malcolm Gladwell offers another categorization of people in social networks [Gladwell 2002:34]:

- **Connectors** exchange information with many people, but don't share deep relationships with them.

- **Mavens** know fewer people, but they tend to invest more time in them and know them better.

- **Salesmen** are masters of interpersonal communication, getting messages across where others can't.

Stephenson claims that Gladwell's (subjective) archetypes of people are different combinations of her own (mathematical) archetypes. And maybe she's right. But I believe that, whichever model one uses, these nonexclusive *archetypes* too easily lead to misunderstanding and a use of *stereotypes,* which would be an overly simplistic approach.

We have observed what communication really means, with information traveling over a relationship from one mind to another, overcoming many obstacles on the way, and requiring a return ticket in the form of feedback. Therefore, I want to offer an alternative (see Figure 12.2).

It is an approach that doesn't categorize people but instead differentiates between people's capabilities. There are nine capabilities of communicators:

- **Connecting**. Some people are good at making connections with other people. They create many pathways through which communication can *potentially* take place. Such people may have many friends on Facebook or LinkedIn; they frequently attend meetings and conferences; and in the office they know just about everybody. Both Hubs and Connectors excel in this capability.

FIGURE 12.2
Nine capabilities of
communicators.

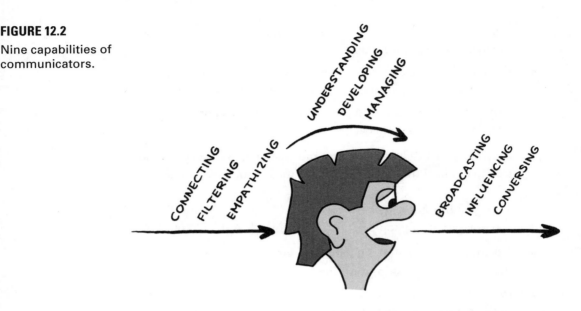

- **Filtering**. Knowing many people doesn't mean that you're actually listening to all their messages. People who are good at filtering not only actively listen to other people's social network status updates, and hallway chatter, but they also know which people and messages to ignore. Someone who is well connected can be bad at filtering qualitatively, whereas someone with only few connections could be listening more intently and selectively. Both Pulsetakers and Mavens are good at filtering.

- **Empathizing.** Actively listening to people still doesn't mean that you care about what they are saying. There needs to be some emotional association to someone's messages to feel interested. For example, a socially challenged system administrator could *care* more about what developers are saying than a social savvy project manager. Both Pulsetakers and Salesmen seem to excel at empathizing with what other people are saying.

- **Understanding.** And then there has to be a real understanding of what is being said. You may be enthusiastic about some architectural issue in your project, and I may be able to empathize with you, but if I don't understand anything about architecture, then I don't know what you *mean*, and I cannot respond properly to what you're telling me.

- **Developing.** Given what you learn, and what you already know, you can develop new information and then pass it along to others. Right now I am developing this list of capabilities by connecting the dots between the works of Cockburn, Stephenson, and Gladwell, while adding my own thoughts to the cocktail. The capability of people for developing (creating, building) *new* information seems to be overlooked in the other models.

- **Managing.** Some people are good at managing (categorizing and evaluating) existing information. They know what is important, and they know to whom they should communicate something and, at least as important, to whom they should *not* communicate something. Gatekeepers perform quite well in this area.

- **Broadcasting.** Then there are people who are experts at radiating information, whether intentional or not. They give away all they know to anyone they meet with either positive or negative consequences. Whether it is about projects, customers, management, or personal relationships, these people can, and will, tell you all about it. Hubs clearly have excellent broadcasting capabilities.

- **Influencing.** But those who send a lot of information may not necessarily be good at also influencing their colleagues. The silent but brilliant software architect, who rarely says a word, may be the best person in the organization, *when* he talks, to really make a difference. Such people transmit messages to fewer people, but (because of their status or power) influencers have a much higher success rate of convincing others. It seems that Mavens are particularly gifted with this capability.

- **Conversing.** Finally, influencers are not necessarily communicators. I am told that some of my blog posts have influenced people, but I have not directly exchanged ideas with many of my readers. This means that I am incapable of steering their actions, and there is no understanding of what they do with the information that I gave them. It seems that both Connectors and Salesmen score well (better than me) in this department.

These are the nine capabilities of communicators in a social network. I think it is more realistic to view a social network as a system of people who communicate with various capability levels in each of these nine areas. These capabilities change over time for each person and fluctuate depending on their areas of interest. This turns the social network into the complex system that we expected it to be! And, as a complex system, the network is prone to many interesting effects.

GREAT ANALOGY: RADIO

Reviewer Jens Schauder suggested an interesting analogy with the principles of radio:

You need proper cables (connecting), you need to prevent amplifying noise (filtering), and you need to be tuned to the right frequency (empathizing).

You need experience working with AM versus FM signals (understanding), you need some amplification (developing), and an equalizer (managing).

And then you can start airing your show (broadcasting), with as little noise as possible (influencing). And if your content is great, your listeners might even interact with you (conversing).

Network Effects

Twitter changed my life. As an introvert, I have never been eager to talk about myself. But on Twitter, it's different. At times, it seems the channel from my brain to my Twitter feed is wider than the one between Holland and Britain. And I have to take care that my social networking activities online aren't taking over my "normal" life in the physical world, where my offline social network has a size comparable to a hotel room in Paris.

Research into network theory and social network analysis has uncovered a number of interesting phenomena in (online and offline) social networks. For example, a **tipping point**[4] [Gladwell 2002] is the moment in time when something which was previously rare suddenly becomes widespread across an entire population, such as the popularity of the Avatar movie, the Susan Boyle video, the Harry Potter books, the Scrum

---

4 http://www.mgt30.com/tipping-point/.

framework, or...*this* book. (I have been twittering about the book until my fingers turned blue, so I'm sure it's not *my* fault if it doesn't fly.) In physics the tipping point is called a **phase transition**,[5] but the meaning is the same: a sudden transformation of a system from one state to another.

A second example is the **strength of weak ties** [Granovetter 1973], which says that information reaches populations better when sent through many weak connections instead of few strong ones. Twitter followers are a perfect example of weak ties. They sometimes talk to me, but they never ruin my good mood with birthday party invitations.

And then there is the example of the **long tail**[6] [Anderson 2008], which says that the sum of the value of sparsely available information can be larger than the value of stuff that is ubiquitous throughout the social network. Or in other words, the Twitterers with few followers are together more powerful (and from a business-perspective more valuable) than the few with many followers.

Finally, I think that one of the most interesting phenomena in small-world networks is the **homogenization effect**. Researchers found evidence that the long tail effect does *not* mean that people's attention is shifting from the "head" (the most popular stuff) to the "tail" (the least popular stuff). Instead, it is the other way around: In a well-connected network, information that gets copied around gets copied around even *more*. What is popular becomes ever more popular. It is also known as the Matthew effect, after a quote from the Matthew gospel: "For unto every one that hath shall be given" [Webb 2007:54].

Homogenization in social groups, in societies, and in organizations, is the mechanism that enables shared culture, fads, and fashions. It is why, despite tremendous diversity in the social network, many people start liking and disliking the same things. It is why there's a good chance that all development managers in the world will either *love* this book or *hate* it. Some researchers call it "social contagion": the carrying over of ideas, likes, dislikes, and desires, from our friends, and from our friends' friends.

> It is becoming clear that a whole range of phenomena are transmitted through networks of friends in ways that are not entirely understood: happiness and depression, obesity, drinking and smoking habits, the inclination to turn out and vote in elections, a taste for certain music or food, a preference for online piracy, even the tendency

---

5   http://www.mgt30.com/phase-transition/.
6   http://www.mgt30.com/long-tail/.

to attempt or think about suicide. They ripple through networks "like pebbles thrown in a pond" […]. By being aware of the effects of social contagion we may be able to find ways to counter it, or use it to our own benefit.[7]

The same researchers found that the homogenization phenomenon usually loses its effect after three degrees in a social network. This means that you copy ideas from your friends, from the friends of your friends, and from the friends of friends of friends. But then the effect fades away.

Nevertheless, we can assume that there is a maximum of three degrees of separation in most if not all organizations, meaning that the homogenization of an idea, fad, or fashion, can easily take place throughout an entire organization.

And now you understand why I have been sharing so much of myself and my projects on Twitter. My 140-character brain emissions tend to increase the number of weak ties with people in the long tail, which has significantly increased the number of people separated from me by just three degrees or less. And now I'm waiting patiently for the tipping point….

Tuning Connectivity

Despite being a broadcaster when it comes to what I do, the bandwidth between my sensory input and my brain seems actually small. Very small. I walk past the people I know without seeing them. I cannot seem to handle having more than five friends at a time. And while listening to someone talk, my brain sometimes registers only the words "You… … … … me … … … … computers … … … … Big Bird … … … …."

It all has to do with balancing connections. The more connections there are between agents in a complex system, the more constraints and restrictions these agents impose on each other. This limits their freedom of movement and reduces their ability to achieve peak performance [Stacey 2000a:114]. It appears that connectivity in a complex system must be tuned. It should be not too much, and not too little.

The average amount of communication between agents in a complex system is more or less constant. No matter how many agents there are in the system, and no matter how many connections they have with

7   Bond, Michael. "Three degrees of separation" New Scientist. 3 January 2009 http://www.mgt30.com/friends/. [Bond 2009a:24-27].

each other, a complex adaptive system finds its own optimal amount of communication.

> It appears that above a certain number of connections, the degree of adaptation decreases. [...] The optimal, and relatively low, number of connections per node (in this instance, considered to be people or groups that define a unique destination in a communication network) does not seem to vary much with network size. As networks get larger, and more nodes are added, the number of connections to each node must remain relatively constant.[8]

There is some optimal quantity of communication in the system. And given our earlier observation of the different types of people in social groups, I think that often people with few interpersonal connections are better listeners, whereas those who know many people filter out a lot more information. That's how they all keep the amount of communication more or less constant. And we must not forget that books, blogs, software, television, newspapers, and all other forms of media also contribute to our communication levels:

> The scarce resource here is not information but rather attention. Given the inherent limits of information processing, agents must actively ignore most of the potential information that they encounter. [...] It may even be the case that agents operate more effectively with less information.[9]

There is a natural way for people to deal with information overload. The more signals people get, the more immune they become to the messages that the signals contain [Gladwell 2002:274]. I believe information overload is therefore never a problem. Just have a look out the window for three seconds, and then close your eyes and try to recall everything that you saw. I'm sure it won't be much. Our brains are naturally wired to ignore almost everything that we receive. There is only a real problem when people's filtering capabilities are not properly trained so that they listen to the wrong things and ignore the good stuff.

---

8 Highsmith, Jim. Adaptive Software Development. New York: Dorset House Pub, 1999. [Highsmith 1999:286].
9 Miller, John H. and Scott E. Page. Complex Adaptive Systems. Princeton: Princeton University Press, 2007. Used with permission. [Miller, Page 2007:94].

Some teams are better able to handle a flood of information than others. Intact teams whose members stay together and regularly work together, for example, invariably hone their team performance strategies and become skilled at dealing with even the most challenging and information-intensive aspects of their work.[10]

Complex systems can find their own optimum when dealing with communication. No governance is needed (or even possible) to manage the amount of information that flows through the social network. But a reasonable thing for a manager to do is to influence which information is available, which connections are formed between people, and how well they are training their sensory filters. And one important lesson to take away here is that teams need time to learn how to filter the information available to them and how to work together. Teams should not be broken up too frequently, or else they have to start all over every time.

Competition and Cooperation

I am a selfish person. Though I gladly do things for other people, and give stuff away for free, I tend to do so when I believe it is in my own *self-interest*. The pursuit of my happiness has led me to offer jobs to unfortunate unemployed souls who needed a second chance, to give projects to people in desperate need of experience, to buy stuff from people in poor countries, and to be a supporter for Amnesty International. All because I'm selfish.

Genes are selfish, too, as Richard Dawkins pointed out some decades ago [Dawkins 1989]. But, despite their selfishness, in the human genome 1,195 genes *cooperate* to produce the heart; 2,164 genes team up to make white blood cells; and 3,195 genes are jointly responsible for the human brain [Corning 2003:107]. They are *teams* of selfish genes, evolving together because, in all their selfishness, they figured out that it pays not to be on their own. Working together increases their chance of survival in the harsh environment of the gene pool.

An interesting form of teaming up within one species is found in the ants called *Pheidole pallidula*, which consists of small ant workers and large soldier ants. When an intruder attempts to enter the nest, the worker

---

10 Hackman, J. Leading Teams. Boston: Harvard Business School Press, 2002. Used with permission. [Hackman 2002:153].

ants pin down the intruder, while they recruit a soldier to decapitate the victim [Anderson, McMillan, 2003:32]. (Don't you just love the things teams can learn from nature?)

There are also many forms of teaming up between *different* species. One example is lichen, which is a partnership, or **symbiotic association**, between algae and fungi. The algae are photosynthesizers, capturing energy from the sun, whereas the fungi have great water-storage capabilities. This symbiotic relationship enables lichen to survive in barren environments. The team of two species can do what neither of the individual species can do alone [Corning 2002:67].

Selfish cooperation is a matter of costs versus benefits, where the small cost of giving or sharing leads to greater immediate or deferred benefits. Some call it **reciprocal altruism**, or win–win reciprocity, or *you-scratch-my-back-I'll-scratch-yours*. It is why many jewelers in Antwerp have snuggled up and settled together in a few streets called the Diamond District. It is why fierce competitors such as Google, Microsoft, and Apple are regularly seen to work together. It is why I'm answering people's questions for free, promoting the books of my competitors, and offering jobs to suicidal kangaroos.

The root cause of the paradox of competition versus cooperation (sometimes referred to as **coopetition**[11]) can be traced back to the 235-year old book *The Wealth of Nations*, by economist and philosopher Adam Smith. He described **division of labor** as the concept of people working together, **specializing** in different tasks, while still working for personal profit. And, as if guided by "an invisible hand," the whole system then tends to improve the lives for everyone involved.

It is the same in organizations. Employees are competitors because they are hired individually. They frequently have eyes for the same job openings, the same cool projects, the same management positions, and the same parking space right near the entrance to the office building. But people team up together because it gives them more joy, more success, and better end-of-year evaluations.

We are all selfish. And the smartest selfish people understand that it is in their own self-interest to work together and be nice to each other. This coincides with the discovery of mathematician Robert Axelrod, who noticed that the game strategy **Tit-for-tat**[12], which tells someone to play nice as long as the competitors play nice as well, is one of the most

---

11 http://www.mgt30.com/coopetition/.
12 http://www.mgt30.com/tit-for-tat/.

successful survival strategies in games and in nature [Mitchell 2009:217]. It also coincides with Christopher Avery's observation that "teamwork is an individual skill" [Avery 2001]. And philosopher Ayn Rand wrote books and essays on what she called the "virtue of selfishness" [Rand, Branden 1970]. Though her rigid doctrine has been criticized by many, at a fundamental level she did have a point.

These examples all tell the same story: Adam Smith's invisible hand gently pushes people into cooperative behavior, *because* they all want the best for themselves.

WHAT ABOUT PEOPLE PUTTING COWORKERS DOWN?

Cooperative behavior does not happen automatically. Some people will never learn. And neither will they be very successful in their life or business.

I am sure that the most successful people on this planet have all learned the power of "coopetition": competition with (selective) cooperation.

Groups and Boundaries

We have seen that individual success will make people want to work together. But then what happens?

When agents in a complex system cooperate, they tend to form subsystems, which is a principle sometimes referred to as **modularity** [Richardson 2004b:79]. In *Small Groups as Complex Systems,* the authors describe four ways in which the formation of groups of people can take place [Arrow 2000:65]:

- **Concocted groups** are groups that are created by an *external* force, in a *planned* manner. For example, a project team is created to build a web site for the CEO's favorite dog, and people are "volunteered" for this team by their managers.

- **Founded groups** are groups that are also *planned*, but the planning is *internal* to the group. For example, some employees get together and decide to launch their own in-company catering service.

- **Self-organized groups** are groups in which the initiative is also *internal* to the group, but formation takes place in an unplanned or *emergent* fashion. For example, the active Twitterers in the company try to promote online social networking.

- **Circumstantial groups** are groups that are formed due to circumstances beyond their own control, *external* to the group, but still in an *emergent* manner. For example, employees stranded together in a broken-down elevator, possibly on their way to the new catering service. (It would be interesting to see their Twitter feeds.)

Managers are often responsible for setting up teams of the first type (Concocted groups). However, real team formation and cooperation can sometimes be hard to achieve in such cases. It is then worth trying to delegate the responsibility of project team formation to the people themselves (Founded groups).

For a group to call itself a "team," two things are important: 1) there has to be a shared goal and 2) there needs to be a group boundary. This boundary can be spatial, temporal, and psychological. Whomever is part of the team can be determined from people's location (for example, everyone in the same room), from the period in time (for example, from now until the end of next year), or from a shared concept in people's minds (for example, all software architects throughout the company) [Arrow 2000:79]. Without an agreement about team boundaries, and too much ambiguity about who is on the team, people cannot act as a team because there isn't one. [Hackman 2002:44]

Key to the successful formation of teams, writes Hackman in *Leading Teams*, is that the team's boundary must be neither too closed (refusing input from outside), nor too open (losing cohesiveness). Hackman uses the term **permeable boundaries**, which is a concept that we also find in systems theory (see Chapter 3, "Complex Systems Theory").

A group acting as a team has a permeable boundary. The boundary is clear and identifiable for all involved, but it is also sufficiently open to allow for new input (ideas, energy, and resources) from the outside. It is neither too closed, nor too open. And so it appears that an adaptive balancing act is not only needed for the connectivity inside a system, but also for the boundary around it.

Hyper-Productivity or Autocatalysis

Only boundaries can turn a system into one that organizes itself. And now that we have discussed boundaries, it is worth looking at what can happen *inside* those boundaries.

The day I wrote this paragraph, I had been drawing screen designs for the website of our business unit, which seemed like a strange thing to do for a team manager. The only reason was that, in our team of five people, I happened to be the one with above-average drawing skills, which enabled our developers to deliver a good looking product faster. Similarly, my work as a manager (and part-time designer) was sped up considerably by our architect, who excelled at turning my designs into readable API documents, which tended to impress the customers we talked to. At the same time, the architect's job was accelerated by our developers who seemed to produce code at the speed of thought and verified his ideas almost before he had finished showing his PowerPoint slides. It seemed we were not just a team. We were an **autocatalytic set**.

An autocatalytic set is a system in which the agents reinforce and accelerate each other's productivity. For example, suppose a number of molecules are in a nice and warm pool of acidic gloop. Some of these molecules will participate in chemical reactions, thereby forming new molecules. And these new molecules in their turn also participate in chemical reactions. Schematically, one can draw a picture like the one in Figure 12.3.

FIGURE 12.3

Each molecule catalyzes and is catalyzed by at least one other molecule.

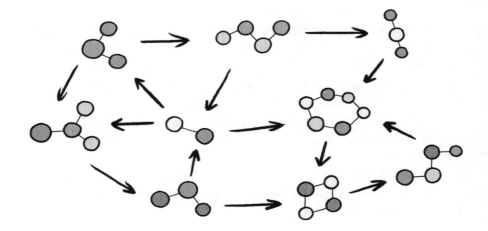

Each molecule in the pool is a participant in a chemical reaction. But each molecule is also the *product* of another chemical reaction. Looking at Figure 12.3, we can imagine a set of molecules where each reaction is accelerated by one of the other molecules (a catalyst) in the set, whereas the catalysts themselves are likewise products of chemical reactions reinforced by other catalysts. In short, the entire set of molecules is catalyzing itself. It is an autocatalytic set.

Theoretical biologist Stuart Kauffman has shown that the forming of such an autocatalytic set is mathematically almost inevitable when diversity and connectivity are increased in a network. Such a heterogeneous system is self-sustaining. It has no need of anything else but itself, and a little energy from outside. There are suggestions that autocatalytic sets contributed significantly to the formation of life on Earth [Kauffman 1995].

The principle of autocatalysis is important. As more diverse people are added to the team, heterogeneity in the team increases. More team members can then play the role of catalyst for the work of some of the other team members, until at some point all work in the team is catalyzed by one or more of the others.

Autocatalysis could be a scientific explanation for the "jelled" teams Demarco and Lister wrote about, and the "hyper-productivity" of software teams that agile expert Jeff Sutherland has frequently referred to.[13] And even if I'm wrong, it still makes an interesting case for support of diversity, connectivity, and specialization in software teams.

A LITTLE MORE IS NEEDED THAN THAT....

And I think you are right! Hyper-productivity is not achieved only by catalyzing each other's work.

Other factors, such as collaboration and competence, are important, too. Some people also refer to *implicit coordination* as a crucial factor, which is the capability of team members to correctly anticipate each other's needs and actions without having to communicate explicitly.

On the day I wrote this part of this chapter, the team I worked with had a planning meeting, and we all noticed how fast we were going with only

---

13 A video of Jeff Sutherland is available via http://www.mgt30.com/hyper-productivity/.

three weeks left for our product launch. Probably none of us thought, "Wow, we sure are autocatalyzing nicely these days," but we certainly felt that each of us was contributing to the productivity of the team. And I'm sure that the question "How am I helping the others go faster?" could have been answered easily by each of us.

Pattern-Formation

The winter of 2009/2010 was one of the coldest in a long time (in the northern hemisphere). For me, it was a time of great joy and great sorrow (see Figure 12.4). Joy, because I love how beautiful the world looks when everything has turned white. And sorrow, because no matter how beautiful the ice crystals are on the windows of my car, I hate having to labor at minus 10 degrees Celsius with an ice scraper.

FIGURE 12.4

Me in the snow.

While busying myself to defrost my car, it was often easy to forget what a wondrous phenomenon snow really is.

> Ice crystals form in the turbulent air with a famous blending of symmetry and chance, the special beauty of six-fold indeterminacy. [...] As a growing snowflake falls

to the earth, typically floating in the wind for an hour or more, the choices made by the branching tips at any instant depend sensitively on such things as the temperature, the humidity, and the presence of impurities in the atmosphere. The six tips of a single snowflake, spreading within a millimeter space, feel the same temperatures, and because the laws of growth are purely deterministic, they maintain a near-perfect symmetry.[14]

Snowflakes are a great example of self-organized pattern-forming (see Figure 12.5). Nature is abundant with other examples, like stripes on a zebra, spots on a butterfly's wings, dunes in the Sahara desert, and leaves on a fern [Waldrop 1992:65]. And there can be pattern-forming in fluids, too. It has been discovered that, superimposed on every ocean, there is a striped pattern of currents, forming 150-kilometer-wide bands that alternately flow from east to west, and from west to east, at a speed of around 40 meters per hour. It is said that no scientist has come up with an explanation for this globe-spanning wave pattern in the oceans [Brahic 2008:10].

FIGURE 12.5

Snowflakes (adapted from unknown source).

---

14 Gleick, James. Chaos. Harmondsworth Eng.: Penguin, 1987. Used with permission. [Gleick 1987:309–311].

Pattern-forming not only happens in a spatial manner. Oscillatory behavior is crucial in living systems, such as the circadian rhythms (or biological clocks) we find in heartbeats, sleep, and the periodic activities of hormone and enzyme systems [Lewin 1999:29]. Another beautiful example in nature, frequently referred to in complexity literature, is a Southeast Asian species of firefly that congregates in trees during mating periods, thousands at a time, all blinking in harmony [Gleick 1987:293].

Patterns in complex systems are emergent events. No single agent in the system is responsible for producing these patterns, but they are there nevertheless.

However, from a complexity viewpoint, not all patterns are alike. There is an important difference between the leaves on a fern and the dunes in the Sahara. Between the harmonious blinking of fireflies in a tree and the perfect concentric ripples I see in a pool of water after my mobile phone drops in. The difference is that some patterns are there for a reason, whereas others exist only as an interesting side effect. There is no purpose to the ice crystals on my car windows, other than to keep me busy. But there is a real purpose to the frantic but steady beating of my heart while my car slips and slides over an icy road.

It is certain that patterns, both spatial and temporal, in team formation and communication occur in your organization. The universe is filled with patterns, so why should they not exist in your development teams? But for patterns to have a *purpose* it is necessary that managers enable them to occur through self-organization. Managing teams to make them crystallize, or orchestrating team members to blink in harmony, is just too much work to do yourself. And it will never look as good.

Before we look at organizational patterns in Chapter 13, "How to Grow Structure," we must finish this chapter with an investigation into the scaling of systems.

Scale Symmetry: Patterns Big and Small

Benoît Mandelbrot was a mathematician who discovered that changes in cotton prices are random and unpredictable, and that the pattern of all price changes is independent of scale: The graphs for daily, monthly, and yearly price changes all matched perfectly. In fact, in *The (Mis) Behavior of Markets*, Mandelbrot argues that similar patterns can be found in all stock exchanges: Prices behave not in a well-mannered way but go up and down in a manner independent of scale [Mandelbrot, Hudson 2006]. And

Mandelbrot knew his subject matter, because he was the father of **fractal geometry**.[15]

Fractals are patterns with a self-similarity across scale (see Figure 12.6), meaning that they look the same no matter how often you magnify a portion of it [Gleick 1987:86]. This self-similarity implies recursion and patterns inside patterns. Fractal-like patterns have been found in classical music with musical patterns on small scales similar to the ones on larger scales. But also in noise on telephone lines, where it turned out that the distribution of errors on a channel was self-similar across seconds, minutes, days, and weeks [Solé 2000:50]. Fractals have been used successfully for computer-generated landscapes, plants and animals in movies, for the reason that fractal geometry looks both complex *and* natural. [Gleick 1987:114]

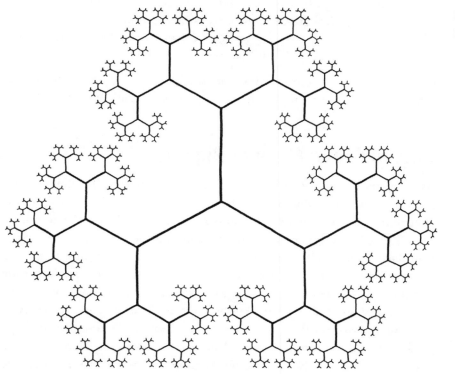

FIGURE 12.6
Fractals.[16]

15 http://www.mgt30.com/fractal/.
16 Image adapted from Jonathan Rees, http://www.mgt30.com/fractal-img/. Reprinted under the Creative Commons License. Please visit http://creativecommons.org/.

Your body has fractals, too. Blood vessels divide and branch almost endlessly throughout your anatomy, and the nature of this branching is fractal. The reason is that blood is expensive and scarce, and needs to reach and feed a huge number of cells. Nature has figured out that a fractal structure is the most efficient way to accomplish this [Gleick 1987:108].

Fractals produce complex structures using just a few simple mathematical rules. And because the patterns are scale invariant (the same for small and big), any efficiency or productivity achieved at a small scale can be matched to equivalent results at *all* scales. That means that, for a big system to work well, it might be a smart idea to look like a small system that works well.

> A complex system that works is invariably found to have evolved from a simple system that worked. A complex [meaning in this context: large and complicated] system designed from scratch never works and cannot be patched up to make it work. You have to start over, beginning with a working simple system.[17]

However, there are some important differences between mathematical systems and systems trying to survive and grow in the physical world.

How to Grow: More or Bigger?

As an employee, I always had a preference for working in small organizations because it is much easier to make a difference in small–business environments. And, in a small company, it is also much easier to annoy the CEO because he actually knows who you are. On the other hand, I do have some trouble working in the smallest of all organizations: the one-person company. Despite it being the most natural environment for making a real difference, it also means that, no matter how you choose to do your work, you can only annoy yourself. Therefore everyone, even those who work on their own, are always looking for opportunities to grow and work with other people. But how? Software developers already know that you basically have just two options for scaling a system: **scaling out** and **scaling up**.

Scaling *out* is the concept of producing many small systems. The size remains the same, but the system grows by producing more versions of

---

17 Gall, John. The Systems Bible. Ann Arbor: General Systemantics Press, 2002. Reprinted by permission of the author. [Gall 2002].

itself. Biologists have found that, for many species, it pays to scale *out*. Large coalitions of male lions are known to take over a pride of females, which is something a single lion can never achieve. A swarm of bees can kill a human being, whereas the sting of an individual bee usually hurts only a little. And among pups of sea lions, much lower mortality rates are found when they are raised in groups, whereas the pups born to solitary mating pairs die far more easily [Corning 2003:17,123].

However, organisms have not only found the benefits of **economies of scale** by working together in groups. Many species themselves have also grown bigger over time, as paleontologist Edward Drinker Cope noted more than a century ago. Species often start small and leave ever bigger descendants, a process now known as Cope's Rule [O'Donogue 2009:39].

Scaling *up* is the concept of one system (or descendants of it) growing bigger over time. Being big has evolutionary advantages. It makes it harder for predators to win an attack, and it is easier to fight off competitors for food or mates. And there's a much better chance of being popular and looking intimidating in a museum.

But there's a downside as well. Big species consume more and breed slower, which means that they have greater problems when times are tough. They are therefore more vulnerable to extinction. Another reason for ending up in a museum.

It appears, for species in nature and organizations in an economy, that the positive feedback loop of getting bigger (with reduced vulnerability) is ultimately negated by the negative feedback loop of becoming slower (with reduced adaptability). The economies of scale are thus pushed down by diminishing returns.

And so it appears that scaling up is a more troublesome strategy than scaling out. When we consider the total biomass in the world,[18] we must recognize that bacteria, plants, ants, and Antarctic krill[19] all have a total mass on earth that far exceeds that of any of the bigger-sized species, such as humans and cattle. We humans like to believe that we are dominating the earth, but by sheer weight the impact of ants is still between 10 and 100 times higher! From a complexity perspective scaling out is definitely better than scaling up. A group of many small systems is more adaptable, and less prone to extinction, than a group of just a few big systems. It seems that Antarctic krill are happier swimming around alive than floating in a jar in a museum.

---

18 http://www.mgt30.com/biomass/.
19 http://www.mgt30.com/krill/.

In Chapter 13, the practical side of the *Grow Structure* view, we see how the concepts of connectivity, boundaries, patterns, and scaling translate to useful ideas on how to grow good organizational structures, thereby improving communication in the organization.

Summary

Miscommunication in organizations seems to be the norm rather than the exception. One reason is that communication requires proper feedback between people, which is often not happening.

We can identify nine capabilities of communicators in an organization, and each of these capabilities can be weak or strong, and different per person. This explains why organizations are highly complex communication networks.

Researchers have identified a number of effects in social communication networks, of which the homogenization effect is an interesting example. It states that the things that are copied in a network tend to be copied even more, which explains how cultures and fashions are born.

The optimization of communication requires that connectivity is tuned. It also requires that competition and cooperation go hand in hand. One result of optimal communication can be an autocatalytic (or a hyperproductive) team.

The structure of an organization contributes heavily to optimal communication. From fractals we can learn that scale invariant structures are efficient and require only a few rules. Another finding is that scaling out (growing many small parts) works better than scaling up (growing one big system).

Reflection and Action

Let's see if you can apply some ideas from this chapter to your organization:

- Discuss the nine capabilities of communicators with your team. Try to find out together who is capable of doing what. Are any capabilities over- or underrepresented? Is there something you can do about that?

- Discuss teamwork with your people. Are people co-operating with each other? Are they doing this because they feel altruistic or because they believe it is in their own self-interest?

Chapter **13**

How to Grow Structure

In all large corporations, there is a pervasive fear that someone, somewhere is having fun with a computer on company time. Networks help alleviate that fear.

—John C. Dvorak, columnist, broadcaster (1952–)

I love structuring things. You can see it in my file folders, my blog, my financial records, and my paper archives. Everything has a place and a function. I even have a neat white box labeled "Jurgen's junk," to keep things separated from another box labeled "Raoul's junk." It's the same with organizations I work for. I want to know what the structure is and what each part is for. Including the junk.

So that's the purpose of this chapter. It gives you an overview of adaptive principles in organizational design and some ideas on the ways to grow a structure in your own organization. I believe better communication follows from better structure; therefore, this chapter focuses on structure. We see that no single structure is the definitive answer for all organizations and that managers should instead focus on an organizational ability for continuous structural change.

The Management 3.0 model specifically refers to *growing* a structure. In complex systems, structure emerges by itself. However, as a manager, being responsible for the direction the self-organizing system takes, you can recognize that some structures are good and others are bad. The level of steering and intervention needed depends on the maturity and competence of the people in your teams.

About Environment, Products, Size, and People

People often ask me, "How should I structure my business and my teams?" (Well, actually they don't, but I expect they might after reading the previous chapter.) Unfortunately, there's no simple answer to that question. At least not a simple answer that also happens to be right. People might as well ask, "What is the best form for a species?" The question makes no sense. One cannot claim that a starfish has a better body structure than a spider. Both species exist, and both have found a niche in which to survive. The spider can't survive in the sea. And the starfish won't survive in my cellar. It is the same with organizations. The "best" organizational structure depends on the environment in which the organization needs to survive.

> Thus we see that in today's environment, *no solutions can be independent of either time or context*. This also applies to organizational structures. To the extent that this is true, there is not—and likely may never be—any single form of organizational structure that provides maximum overall effectiveness.[1]

But the structure of an organization not only depends on its environment. The second factor in organizational change is the type of products. **Conway's Law**[2] says:

> Organizations which design systems [...] are constrained to produce designs which are copies of the communication structures of these organizations.[3]

Conway's interesting observation easily leads to the conclusion that an organization must be adapted to the kinds of products that are being produced [Poppendieck 2009:67]. Therefore, a second driver for organizational design is the set of products developed in the business.

The third relevant factor contributing to organizational structure is the size of the organization. While an organization grows, it regularly needs restructuring to accommodate for its new size, even when environment and product types remain unchanged.

> As a rule, every time a company grows by 50 percent, you should evaluate whether organizational changes are required, and by the time growth reaches 100 percent, you should already have made changes to accommodate that growth.[4]

---

1   This text was published in Organizational Survival in the New World, Alex Bennet and David Bennet, page 9, Copyright Elsevier, 2004. Used with permission. [Bennet 2004:9].

2   http://www.mgt30.com/conway/.

3   Reprinted under the Creative Commons License. Please visit http://creativecommons.org/.

4   © 2009 by Louis Testa and No Starch Press, San Francisco, CA, page 54. Used with permission. [Testa 2009:54].

And finally, the last driver for organizational change is the people. It is no coincidence that new managers and new teams, even when all else remains constant, often result in a restructuring of an organization. Different people need different structures to work with.

Changes in the environment, changes in product types, changes in company size, and changes in people, all lead to (or *should* lead to) changes to the organization's structure. A business that does not change with the times creates its own bubble of reality in which a lot of effort is wasted on stuff that has no value to anyone. A famous example of this phenomenon is **Parkinson's Law**, which says that "work expands so as to fill the time available for its completion." When existing structures in an organization are not abandoned, they will just keep inventing new work simply because they have the capacity available for it.

The people with whom I've worked know that I don't mind regular changes to teams and departments. It's not that things must change for the sake of change. But neither do I think that a structure is better off unchanged for the sake of stability. And when I leave an organization for another job, it doesn't bother me (that much) when my legacy is overhauled again by my successor. Times change with new competitors, new products, new employees, and new managers. I would be worried if a business *stopped* responding to such changes.

I don't believe managers need an overview of best organizational diagrams. What they need is advice on how to achieve adaptability. Species are all different, but they have one thing in common: The principles of adaptability are built into their DNA. That is what we're looking for. We want to know how to have an adaptable business so that it is easier to let an organization morph into different structures depending on context, products, size, and people.

When researching a number of books covering business structures, I noticed that many of them have a description of the "standard" hierarchical functional organization and then go on to describe "alternative" structures that are supposed to be better [Augustine 2005]. Or they describe different organizational archetypes or "forms," where the forms emerge as a result of their environments [Mintzberg 2009:106]. I will attempt a different approach. I will focus on a number of guidelines for adaptable organizations, and you can use these guidelines to grow your own organizational structures.

I believe that, similar to the forms of species, there are a few basic successful patterns with a large number of variations. None of them are intrinsically "better" than any of the others. The starfish is not better than the spider. Though, I must admit, a poodle is better than a Chihuahua.

Consider Specialization First...

Suppose you are the publisher of a magazine about cooking. It's a glossy magazine with recipes, restaurant reviews, and lots of pictures of expensive cutlery and celebrities tasting trendy oysters. The magazine is released every month, and you have a huge list of recipes and restaurants, and celebrities waiting to make their appearance in one of the upcoming editions. Getting a new edition out the door is always a stressful experience. The celebrities can never commit to any culinary photo shoot. The chefs always complain about the way their dishes are depicted. And some of the recipes are so bad, you wouldn't even want to cook them for your neighbor's dog.

Now the editor walks up to you and tells you he has the solution to all problems. It is called generalization. It's really simple and very effective, he says. The different roles of all people working on the magazine will be turned into one generic role called "team member." There are no real specialists anymore, as everyone on the team is allowed to do any of the jobs needed to get a new edition of the magazine out of the door. The writers are allowed to do the photo shoots, whenever they happen to be in the vicinity of a celebrity. Any chef, with at least one working finger left, is allowed to type restaurant reviews. And if the photographers are finished with their work, they can help out writing and cooking recipes. With such a team of generalists, explains the editor, making a new edition of the magazine will be much less stressful (see Figure 13.1). So...what do you say?

This is what I would say, "Are you completely mad?" If I'm on an operation table having my eyelids corrected, would I want the nurse to take over when the surgeon is having trouble keeping up with his schedule? Would I say, "Yes, thank you nurse, and why don't you remove my tonsils while you're at it?"

I believe generalization is a fine idea. But specialization is your *first* friend. Research has confirmed that teams of specialists are more productive than teams of generalists [Anderson 2004:271]. Building teams of only generalists ignores everything society has learned in the last 235 years, ever since Adam Smith pointed out that specialization leads to higher productivity and prosperity. Specialization is the reason why software developers do not bake their own bread, fix their own clothes, or grow their own food, a few exceptions notwithstanding. The larger an economy or organization is, the more people will want to (and be able to) specialize in what they are good at. It is a mechanism that has proven to work well, not only for individuals but also for the whole world.

FIGURE 13.1
From specialist to generalist?

...And Generalization Second

On the other hand....

Specialization does have its problems. It can lead to bottlenecks when specialists cannot cope with demand and others cannot take over for them. After all, I once *did* design a corporate web site myself, including interaction design *and* graphics design because our regular designers were unavailable for weeks. And it can lead to stagnation when the specialists are unable (or unwilling) to pick up work that they are unfamiliar with. For example, I once *did* ask a software developer to help me carry out some marketing activities I could not have done on my own. Our marketing efforts would have stalled if he had not willingly co-operated.

I have no use of people telling me they have a "broad range of skills," meaning that they never specialized in any specific area. I clearly prefer specialists over generalists. But I like it even better when the specialists have a few extra areas in which they have built up some knowledge and expertise. Fortunately, I'm not alone in that opinion.

> A generalizing specialist is someone who: 1) Has one or more technical specialties […]. 2) Has at least a general knowledge of software development. 3) Has at least a general knowledge of the business domain in which they work. 4) Actively seeks to gain new skills in both their existing specialties as well as in other areas, including both technical and domain areas.[5]

A **generalizing specialist** does one kind of job very well and some other jobs adequately. With generalizing specialists your teams enjoy the benefits of high productivity, while lowering the risk of bottlenecks and retaining flexibility. Generalizing specialists are sometimes called **T-shaped people**. They have a principal skill that is the vertical leg of the T, but they are also inquisitive and interested in branching out into other skills. Such people are valuable because they can explore insights from multiple perspectives. [Brown 2005]

When hiring people and putting together teams, look for T-shaped people. Always check if they are specialists in at least one useful area, and then verify that they are willing and able to pick up other kinds of work as well. If you're looking for a software developer, make sure it's a good one. But also ask some questions about graphics, design, hardware, and maybe even marketing.

AND SPECIALIZING GENERALISTS? DO THEY EXIST?

They certainly do. They are people who do many jobs reasonably well but have a tendency to do one or two jobs significantly better. They are very much like generalizing specialists but still less of a specialist and more of a generalist. I would consider them almost as valuable as generalizing specialists.

---

5 Ambler, Scott "Generalizing Specialists: Improving Your IT Career Skills" http://www.mgt30.com/specialists/. Agile Modeling. Reprinted by permission of Scott Ambler. [Ambler 2010].

Widen People's Job Titles

In my job as chief information officer, I sometimes clashed with HR people over the chaotic growth of job titles in some parts of the organization. For business units as small as 10 people, I saw never-ending streams of job titles flying by, like Content Developer, Content Manager, Web Editor, Web Designer, Interaction Designer, Front-end Designer, Front-end Developer, Web Manager, and Front-end Manager. I'm sure Interaction Developer had slipped in there somewhere as well. What was the use of all these different titles? I have no idea. And neither did the ones involved. I repeatedly told people that having fewer job titles is better. And all those developers and designers could have been called Esteemed Employee, as far as I'm concerned.

The team I was working on (while I wrote this) had four great people in it. One of them knew all about the API that we were developing. He decided what the interface looked like, how it was deployed, and how it was kept consistent over multiple releases. He was our leader when it came to our programming interfaces. The second person was our youngest team member. But he had proved himself as a promising architect. Our third team member knew all about social media and e-commerce. He was our leader when it came to online marketing and communication strategies. And finally, yours truly played the role of the Product Owner, making decisions about features and priorities, and keeping the others busy so they didn't get bored and started blowing things up.

Each of the members in our team was a leader. We played roles that matched our specialties, but they were not our job titles. We had no titles for Interface Programmers, Software Architects, Marketing Consultants, or Product Owners. In fact, we took over each other's roles whenever the need arose. (And this was a real necessity with me traveling up and down between conferences around the world.)

For improved organizational adaptability, I believe it helps not to lock up responsibilities in job titles. Instead, you need to keep those titles as widely applicable as possible. People's official job titles don't change easily (sometimes only once every few years); therefore, it is wise to decouple job titles from day-to-day responsibilities. For example, the title Software Engineer gives you more freedom in moving responsibilities around than the title Information Analyst. Even when someone asks to be called an Information Analyst, tell her that her contract will say Software Engineer, and that Information Analyst will be her role. For now.

The wide job titles *can* be used as formal boundaries for the informal roles. For example, the job of a Software Engineer can include anything ranging from design, development, and testing, to project management and support [Abran 2004]. Therefore, a Software Engineer in your organization might be allowed to pick up a diverse bunch of roles like Programmer, Tester, Support Engineer, and Business Analyst. But no person with a job title outside the boundary of Software Engineer (like Account Manager or System Administrator) would ever be given such roles.

Flexibility of people is exactly the reason why Scrum calls everyone simply a Team Member. It underlines the requirement that people feel a responsibility to do anything needed to ship their product, no matter their official job titles. Nobody should be able to say, "I won't do that. It's not my job." If releasing a successful product involves cleaning your customer's keyboard, then cleaning keyboards *is* your job. Some organizations even go as far as to have just the title Associate for everyone in the company. It teaches people to be flexible while getting things done.

Note that the idea of widening job titles actively supports the concept of generalizing specialists. People *should* specialize in something, but they must be flexible enough not to claim exclusive job titles in support of their specialization. Such specialist job titles would mean responsibilities get locked into the title and into the person. And that's not what you want in an adaptable organization.

What you want is a small set of job titles and perhaps a few guidelines on which informal roles go with which titles. Any initiatives that tend to increase the number of job titles in the organization, and requests to formalize roles and responsibilities, should be nipped in the bud.

For years, my job title had been CIO, which is a great title because the letters can stand for almost anything. (Depending on the context, the "I" has stood for Information, Ideation, Imagination, Innovation, Inspiration, Insubordination, Interaction, Intimidation, Illustration, and Idolization.) But the things I've specialized in, and the projects I did, often had nothing to do with my title. It was just stuff that had to be done.

Cultivate Informal Leadership

Leaders in a team are sometimes called Leads or Chiefs, like technical leads, project leads, chief programmers, and chief architects. What these people have in common is that they are not the line managers of the others in their teams. Informal leadership is bestowed upon people because of credits earned or commitments made. Or maybe even as a practical joke. It is a responsibility that is completely separate from line management [Testa 2009:53]. When several people take up leadership in different areas, we might call it distributed informal leadership. Informal leadership follows logically from working with generalizing specialists and using wide job titles.

You can actively cultivate informal leadership in your teams by supporting emergent leadership positions, but it is best to refrain from directly assigning such roles yourself. Allow the teams to decide whether they want to appoint Technical Leads, Project Leads, or some other leading role. (Note that many teams tend to flounder when there's no strong leadership inside the team. You may need to push them and help them in solving their own leadership problem.)

None of the roles mentioned would involve a management layer. In fact, that is precisely why informal leadership contributes to the adaptability of an organization. By abstaining from a management layer of Chief Somethings and Lead Whatevers, you make it much easier for the organization to add, move, and delete such responsibilities. Whenever there's a need for a Chief Graphics Designer, she can be appointed on the spot. And when the need fades away, so does the role. Not the person. If the role was a formal job title, the person would have to be kept busy, or she would have been asked to formally change her job, or else she'd have to bet fired for lack of work. All these are unpleasant measures that suck productivity out of the organization.

Generalizing specialists, widening job titles, and informal leadership are different but related concepts (see Figure 13.2). Though they tend to reinforce each other, you can introduce one before introducing the others, which might be necessary when gradually changing a bureaucratic organization to a more adaptable one. But please don't ask me what order would be best in such cases. My experience is mainly with organizations in which people were flexible and passionate enough to swallow them all at once.

FIGURE 13.2

Different but re-
lated concepts.

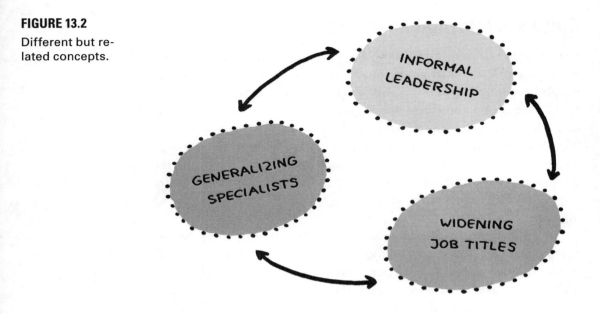

Watch Team Boundaries

In Chapter 12, "Communication on Structure," we saw that people tend
to form groups. And when a group is small enough and has a shared purpose, we may call it a team. The concept of a team is very useful because
it is a way of identifying a number of people as one entity. In psychology
they call that chunking:

> The idea of "chunking": a group of items is perceived as
> a single "chunk". The chunk's boundary is a little like a
> cell membrane or a national border. It establishes a sepa-
> rate identity for the cluster within. According to context,
> one may wish to ignore the chunk's internal structure or
> take it into account.[6]

In my last job, with many small projects and dozens of developers and
testers in multiple locations, team formation was always a challenge. We
changed our team formation approach more often than Madonna changes
her image. But management of team boundaries is an important part of a
manager's responsibilities, and it's important to try and get things right.

---

6 Hofstadter, Douglas. Gödel, Escher, Bach. New York: Basic Books, 1979. [Hofstadter
1979:288].

After all, teams don't operate well when people don't know what the teams are and who they can rely on.

There are three aspects to boundary management: the way teams are structured, how individuals relate to teams, and how teams change over time. Self-selection of teams is possible in organizations in which people have a high level of "empowerment maturity" (see Chapter 7, "How to Empower Teams"). In such an organization you create a pool of potential team members, and then you leave team formation to the group. There might be projects that many people want to be on and projects that nobody wants to do. The great thing is that the group has to find its own rules for team selection, and as a manager you can just enjoy the heated discussions from the sideline. Self-selection of teams is something I have rarely seen in real businesses. It *is* worth considering, but you have to be sure that people understand *how* to form teams. One team of 30 developers and one team of 20 testers might not be a good option. Just consider the example of popular boy bands: Though they *can* have 30 members, in which case we tend to call them boy *choirs*, with such a size they rarely have the agility to keep up with trends in entertainment as much as a small team can. So to increase their chance of success, you might want to define and discuss some constraints on team formation first, concerning size, diversity, and other parameters.

How individuals relate to teams is another constraint you should take into account. Is a person allowed to be a member of more than one team? It is common for people not to perform as well as they could when they are asked to spread their loyalty across multiple teams. Mick Jagger never joined the Jackson Five to complement the Rolling Stones, and for good reasons. Such situations lead to task-switching, conflicts of interests, loss of commitment, and loss of motivation. Try to make sure that every person is dedicated to just one team. People cannot act as a team when they do not know what the team is. They may occasionally assist other teams and help out with other people's projects or perform some duets, but each person should have exactly one base team to return to.

Finally, the time span of a team is also an important issue. Research shows that teams perform much better when they are long-lived. Not just in software development [Larman, Vodde 2009:149/153] but also in other businesses, like airlines [Hackman 2002]. It is best for teams to exist for as long as possible because it takes time for communication paths and rules in a team to grow and pay off. It also takes time for them to learn, as a team, which information is important for them and which is not. Just think of this: What is the best pop group ever? And how long did they stay together? More than a few years? Yes, I thought so. When projects in your organization are by their nature short, try to keep people together in teams with longer life spans, where the same teams work on one project after another.

The Optimal Team Size Is 5 (Maybe)

What is the optimal team size? This is one of the most interesting boundary issues and an important question people have been discussing ever since they teamed up and killed the first mammoth.

I once attended an inspiring conference session hosted by social complexity expert Joseph Pelrine, who told his audience that the sizes 5, 15, and 150 have been mentioned in (or can be derived from) scientific research as being optimal sizes for social groups.

The Agile movement, with Scrum as the leading method at the time of writing of this book, often mentions a preferred team size of "7 plus or minus 2" (which is just a software developer's way of saying "between 5 and 9").

Research into optimal group size for decision making revealed that only numbers below 20 appear to work well [Buchanan 2009:38-39]. Anything from 20 and up can hardly be called a *team*. When the number of people is too large, we should just call it a group. (I'm writing this text secretly while attending sessions at the Scandinavian Developers Conference, which has 600 attendees. That's a group, not a team.)

Buchanan's article makes an exception for team sizes of 8, which do not appear to work very well. That's because eight people frequently find themselves in a deadlock situation over their decisions. It is said that King Charles I, the only British monarch ever to work with a council of eight members, made decisions that were so notoriously bad that he lost his head [Buchanan 2009:39].

Considering these findings, we can easily see that there's only one optimal team size that satisfies all conditions:

Five

Five is one of the three optimal sizes mentioned by Joseph Pelrine. Five also falls within the preferred range of sizes for Scrum teams. Five is less than 20 and yet unequal to 8. Five is also closest to the optimum of 4.6 team members that professor J. Richard Hackman found in his research [Hackman 2002:116-122]. And best of all, 5 happens to be my lucky number. So it must be true.

Five is also my default answer to any question that I cannot answer without more information. You see, I actually cannot tell you what the optimal team size is! Let's revisit Kurt Lewin's equation for a moment (discussed in Chapter 10, "The Craft of Rulemaking"), and you will see why:

$$B = f(P,E)$$

As discussed earlier, this equation means: *a person's behavior is a function of his or her personality and his or her environment.* And because communication is part of a person's behavior, a different version of this equation could look like this:

$$C = f'(P,E)$$

It means *a person's communication is a function of his or her personality and the environment.* And when we're talking about a whole group of people, and realizing that team size is a communication issue, we can rewrite the equation to look like this:

$$S = f''(\{P\},E)$$

This version means *the optimal size of a team is a function of the set of people's personalities and their environment.*

In other words, the value of S can be anything! For the Apollo 11 moon landing, the optimal team size was 3. In rugby, the team size is 15. Apparently, the optimum for team size depends on the project, the people, and their environment. But statistically, across all teams in all businesses, the optimum could be 5, and a few numbers close to 5. And if we want to describe this as a range, we could say "between 3 and 7" (or for software developers, "5 plus or minus 2"), which neatly cuts off the 8 (see Figure 13.3).

FIGURE 13.3

Optimal team size: 5 plus or minus 2.

So, what can we learn from this?

My suggestion is not to *impose* one "preferred" team size on people; although, you might want to add some constraints to team formation. For example, anything upward of 20 is not allowed, with a *suggestion* to have 5 plus/minus 2 members per team. Then allow self-organization to do its job, and let the people (within their real environment) figure out what their optimum is. Do they want to cut a team of 7 into two teams of 3 and 4? Sure, why not? Are they merging two teams into one big team of 15? Fine, let them see if that works for them. Just make them aware that they might want to reconsider things when the environment *or* the set of personalities in the team has changed. One final world of advice: Keep your axe ready in case they come up with a team size of 8 (plus or minus 0).

Functional Teams versus Cross-Functional Teams

Whether team formation is done by the manager or by the teams, one important question needs to be answered, "*How* should people be grouped together?" Basically there are two main options to choose from: group people by *similar function* or by *similar business*.

Grouping people by similar function means that you put developers with developers, testers with testers, and project managers with project managers. Such groups are called functional units, and the driving motivation behind this kind of structure is efficiency and functional learning [Larman, Vodde 2009:243]. It is easiest for writers of user stories to learn how to be efficient user story writers when they're all put together in one department called User Story Writing.

Grouping people by similar business means that you put everyone together who works on the delivery of the same business value (the same feature, the same product, or the same customer). Such groups are sometimes called cross-functional units because all people involved in the same project(s), from user story writers to binary assembly deployers, end up in the same group.

In Chapter 12, "Communication on Structure," we discussed that good communication is both hard and crucial for any organization. It is therefore imperative that we let communication be one of our guiding principles when choosing between the two variants. Which people need each other most often? The ones with the same job titles? Or the ones working on the same project?

If you were to analyze daily communication between employees, it would quickly become clear that most of that communication is oriented around the business and not around the function. People with different functions but working on the same projects need to communicate more frequently than people with the same functions who work on different projects (see Figure 13.4). We can thus conclude that for *projects* cross-functional teams are a more suitable solution to the grouping problem.

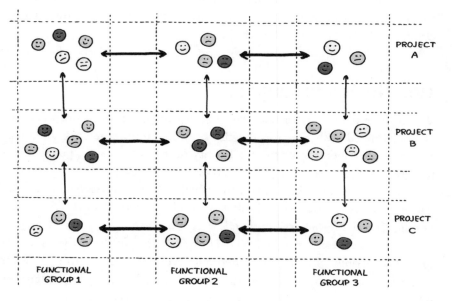

FIGURE 13.4

More communication in projects than within functional groups.

It has been reported that in organizations where people are grouped by function (sometimes referred to as **functional silos**), there are too many dependencies between the functional teams. Delivering even the smallest piece of business value (like one feature of a product) requires communication and coordination across multiple teams [Poppendieck 2009:68]. Functional silos therefore have a high interaction penalty [Augustine 2005:26].

When you build teams *across* the functional silos and not *inside* the silos, the interaction penalty is lower but *not* zero. Donald Reinertsen lists three problems with cross-functional teams: suboptimization at the project level, inefficiencies due to lack of coordination across projects, and reduced expertise because of limited knowledge sharing across specialists [Reinertsen 1997:104]. So it appears that with cross-functional teams the penalty is paid for synchronization of standards, methods, and approaches within one functional discipline across different teams. For example, it will take a quality assurance manager more effort to co-ordinate best practices in testing, when the testers and QA people are spread over multiple teams. But the price being paid here is generally lower than in the case of functional units.

There are several other advantages to cross-functional teams (varyingly referred to as feature teams, project teams, organic teams, or product teams). Several experts report improved design decisions, reduced waste from hand-offs of intermediate products, improved speed, improved adaptability, simplified planning, and focus on delivering value [Cohn 2009:182–188] [Larman 2009:154].

Two Design Principles

When there is more than one team in your organization, things need to be coordinated. Whether it is the choice of logging framework, the location of the refrigerator, or the availability of the demo room, people need to agree on things that are shared across multiple teams.

Psychologist Fred Emery distinguished two basic patterns for coordination of activities across multiple teams. He named them the *first design principle* and the *second design principle*.

In the first design principle (DP1), the location of the fridge is determined by people who are positioned one level above the teams. They are either the line managers of the teams or else a dedicated Fridge Manager who is appointed by the line managers. Either way, the teams have no say in the location of the fridge. Only the Fridge Manager is authorized to decide (see Figure 13.5).

FIGURE 13.5

First design principle: a manager coordinates.

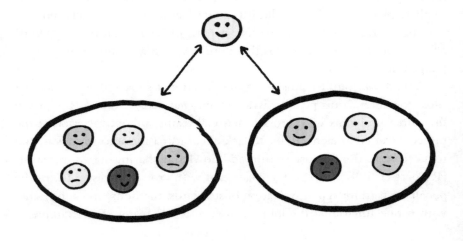

In the second design principle (DP2), regulation of the location of the fridge is built into the teams themselves, meaning that the teams take care of coordination across their boundaries. In practice, this means that teams have to negotiate with each other and agree on some rules, such as voting on the location of the fridge, pricing the availability of the fridge, daily fridge rotation, or fridge roulette. The teams may even agree on their own Fridge Manager and bestow authority on her to make decisions for the teams. With DP2, the authority ultimately lies with the teams, not with the line managers (see Figure 13.6). (And then informal emergent leadership inside the team could become a necessity to prevent a consensus culture with endless discussion.)

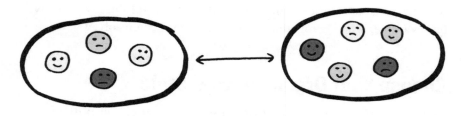

FIGURE 13.6
Second design principle: The teams coordinate.

The second design principle closely resembles the solution that complexity scientist Stuart Kauffman describes as "patches":

> Kauffman says break up the organization into patches, yet emphasizes that these patches must interact. This advice is different from the old management standby of the independent, self-sufficient business unit. It is in the nature and quantity of the interactions that Kauffman finds that the organization as a whole can be moved toward a global optimum, even though each patch is acting selfishly. Interactions require language or some other mechanism of fairly continual communication. He stresses that the patches must be coupled. In management jargon, the pieces must communicate, and not just at quarterly review sessions.[7]

In this analogy, patches are self-organizing teams, not controlled departments. The adaptability of these patches (DP2) compared to hierarchical management (DP1) follows directly from the organic way of problem

---

7 Lissack, Michael R. "Complexity: the Science, its Vocabulary, and its Relation to Organizations" Emergence. Vol. 1, Issue 1, 1999. Used with permission. [Lissack 1999:114].

solving. Every team tries to solve one part of a bigger problem. But because of the couplings between teams, the solution found in one team will change the problem to be solved in adjacent teams. And the adaptive moves of those teams in turn will alter the problems to be solved by other teams. Ultimately, you end up with an ecosystem of teams, or patches, solving a big problem together. [Kauffman 1995:252]

It is clear that the principle of patches (DP2) is the best option for decisions on the choice of logging framework, the location of the refrigerator, the availability of the demo room, or anything else that needs to be coordinated across teams. When some issue needs to be resolved across multiple teams, tell them to coordinate the solution among themselves. DP1 (that's *you* or some other manager making the decision for them) will only be a viable solution when you realize that DP2 doesn't work well. For example, when competence issues have not been resolved yet.

Choose Your Organizational Style

There is a tremendous amount of praise in literature, and in the blogosphere, for cross-functional teams. It sometimes seems as if it is the best idea since cross-personal interaction. And cross-personal interaction *is* a great idea, until you find out you caught some social disease you would rather have avoided.

I am glad that I have little experience with social diseases, but I do know that at least part of the praise for cross-functional teams is undeserved. There are a number of misconceptions because some authors associate functional teams with hierarchies and cross-functional teams with organic networks. But this is both unrealistic and unfair.

Functional teams require coordination across team boundaries about the projects they are doing, and the business value delivered to customers. On the other hand, cross-functional teams require coordination across team boundaries about practices, standardization, and shared resources, for any similar kind of work that is carried out in different teams. So the question is, "*How* is this coordination across teams taking place?"

In the previous section, we saw that you have two options for coordination: DP1 and DP2. Both can be applied to either functional teams or cross-functional teams. These 2x2 options result in four organizational styles, as shown in Table 13.1 and Figure 13.7.

Style	Team Structure	Design Principle	Description
1	Functional	DP1	Coordination between functional teams is performed by managers (typical hierarchical functional silos).
2	Functional	DP2	Coordination between functional teams by the teams themselves (for example, self-organized sysops teams each dedicated to a piece of an infrastructure).
3	Cross-functional	DP1	Coordination between cross-functional teams by a project manager or other authorities above the teams.
4	Cross-functional	DP2	Coordination between cross-functional teams by the teams themselves (for example, a "Scrum of Scrums").

TABLE 13.1

Four organizational styles

In general, cross-functional teams work better than functional teams, and DP2 works better than DP1, and therefore organizational style 4 is the preferred option for many Agile consultants. But, as always, it depends on the context, and you may want to choose one of the two reasonable alternatives (organizational styles 2 or 3), either because team maturity or prevailing communication paths require it, or to facilitate a gradual organizational transition from style 1 to style 4 (see Figure 13.7).

I have known cross-functional teams that were so young and inexperienced (may I even say irresponsible?) that they could have infected half the company with their problems, if management had let them. Fortunately, organizational style 3 saved the day there. And I have known productive specialist teams responsible for components or assets that were too risky to distribute over multiple teams. (Access to other people's bank accounts is one that comes to my mind.) Yet these small specialist teams were mature enough to organize their own cross-team coordination without a manager.

FIGURE 13.7

Quadrant of organizational styles.

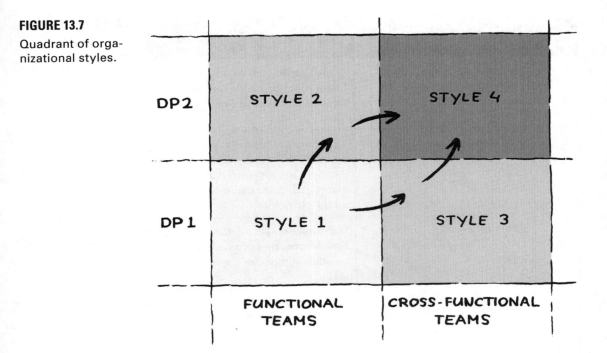

Cross-functional teams without management coordination are a great idea. But they can both solve *and* introduce problems. Good managers need to be smart enough to think of their own best approach to an organizational style that is both adaptable *and* safe.

Turn Each Team into a Little Value Unit

The last team of system administrators I worked with was a great team. I really like them, but I think I was their worst customer. It's not that I was behaving badly. (Well, usually I wasn't.) It's just that my aura has an unpredictable effect on electromagnetic fields. People have seen reliable software crash whenever I passed by, and even the sturdiest operating system has an increased tendency to reboot unexpectedly in my presence. And remember those many times you saw a Fail Whale on Twitter? Yes, that was probably me having logged in before you. That's why I liked my system administrators so much. Because no matter how many problems I generated for them, they always treated me as a customer.

It is often claimed that cross-functional teams solve the problem of local optimization, which happens when functional teams optimize their own efficiency. This hurts the overall performance of the business. For example, a testing team may optimize testing procedures, making sure that all testing for a project is performed in one short period of time. Such an "efficient" practice doesn't take into account the dramatic effect this has on the development and support phases of the projects. But is this really a problem of functional structure? Or is it an example of the testing team not treating the development and support teams as their customers?

The opposite problem is that cross-functional teams tend to optimize for their own projects, which can also hurt the overall performance of the business. For example, there may be problems when different project teams all decide to choose their own architectures and third-party components. This increased variation of technologies makes it difficult for the organization to support all those projects. And I'm sure that when I allowed project teams to purchase their own computers and install their favorite operating systems and development environments, my friendly team of system administrators would have skinned me alive.

But most software developers I have worked with wouldn't dream of inviting system administrators into their cross-functional teams. And that's not because they don't like them. It's because communication within a team of system administrators is usually more intensive than their communication with project teams, even though infrastructure is often an important part of many business solutions. Therefore, it makes more sense to keep these people together in their own functional group, despite the communication penalty paid on any cross-functional communication.

What's important is that every team, both functional *and* cross-functional, should see itself as *delivering value* to a customer, no matter whether that customer is an internal or external one. Our team of system administrators saw itself as a small business unit that tried to serve its customers, by delivering something valuable. And that's why we liked them. They made the other teams feel important, because to them we *were* important, no matter how often I crashed our systems or brought down our servers. Functional teams *and* cross-functional teams should be run as little value units. Then they are truly fractal teams, and there is no limit to the number that can be formed [Leffingwell 2007:96].

Move Stuff out to Separate Teams

The nice thing about not being directly involved with any method, framework, alliance, or consortium, is that I can be a heretic and say anything I want. The worst thing that can happen to me is that I'm being flamed and grilled when I'm on a conference panel. That is why I have fire-resistant gel in my hair. But I've noticed there's a market for contrary ideas. And as a firm believer in markets, I love exploiting opportunities of dissent whenever I can. Like in this case.

I believe it is *sometimes* better to move specialist work to (functional) specialist teams. This could be necessary for project management, architectural components, user interface design, hardware design, testing, or any other work that deviates significantly from standard activities in a project team. This goes against "accepted" thinking in the Agile community because many strong voices suggest that all work, from story to binary, should better be done by cross-functional project teams, including coordination of efforts across multiple teams. The Scrum of Scrums is a good example. It says that each team sends a person to a daily Scrum of Scrums meeting, and these people then coordinate the work across the teams. Such suggestions have been made for Scrum Masters, technical leads, user interface designers, and lead testers.

But I believe it is simply a matter of balancing communication. If it turns out that user interface designers need each other more often than they need the team members working on delivering business value to customers, then it is right for them to sit together and form their own team. Likewise, project dynamics in a company may be so intense or complex that project leads of different teams require intense collaboration. Then it might be better for them to get together and form their own team. Perhaps even a Project Management Office.

BUT...five things are important here:

- First, when some responsibility, like project management, architecture, or GUI design, is moved outside the project teams, every (cross-functional) project team needs a communication interface to the (functional) team that is formed around the specialist activity [Leffingwell 2007:108]. One can think of regular attendance of the specialists in the project teams' stand-up meetings and/or some designated representative from the project teams in the specialist team. Plenty of options are available and should be applied to address the issue of the bandwidth of communication between the project teams and the specialist team.

- Second, the people who are moved into a specialist team must see themselves as value units, just like system administrators are *servicing* project teams, not *controlling* them. Specialist teams should consider project teams to be their "customers," not their subordinates, and organize their processes accordingly. They sell their services to their colleagues in the other teams, just like I'm trying to sell my dissenting views to you. (I'm glad you invested in this book *before* you got this far.)

- Third, the project teams should decide whether the specialist team is actually delivering any value. Such a market approach would counterbalance the tendency for support units to suboptimize at their own level. For example, in my last position I could choose to go to our unit of expert interaction designers, or I could choose to do interaction design myself. It all depended on how well (and how soon) our interaction design unit was able to service me and my project. (And note: I have developed some skills in dissent *and* design.)

- Fourth, we know that the total amount of communication in a complex system remains (more or less) the same, no matter how the system reorganizes itself. Therefore the teams and their managers will figure out how many points of contact with other teams they can handle. Both too little and too much is bad for the adaptability of the organization.

- Fifth, a team of specialists can be virtual instead of physical. It can be just a matter of getting all user interaction designers together once in a while, and allowing them to agree on common standards and approaches across the cross-functional teams where they actually do their work. Such virtual teams are called **communities of practice**, and they are a good compromise, bridging the need for cross-functional teams *and* the need for coordination among specialists [Augustine 2005:71–73] [Larman, Vodde 2009:252/253]. (Note: Some organizations have **centers of excellence** with a similar purpose; although these COE tend to be a bit more formal in nature.)

It is possible, and perhaps even preferred, that the formation of specialist teams is a result of self-organization. Specialist teams form themselves organically in an attempt to solve a problem that is shared across multiple teams. For example, a continuous integration (CI) team forms itself as a spin-off in an attempt to provide a more professional CI service to the other teams. Team members from the various project teams then have a choice of full-time, part-time, and/or rotating membership [Highsmith 2009:272/280]. Another example is that of a component team, which designs, builds, and delivers an architectural part of a solution to the project teams, whereas the project teams together act as customers to the component team [Cohn 2009:185]. The primary reason for the formation of specialist teams is efficiency and effectiveness (productivity through division of labor).

We can even imagine that these specialist units grow and form their own little hierarchies. They may even have a number of rules that apply to project teams *if* these teams decide to make use of their services. But like in any market environment, the specialist teams (and their rules and hierarchies) can and should be dissolved as soon as the need for them evaporates.

In each of these examples it is clear that the project teams are consuming and the specialist teams are providing (see Figure 13.8). And so it should be the same with a project management office (PMO), *if* it exists. A PMO is in the business of *servicing* project teams in getting projects organized. Project managers, like user interface designers, architects, and system administrators, are *not* line managers. And nobody should ever be expected to "report to" the PMO. Instead, the PMO should respectfully *ask* the teams for information and *deliver* something that the teams and their customers can actually use.

FIGURE 13.8

Project teams serviced by specialist teams.

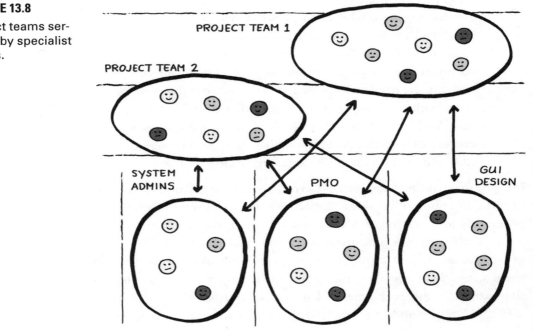

WHAT IF THE PMO SERVES TOP MANAGEMENT?

That would not be consistent with the picture painted here. The PMO cannot see both the project teams and the management team as their customers. This would lead to a conflict of interest, and usually the project teams get to draw the shortest straw.

I am convinced that project *teams*, not project *managers*, should be held accountable for the results of a project. This requires that top management should work with teams, not with a PMO, either directly or through line management. The PMO, like System Administration and Human Resources, is there to help and coordinate—not to control.

Move Stuff up to Separate Layers

Management hierarchies are like taxi drivers. They are both necessary and evil. Necessary because there needs to be some traceable line of authority between employees and the owners of an organization. And evil because hierarchies are too easily abused, in which case they have terrible effects on information flow. This follows (theoretically) from Emery's first design principle and (practically) from empirical evidence. An example of the latter is found in Malcolm Gladwell's book *Outliers*, in which he described that there is a strong correlation between plane crashes and hierarchical cultures (because of bad communication in cockpits) [Gladwell 2008]. But that doesn't mean that there should be *no* hierarchies. If hierarchies were all bad, we wouldn't find them all around us in nature, as indicated by the **Hierarchy Principle**:

> Complex natural phenomena are organized in hierarchies wherein each level is made up of several integrated systems.[8]

The question is then how to use the benefits of a hierarchy without allowing it to work against us. To me the chain of authority seems to be a valid reason for the existence of a management hierarchy. The owners of

---

8   Skyttner, L. General systems theory: Ideas and applications, River Edge, NJ: World Scientific. 2001. Used with permission. [Skyttner 2001:93].

an organization hire someone to run their business, and this person hires some other people to delegate part of that work to, and so on. This is a hierarchy. There's no denying it. It is a tree-like structure to facilitate the flow and division of authority.

> The purpose of organization is to reduce the amount of communication and coordination necessary; hence organization is a radical attack on the communication problems.... A tree organization really arises as a structure of authority and responsibility. The principle that no man can serve two masters dictates that the authority structure be tree-like. But the communication structure is not so restricted, and the tree is a barely possible approximation to the communication structure, which is a network.[9]

What we need is a happy marriage of the formal hierarchical structure with the informal network structure [Augustine 2005:48]. Management must acknowledge that information flows through the network and not through the hierarchy. This is not something to be blocked or controlled. Instead it must be nurtured. The hierarchy is needed for authorization; the network is needed for communication (see Figure 13.9).

FIGURE 13.9

Both network (for communication) and hierarchy (for authorization).

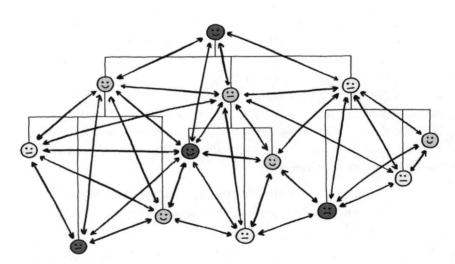

---

9   Brooks, Frederick. The Mythical Man-Month. Reading: Addison-Wesley Pub. Co, 1975/1995. Used with permission. [Brooks 1995:78–79].

Organizational psychologist Elliott Jaques, creator of Requisite Organization Theory, discusses in his works that hierarchies do have a function; although, they are usually badly designed [Jaques 1998]. One important requirement for each management layer is that it must add value to the organizational structure. Just like natural hierarchical layers have new emergent properties at each higher level that did not exist at the lower layers, so must each managerial layer in an organization take care of stuff that the lower levels don't normally concern themselves with.

For example, Jaques describes that each higher level could deal with a different organizational time span [Jaques 1990]. The lowest level deals with all issues that take between 1 day and 3 months to solve; the second level has a time horizon of 3 to 12 months; the third level has work spanning 1 to 3 years, and so on. A project team (usually) has no time to wonder what needs to be done for a business to be successful in 5 years' time. And there are other examples, too, such as hiring people, forging strategic alliances, and balancing budgets, all of which are things that project teams are unlikely to address by themselves. However, it must be noted that management experts don't agree on this matter. Some have noted that even CEOs tend to busy themselves with day-to-day concerns [Mintzberg 2005:110].

I think the real lesson here is that there needs to be *some* separation of concerns between management layers, regardless of whether this separation is by nature temporal, spatial, or anything else. Jaques has shown that organizational problems are often the result of different management layers not clearly adding value. The requirement of adding value is a great starting point when making decisions on management layers. Whenever someone suggests adding a new management layer, ask yourself the question, "What is this layer going to solve that the lower or higher layers cannot do themselves?" If you cannot clearly answer this question, then *don't* add the managers!

How Many Managers Does It Take to Change an Organization?

A trendy thing to say is that having fewer managers is "better" and organizations should be "as flat as possible." True. We all know that. We read it all the time. But the first question people then come up with is, "How many managers should there be?" And the documented answers I could find range from one for every team [Testa 2009:52] to one for every 100 employees [Larman 2009:241].

But I think the question is a wrong one. The ratio of managers to subordinates in an organization is not some constant you can define. Instead, this ratio is the *outcome* of the measures that managers take when growing the structure of their organization. How many teams are cross-functional and how many are functional? Where is the first design principle applied and in which cases the second? And how free are employees in choosing the teams they want to work for and work with? It is managers who make these decisions. And it is managers who bear the consequences.

> It is a fantasy—a tempting and pervasive one, but a fantasy nonetheless—that it is possible to have great teams without the bother of creating enabling team structures. We hope that markets will make hierarchies unnecessary. That we can have networks rather than organizations. That boundaryless social systems can accomplish work efficiently and effectively. And, when some kind of structure actually is needed, that self-organizing processes of the kind celebrated by complexity theory will create them automatically.[10]

The first concern for managers is growing the best team structures. It makes no sense to discuss the best ratio of managers to subordinates in an organization. But it does make sense to discuss the best rationale for organizational design. The ratio will simply follow the rationale.

Create a Hybrid Organization

The mixing of project teams with specialist teams, and hierarchies with networks, can be called a **hybrid organization**. It is said that hybrid organizations avoid the disadvantages of both functional teams in a purely hierarchical environment and autonomous project teams in a purely networked environment. Companies with less rigid cultures, many projects, and the need for speed, typically arrive at hybrid solutions [Testa 2009:370] [Reinertsen 1997:106].

Some forms of hybrid organizations are called **matrix organizations**. But although I've used that name in the past, I prefer not to use it

---

10 Hackman, J. Leading Teams. Boston: Harvard Business School Press, 2002. Used with permission. [Hackman 2002:130].

anymore. In the available literature on this topic, the term matrix organization for many people seems to imply two organizational "dimensions": line management and project management. Some authors describe the "problems" of matrix organizations, which are conflicts of authority between line managers and project managers, the question of who is the real boss, nasty political situations, and a perceived overhead in the number of managers. [Jones 2001]

Some authors report problems with morale in matrix organizations. If the project manager is in control, the line manager feels demoralized for having responsibility but no control. And it is the same the other way around, with "strong" line managers and "weak" project managers. But I believe all that is just a big misunderstanding. One shouldn't blame the chainsaw for holding it at the wrong end.

The reported problems with matrix organizations are a result of incorrectly implementing hybrid organizations. In a proper implementation, there is *one and only one* line of authority, and it flows through the hierarchy of line managers. Project managers are there to *serve* the teams, not to control them. Project managers are there to manage *projects*, not *people*. I am convinced that the position of project managers should be no different than that of software architects and QA managers, who all have their own responsibilities. By the way, this also makes it clear that there are usually more than two "dimensions" in a hybrid organization. Only one line goes up (through line management), but many lines go sideways.

The Anarchy Is Dead, Long Live the Panarchy

Big projects have a higher chance of failure than small projects, primarily for sociological and communicative reasons [DeMarco, Lister 1999:4]. Some sources even claim that the odds of successful completion of a project disappear almost completely with large-scale projects [Yourdon 2004:4].

But I'm an anarchist and an optimist. I believe we *can* solve these problems by breaking things down and then blowing them up—figuratively speaking, of course.

Agilists and anarchists break up big projects into small projects, and they break up large organizations into small organizations. Then they blow things up by scaling the small working parts to similar-looking big working parts [Highsmith 2009:272]. An Agile organization is the inverse of bureaucracy through top-down planning. It is adaptability through bottom-up growth.

With the rise of global markets, the Internet, social networks, and other network-like developments, there is a global trend that looks similar to the emergence of Agile organizations. On a transnational scale, such a network is called a **panarchy**.[11] I love the word because it is just one letter removed from my natural state of mind.

> The emerging **complexity** of our social and political structures, composed of many interacting agents, combined with the increasing importance of **network forms of organization**, enabled by technologies that increase **connectivity**, propels the world system towards a transformation that culminates in a global political environment that is made up of a diversity of spheres of governance, the whole of which is called **panarchy**. To clarify, global linkages between individuals and groups create transnational networks consisting of shared norms and goals. [...] Panarchy is governance as a complex adaptive system of anarchical networks that relies on diversity and resists hierarchy in order to function and adapt.[12]

A panarchy is a system of overlapping networks of collaboration and authority. As an individual, I subject myself not only (unwillingly) to the authority of my government, but also (willingly) to that of my bank, my Internet and energy providers, Twitter, Facebook, and LinkedIn, sports and game clubs, nonprofit and charity organizations, and foreign governments when I'm traveling abroad. (And other people can add religious organizations to that list.)

There are many sources of authority in the world, and as an individual I choose to subject myself to the rules and norms of any group or organization that I want to participate in. The only one I cannot choose directly is my government. (Unless I pick up my stuff and move somewhere else.)

These days being an anarchist is not what it used to be. I now call myself a panarchist. A panarchist is an anarchist who is acting peacefully. Brian Marick, one of the original signatories of the Agile Manifesto, has similar ideas and calls it *Artisanal Retro-Futurism crossed with Team-Scale Anarcho-Syndicalism*.[13] But I think the word panarchy is easier. And I hope the stickers are cheaper.

---

11 http://www.mgt30.com/panarchy/.
12 Hartzog, Paul B. "Panarchy: Governance in the Network Age" http://www.mgt30.com/network-age/, 2009. Reprinted by permission of Paul B. Hartzog. [Hartzog 2009].
13 http://www.mgt30.com/arxta/.

The rise of global network governance is a process that is to some extent shaped by states, but it is not controlled by them, and it is also shaped by corporations, individuals, non-governmental organizations, and other groups. It is as yet unclear if any one of those entities trumps the others, although realists would claim the state holds the trump card, and Marxists would claim that it is capital that is in the driver's seat. History has shown that ultimately it is the people who are in charge, and the new connective technologies have only increased their power and ability to organize collective action.[14]

We can now understand why true Agile organizations are panarchies. And because they are networks of value units we may also call them "value networks." They have multiple sources of authority within the Agile organization, including those dealing with architecture, GUI design, project management, and infrastructure. Each value unit can subject itself, *willingly*, to the rules and norms of some specialist groups. But they can also form such functional teams themselves or simply decide to do everything inside their own team. There is plenty of freedom to be anarcho-syndicalist or peacefully anarchist. The only choice people usually cannot make themselves is that of line management. Unless they move to another organization.

A value network is an organic approach to organizational design, resulting in a fractal-like structure of small hierarchies that are all superimposed on one another in one big network. And because it favors scaling out over scaling up, there is no end to the growth of a panarchy.

Have No Secrets

Now that you know what your choices are in designing your organization it is time to spend the last few pages of this chapter on the communication flowing through the structure you created.

As I wrote earlier, most problems in software projects are the result of bad communication. For proper communication people need good information, good relationships, and good feedback.

---

14 Hartzog, Paul B. "Panarchy: Governance in the Network Age" http://www.mgt30.com/network-age/, 2009. Reprinted by permission of Paul B. Hartzog. [Hartzog 2009].

In many organizations, people lack good information, which usually results in people *inventing* it themselves. When they don't know how well their project is doing, they will try to guess. When they don't know how other teams are performing, they will make assumptions. When they don't understand what their colleagues contribute to the organization, they will invent their own reasons. And when they don't know anything about their manager's personal life, they will gossip about it.

To prevent such problems, you should make information available and accessible. And in general, *more is better*. Give everyone access to the Internet, all network folders, project information systems, and source control systems. Make books and magazines available, promote your company's intranet, and publish time registration reports, project burn charts, profit and loss figures, and other kinds of corporate information. Withholding information is (in general) a bad thing. Don't just assume that nobody will be interested in something. You may be right, but keeping information to yourself is not a good thing, because people *will* communicate *something*, and it can only mean that *other* (mis)information gets passed around. And opening up not only applies to your information systems. You have to be honest yourself as well because talented people want to hear the truth about themselves and about the organization. [Kaye, Jordan-Evans 2008:204]

I have often tried to make sure that plenty of information is available for everyone. I want people to see who is working on which projects and which features, bugs, and issues are handled by whom, and what the team members' evaluations are of those projects.

In tough economic times, it is particularly important to make everyone understand what the organization's financial performance is. As Jack Stack wrote in *The Great Game of Business*, only when employees care about financial figures, they will think of ways to improve them [Stack 1994].

Some great managers argue that, ultimately, even people's salaries should be made public, including the salary of the manager. After all, if you cannot explain a person's salary to everyone else in the organization, how can you expect people to trust you as a manager?

I think I can agree with that. But I also understand that you cannot change an organization's culture overnight. It would be unwise to start communicating people's secrets when there's no culture of doing so. But you have to start *somewhere*. Jack Stack lists ten "Higher Laws of Business," of which the last is called "Shit rolls downhill." It means that changing an organization begins with changing management.

Well, *someday* I hope to be a great manager. So I have made sure that my personal "secrets" are published throughout this book. Have you spotted them?

Make Everything Visible

I once started following Ashton Kutcher on Twitter. I didn't really think about the decision for long. It was just that Ashton was the first person in the world to have 1,000,000 followers on Twitter. So, except for the looks, there had to be *something* interesting about this guy, right?

Ashton Kutcher was visible. Stories about his race with CNN to be the first with a million followers could be found all over the Internet. For someone like me, reading many social networking blogs, it was very hard *not* to see this. *That's* why I followed Ashton Kutcher.

So, how do you make people follow practices? Easy. Make them *visible!*

Last year, some managers and I introduced "big visible charts" in the form of task boards for every development team. Anybody walking around the office could easily see them. So, when other (nonsoftware development) teams noticed these task boards, they wanted them as well! *They saw and they followed.* And this principle doesn't just work for task boards. *Any* visible process is an **information radiator**.

My last team did its stand-up meetings in our open office space as well. We first considered doing stand-ups in a more secluded area so as not to disturb our colleagues while discussing our project for 15 minutes. But we decided against that. Then it soon turned out that, again, other teams (including nonsoftware development teams) started following the same practice. They saw our teams doing stand-ups every morning, and they decided to try this interesting practice, too.

To see is to follow....

People copy each other's behaviors, sometimes for no other reason than just seeing them. It's a human thing. It's why I started following Ashton Kutcher. And it's why teenagers start smoking. Scientists say humans often mimic each other unintentionally. But this fact can be used intentionally, too. Mimicry has a great potential to be used for influencing interpersonal persuasion and communication. You can use mimicry to your advantage by making sure that good behavior is visible. If you want people to write better code, plaster the best code you have all over your coffee machine. If you want other people to follow Scrum practices, post times and locations for sprint planning and review meetings on your company's public calendars. If you want people to use proper source control and branching techniques, draw the source control tree and its branches on your office walls.

People follow what they see, and you must show that which is good.

And perhaps you should refrain from showing examples of bad behavior in your office. People might (unintentionally) follow them.

Connect People

In his book *Fired Up or Burned Out,* Michael L. Stallard shows us that one of the best ways to achieve organizational excellence is to "connect with people." And in their book *Love 'Em or Lose 'Em,* Beverly Kaye and Sharon Jordan-Evans describe the concept of "creating connections," which they call one of the 26 engagement strategies [Kaye, Jordan-Evans 2008:113-122].

Creating and maintaining meaningful connections with employees (and *between* employees) is not just some fancy way of making managers seem more human. As we saw in Chapter 12, the need for connections is rooted in complexity theory.

Resilience and innovation in an organization are the result of people having good relationships with each other so that information flows freely and undistorted. You have to make sure that people enjoy working together. Remove cubicle walls, have informal meetings, facilitate coffee and smoke breaks, and stimulate that people enjoy each other's company at lunch or dinner.

And try and engage in more meaningful relationships with your employees. It doesn't mean you have to be close friends with everyone. That's not even possible. But simply knowing a little more about their life, their families, their home, and their hobbies (and them knowing some more about yours) would be a great start.

Aim for Adaptability

At the beginning of this chapter, I noted that no single structure is the definitive answer for all organizations. Not cross-functional teams, not matrix organizations, nor whatever. The most important thing to take away is that you need to work on the organizational ability to change. It should be OK for functional teams to morph into cross-functional ones and back. It should be OK for teams to spin off specialist teams, and then break them up again later when they have no need of them anymore. It should be OK for management to try the second design principle in some part of the organization, and then replace it again with DP1 if that didn't work out well. It is only natural that complex adaptive systems constantly revise and rearrange their building blocks as they gain experience. In organizations it is no different [Waldrop 1992:146].

Organizational adaptability calls for a minimum specification of organization. The less that is defined and frozen into formal charts, contracts, and procedures the better.

> Applying a "barely sufficient" principle to your team's organizational design will afford it the flexibility and freedom to self-organize. At times, some managers have tended to go overboard in attempts to comprehensively define organizational elements such as roles, responsibilities, policies, and procedures. Instead, a holographic structure limits design to just the critical minimum specifications.[15]

You know you have achieved organizational adaptability when employees stop complaining about reorganizations and start suggesting new structural changes. Then you can simply enjoy watching the organization grow, and you will have achieved the purpose of the fifth view of Management 3.0.

Summary

Because of changes in the environment, organizational size, products, and people, it is important to change organizational structure regularly. Implementing the concepts of generalizing specialists, wide job titles, and informal leadership greatly improves organizational adaptability.

Team boundaries need to be watched carefully because people cannot identify with a team if team membership is unclear or unstable. Various research studies seem to indicate that between three to seven people is a good team size.

Teams can be organized as either functional or cross-functional units, with the latter being the most obvious choice for optimal communication,

---

15 Augustine, Sanjiv. *Managing Agile Projects*. Upper Saddle River: Prentice Hall Professional Technical Reference, 2005. Used with permission. [Augustine 2005:58].

though exceptions may exist. Communication between teams happens either via managers or primarily via the teams themselves. Again, the latter is usually preferred.

Organizational structure is most adaptable when teams work as value units, considering other teams as their customers to whom they must deliver value. New teams can be constructed when there is demand, but they must be dissolved when demand among other teams evaporates. Management layers can be beneficial to an organization provided that they too truly add value.

With authority flowing through teams from different directions, we have what is called a hybrid organization. We may also call this a panarchy or value network, when the organization primarily works as a network, with (optionally) multiple overlapping hierarchies.

Last but not least, for optimal communication it is important that managers have as few secrets as possible, make all information they have visible, and make an honest attempt at connecting with their people.

Reflection and Action

Let's see if you can apply some ideas from this chapter to your organization:

- Consider the people in your team. Are they generalizing specialists (or specializing generalists)? If not, what will you do about that?

- Review the official job titles in your organization. Are they wide enough to cover different roles? If not, come up with a plan to change them and make them wider.

- Consider leadership in your team. Are there informal leaders among the team members? Are these leadership roles dynamic enough so that they can change easily when needed?

- Review how teams are constructed in your organization. Are the teams small enough so that people can feel they are really part of a team? Does team membership last long enough for rules and leadership to emerge? Are the teams cross-functional?

- Review the quadrant of organizational styles. Which style are you using now in your organization? If it's not the fourth style, do you have a plan for getting there?

- Discuss value with your team. Does the team see itself as a value-delivering unit? Do they feel that other teams also consider themselves as value units? If not, can you do something about that?

- Review the management positions in your organization. Are all of them adding real value? If not, can you address or influence this issue?

- Draw the organizational structure of your business. Does it look like a hierarchy or like a value network?

- Check your own social skills. Are you connecting with people regularly? If not, how will you change that?

Chapter **14**

The Landscape of Change

What we call "progress" is the exchange of one nuisance for another nuisance.

—Henry Havelock Ellis, sexologist, physician (1859–1939)

My partner and I have camped in Sweden for a week. And we've noticed that, even with a big Volvo full of camping gear, food, clothes, and toiletries, "surviving" in the wild, and adapting to new environments, is a challenge.

The sixth view of the Management 3.0 model is called *Improve Everything*, meaning that the topic of this chapter and the next is **improvement**. And like the north of Sweden, this topic is the beginning of the end. In this chapter, we review concepts involving the survival of systems in changing environments, and then we move on to some practical implications in the next chapter, and my conclusions in the last.

So, let's pick up our hiking gear and start climbing this final mountain!

The Environment Is Not "Out There"

It is said that there are billions of mosquitoes in the north of Sweden. But I don't think this is true. I believe there are actually only 1,217 specimens. But they have unimaginable powers of smell and flying.

I am convinced of this because no matter where you go in Sweden, you will *not* see any mosquitoes *until* you get out of your car to expose the delicious scent of your bare skin to the air. And then they come. From all over Sweden. Within a few minutes all 1,217 mosquitoes will have arrived to buzz all over you, trying to get to those bare patches of skin that they sensed from the other side of the country. The Swedish mosquitoes have developed supersonic flight because there are virtually no humans living in the northern part of Sweden. I'm sure it is impossible for billions of mosquitoes to survive there. There are only enough humans to feed 1,217 of them. And I fed them all in five days.

Wherever I went in the wild north of Sweden, I always saw a dense cloud of mosquitoes *because I was there*. The introduction of me into the environment *changed* the environment. And if *I* wasn't there, then neither were the mosquitoes. In other words:

> The introduction of a system into an environment *changes* the environment.

I put this on a separate line because I believe this is one of the most important concepts in complexity science. *The environment that a system experiences, is not the same environment that would exist if the system wasn't there.* This is the primary reason that it is hard to "plan" for the introduction of something new based on the current state of an environment. The introduction itself will *change* that environment, possibly rendering the whole plan useless.

> Acting should precede planning because by acting we take part in constructing the environment. The environment is not "out there," separate from us. We can help to create the environment. [...] The Spanish have a phrase which nicely captures this connotation: *"Compañero, no hay camino. Se hace camino al andar."* A suitable translation is: "My friend, there is no road. You make the road as you walk."[1]

The environment "out there" without your software product is different from the one that will exist after your product is introduced. The users of your product will change their working habits when they start using it. They will come up with change requests and unforeseen requirements. Other products will exchange value with yours, possibly forming alliances, or even symbionts.[2] Parasites will rush in and try to bleed it. Competing products will adapt their strategies and try to squash it. And I might try to blow it up. Not intentionally, of course.

It is impossible to fully "plan" a software development method (in the sense of using some project "typology" with corresponding "best-matching" models). We first have to experience how the environment responds to a new system before knowing how to operate in it.

---

1   Dent, Eric B. "Complexity Science: a Worldview Shift" Emergence. Vol. 1, Issue 4, 1999. Used with permission. [Dent 1999:13].
2   http://www.mgt30.com/symbiosis/.

The environment decides how to deal with an intruder. And that is why any software development approach needs to take into account the *real* actual environment. By experiencing it. And feeding back the lessons learned into the project.

> It is thus seen that a project cannot be viewed independent of its surrounding context as well as its history. Further, an understanding of the context is in itself not sufficient to prescribe a method (as posited by the project typology approach). Rather, the method to manage the project is embedded in the context and one must allow the *emergence* of such a method through interaction between the actors and the environment.[3]

Before our wild adventures in Sweden, my partner and I had bought several liters of insect repellent, shirts with long sleeves, and thick socks. It was the actual experiences of earlier visitors that had prepared us for the dense cloud of 1,217 mosquitoes that travels all over Sweden. Next time, I will bring pants of steel.

The Fear of Uncertainty

Speaking of traveling and planning.... A year earlier, my partner and I went to Cuba, where we unexpectedly visited a famous tobacco plantation. This happened because we had picked up a young hiker who turned out to be one of the workers at the plantation. But we had done so reluctantly, and a bit scared, because travelers are regularly warned *not* to take any hikers for a ride. Two years earlier, my good friend Nadira was robbed of all her personal belongings after picking up hikers in Cuba. It shows that, as a traveler, you have to deal with uncertainty. Picking up hikers can get you either robbed or rewarded. How can you tell the difference in advance?

In *Complexity: A Guided Tour,* Melanie Mitchell explains that two important factors contribute to the crucial role of uncertainty in complex systems [Mitchell 2009:20]. The first is **Heisenberg's Uncertainty Principle.**[4] It states that certain physical properties of elementary particles, like

---

3   Pundir, Ashok K, L. Ganapathy and Narayanasamy Sambandam. "Towards a Complexity Framework for Managing Projects" E:CO. Vol. 9, Issue 4, 2007. Used with permission. [Pundir 2007:22].
4   http://www.mgt30.com/uncertainty/.

position and momentum, cannot be known at the same time. The more precisely one knows a particle's position, the less precisely one knows its momentum, and vice versa. The Uncertainty Principle shows there's a pattern of uncertainty woven into the fabric of reality. This would only have been a mildly interesting statistical oddity, if it weren't for the second factor: the Butterfly Effect.

The **Butterfly Effect**,[5] usually attributed to Edward Lorenz, is a metaphor for the sensitivity of a system to (uncertainty in its) initial conditions. It is said that the flapping of a butterfly's wings in China could, theoretically, cause a thunderstorm in the United States. I've noticed that the metaphor is cited in many books on chaos and complexity theory. And sometimes the butterfly is in China, sometimes in India, sometimes in Brazil. But, strangely enough, the thunderstorms always end up in the United States. It made me wonder if chaos theorists have uncovered a global network of terrorist butterflies trying to aim thunderstorms at the United States. (During our vacation in Cuba, we actually got to experience a hurricane passing over the island. And I could verify that it was indeed heading for Florida. From its trajectory I estimated the butterfly to have been located on the island of Aruba.)

We must accept that our business landscape in the 21st century is as uncertain as it is complex. And it's not getting any easier. However, uncertainty may be natural, but for many people it's not welcome. It is certainty and safety what they hope to see in their future. And attempts at achieving certainty can lead to **decision paralysis** [Heath 2007:34-37]. We don't know what to decide because we are not certain of the outcome. Do we implement a scalable architecture now or later? Should we use Html5 or Flash for our front-end development? Shall we pick up the hiker or not? Will we end up at a cigar factory or at a police station?

When people are *finally* brave enough to make a decision, they often favor risk avoidance over opportunity seeking. They look at uncertainty as something that is more likely to have a negative outcome than a positive one. (Or they estimate the cost of potential problems to be greater than the benefit of positive outcomes.) A good example is the often cited "threat" of non-native species being transported by humans from one ecosystem to another. Many environmentalists are actively trying to address this "threat." But research has shown that only in a few percent of the cases non-native species had a significant and bad effect on existing

---

5 http://www.mgt30.com/butterfly/.

ecosystems [Davis 2009:26]. In most other cases, the effects of "alien" species on native ecosystems were neutral, or even positive. (It is interesting to note that the honeybee is the official symbol of several states in the United States, but it is a non-native species because it was introduced in North America from Europe in the 1600s. Perhaps the bees got there with a thunderstorm.)

Uncertainty is found in the tiniest parts of reality, and the sensitivity of complex systems to uncertainty can have far-reaching consequences. Fear of this uncertainty is common, understandable, and sometimes even necessary. But we should not allow it to turn into fear of change itself.

Laws of Change

The quote "change is the only constant" is attributed to the Greek philosopher Heraclitus.[6] And it is said that only those who "embrace change"—the subtitle of Kent Beck's bestselling book *Extreme Programming* [Beck 2005]—can survive.

Software products must often be adapted to environmental changes. The introduction of the Euro[7] as Europe's official currency in 2002 required businesses throughout the continent to spend millions of French francs, German marks, Italian liras, Spanish pesetas, Austrian schillings, Portuguese escudos, and Dutch guilders on software changes.

Several authors have suggested that successful software products often require *more* maintenance than the unsuccessful ones [Brooks 1995] [Glass 2003]. One reason is that people use their favorite software in innovative ways and unanticipated situations. For example, mobile phones in Africa are used as a banking system, enabling cell phone payments among low income people who don't have a bank account. Another reason is that successful software tends to outlive the hardware and business processes that were considered during its initial creation. For example, many software products were never expected to reach the end of the 20th century, meaning that they had to be fixed because of the Year 2000 problem[8] (often incorrectly called the millennium bug).

Environmental change is so fundamental to software development that it was inevitable that I would find a number of laws about it. And lo

---

6   http://www.mgt30.com/heraclitus/.
7   http://www.mgt30.com/euro/.
8   http://www.mgt30.com/y2k/.

and behold, Professor Meir M. Lehman proposed eight laws of software evolution:[9]

1. **Continuing Change**: A system must be continually adapted or else it becomes progressively less capable of satisfying its users.

2. **Increasing Complexity**: As a system evolves its complexity increases unless work is done to reduce it.

3. **Self-Regulation**: The system evolution process is self-regulating with product and process measures closely following a normal distribution.

4. **Conservation of Organizational Stability**: The average activity rate (maintenance) in an evolving system is invariant over its lifetime.

5. **Conservation of Familiarity**: As a system evolves all people involved with it must maintain mastery of its content and behavior to achieve satisfactory evolution.

6. **Continuing Growth**: The functional content of a system must be continually increased to maintain user satisfaction over its lifetime.

7. **Declining Quality**: The quality of a system will decline unless it is rigorously maintained and adapted to operational environment changes.

8. **Feedback System**: Evolution processes constitute complex feedback systems and must be treated as such to achieve significant improvement over any reasonable base.

I have minor issues with a few of Lehman's laws (and with the third law in particular[10]), but I think the main message is clear and sound: A system that is used undergoes continuing change or else it degrades in effectiveness. And when the system is changed, the changes inevitably increase complexity in the system unless work is done to reduce it.

But perhaps most interesting is Lehman's observation that the effort needed to change and adapt the system is (roughly) constant throughout its lifetime. Again it seems that change is the only constant....

---

9 http://www.mgt30.com/lehman/. Reprinted under the Creative Commons License. Please visit http://creativecommons.org/.

10 I believe most product and process measures follow a power law distribution, not a normal distribution.

Every Product Is a Success…Until It Fails

How do we know if a software product is successful?

Industry reports like the famous (or infamous) CHAOS report of the Standish Group often claim that only a small number of software projects are "successful." But what does that mean? People have been struggling to find a proper definition for years, and they are still not in agreement. One traditional view has it that a product is successful when it is delivered on time, within budget, and according to specifications. Others say that a product is successful when it matches a customer's expectations, generating a return on its investment in the form of business value created. Another view is that a product is successful when all stakeholders are happy.

Do you think dinosaurs were successful? And do you think humans are successful? I suspect that many people would answer "no" to the first question and "yes" to the second. However, dinosaurs ruled the earth for about 160 million years,[11] whereas the family of *hominidae*[12] (all species of great apes) has existed only for six million years—with humans wreaking havoc on the planet's surface for less than 200,000 years.[13] I think humans still need plenty of time to prove that they are more successful than dinosaurs (see Figure 14.1).

FIGURE 14.1

Dinosaurs versus great apes.

And do you think horses are successful? My daughter probably does, but she wouldn't have found the late and great paleontologist Stephen Jay Gould on her side. Several times in his works, Gould pointed out that

---

11 http://www.mgt30.com/dinosaurs/.
12 http://www.mgt30.com/hominidae/.
13 http://www.mgt30.com/human/.

almost all species of wild horses[14] (of the *Equus ferus* family tree) have vanished from the earth [Gould 2002]. Only *Equus ferus caballus* (the domesticated horses) can be considered successful in the sense that they have adapted and allowed *Homo sapiens* to sit on them, which is likely to have prevented their extinction.

I think it is apt to say that every species is a success until it fails and goes extinct. Given the fact that 99.9% of all species are now extinct, failure appears to be in abundance. I therefore prefer the following definition for the success of software products:

> A software product is a success, until it fails.

Yes, I know it sounds silly. But the universe *is* a bit silly at times.

Some products that I have contributed to were a success for only a very short time, until the customers canceled them because they finally figured out what they really wanted. (Which was, of course, something completely different.) Even though these products never made it to their first release dates, team members and customers had been working happily together, but the business case changed and they ran out of budget. I have known other products that were on time, within budget, and according to specifications when, at the time of their first release, it appeared that they could not live up to our customers' expectations. Did they fail? Not really, because we found ways to recover from our errors, adapted to the new feedback, and delivered versions that won back our customers' trust. I've also known products that were still being funded, several years after their first release date, even though they never returned their investment. Apparently they were able to postpone their failure by hanging on to some stakeholders' support. Maybe some stakeholders see value in these products because it gives them something that was never anticipated. Maybe they just enjoy spending cash.

Success is the continued absence of failure. In my opinion, other definitions are insufficient. Products can be of some value to someone, even though they are not on time and within budget; even though they never returned their investment; and even though they may not satisfy all stakeholders. Species are successful until they go extinct. My car is successful until the day it fails to please me. Products are successful until the day they have lost all users. The principles of embracing change and continuous improvement are intended to postpone the inevitable moment of losing the last user. But all software products *will* fail someday. I'm 99.9% sure of that.

---

14 http://www.mgt30.com/horse/.

Success and Fitness: It's All Relative

A product is a success, until it fails. At this time, I consider my car to be a success. The blue lights shining on the pedals, and the sound system pounding on my eardrums, have contributed significantly to this perception. But I'm sure some other cars would have been an even bigger success, possibly with even prettier lights and heavier sound, if only the size of my wallet had matched the size of their price tags. I also know other people would never care for my car. They have other criteria to measure their favorite vehicles against. Some feel happiest when driving a second-hand, pink mini-bus, without a sound system. Some don't even care for blue lights on the pedals.

When discussing the survival of species, biologists sometimes talk of **fitness**. Fitness is a system's ability to exist and to prosper. Like success, fitness is relative. There is no absolute fitness in nature because there is no common scale to measure it against. Fitness depends on the niche a species is filling, the environmental conditions that it has to cope with, and any other species that happen to exist in that same environment. Penguins are a success in the harsh climate of Antarctica. Cows are a success in the context of the farm.

The fitness of a species is determined not by its good legs, eyes, wings, fins, or udders, but by its ability to meet the requirements of its environment. And the fitness of a product is determined not by its ability to operate as intended, but by its ability to consume people's time and/or money, in a certain context, transforming it into some kind of value for some stakeholders. Just like the fitness of my car is not determined by its ability to drive well, but by its ability to please *me*. There's a difference.

How to Embrace Change

I spent a number of pages explaining that uncertainty is expected and that we need to embrace change. Perhaps I've bored you to tears, and perhaps you're now more eager to embrace sleep instead. So let's try and wake you up by discussing the *how* behind uncertainty. *How* must we deal with an uncertain environment? *How* should we manage this continuous change? Sadly, there is no single recipe. Change management is highly situational and depends both on the environment and the organization [Bennet 2004:10].

Nevertheless, many people assume that change can be harnessed by implementing *processes*. This has led to the concept of continuous *process improvement*, which is what we find at the core of many models and frameworks.

But I believe a focus on process is a too narrow approach to managing change. We need continuous *business* improvement, not just process improvement. From a complexity perspective uncertainty cannot be dealt with by (only) implementing processes. Uncertainty applies to the whole system *including* the execution of any processes. But how can one improve a system in which everything is unpredictable, including the processes?

> Complex problems are those that behave unpredictably. Not only are these problems unpredictable, but even the ways in which they will prove unpredictable are impossible to predict.[15]

The answer is in critically considering the whole system and not just processes. In Chapter 11, "How to Develop Competence," we discussed seven dimensions of software projects: functionality, quality, tools, people, schedule, process, and business value. I am convinced that *all seven dimensions* must be candidates for improvement when operating in a changing environment. Change management is not just achieved with process improvement. You also need continuous attention to functionality, quality, tools, people, schedule, and business value.

Managing change requires that one can reinvent oneself. Changing only processes (or only functionalities, like some development methods do) is like limping with a crutch under one arm and the other tied to a rock.

Adaptation, Exploration, Anticipation

The business unit I was leading at the time of writing was a fine example of a system trying to survive. As a young startup business, our prime objective was to find paying customers. We anticipated in which places we could find them, and we adapted when it turned out they weren't there. (Regrettably, the second often followed the first. For many startup

---

15 Schwaber, Ken. Agile Project Management with Scrum. Redmond: Microsoft Press, 2004. Used with permission. [Schwaber 2004:2].

businesses survival is a long process of learning what doesn't work.) And sometimes we simply experimented, not knowing whether the results would be good or bad, only to learn what worked and what didn't.

In most Agile methods, this learning takes place in the form of increments and reflections, both of which are done iteratively. An increment is a new release of a product into its intended environment, and its main purpose is to invite feedback that enables learning, adaptation (looking backward) and exploration (trying things out), while reducing the need for anticipation (looking forward) to a manageable level. The released product influences the environment, and the environment then responds to it in some (possibly unexpected) ways. The knowledge gained is used to adapt, to anticipate what will be needed in the next release, or to continue exploring when we still don't know.

Reflections (often called retrospectives) are used to understand whether the project is operating in the right way and how to improve parts of it to be more successful. The last team I worked on delivered many increments of our tools, some of which were successful, and some of which failed miserably. And we had plenty of reflections on how we ran our business, some of which were rather painful, and some of which hurt like hell.

Increments and reflections are an example of **double-loop learning**,[16] a concept proposed by business theorists Chris Argyris and Donald Schön. An often cited example of double-loop learning is the simple thermostat combined with a human operator (which I will repeat here, for lack of inspiration). The thermostat adjusts itself frequently based on the information about room temperatures that it gets from the environment (the first loop, *using* a model of the environment). But the thermostat is operated by a human being who modifies its settings based on her earlier experiences with comfortable temperatures *and* anticipated changes such as holidays or weather forecasts (the second loop, *refining* the model of the environment) [Augustine 2005:170].

I think that continuous improvement in a business environment takes place in two loops, and involves adaptation, exploration, and anticipation (see Figure 14.2).

---

16 http://www.mgt30.com/learning/.

FIGURE 14.2

Double-loop learning versus improvement.

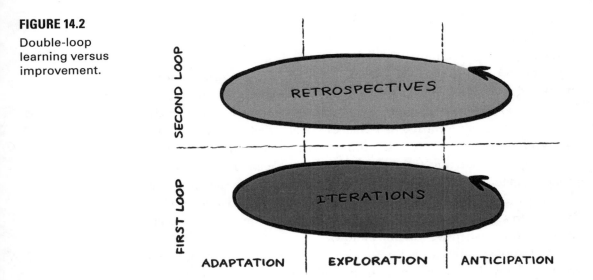

Though adaptation is often mentioned as a key component in Agile software development, we shouldn't forget the role of exploration and anticipation in our businesses. We not only need to solve problems. We also must try new things just to see what happens and innovate by developing solutions to issues that we *think* will be important (in the next release, or shortly thereafter).

> We expect uncertainty and manage for it through iterations, anticipation, and adaptation (Declaration of Interdependence).

DOESN'T ANTICIPATION VIOLATE AGILE?

Anticipation is like alcohol. It is healthy when used in a small dose. But it is addictive, and most people use far too much of it.

Agile software development does not reject anticipation. But it tries to reduce it to the smallest possible amount, where it is still beneficial instead of harmful.

In my former little startup business, we did plenty of adaptation, exploration, *and* anticipation. Frankly, I did so much double-loop learning with my team that my brain thought it was on a roller coaster. But one question that sometimes came was, "Are we really improving at all? Or are we just keeping up with the rest of the world?"

The Red Queen's Race

Despite our efforts to improve, it sometimes seems to have no effect whatsoever. Developers are never completely happy with the tools they are using. Users are never fully content with the software we build for them. And team members are never quite satisfied with the processes in their software projects. Why is that? The answer can be found in an old children's book from the 19th century.

Success is the postponement of failure. Scientists have found that the ability of families of species to survive does not improve over geological time. From the fact that the risk of extinction in ecosystems has never dropped, it follows that species have never succeeded in becoming any better at avoiding it. It seems as if the goal of evolving species is not to lower the chance of failure, but to change only when it is really necessary. There are crocodiles, pandas, sharks, sturgeons and horseshoe crabs, often called **living fossils**[17], which have barely changed an eyelash in a million years. Apparently, their environments didn't require them to change. When environments don't change, species don't bother with the effort either.

And when species *do* change, it is usually not because of the weather. Species are linked inextricably with each other, and they need to adapt to each other's changes. For example, plants might evolve tougher surfaces and chemical repellents to fend off hungry insects, while at the same time the insects evolve stronger jaws and chemical resistance mechanisms. Species change to remain in the game. It is like an evolutionary arm's race, which has been given its own colorful name: **The Red Queen's Race**.[18] The term is taken from Lewis Carroll's *Through the Looking-Glass*, where the Red Queen said to Alice (see Figure 14.3):

> It takes all the running you can do, to keep in the same place.

The Red Queen's Race is an evolutionary hypothesis describing that a complex system needs continuous improvement to simply maintain its current fitness, relative to the systems it is co-evolving with. Some scientists claim that the Red Queen's Race, or the principle of co-evolving species, is an even more important driver of evolution than any other kind of environmental changes.

---

17 http://www.mgt30.com/fossil/.
18 http://www.mgt30.com/red-queen.

FIGURE 14.3
Alice and the Red Queen.

The Red Queen's Race explains why most users are never completely satisfied with the software products they use. After all, even though the products get more features with each release, the users keep adding new requirements. This closely parallels Lehman's sixth law, which states that a product must keep growing just to maintain the same level of user satisfaction. It is also reflected in the **Kano quality model**,[19] which says that any product feature viewed as an exciting capability will soon be expected as standard functionality.

Many software products do not evolve to become better at what they do. They evolve to postpone the (inevitable) moment that they will be discarded. Success is the postponement of failure. And when environments don't change, software vendors don't bother changing their products either. And why should they? Lack of strong competition is why Microsoft did not release any new versions of *Internet Explorer*, after version 6, for more than five years. One might even argue that the threat of being pushed back by competing products is an even more important driver of software evolution than the new requirements of existing users. A vendor can ignore its users, but it cannot ignore its competition.

---

19 http://www.mgt30.com/kano/.

> Over the coming decades the adaptability of every soci-
> ety, organization, and individual will be tested as never
> before. [...] Hence the most critical question for every
> 21st century company is this: Are we changing as fast as
> the world around us? As we've already seen, the answer
> for many companies is "no."[20]

My current car cost me twice as much as my first one, and it has ten times the number of features. But has it made me any happier? Only for a short while, I'm afraid. The fact that it has just one parking sensor in the rear, and not on any of the other five sides, is a bit of a challenge for me. And the heating in the seats takes way too long to climb to a comfortable temperature. And the brightness of the blue lights on the pedals cannot be adjusted.... Day by day, ever so slowly, my car is falling behind in the Red Queen's Race.

Can We Measure Complexity?

Lehman's sixth law states that software systems must keep growing new features to satisfy their users, and the second law states that complexity will keep increasing unless work is done to reduce it. And I can attest to that. The intranet application that I once built over a period of five years had grown into a semi-conscious entity that even I had trouble under-standing. Is this increased complexity a trend for all complex systems? Is it normal for systems to become more complex over time?

The issue of increasing complexity has been fuel for heated debates among scientists. Some have claimed there is no such thing as an innate drive in systems for increased complexity, whereas others say that life on earth, and human society in particular, are proof of things becoming more complex. And then there's another group that says the whole discus-sion is moot because we don't even know how to *measure* complexity, and thus we cannot say whether one thing is more complex than another.

Let's join the debate at the end: measuring complexity. It is true that there is no single measure of complexity that scientists agree upon. Many metrics have been proposed, from the number of agents and connections to the number of potential states in a system, from the level of entropy to a system's "computational capacity," and from degrees of hierarchy to

---

20 Hamel, Gary. The Future of Management. Boston: Harvard Business School Press, 2007. [Hamel 2007:42].

"fractal dimensions" [Mitchell 2009:94–111]. And, like all features in my intranet application, all metrics have been found wanting.

But lack of a common measure for complexity doesn't mean that we cannot recognize some systems as being more complex than others. Justice Potter Stewart once famously wrote, "I know it when I see it," referring to hardcore pornography, which he found unable to define but didn't have any trouble recognizing. It is the same when comparing a human brain to that of a chicken. Or when comparing my intranet application to the NASA space control center. I don't know how to prove that one is more complex than the other. But I know it when I see it.

Are Products Getting More Complex?

Now back to the original argument: Do systems really have a tendency of becoming more complex? Some scientists say "no." There are plenty of examples of species having *lost* functions over time. For example, the ancestors of brainless starfish had a brain. But starfish don't, and nobody knows why [Le Page 2008:29]. (Some believe the same applies to managers.) It is also known that primates lost the ability to synthesize their own vitamin C around the time they adopted the habit of eating fruit. However, this also meant they had to re-evolve a trait they had previously lost: color vision [Corning 2003:176]. And despite the many more complex species roaming the face of the earth, a great number of species of simple bacteria are still the most successful in terms of sheer biomass.

The concept of "increased complexity" in species was famously discussed (and vigorously rejected) by Stephen Jay Gould [Gould 1997]. He used the metaphor of the "Drunkard's walk" to explain that a species can become either more complex or less complex, just like a drunkard can sway to the right or to the left. He wrote that there is a "wall" on the left side, because there is no such thing as negative size, negative weight, or negative complexity (see Figure 14.4). Therefore, if you let hundreds of drunkards start from a door near the wall (minimal complexity), the average direction of all of them will show a tendency to the right, despite that each drunkard is just as likely to step in either direction.

Despite Gould's wonderful metaphor, I believe there *is* a tendency of increased complexity in systems. And the arguments against it stem from misunderstandings.

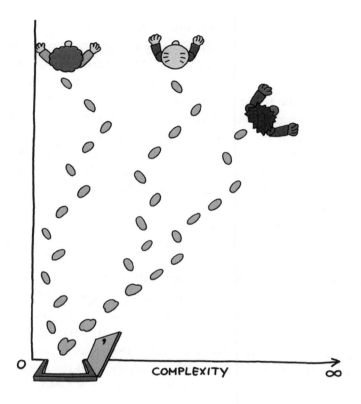

FIGURE 14.4
The drunkard's walk.

First, the argument against increased complexity is often confused with the argument against progress. As we've noted before, higher complexity doesn't mean higher fitness. Complexity is a way to "stay in the game" in the Red Queen's Race. Throughout history people have believed in biological "progress," or increased perfection, culminating in the "most advanced" of all species: humans. Scientists such as Gould have rightfully argued against such ideas, and in doing so they seem to have dismissed the innate drive of systems toward increased complexity. But the nonsense of progress doesn't rule out a tendency toward complexity.

Second, there is no single measure of complexity. Measuring brain size and intelligence of species is just one way of looking at complexity. We know that microorganisms are still the dominant form of life on earth. *But* the complexity of the bacterial and viral worlds has exploded over geological time, even though the individual specimens are all relatively simple. It is only a matter of scaling out instead of scaling up. The microbiological world might have achieved a level of complexity similar to humanity, only in another dimension.

Third, is the growth of a complex system as likely as shrinkage? When a drunkard moves across a street, is a step to the right just as likely as a step to the left? Fortunately, I cannot tell from personal experience. But with evolution a step to the left is not as likely as one to the right. Just think of it: How do researchers find out that brainless starfish once had a brain? Or that primates once had the ability of synthesizing vitamin C? They know because the remnants of those functions still linger in DNA as pseudogenes. The functions are lost, but the coding is still available in the schema, dormant and waiting to be activated. That's how species can "re-evolve" traits that they've lost earlier. They simply switch the genes back on! And thus it appears that loss of a function in a system doesn't mean that the system has become less complex. It might have become *more* complex because a new function was *added* to switch the "lost" function off and on.

Fourth, the **second law of thermodynamics**[21] states that entropy (or disorder) in a system tends to increase over time. Although, strictly speaking, this is only true for closed systems, we *can* recognize entropy in our genome in the form of junk DNA.[22] This junk has no effect whatsoever. Most of it is just waste accumulated over time. But I'm certain (though I cannot prove it) that it adds complexity to the system. Only a few genetic mutations are sufficient to reactivate junk DNA, with unpredictable consequences as a result.

And finally, one last argument that favors a trend of increasing complexity of systems is our earlier observation that a system's internal models must represent the environment in which it tries to survive. If the environment gets more complex over time, the system tends to evolve and become more complex as well. It takes complexity to deal with complexity, and the selection pressures that favor higher complexity may be strong [Gell-Mann 1994:245].

Given these five arguments I now dare claim that many living systems *do* become more complex over time. And I never thought I would ever be able to disagree with Gould because to me he was one of the smartest people on the planet. But now I disagree. So perhaps there is some progress after all.

---

21 http://www.mgt30.com/2nd-law/.
22 http://www.mgt30.com/junk-dna/.

The Shape of Things: Phase Space

When I was 15 years old, I was fascinated by books about the shape of the universe. (Other guys of my age were more interested in other shapes. But I've always had an eye for the bigger picture.) The things I read about special relativity and the expanding universe led me to try to draw my own four-dimensional object on paper (see Figure 14.5).

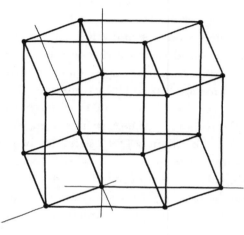

FIGURE 14.5

A four-dimensional cube (or "hypercube").

I created the object in Figure 14.5 by shifting an ordinary cube into an imaginary fourth dimension, and then connecting the 16 corners, just like one creates a cube by shifting a square in a third dimension, and then connecting the 8 corners. I was thrilled at the time that it was so easy to draw what was in fact a 2D projection of a 3D projection of a 4D object. It was my favorite shape at the time (until I found out other shapes were more important, when I finally started dating.) But when I showed my drawing to my physics teacher, he told me it was complete nonsense. I felt defeated and misunderstood. Years later I learned that the thing I had "invented" is called a *hypercube* and that my physics teacher missed a great opportunity for learning from a student.

A hypercube is yet nothing when compared to the "shape of improvement" in a complex system. When evaluating the many states of a dynamic system, researchers imagine each variable in the system to be an axis in a multidimensional space. A small system with just three variables is represented as a **phase space** in three dimensions; and a system with 20 variables has a phase space of no less than 20 dimensions. I'm afraid that even I would not be able to draw such an object. And that would still be just a small one. Many complex systems consist of thousands or more variables, with a corresponding phase space of a mind-boggling size.

For example, seaweed has roughly 1,000 genes. Suppose, for the sake of simplicity, that each of those genes comes in just two varieties: green leaves versus brown leaves, big leaves versus small leaves, flat leaves versus wrinkled leaves, and so on. The number of possible states of seaweed would then be 2^1000, or one thousand dimensions with two possible values in each dimension [Waldrop 1992:167]. (Human DNA is estimated at 25,000 genes, and it has more than two variants per gene. Can you imagine drawing a hypercube for that phase space?)

A specific instance of a system is said to be in one location of its phase space. (Each variable has one specific value.) When any of these variables change, the system is said to move through its phase space. Switching one gene in seaweed DNA (for example, a mutation from green leaves to brown leaves) will move seaweed DNA from one point to a neighboring point in its phase space. But changing many different variables at the same time (for example, mixing the DNA strings from mommy seaweed and daddy seaweed into a brand new DNA string for baby seaweed) is like a hyper-jump through phase space.

By visualizing change as a journey through a space it becomes easier to recognize and discuss the patterns of continuous improvement. It also becomes easier to see which shapes are important, and which ones are not.

Attractors and Convergence

OK, now it gets a bit more mathematical. Just hold on tight, and I'll try and steer you through this challenging landscape. Trust me; the scenery will be worth it.

When complex systems change, the journeys they take through their vast phase space typically fall in one of a few categories. Consider the example of the Game of Life, described in Chapter 8. Regardless of the initial state of the game, after a number of steps, the system ends up in a stable situation, in all but a few cases. The stable situation at the end is either one stationary state (a "still life"), or it is an everlasting cycle of a small number of states. We say that the stable situation is an **attractor** for all other states that lead into it. And the collection of all trajectories that lead to an attractor is called its **basin of attraction** (see Figure 14.6). Because each system usually follows trajectories that lead into attractors, the attractors lure the system into small regions of its entire phase space. Despite the vast range of possible states of the system, it finally settles into one of just an orderly few.

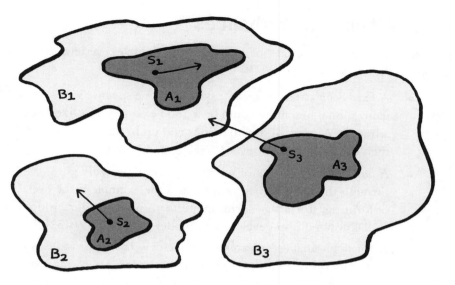

FIGURE 14.6

Attractors (A), basins of attraction (B), and disturbances (S).

Are you still with me? Good. Let's make it a bit more concrete with the example of seaweed.

Theoretically there are 2^1000 possible versions of seaweed DNA. That's a lot, actually. It's quite a bit more than the number of atoms in the universe. However, the number of real observable forms of seaweed is extremely small because all other forms are unstable and, within a few generations, would either die out or change and end up in one of the few stable forms. It doesn't matter that an uncountable number of forms of seaweed is *theoretically* possible. In *practice*, the environment forces seaweed to end up in one of a small number of forms that are actually feasible for that environment.

Some scientists think that **convergence**,[23] which is the fact that biological solutions like eyes and wings have been "invented" several times independently, is a good example of the concept of attractors [Lewin 1999:73]. In biological morphology there is an attractor of "things that have four legs," and an attractor of "things with two wings," and so on. Five legs and one wing are valid forms, but they are not stable (except perhaps in the vicinity of an unstable nuclear power plant).

And so I believe that to make a software project work well in its environment, we must make sure that what works *well* is also *stable*. Because projects will converge on stable forms, but that doesn't mean those forms also work well.

---

23 http://www.mgt30.com/convergent/.

Stability and Disturbances

Following are three kinds of attractors in complex systems [Gleick 1987:269]:

- A *fixed point* attractor keeps a system in one specific state. An organizational hierarchy could be a good example of a fixed point attractor. Almost all organizations end up in that structure, and then they stay there forever [Waldrop 1992:169].

- A *limit cycle* is an attractor where a system repeatedly goes through the same sequence of states. One example is the cycle of forming, storming, norming, performing, and adjourning, a well-known group development model [Arrow 2000:152].

- A *chaotic or "strange" attractor* is a trajectory that refuses to end up in any of the other two kinds of attractors. An example of a strange attractor could be a chaotic startup business desperately running from opportunity to opportunity, never settling in a stable situation until the environment finally allows it to do so.

An attractor typically drains an enormous basin. Now suppose that, somehow, the stable system is disturbed. Suddenly the state of one of its variables is arbitrarily switched from one value to another. (For example, one development practice is replaced by another.) Figure 14.6 shows that most of these perturbations have no serious effect on the system. It simply stays in the attractor (S1), or it is pushed out of the attractor but finds itself in the same basin of attraction (S2), meaning that the system will still end up in the same attractor anyway. Only when the variables in the system are pushed far enough will the system be pushed from one basin of attraction to another, thereby ending up in another attractor (S3).

Stability, or **homeostasis**, is an important property of complex systems. No matter how you push and prod, some systems keep on doing whatever they did before. Doesn't that sound familiar? Doesn't that sound eerily like the time you tried to introduce Agile development practices in a group of people, and the group simply fell back into their old habits? Doesn't that remind you of the time you wanted to change an organizational culture, and the organization simply resisted all your efforts?

Like any other kind of complex system, a group of people can get stuck in an attractor. This can be either good or bad. It is good when great performance keeps the group locked in that state. It is bad when other factors, like an organizational culture, keep a group in a "bad" attractor, preventing them from performing better. The forceful introduction of "change" into such an organization will rarely have an effect. Even if you can push the group out of their attractor, the big basin of attraction around it will simply let them slide back in!

So, what is the solution? How can we make change management work? I believe the answer should be found not in the system but in the environment. The attractors in a system depend on the environment. When the environment changes, the attractors change along with them. Some environmental changes disturb attractors so much that they dissolve altogether, and the system automatically finds itself on a path to another attractor. Maybe even a brand new one.

When changing teams and organizations, the trick is not to try and push them out of their current behavior. That's just too much work with far too little results. A better idea is to change parameters in the environment so that their current situation becomes unstable and disappears all by itself.

Let me give you an example... In several software development teams I have tried to introduce test-driven development (TDD), without any success. Legacy code, technical platforms, team culture, and customer contracts all seemed to conspire against me. Even when team members were willing to adopt TDD, they simply couldn't sustain their heroic attempts at practicing it. However, I then started from scratch with a new team, with a different business model, different technologies, a different architecture, and most important...different customer contracts. The people in my new team were the same people I worked with before. But I changed the *environment* instead of trying to change the team. And the team could then find a stable state that *included* TDD. Practicing TDD was suddenly very easy.

Fitness Landscapes

I will now further challenge your imagination by asking you to visualize one extra dimension that we are going to add to a system's phase space. This extra dimension will correspond to the "fitness" of the system. (Actually, there is no absolute measure for the fitness of a system [Waldrop 1992:259]. But, again, we *can* recognize that one system is better suited to a certain environment than another. We know it when we see it!)

In Figure 14.7, I visualized the combination of fitness and phase space using just two dimensions. The horizontal dimension represents the location in a system's phase space (as if I folded all dimensions of phase space into one simple line). The vertical dimension represents fitness. The result is what system theorists call a **fitness landscape**. It plots how good the performance of a system is, relative to its current state. It looks a bit like the Swiss Alps. But without the toll roads.

FIGURE 14.7

An adaptive walk across a fitness landscape.

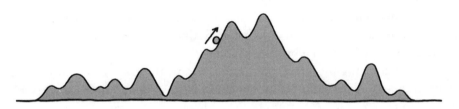

When we change one part of a system into something else (one gene, one employee, one team member, one practice), the system moves to the left or to the right on the fitness landscape, thereby either increasing or decreasing its fitness. The systems that can find the highest peaks on the fitness landscape are the ones best able to survive. And those with the ability to repeatedly tune their own internal organization are said to be doing an **adaptive walk** across their fitness landscape. An adaptive walk is the process by which a system changes from one configuration to another to stay fit. Software projects do their adaptive walks by repeatedly changing features, qualities, people, tools, schedules, and processes. It's like hiking through the Swiss Alps. And it can be just as strenuous.

The form of a fitness landscape depends on both the system *and* its environment. Therefore survival strategies from one system cannot be easily translated to another. And outside consultants who rely on approaches that worked for other groups or organizations, with very different fitness landscapes, may be in error when they apply the same approaches to a new group with a new fitness landscape. [Arrow 2000:182]

The message here is never to *blindly* trust anyone's advice on how to improve your project. By definition, other people's fitness landscapes are different than yours. It's *your* hike. Nobody else can walk for you.

Systems adapt to their environment and to each other. When two or more species, businesses, or products keep adapting to each other's moves across their fitness landscapes, we say that they are **coevolving**. And we can consider the internal structure of each system to be a code for the environment and the other species that it is evolving with.

The environment of any given species of organism includes a huge number of other species, which are themselves evolving. The genotype of each organism, or else the cluster of genotypes that characterizes each species, can be regarded as a schema that includes a description of many of the other species and how they are likely to react to different forms of behavior. An ecological community consists, then, of a great many species all evolving models of other species' habits and how to cope with them.[24]

Because of changing environments, and coevolving systems, we must realize that fitness landscapes are never static. It's as if they are made of rubber [Waldrop 1992:310]. While you're doing your adaptive walk over the landscape, you notice that some peaks are dropping, other peaks are rising, valleys are moving around, and each of your steps can have unexpected consequences, like walls forming in front of you and cliffs disappearing behind you. This is the main reason why you have to continuously evaluate your strategy, again, and again.

And is this also like the Swiss Alps? Not really, I suppose. Unless you had a bit too much wine with your fondue.

Shaping the Landscape

Are fitness landscapes easy to walk through? How hard is it to find a peak? Do we need Nordic walking poles or Swiss Army Knives?

The shape of a fitness landscape is directly related to the interconnectedness of a system. This is not difficult to explain. Imagine that all parts in a software project (people, tools, practices, and so on) have absolutely no influence on each other whatsoever. In that hypothetical case, replacing one person, tool, or practice with another would have no consequences for any of the other parts. Each individual part would simply have its own isolated effect on the system's fitness (either positive or negative). And it would mean that there would be one and only one best configuration for the entire software project, namely the one in which each individual part had a positive effect on the system's fitness. This optimal configuration would correspond to the single highest peak in the landscape of Figure 14.8a.

---

24 Excerpt from The Quark And The Jaguar by Murray Gell-Mann, page 237. Copyright © 1994 by Murray Gell-Mann. Reprinted by permission of Henry Holt and Company, LLC. [Gell-Mann 1994:237].

Unfortunately, this situation is as unlikely as a St. Bernhard dog saving your project with a barrel of brandy. There is always a level of interdependence between agents in a complex system. Genes for feathers and genes for wings are related in such a way that they have a combined effect on an animal's fitness. And it's the same with various combinations of features, qualities, people, tools, and practices in software projects. Remove one part, and other parts will then also stop working.

FIGURE 14.8

Three adaptive walks: a) simple; b) rugged; and c) moderate.

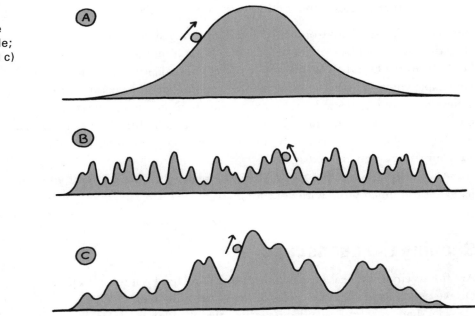

Researchers have found that, with a *large* number of interdependencies between the parts in a system, its fitness landscape looks like a rugged terrain of many small peaks, not one of them clearly being the highest (see Figure 14.8b). They call this the **complexity catastrophe**, which tends to limit the chance of a system to achieve optimal fitness. Simple changes in the system lead to wildly fluctuating performance because a step to the left or to the right in such a landscape easily leads to a fall off a cliff. Therefore it appears that the ruggedness of a fitness landscape (and thus the number of connections between the parts in a system) is an important aspect for survival strategies of complex systems.

The lesson here is that systems shouldn't have too many interdependencies, and the ruggedness of the fitness landscape should be moderate (see Figure 14.8c). This is the case when there is only a moderate inter-dependence between features, qualities, people, tools, and processes in a software project. Changing any one of these has *some* effects for other parts in the system, but nothing too drastic. From this, it also follows that software development methods should mainly consist of *loosely coupled* practices so that continuous improvement is possible without the fear of sliding down the Matterhorn at every single step.

Directed versus Undirected Adaptation

In *Small Groups as Complex Systems,* the authors distinguish between directed and undirected adaptation [Arrow 2000:175-176]. **Undirected adaptation** (or, in my words, adaptation and exploration) is what we find in biological systems. The search of species across their fitness landscape is not an intelligent one. DNA is mutated in random ways, and species do their adaptive walks in all directions, including every wrong one. But *natural selection* comes to the rescue by killing the offspring that inadvertently ended up in the wrong direction. (If only leading people was that easy....)

Directed adaptation (or, in my words, anticipation) is what we usually find in human systems. A software team cannot afford to try out every combination of features, people, tools, and processes. In this case not natural selection but *conscious selection* comes to the rescue. Humans have the intellectual capacity to make an educated guess where the higher peaks in the landscape are. They balance features against qualities, they fire and hire employees, they discard and select tools, and they learn from experts about what works elsewhere.

Besides directed adaptation, teams are also (unintentionally) involved in undirected adaptation. Teams can gradually change their practices without specifically meaning to do so. They may do things differently from iteration to iteration without following a conscious change strategy, and over time all these small changes can accumulate and account for a substantial movement across their fitness landscape. [Arrow 2000:175]

And interestingly enough, genetic engineering has (intentionally) brought directed adaptation to the biological world, with artificial evolution greatly accelerating change in crops and cattle [Kelly 1994:3].

In scientific literature the adaptive part of complex *adaptive* systems is widely associated with undirected adaptation. But that's only because there's a bias among scientists toward things that they can jam under a microscope. It doesn't mean that complexity science applies only to systems with nonconscious agents. On the contrary, the mechanism by which a system moves over a fitness landscape, whether by natural selection or conscious selection, has little relevance to the dynamics of the landscape and the strategies of the system.

And so we now consciously finish this chapter and move on to the next one where we learn how to put *Improve Everything* into practice.

Summary

Contrary to what many people believe, an environment cannot be seen independent of the systems that inhabit it. If you introduce a new software product in an environment, the environment will change, and consequently the requirements for the product will change with it.

People have a natural resistance to change, and most often they see change as a negative thing. But all change can be positive or negative and the effort to improve to cope with environmental changes is more or less constant. Ultimately, every product is doomed to fail, and success can be defined as postponement of that failure for as long as possible.

The three approaches to continuous improvement are adaptation, exploration, and anticipation. Projects need all three of them in neverending cycles. Such continuous improvement is sometimes called a Red Queen's Race: You improve in order not to fall behind.

Sometimes teams or organizations seem unable to change. It is said such systems are stuck in an attractor, and the best way to get them out might be to modify some parameters in the environment so that the attractor becomes unstable.

The effort to find the best configuration of a project, given a certain environment, can be considered as an adaptive walk over a fitness landscape. It is best when a project consists of loosely coupled parts (people, tools, and practices) because continuous improvement is easier when parts can be replaced without disturbing the rest of the project too much.

Reflection and Action

Let's see if you can apply some ideas from this chapter to your organization:

- Review your improvement process. Are you applying each of the three improvement approaches (adapting, exploring, and anticipating)?

- Review your team and process. Are there many interdependencies between them (people or processes only working well in combination with others)? Can you break some interdependencies so that it is easier to change things and improve?

Chapter **15**

How to Improve Everything

The reasonable man adapts himself to the world; the unreasonable one persists in trying to adapt the world to himself. Therefore all progress depends on the unreasonable man.

—George Bernard Shaw, playwright (1856–1950)

When you read literature about process improvement or quality improvement, you are bound to be confronted with a model of some kind. So many models exist in this business that it wouldn't surprise me if some of them founded their own agency. Most of the models look pretty, in pictures. But when you get to know them directly, I fear that many of them lack some depth.

Five of the best known improvement models are depicted in Figure 15.1, where I distilled from them a basic pattern for an improvement process. I'm calling it SLIP (Simple Linear Improvement Process), and it consists of eight steps.

> **NOTE:** My mapping of existing models to my own model is subjective. Other people could make mappings in different ways.

It is easy to see that these models all follow a similar pattern, which the SLIP model presents as eight different steps:

1. We analyze our current situation and determine what the most important **problem** is. (For example, we're getting fat.)

2. We define a **goal** that can help to get us out of the problematic situation. (We want to weigh 10 pounds less.)

3. We define a **metric** that can tell us whether we succeeded. (We retrieve our old diet scale from the attic.)

4. We identify an **improvement** that can take us in the direction of the desired goal. (We decide to run and eat healthier.)

5. We realize an **implementation**, possibly in a small controlled experiment. (We buy running shoes and a cook book.)

6. Then there is the **execution** of our day-to-day operations that can result in actual measurements (run daily, eat healthy food).

7. Then there is an **analysis** of the measurements to verify improvement. (Oh dear, only one pound in three weeks?)

8. Finally, the analysis enables **learning**, about the problem, the solution, and the metrics. (Never trust an old diet scale.)

After Step 8, we return to Step 1, either to determine that the same problem still exists (we're still fat), or that another problem is now the most pressing one. (We need a new diet scale.)

However, the implicit assumption many people make when working with these improvement models is that each iteration should, in principle, improve the current situation of a system. Whether intended, the models lead people in a *linear* fashion, step-by-step, through the fitness landscape, where it is assumed that every step should lead people to a better position on the landscape, with higher fitness, and a slimmer waist line.

FIGURE 15.1

SLIP, based on five improvement models: PDCA[1], QIP[2], AMI[3], IDEAL[4], and DMAIC.[5]

SLIP	PDCA	QIP	AMI	IDEAL	DMAIC
DETERMINE PROBLEMS	ACT	UNDERSTAND	ASSESS	INITIATING	DEFINE
SET GOALS	PLAN	GOALS	ASSESS	INITIATING	DEFINE
DEFINE METRICS	PLAN	GOALS	ANALYZE	DIAGNOSING	MEASURE
IDENTIFY IMPROVEMENTS	PLAN	CHOOSE	ANALYZE	ESTABLISHING	IMPROVE
IMPLEMENT IMPROVEMENTS	DO	CHOOSE	METRICATE	ACTING	IMPROVE
EXECUTE PROCESSES	DO	EXECUTE	METRICATE	ACTING	CONTROL
CHECK MEASUREMENTS	CHECK	ANALYZE	IMPROVE	LEVERAGING	ANALYZE
LEARN FROM RESULTS	ACT	PACKAGE	IMPROVE	LEVERAGING	ANALYZE

1 The Plan-Do-Check-Act process, also called Deming/Shewhart cycle, see http://www.mgt30.com/pdca/.
2 The Quality Improvement Paradigm, by NASA and the University of Maryland, see http://www.mgt30.com/qip/.
3 The ami method, created in Europe [Pulford 1996].
4 The IDEAL model, by the Software Engineering Institute, see http://www.mgt30.com/ideal/.
5 The DMAIC project methodology, part of Six Sigma, see http://www.mgt30.com/dmaic/.

Linear versus Nonlinear Improvement

Fitness landscapes aren't usually that accommodating to linear progress. With step-by-step improvement, it is easy to get stuck in a local optimum. How do you move from one peak of relatively good performance to another peak of much better performance, when everything between the peaks is just one big valley of misery (see Figure 15.2)?

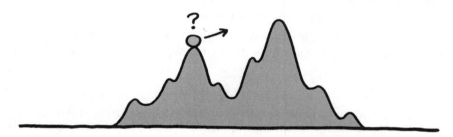

FIGURE 15.2

How to escape the local optimum?

This is a common problem in all improvement efforts. It is why people sometimes say that things go "one step back, two steps forward," or "things have to get worse before they get better." The adaptive walk of a complex system through its fitness landscape is not always an easy one. Standard process models do not explicitly address the fact that plenty of iterations, even though they *are* in the right direction, will only make matters *worse*. Hopefully for just a short while, of course.

> This characteristic of change—its lack of linearity—is the second key factor that renders the majority of methodologies for "managing" change ineffectual. The inevitable, associated attempts to force-fit approaches to change into linear continua have also played havoc with approaches to managing product lifecycles, systems development lifecycles, and the like. [...] Business theory is turgid with product lifecycle models, most of which fail to describe the nonlinear, unpredictable nature of the life of a product, especially in our increasingly complex market, consumer, business, and economic landscapes.[6]

---

6   Falconer, James. "Emergence Happens! Misguided Paradigms Regarding Organizational Change and the Role of Complexity and Patterns in the Change Landscape" Emergence. Vol. 4, Issue 1/2, 2002. Used with permission. [Falconer 2002:122].

Linear improvement is easy. But what if the hill that a team is climbing is only a small one on the fitness landscape? What if the team finds itself in the (small) Belgian Ardennes instead of the (big) Swiss Alps? Teams need more than just step-by-step improvements. It would be wise of them to get to a mountain range first, in a couple of radical jumps, *before* taking smaller steps to the top.

In *Making Innovation Work*, the authors write that an innovative business not only needs *incremental innovation*, but also *radical innovation* [Davila 2006:51–55]. And although most literature on Lean software development preaches *kaizen* (gradual improvement), only few of them mention that teams also need *kaikaku* (radical improvement) [Middleton, Sutton 2005:31].

> Thus, when approaching a problem situation, it might require radical improvement to start with (kaikaku), then be continuously improved (kaizen).[7]

WHAT ABOUT ADAPTATION?

Whenever I speak of continuous improvement, I mean *adaptation*, *anticipation*, and *exploration*. Adaptation is reactive: responding to a change in the environment. Anticipation is proactive: imagining a higher position on the landscape and moving in that direction. Exploration is interactive: doing something different just to experience what the effect is, and not because either the environment required it or because we imagined good results.

Nonhuman systems improve only by responding to the environment (adaptation) and randomly trying things out (exploration). But social teams use their imagination to predict good results (anticipation). Continuous improvement covers all three approaches.

The rest of this chapter does not use any of the existing improvement models. Instead, it focuses on some dimensions that most models seem to be missing. I choose to send a more complex model onto the catwalk. Together, we can figure out how to translate our findings into practical continuous improvement efforts, and whatever model it is that we prefer to work with in our daily jobs.

---

7   Taken from the Improvement Encyclopedia at: http://www.mgt30.com/kaikaku/.

Know Where You Are

When my partner and I are on vacation, driving around in a foreign country, I am usually best at estimating how to get from one landmark to another, calculating the duration of travel between two places, and figuring out what the silly symbols on the maps could possibly mean. Unfortunately, I am also the one most easily misled by crooked turns, sneaky exits, and invisible signage. My partner, on the other hand, usually has no idea where he's going and has held the map upside down on several occasions. But, being smarter than me, he *knows* that he sucks at this kind of stuff. While I *think* I know where I'm going and how to hold a map, far too late I realize that the environment is playing games with my overconfidence. This makes it irrelevant who is actually driving. Either way, we get lost.

When trying to improve the current situation of your team, the first thing to do is to make sure you *know your current position*. You cannot find your way to the next B&B, or the next successful product release, if you have no idea where you are. Mike Cohn calls it *developing awareness* [Cohn 2009:23–26], and Tom and Mary Poppendieck call it *exposing problems* [Poppendieck 2009:169–172]. You have to look around you and be aware of your current situation and its most pressing problems, or else you're just going around in the dark, never knowing if you're getting any closer to your intended target. Improvement then depends on luck and coincidence.

Agile literature is teeming with suggestions on how to understand your current situation. Burn charts, value stream mapping, 5-Whys, retrospectives, and dozens of other tools and techniques are available to assist you in understanding your progress and your problems. Several additional volumes to this book would have been necessary to describe the many options available to you. But I had to restrain myself here. I knew the goal of this book very well, and any more detours would have seriously hurt my progress. For now I will only point out that managers should actually *go to the workplace* [Poppendieck 2009:172] to experience first-hand, with their own eyes, what the most important problems are.

We were once driving in the mountains between Argentina and Chile. Not long after we passed a lake that tried to confuse me by being on the wrong side of the road (which was compensated by the fact that my partner held the map upside down), we encountered a man and his car, stranded in the middle of nowhere. The guy had run out of fuel, several hours away from civilization. Of course, *we* had done our calculations.

We knew our position, our destination, and how much was needed to get there. And we knew it was safe enough to lend the guy half of our spare jerry can of fuel. And off he went, driving like a maniac. We were barely able to keep up with him, while he tried to get to the next gas station before he ran out of fuel again. It seemed this person didn't understand how he got into problems, nor how to improve.

Travel Tips for Wobbly Landscapes

In the previous chapter, we saw that fitness landscapes have a tendency to change. It is hard to give accurate directions when mountains run faster than alpacas and vicuñas. But a few basic principles for continuous improvement are easy enough to understand, if you're willing to accept that the scenery will sometimes have moved to the other side of the road.

- From a valley, you can often see only the mountains directly around you, and not the (sometimes higher) peaks behind them. But you needn't worry about that. If you climb any of the nearby peaks first, you will be in a much better position (and shape) to oversee the bigger landscape.

- The longer it takes you to travel to any of the other peaks in the fitness landscape, the higher the chance that it will be gone by the time you get there.

- You probably cannot directly see the best peaks. But at the very least, you should understand where the mountain ranges are. And a valley in a mountain range can still be higher than a hill in the flatlands.

- You can trust that each of the peaks in the mountains will be high. It doesn't matter much which one you climb, if your goal is just to climb.

- Finally, only when you've reached the summit of one of those peaks, it can be easier to see which of the other peaks is *really* the highest.

Let's review these concepts with a more practical example (see Figure 15.3). Suppose you are responsible for a team with an old-fashioned process and terrible performance....

1. Before completely changing the whole team and their process, perform a number of small steps to get them in a better position (with better discipline, coding guidelines, daily communication, and so on). It will be easier for them to see, understand, and accept radical change when they are in a better shape.

2. After the small changes, the team will be ready for more drastic changes to the way they work (for example by adopting XP, Scrum, or Kanban). But do this incrementally in small "jumps" of a few days or weeks. Don't do a big reorganization that takes months to complete because the intended "better" position might have vanished by the time you get there.

3. Your "radical jump" (for example: implementation of standard Scrum-by-the-book) doesn't have to land you on a perfect spot right away. Even when you end up with (relatively) bad performance after a big change, this should only be a temporary issue. If you're smart and well-informed, the direction of your radical change (kaikaku) was probably fine, and you will have ended up in a mountain range. Gradual step-by-step improvement through retrospectives (kaizen) can then get you climbing up a mountain side in no time. And there are multiple ways of achieving good performance in a team. Don't worry too much whether Scrum is the best choice. Just pick a good method, and optimize the team's performance.

4. When performance is optimized, the team is in a better position and shape to look at the landscape around it. The team might then consider a semi-radical change to one of the other methods (such as XP or Kanban), if it thinks that gives it even better performance.

5. Finally, after it makes the jump to a great-looking peak, the team can use step-by-step improvement again to achieve global fitness.

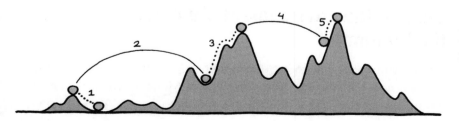

FIGURE 15.3

Stepping and jumping through the fitness landscape.

And when it finally reaches the summit of the highest peak in the landscape, the team must remain vigilant. Because either the peak may be moving, in which case it needs to walk along with it, or it may be slowly dropping, in which case the team needs to prepare to jump to another one.

The drop in performance that a team often experiences after any kind of change is depicted in the **Virginia Satir change curve** (see Figure 15.4) [Satir 1991]. From a complexity perspective, our interpretation can be that such a team jumps across its fitness landscape and lands in a valley somewhere between the mountains. Regular continuous improvement will then get the team on its way to a higher peak. The bad performance is just a temporary issue; one that is hard to prevent.

FIGURE 15.4

Virginia Satir
Change Curve.

Source: Satir, Virginia et al. The Satir Model. Palo Alto: Science and Behavior Books, 1991. Used with permission. [Satir 1991].

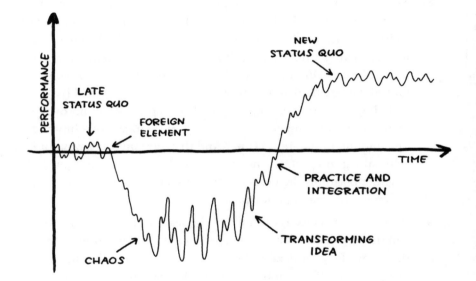

A similar finding was offered by Robert L. Glass, who described that learning a new tool or technique usually *lowers* quality and performance initially, before it goes back up [Glass 2003:23].

Change the Environment, Summon the Mountain

"If Mohammed can't go to the mountain, let the mountain come to Mohammed." This quote from the story of Mohammed turns out to be wrong because the actual quote is the opposite:

> If the hill will not come to Muhammad, then Muhammad will go to the hill.[8]

Interestingly enough, the rewording of the quote underlines its new meaning, which is that humans have an uncanny ability to make the impossible happen, and to change the environment (and quotations) to suit their purposes.

While discussing our travels over fitness landscapes, we might almost forget that we can *change* the fitness landscape, thereby significantly shortening the path from our current position to a peak of high performance. We can make the mountain come to *us*, instead of traveling the whole distance to the mountain. (Or we could compromise and arrange a meeting halfway, say at the parking lot of KFC.)

As a manager, you have the power to change the environment in ways that make it easier for teams to perform better. Contracts with customers and vendors can be reconsidered and renegotiated. Corporate departments, like Human Resources, Recruitment, Facilities, Finance, and Marketing may have to be dealt with so that their policies *support* rather than *obstruct* self-organizing Agile teams [Cohn 2009:38–39]. And the organizational structure, discussed in Chapter 12, "Communication on Structure," and Chapter 13, "How to Grow Structure," is an extremely important aspect of the environment. A switch from functional to cross-functional teams, or from hierarchical to networked decision making, is like moving *Ojos del Salado* from the Andes to Amsterdam.

But one aspect trumps all others. And that is the *willingness to change*.

All too often, I have heard of employees in various organizations complaining about change, and things "never staying the same." One reorganization has barely finished, and the next is already being prepared. But reorganizations are not the problem. The problem is people experiencing change as a negative thing. And management can help teach them that it's not.

The people in your organization should *want* to change. And you can help them with that, by turning the environment into one that invites rather than subdues continuous change. Think of *open office spaces* and *movable desks*, which make it easier for people to relocate to places that best suit their current projects. Think of *job rotation*, which makes people more flexible in their attitudes toward other people's work. Think of occasional

---

8 Taken from Wiktionary, the free dictionary, at: http://www.mgt30.com/muhammad/.

team member exchanges, and *swapping management positions*, so that people learn to work with different colleagues. And instead of people and jobs, you can also *move projects around* so that teams learn to adapt their practices to different projects. By institutionalizing continuous change of the environment in your organization, you create a culture of comfort despite uncertainty with people who can see opportunities and not only threats.

This brings me to the topic of communication about organizational change. You must try and make people understand that continuous change should be the *default* behavior of an organization. Standing still is the *exception*. It is therefore perhaps smart not to talk of "reorganization" because this sends the signal that change is an exception to regular "organization." And don't give names to change initiatives, like "Quality 2012" or "The Agile Road." Again, this only emphasizes that organizational change is something "special," with a beginning and an end [Cohn 2009:34]. If you treat change as an exception, as something special, people have good reasons to become demotivated when they come to realize that it actually never ends.

People often experiment with change by setting up pilot projects. But pilot projects for organizational change are useless when carried out in a separate and safe sandbox environment. The complexity of a problem usually exceeds that of "tiger" teams, task forces, and other ad hoc problem-solving groups tasked with solving a problem in a safe environment [Dent 1999:14]. The idea of experimentation itself is good. An experiment is like sending a scout across the fitness landscape with the task of investigating any dangers before the rest of the troops get there. But a sandbox is not the real environment. It won't respond to scouts in the way a real environment would. For example, it doesn't mean anything when you "try" the Kanban framework on a side-project that has no real importance or priority in the organization. Your findings will be neither relevant nor predictive for real projects.

Sandboxes are for learning *without* dangers. Scouting is for learning *about* the dangers. Don't send your scouts to investigate a sandbox. Their pilot projects must be the *real thing*, or else the only thing you will learn is how to remove sand from keyboards.

Make Change Desirable

I don't mind changing if it makes me feel better. I changed the style of my presentations from photos to drawings because simple drawings seemed to be fashionable. I tried to change the way I communicate through Twitter and Facebook because I trusted experts who said it would improve my business. I bought Google's Nexus One smartphone because it gave me the status of being the first (and virtually only) one to own that device. And I joined a political party at a time when it was doing well because it's nice to associate yourself with winners.

People change their behaviors when new behaviors are desirable. You can use that principle in a variety of ways when you're helping teams in your organization change the way they work:

- Make the desired behavior seem fashionable so that people associate not-changing with being a cranky old conservative.

- Make room for trusted experts to share their passion and experience because passion tends to rub off on other people.

- Celebrate small successes because it will make people associate (good) change with winning, happiness, and free drinks.

- Let the change address people's intrinsic desires, like curiosity, idealism, independence, social contacts, or status (see Chapter 5, "How to Energize People").

- Associate change with something else that is desirable. Coat the medicine in an irresistible flavor—dark chocolate, for example.

In this context, it is interesting to refer to Chapter 12, "Communication on Structure," and the various types of communicators among employees in an organization. Some change management experts suggest that you analyze the social network in an organization to identify hubs, pulsetakers, connectors, and salesmen, and work with them to spread new behavior across a company [Manns, Rising 2005]. You can also refer to Everett Rogers' **innovation curve**[9] (see Figure 15.5) and start with the *innovators* who are eager to try something new. Then work your way through the *early adopters, early majority,* and *late majority.* In the meantime, ignore the *laggards* who keep resisting the change until everyone else has adopted it.

---

9 http://www.mgt30.com/diffusion/.

FIGURE 15.5
Innovation
Adoption Curve.

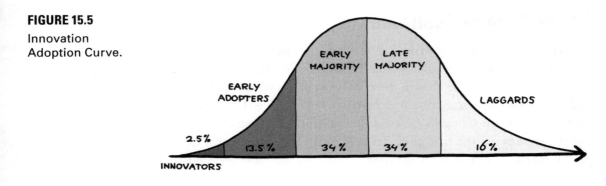

Considering complexity theory, a word of warning is justified for organizational harmony, which you should *not* strive for. Quite often, managers assume that change is successful when people are persuaded to hold the same beliefs. But this means removing or suppressing differences crucial for the emergence of spontaneous creative change [Stacey 2000a:105].

Internal conflict is a natural state for complex systems, and this includes disagreements on how to change. Your goal is *not* to make everyone have the same ideas and opinions. Your goal is to let teams find a better position on the landscape by allowing them to *use* their conflicting ideas and negotiate their differences so that they can move ahead together. In my last team, debates over mobile phones and social networks were a daily recurring theme. But it was the internal conflict itself that helped us to be more mobile as a team and more socially connected.

Make Stagnation Painful

I once experienced a little personal disaster that resulted in 100 gigabytes of data being wiped from both my hard disk *and* my backup disk. Fortunately, I recovered the most crucial part of what I had lost (including early notes for this book). And despite the panic at the time of my realization (as if I dropped down a sink hole), I can say that the situation after the catastrophe was better than the one before.

Reconstructing my data folders required me to rethink the folder hierarchy, to clean up old junk I never used, to improve file and folder naming, and to clearly separate vital data from merely interesting data. Before the crash my data storage situation was a bit messy. The catastrophe motivated me to spend a lot of time creating a new situation that was much better than before. But why didn't I do all that earlier? It would have saved me a lot of trouble.

Here's what I think: The perceived value of change is proportional to the pain that a person experiences when *not* changing.

Why are buildings reinforced *after* the latest earthquake? Why do I improve my dental care only *after* I lose a tooth? Why do I refactor my code only *after* I encounter tough design problems? Why do team members communicate better only *after* the customer hits them on their heads with a dead fish?

It's because value is subjective. The value that we attribute to change increases significantly after we've experienced pain. And the bigger the pain, the higher we value the change we need to go through to prevent the pain. It's not logical, but it's human. The value we place on a transformation is not correlated to the business value of its results. Instead it is correlated to the intensity of the pain we experience for not doing it.

That's why people (like me) change when they feel pain. No pain, no gain. And that's why managers (like me) sometimes try to find devious ways of inflicting "pain" on others to motivate them to change. The pain is just another way of making sure that the change looks more desirable. So, if none of the suggestions for desirability given in the previous section seem to work, turn up the heat and make sure that people *feel* a reason for change.

Honor Thy Errors

Errors are an essential part of biology. DNA is under constant attack from chemicals, radiation, and copying errors. Each human embryo contains 100 or more mutations, most of them neither beneficial nor harmful [Le Page 2008:33]. But even when errors have no important or immediate effects, they enable a system to acquire crucial knowledge for unexpected situations down the road.

Last year, my partner and I were driving to see our friends Devika and Rudie, who live on the other side of our little country. We would be staying there for the night. Halfway through the journey, I took a turn onto a wrong highway, and I didn't notice this until at least 15 minutes later. Not willing to be blamed for a bad sense of direction, I didn't tell my partner anything. I just hoped, and prayed feverishly, that another highway would take us back in the right direction, without us having to go all the way back. Fortunately, luck was with me, and I could stop sweating. My little detour had cost us no more than 10 minutes on a trip of 2½ hours. My partner (having a sense of direction far worse than mine) never noticed a thing, and our friends even complimented us on our speedy arrival. Because everybody was happy enough, I saw no point in telling anyone we could have been there 10 minutes earlier.

The next day, on the way back home, traffic information on the radio told us that we were to expect a nasty traffic jam located exactly on the part of the highway that we had accidentally never seen the day before. So, I told my partner not to worry, because, being the knowledgeable and experienced driver that I am, I knew a little detour that would only cost us 10 minutes extra and would save us the trouble of ending up in the middle of the traffic jam. And so it turned out that I used the new knowledge that I had acquired because of a previous error. My partner's complete lack of directional skills guaranteed that he never recognized the detour from the day before, and my reputation as an experienced driver survived yet another day.

Errors are not unwelcome in software projects. Though there can be some direct costs associated with them, the benefits of the opportunity for learning are often much higher. So, don't worry too much if your software project took a wrong turn somewhere. Correct the mistake and cherish what you've learned.

The Strategy of Noise

Mutations[10] in complex systems, whether or not intentional, are "chance processes." First, there is the mutation, and then the environment decides whether or not the change is a good one. And only by chance will the mutation turn out to be good [Gell-Mann 1994:67]. But no matter what their results are, mutations invite learning about what works and what doesn't. Errors should therefore not be seen as something to be avoided, but as a learning mechanism [Weinberg 1992:181].

In *Managing the Design Factory*, Donald Reinertsen showed convincingly that we cannot maximize information by trying to maximize our success rate [Reinertsen 1997:71–79]. The idea that you learn very little if you try not to make any mistakes is a view shared by many complexity thinkers.

---

10 http://www.mgt30.com/mutation/.

> Error, whether random or deliberate, must become an
> integral part of any process of creation. Evolution can be
> thought of as systematic error management.[11]

This idea gives some software development experts a good reason to
preach the opposite of defining the perfect process for software development because every mutation in a project, and every failure, is an opportunity for the team to learn more about its fitness landscape (and how the
landscape adapts to its changes). The more the team members know about
it, the easier they can navigate it.

> The opposite approach [to a defined process] would be
> one in which every new undertaking is run as a pilot
> project. To the extent that there was a standard way to
> carry out the work, that would be the only way you
> *weren't* allowed to carry it out. The standard would be for
> at least one part of the effort to be run in a nonstandard
> way.[12]

6,000 years ago, metallurgists figured out that the heating of metals, and
the subsequent cooling, causes changes in their properties, such as increased strength and hardness (of the metals, not of the metallurgists).
This technique is called **annealing**.[13] The atoms in the metals are intentionally disturbed by the heat, and when the material cools, the atoms settle down in more regular patterns. It is a form of "stress relief," in which
the intentional disturbance from outside helps the system to achieve an
equilibrium state more easily than it can do by itself.

Complexity researchers have found that similar things happen in
complex systems. Errors and noise in a system, often caused by the environment, stir the system and enable it to break free from suboptimal
results, after which it can settle more easily in a better position. The scientists call it **simulated annealing**,[14] where a bit of randomness helps a
system to better find a global optimum [Miller, Page 2007:24] [Lissack
1999:115-116].

It's as if a system gets pushed and shoved on its fitness landscape, which
is great when it was stuck on a small hill, not daring to go down the slope

---

11 Kelly, Kevin. Out of Control. Boston: Addison-Wesley, 1994. Used with permission.
[Kelly 1994:470].
12 DeMarco, Tom and Timothy Lister. Peopleware: Second Edition. New York: Dorset
House Pub, 1999. [DeMarco, Lister 1999:119].
13 http://www.mgt30.com/annealing/.
14 http://www.mgt30.com/simulated/.

(see Figure 15.6). After such a push, the system may suddenly find itself in a valley, and from there, it can find its way to a higher peak. Simulated annealing shows us that imperfection is a useful way to navigate the fitness landscape [Miller, Page 2007:108].

FIGURE 15.6
Mutation: being pushed around in the landscape.

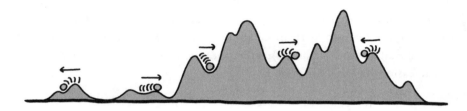

ISN'T IT THE OTHER WAY AROUND?

I draw fitness landscapes as biologists usually draw them, with the fittest positions at the top because it looks more intuitive to have high positions mean "good."

However, physicists are known to draw them the other way around: with the best positions at the bottom. The concept of simulated annealing actually better fits these mirrored versions of fitness landscapes. Because "shaking" the system then results in things rolling downhill into the "good" valleys thanks to gravity.

Just remember that, no matter how you draw them, the fitness landscapes are just metaphors. In reality there's no mountain range, no shaking, and no gravity. There's only impossibly complex mathematics.

In software development, a similar concept of "less perfection" and "noise in execution" enables a team not to get stuck on a local optimum and to find ways of achieving higher performance. DeMarco and Lister have called for a policy of "constructive reintroduction of small amounts of disorder" [DeMarco, Lister 1999:160]. I might call it "performance improvement by imperfection."

The Strategy of Sex

Mutation is experimenting by repeatedly changing individual parts in a software project to see if the results are good or bad. But it is not the only strategy available to a team. Another strategy is sex. Or maybe I should say **cross-over**,[15] which is the better scientific term.

Cross-over is nature's way for species to find higher peaks in a fitness landscape by performing big jumps instead of step-by-step walks. A child receives half of its genes from its mother and the other half from its father. Both mother and father are fit specimens, each of them positioned somewhere at or near a peak in their fitness landscapes. (If they weren't they would be sick or dead and would find it hard to reproduce.) The random mixture of genes that the child ends up with puts it somewhere halfway between the mother and the father on its fitness landscape. If this happens to be a valley, the child is going to be less fit than both its parents. But there's also a good chance that it is an even higher peak than the ones its parents are on. From a complexity perspective, two systems produced a third and made it jump to a new position on the landscape (see Figure 15.7)!

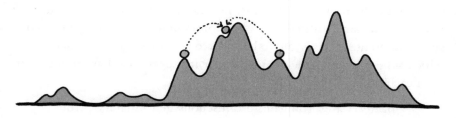

FIGURE 15.7
Cross-over: jumping across the landscape.

The strategy of having sex works well because peaks in a rugged fitness landscape tend to cluster around each other. This is why people use cross breeding to produce superior corn plants or race horses [Holland 1995:66]. They take two top performers, mix their genes, and end up with offspring that might perform even better than both its parents.

Mutation is nature's way of experimenting. It is about carefully taking steps in new directions by randomly changing small parts of a system. Crossover is nature's way of recombining proven best practices. It is about jumping around, in a relatively safe way, and exploring the details of a territory already broadly known [Miller, Page 2007:184].

---

15 http://www.mgt30.com/crossover/.

So, you're wondering about the message in all this for teams? My suggestion is to consider "cross-breeding" teams and project approaches. When you start a new project, try to mix a good method from one earlier project with another good process from a second project. Or create new teams out of old ones, when team members have been together for a long time, and their learning rate is decreasing. Such cross-pollination could give you offspring that outperforms even the fittest parents.

The Strategy of Broadcasts

But mutation and sex are not the only two strategies that enable species to navigate their fitness landscapes. Interestingly enough, a third strategy has been overlooked for a long time in the evolution of multicellular organisms, whereas it appears that it has always played a major role in the bacterial world: **horizontal gene transfer (HGT)**.[16]

Microbes exchange information with each other by flinging bits of genome around. Research has shown that typically 10% of bacterial genomes are acquired from other species. Renowned microbiologist Carl Woese even thinks that HGT was the dominant form of evolution before sexual reproduction took over for the multicellular branches in the tree of life [Buchanan 2010:34–37]. The promiscuous sharing of genetic code across different species is said to have led to a "unified genetic machinery," which subsequently made it much easier for species to share innovations with each other.

> Bacteria are profligate, promiscuous gene-sharers—true practitioners of genetic communism. [...] Sometimes bacteria engage in "sex," exchanges of genetic materials via direct cellular "bridges." At other times bacteria simply broadcast various gene-bearing plasmids and virus-like fragments as free agents: "To whom it may concern." In either case, the result is an uninhibited flow of genetic information. One consequence of this gene-sharing behavior is much greater collective adaptability.[17]

---

16 http://www.mgt30.com/hgt/.
17 Corning, Peter. Nature's Magic. Cambridge: Cambridge University Press, 2003. [Corning 2003:52].

Is there a way to translate this idea to software development teams? Of course there is, and it seems we do it all the time. Teams share practices with each other, exchange team members, copy each other's features, and talk about their experiences with tools. Sometimes this is done in one-on-one exchanges; other times it is through a broadcast via articles, blogs, presentations, or podcasts, "to whom it may concern." (It seems that this book is an example of horizontal transfer in action!)

Recent research has shown that the copying of ideas is the most successful of all strategies. In a tournament with virtual agents, submitted from a variety of academic disciplines, it appeared that the most successful agents spent almost all their learning time observing rather than innovating [Macleod 2010]. This would indicate that teams should spend most of their (learning) time copying ideas from other sources. Only a little time should be spent on inventing their own.

It seems evident to me that organizations need all three strategies for continuous improvement: mutation, crossover, and horizontal transfer. They need mutation for gradual and innovative improvements in unknown and potentially dangerous territory. They need crossover for more radical improvement, by recombining different methods and teams that are each good performers in their own right. And they need horizontal transfer to copy innovations between teams, which enables them to walk in "new" directions that are already familiar to others (see Figure 15.8).

FIGURE 15.8
Horizontal transfer: following another on the landscape.

In practice, the three strategies mean that you let teams use retrospectives (or other techniques) to explore their fitness landscapes by continuously mutating features, qualities, practices, tools, people, schedules, and business value. Whereas on another level you use "continuous reorganization" to recombine best teams and project approaches to find out which of that offspring performs even better. And the promiscuous sharing and copying of ideas, people, and tools is the third strategy for achieving overall high fitness.

DO YOU MEAN TEAMS ARE ALWAYS CHANGING?

Actually no, I'm exaggerating. I'm just trying to make a point here. One year it's the team structure, another year it's the standard processes, and the next year it's management layers or business units. In a healthy organization there's always something under (re)construction.

I don't mean that teams themselves should always be reorganizing. This would contradict the requirement that teams should be stable over a longer period of time, as described in Chapter 13, "Grow Structure."

Computer simulations show that the combination of mutation, horizontal transfer, and crossover is a great approach to achieve global optimal performance [Buchanan 2010:36]. We can assume that the same applies to teams and organizations. Use mutation to invent new stuff. Use horizontal transfer to copy innovations from other teams. And use crossover to discover best-of-breed solutions out of the available combinations.

BUT SPECIES ARE DIFFERENT FROM BUSINESSES!

True, biological evolution is undirected while business improvement is directed (see the end of Chapter 14, "The Landscape of Change").

Species produce multiple siblings so that one or two end up going in the right direction. But in a business we must use anticipation to achieve similar results. Both species and businesses can either fail or succeed. In terms of practical results, I see no difference between these approaches.

Don't Do Copy-Paste Improvement

In the previous chapter, I warned you of simply copying other people's "best" practices, and following the advice of consultants, without consideration for your specific context. The fitness landscapes of other teams may be different from your own. Sharing innovations through horizontal transfer is a great strategy, but it requires that you verify whether the innovations actually make sense in your situation.

I have trouble with people *adopting* other people's opinions and arguments without *adapting* them to their local context. Some forget to analyze a new situation before applying copied ideas. And some people accuse others of having a wrong approach to software development or management, without investigating if their ideas can actually survive in the context of the accused. We could call this *copy-paste improvement*.

Examples?

"You shouldn't do fixed price, fixed scope contracts, because…."

That sounds sensible, but it doesn't help me if fixed price contracts are the only ones my customers want. Are you suggesting that I should just give up my business?

"Big upfront requirements are wrong, because…."

Could be, but my customer just handed me a 500-page requirements study and he pays me to implement it. Are you telling me to decline this project?

"Teams must be cross-functional and collocated, with all roles represented in the team because…."

That would be nice, but our customer just contracted another party for front-end design, on the other side of the country. Shall I ask them to move to our offices?

"You have to do iterations of two weeks each, because…."

OK, but that advice doesn't help me much when I have a very short project that lasts for only two weeks.

I appreciate any kind of advice from any source, including ideas that don't translate well to my context. It is an opportunity to learn and to understand how our situation compares to, and differs from, the world outside.

Despite popular terminology, I believe there is no such thing as a "bad gene" or a "good gene." The effects of genes on an organism are context-dependent. It depends on the other genes and on the environment. Even the most malicious genes can turn out to be beneficial to some organisms in some environments. My late Persian cat Poesie (see Figure 15.9) possibly couldn't have survived in any environment, except in the hands of a loving owner with a large comb.

Likewise, development and management practices are context-dependent. You shouldn't tell people what to do without fully understanding their context first. Even if you're right in 95% of the cases, people will only be digging their heels deeper in the sand when you don't acknowledge that their situation is slightly different.

FIGURE 15.9
Tribute to Poesie.

I am usually in favor of trying to adopt practices "by the book" *if and only if* it is immediately followed by a learning process on how to tune those standard practices to the local context. However, sometimes this approach just doesn't work. Sometimes significant adaptation is needed *before* adoption because straight implementation of the practice directly from the book is clearly impossible.

That's why I suggest that you don't apply *copy-paste improvement*. Use only *copy-paste special…* and then carefully select your options. (But never lose sight of the real benefits of the original practices. Too often, great new approaches are watered down far too much to "fit" an existing organization, and then they completely lose their power to have a useful impact.)

Some Last Practical Tips for Continuous Change

I find it difficult to come up with more concrete tips for continuous change. As noted in Chapter 14, "The Landscape of Change," the nature of complexity makes it nearly impossible to describe approaches that work for most organizations. However, I will try and give you a few simple pointers that you can decide to dig in to and mold to your own situation.

- Use regular **retrospectives** to discuss the current situation and how to improve on it. These retrospectives can be done at multiple organizational levels, not just at the team level. You can see to it they not only deal with *adaptation* (responding to experiences), but also with *exploration* (experimenting around), and *anticipation* (preparing for expectations). That way, you can ensure that people's double-loop learning efforts look both backward and forward. A ton of advice on retrospectives can be found in the book *Agile Retrospectives* [Derby, Larsen 2006].

- Maintain an **improvement backlog** for different teams, and at various levels in the organization, and make it visible for everyone. This helps people to keep track of ideas that have yet to be implemented. As with any other normal backlog, old unimplemented ideas may be replaced by newer ones at any time [Cohn 2009:62–63]. You may find it necessary to reserve some capacity in people's schedules each month for your continuous improvement efforts; otherwise, the ideas on the backlog may get discussed but never implemented.

- Use an explicit multistep **improvement cycle**. You can use the eight steps that I described in the SLIP model or any other cycle that you find valuable. As with any normal task board, like in Scrum and Kanban, the items from the improvement backlog must pass through the different steps in the workflow, which helps people to not forget any important steps (like measuring and verifying improvement).

- Set up a **transition team** (sometimes called an Enterprise Transition Community, or ETC) with the task of promoting and supporting change across an organization. The team should have senior people and representatives from all parts of the organization that are to be transitioned. The goal of this team of "change champions" is not to impose change on people but to guide them in their transition [Cohn 2009:63–70]. As discussed earlier, the endless nature of change may require that a transition team has a semi-permanent character.

- Learn about the **Kanban** method as a great framework for your continuous improvement efforts. Kanban is a change management approach that uses work-in-progress limits as a control mechanism to introduce change, and a visualization of value streams (or value networks) as a way to confront teams with the need for change [Anderson 2010].

- Suggest to the people in your organization that they initiate their own **improvement communities** around topics that transcend multiple projects, such as testing, architecture, or user interface design [Cohn 2009:70–78]. As a manager it is best not to install such communities yourself because teams are supposed to self-organize their own communities based on their own needs. Though, of course, you can assist them if needed. (In this respect they are similar to the self-selected specialist teams that we discussed in Chapter 13, such as continuous integration teams and component teams.)

I am sure people can think of plenty more tips for continuous improvement. But the ones in this chapter are enough to get you started.

Keep on Rolling

Changing environments, and the Red Queen's Race of coevolving systems, have huge implications for fitness landscapes. They make it seem as if they are made of rubber. (Rollerblades would work well in such landscapes.) The peaks and valleys are always on the move and forever rising and falling. A system that was fit yesterday may be unprepared for the environment of tomorrow. Today's best practices can be tomorrow's worst practices. Species, businesses, and teams have to keep changing, because it takes all the running (or skating) they can do just to stay on top of a moving peak. And when a peak turns into a valley, they need a radical jump to another one.

In stable environments, the fitness landscape doesn't change much. After an organization has found a peak, it can comfortably stay there for a while, making sure that it exploits its current situation in the most efficient and effective ways possible. But in stable environments, systems tend to lose the capability to change. People forget *how* to change when the environment has always seemed the same for them. The danger is that they may not notice it when their comfortable peak is dropping slowly and turning into a valley. Contentment with the success of your business may be your worst enemy. Your once brilliant colleagues suddenly turn out to have fallen behind the times. The tools you were using are not giving you the best results anymore. Your favorite development method, once a great asset, has slowly turned into a liability. And the roller blades got rusty, or lost.

This is why being Agile is about survival.

The Agile Manifesto never said you should stick to XP or Scrum or any other method. It says you must understand and embrace change. This is why improvement of features, qualities, people, tools, schedules, and processes never stops. It is your way of life. Don't ever be content. Keep changing! Keep rolling! And take a break sometimes to review the landscape and check what the peaks are doing. Then pick up your skates and resume the race.

This brings me to the end of the *Improve Everything* view, and (almost) to the end of this book. We've discussed people, empowerment, alignment, competence, structure, and improvement. The only topic left for me to discuss is the Management 3.0 model itself.

Summary

Most models for continuous improvement are linear, but software project teams are nonlinear complex systems. That means improvement is sometimes a matter of doing one step back and two steps forward. Software teams must go through both gradual changes and radical changes, performing both small steps and big jumps, to navigate their rugged fitness landscape.

One way to navigate a fitness landscape is simply to change it. This means purposefully changing the environment (including customers, top management, and various departments) so that teams can better find their optimal performance. Another way for managers to drive change in an organization is to make change desirable and to make stagnation painful.

There are three strategies for achieving optimal performance: experimenting by changing individual practices, mixing collections of best practices from previous top performers, and learning from others who broadcast their best practices to whom it may concern.

No matter which strategies you employ, it is important to realize that continuous improvement is indeed continuous. It never stops.

Reflection and Action

Let's see if you can apply some ideas from this chapter to your organization:

- Create a backlog and workflow for improvements. Use the SLIP model, or another improvement model, to define and track the phases for each improvement. (But don't be surprised if individual changes don't lead to improvements immediately and only seem to make things worse at first.)

- Discuss necessary changes with your team. Are the changes made desirable enough? Is stagnation made painful enough?

- Review problems that your team cannot seem to get rid of, despite all the solutions they've tried. Try to find ways of changing the environment instead of the team so that the attractor in which they are stuck dissolves.

- Make it a habit of discussing errors with your team. Discuss what valuable things you've learned from those errors.

- Try experimenting with change just because you can. Without pressure from the environment, and without knowing if the direction is the right one. Discuss what you've learned.

- Try mixing the software development approaches from different teams. Can you make a great new process out of two good ones?

- Discuss with the team how it picks up interesting practices from other sources. Make sure there is a continuous input (and output) of ideas.

- Make sure that every team regularly performs retrospectives.

- Set up a transition team with the task of supporting change in your organization.

- Suggest people to set up improvement communities around topics that concern multiple teams.

Chapter 16

All Is Wrong, but Some Is Useful

The pure and simple truth is rarely pure and never simple.

—Oscar Wilde, writer, poet (1854–1900)

I feel I am unable to properly finish this book. It appears that every description of Agile management is incomplete, and every conclusion I write may be wrong.

Embracing complexity thinking is like marrying a black hole. To keep your sanity, it would be best to stay far away. But it's very attractive. You can't help being sucked in, and then everything you believed in is either negated or compressed to nothing. And there are plenty of things I believe in.

The Six Views of Management 3.0

I believe that linear thinking often leads to incorrect conclusions (refer to Chapter 1), and that both Agile software development and complex systems theory share a foundation of nonlinear thinking (refer to Chapters 2 and 3). I think that people are the most important parts of an organization and that managers must do all they can to keep people active, creative, and motivated (refer to Chapters 4 and 5). I believe that teams can self-organize, and that this requires empowerment, authorization, and trust from management (refer to Chapters 6 and 7). I explained that self-organization can lead to anything, and that it's therefore necessary to protect people and shared resources, and to give people a clear purpose and defined goals (refer to Chapters 8 and 9). I also believe that teams can't achieve these goals if team members aren't capable enough, and that managers must therefore contribute to the development of competence (refer to Chapters 10 and 11). Many teams operate within the context of a complex organization, and thus I am convinced it is important to consider structures that enhance communication (refer to Chapters 12 and 13). I also think that people, teams, and organizations need to improve continuously to defer failure for as long as possible (refer to Chapters 14 and 15). Finally, I think a conclusion as described here is simple to understand, which means it is probably wrong (this chapter).

Figure 16.1 depicts Martie, the Management 3.0 model. Martie has six views:

- Energize People
- Empower Teams
- Align Constraints
- Develop Competence
- Grow Structure
- Improve Everything

FIGURE 16.1

Martie, the Management 3.0 model.

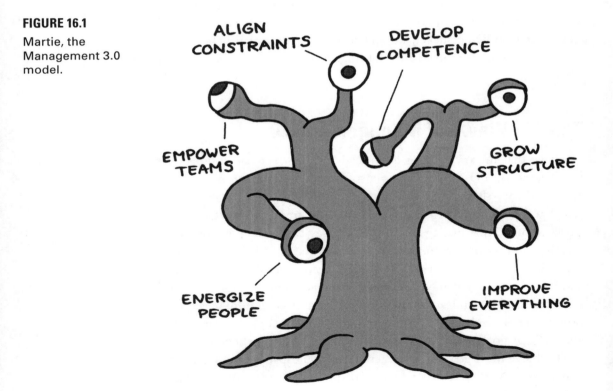

I specifically use the term "views" instead of "principles" or "pillars" because it stresses the idea that it is one and the same system, with viewpoints from different angles. For example, the concept of a Community of Practice (refer to Chapter 13) fits in at least three views in my model (*Develop Competence*, *Define Structure*, and *Improve Everything*). Similarly, the suggestion for a team to define its own Team Values (refer to Chapter 5) touches upon *Energize People*, *Empower Teams*, and *Align Constraints*. The six views are different ways of looking at the same things.

But no matter how accurately I try to summarize the contents of this book, and how well I try to draw my illustrations, complex systems theory tells me that every simple description I have for management of Agile organizations will be incomplete. Negated by complexity thinking. Compressed to nothing.

It could make me very sad, but you've made it this far into the book, which helps to relieve the pain.

Yes, My Model Is "Wrong"

The cause of my looming misery is the concept of **incompressibility**:

> There is no accurate (or rather, perfect) representation of the system which is simpler than the system itself. In building representations of open systems, we are forced to leave things out, and since the effects of these omissions are nonlinear, we cannot predict their magnitude.[1]

Allow me to try and rephrase that in my own words....

In Chapter 3, I depicted chaos theory as the heart of complexity theory. The Butterfly Effect (the foundation of chaos theory, discussed in Chapter 14) shows us that even the tiniest deviations in a complex system can have far-reaching consequences. When we try to model and describe complex systems, we *have* to leave things out; otherwise, we get crushed by all the details. But in a complex system, the details make all the difference, and when we leave them out, the results can be unexpected!

According to the concept of incompressibility, the only accurate description of a complex system is the system itself. Anything simpler is incomplete because it ignores important details. And thus my simple

---

1   Source: Cilliers, Paul. "Knowing Complex Systems" Richardson K.A. Managing Organizational Complexity: Philosophy, Theory and Application. Greenwich: Information Age Publishing, 2005, page 13. Used with permission. [Cilliers 2005:13].

Management 3.0 model is incomplete. Sorry to disappoint you. If you wanted a book with a simple conclusion, you picked the wrong one.

Fortunately, Gerald Weinberg, one of the earliest systems thinkers, comes to our rescue with his **Complementarity Law**:

> Any two points of view are complementary.[2]

Even though models of complex systems are usually incomplete, they can still be valid and useful because they give us complementary (and possibly contradicting) viewpoints [Richardson 2004a].

There is no single theory of evolution. Instead there are multiple complementary, competing, and sometimes conflicting models. And yet, this collection of models has a tremendous descriptive and predictive power [McKelvey 1999:19]. In physics we see something similar: The wave and particle models are both accepted because each produces accurate descriptions and reliable predictions. Apparently, physicists don't consider their conflicting explanations to be a failure.

My suggestion is that the same applies to models of software development. Scrum, Kanban, and XP are complementary, competing, and conflicting models. But this is not a failure. We simply have to be careful and critical in our usage of these models and the knowledge that we gain from them.

> As far as complex systems are concerned, our knowledge will always be contextually and historically framed. It is also not claimed that there is something wrong with modeling complex systems. [...] However, we should be careful about the claims made about the "knowledge" we gain from many of these models. [...] In order to gain "knowledge" from complex models they have to be interpreted, and these interpretations will always involve a reduction in complexity. Thus the main argument is not that there is something metaphysically unknowable about complex systems, but rather that we cannot "know" a system in all its complexity.[3] [Cilliers 2002:78]

There will always be coexisting and conflicting models of management, each with its own strengths and weaknesses *because* organizations and

---

2   Weinberg, Gerald. An Introduction to General Systems Thinking: Silver Anniversary Edition. New York: Dorset House, 2001. [Weinberg 2001:120].

3   Cilliers, Paul. "Why We Cannot Know Complex Things Completely" Emergence. Vol. 4, Issue 1/2, 2002. Used with permission. [Cilliers 2002:78].

software teams are complex. Incompressibility makes it so. There will never be one Theory of Everything (TOE) for managing organizations or developing software (a secret hope I had already left behind me in Chapter 1). Instead we need to work with a patchwork of theories, methods, and frameworks [Richardson 2008:17]. Apparently, the body of knowledge of software development is as ugly as the body of knowledge of systems (refer to Chapter 3). Though, perhaps, the tutu is of a different color (see Figure 16.2).

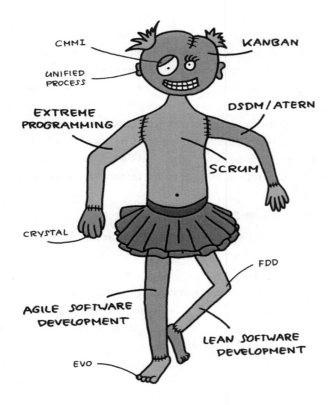

FIGURE 16.2

The body of knowledge of software development.

But Other Models Are "Wrong," Too

Whenever I fail a test, I find comfort that I'm not the only one. Likewise, it pleases me to know there are other models for managing organizations, and that they are just as "wrong" as my Management 3.0 model. Shared pain is half the pain. Though in this case, shared pain could even turn into joy. We learned from Weinberg that multiple incomplete models are less incomplete than one. So perhaps two or more wrongs *do* make a right....

The Toyota Way

The Toyota Way[4] was published in 2001. It is a set of behaviors that underlie Toyota's managerial approach and production system. The Toyota Way consists of two main principles: *Respect for People* and *Continuous Improvement*, which nicely align with two views in my own model (Energize People and Improve Everything).

Professor Jeffrey Liker analyzed Toyota's management philosophy and expanded it into 14 more detailed principles [Liker 2004]. Some of them, such as *long-term goals*, *growing leaders*, *developing people*, and *relentless reflection*, are adequately covered in my Management 3.0 model. Other principles, such as *continuous flow*, *pull systems*, and *slow decisions/rapid implementation*, are useful for many organizations, but I prefer to see them as good techniques for workers, not as core principles for managers.

One interesting difference is that organizational structure (the *Grow Structure* view of my model) seems to be missing in The Toyota Way. I won't claim that this is reason for a recall of The Toyota Way, but I do think the structure of a complex system is too important to ignore, and it is one of the keys to making Agile organizations actually work.

Deming's 14 Principles

In his book *Out of the Crisis*, Management Professor W. Edwards Deming offered 14 key principles for managing and transforming organizations [Deming 1986]. Deming's principles have been cited in literature countless times and are a source of inspiration for many Agile and Lean managers around the world.

It turns out that the six views described in this book, and the examples and techniques I've given to support them, cover almost all Deming's principles. *Constancy of purpose, Leadership for change, Cease dependence on inspection, Improve constantly, Institute training, Institute leadership, Drive out fear, Break down barriers between departments, Eliminate exhortations of workers, Pride of workmanship, Education and self-improvement*, and *Transformation is everyone's job* have all been addressed in earlier chapters in one way or another. Only the principle *Minimize total cost* has not been addressed here, but hopefully you didn't find the book too expensive.

There is also a concern regarding Deming's principle *Eliminate management by objective*, which seems to contradict some of the ideas in my views of *Align Constraints* and *Develop Competence*. However, Deming's

---

4 http://www.mgt30.com/toyota/.

problem with objectives was about the use of incentives and the lack of a systemic view among managers, both of which are sufficiently addressed in this book.

Mintzberg's Six-Plane Model

Professor Henry Mintzberg is one of the world's best thinkers and authors on business management. In his book *Managing* he presents a new model he developed over many years [Mintzberg 2009:48]. Mintzberg's model describes management taking place in three "planes," with two main activities per plane: the *action plane (doing and dealing)*, the *people plane (leading and linking)*, and the *information plane (communicating and controlling)*.

Comparing my Management 3.0 model with Mintzberg's model, it seems that they overlap halfway. This book has covered the activities leading, communicating, and doing well enough, I believe. But my model has little regard for the other half (linking, controlling, and dealing) that in my opinion are not necessarily a manager's responsibilities and can easily be delegated to teams. On the other hand, Mintzberg's model doesn't mention half of the topics from the Management 3.0 model: structure, competence, and improvement, whereas I am convinced that these are crucial for Agile organizations.

The different viewpoints can be explained with the observation that Mintzberg created his model with input from management practice. It shows what managers are *actually doing*. Instead, I created my model with input from scientific theory (and from my car). It shows what managers *should be doing*.

Hamel's Five Principles

Gary Hamel, one of the *other* best thinkers and authors on business management, outlined five "21st century management principles" for building companies that are fit for the future in *The Future of Management* [Hamel 2007]. His principles are *Life (Variety)*, *Markets (Flexibility)*, *Democracy (Activism)*, *Faith (Meaning)*, and *Cities (Serendipity)*.

Though the naming of these five principles seems a bit vague, I recognized most of the ideas underlying Hamel's principles (*experimentation, mutations, Darwinian selection, networks instead of hierarchies, distributed leadership, inspiring goals, caring people, diversity, creativity, innovation,* and so on) because they have all been discussed in this book.

The only topic I feel is missing from Hamel's model is the development of competency. Like the original Agile Manifesto, Hamel's model seems to assume that excellent employees simply drop from the sky on a parachute, with no price tag on them. This, unfortunately, has never been my own experience.

And Many More...

There are dozens, if not hundreds, of models for management. I chose to review and compare only a few offered by the most highly respected and knowledgeable sources. (I didn't want you to suffer reading through *142 Leadership Laws from Priests, Reverends, and Military Commanders*.) The point I make here is that, though none of the models are perfect, there can be significant value in each of them.

The Fall and Decline of Agilists

Not only management is faced with a multitude of competing models; we also have a similar situation in software development.

Agile experts regularly tell people that to do Scrum or XP correctly, "developers *must* refactor their code." Some claim that "everybody needs unit tests," that "Scrum makes things worse by ignoring engineering practices," and that "you're not Agile if you don't practice build integration every day." According to these experts, being Agile is *not* about being adaptable and doing whatever it takes to make your project a long-lasting success. Apparently, Agile is about following practices X, Y, and Z. Except, it isn't.

> *Agility is about staying successful in ever-changing environments.*
> *[me]*

That's it; there's little more to it.

I believe there is one best practice for all organizations, and that is to throw out any "expert" who claims that practice X is best for all organizations. Quite likely, practice X happens to be something this person is very good at and is willing to assist you with for a considerable consultancy fee. (In case you're wondering, I don't get paid for throwing out experts.)

Some Agilists have suggested that perhaps we should give up on the "Agile" brand name. After all, it's never been clearly defined, which has allowed a lot of dysfunctional projects to call themselves "Agile." But what these Agilists *mean* is that it has never been clearly defined which practices are the core of Agile. And rightfully so, because there are none!

If there were, it would mean prescribing one survival strategy for all systems, which would defeat the concept of complexity (and more specifically the game theory part of complexity science.) Agile has never been some specific set of practices. Nowhere on the Agile Manifesto does it say that you have to do automated testing, pair programming, or refactoring. (I wouldn't know how to write a book in an Agile way if these practices were actually required.) In fact, an "Agile practice" should be considered a contradiction in terms as soon as people consider it to be mandatory!

It seems reasonable for us to expect from Agile experts that they understand the basics of complexity theory. After all, it is one of the roots of Agile software development. If people understood this, they wouldn't be telling us silly things like, "Do practice X or you won't be Agile" and "You're not doing Scrum right if you don't do Y." Unfortunately, that is not how things seem to be these days. Agilists argue over Lean versus Agile, XP versus Scrum, Kanban versus Scrum, and who-knows-what-else-and-my-mother-in-law versus Scrum. (At the time of writing, Scrum is still the norm. If you find some faults with Scrum, people will probably think you're smart.) But, *every* model is incomplete. Pointing out failures in a model is actually quite easy. It's not very helpful though.

We are faced with a global armada of Agilists who know words like *emergence* and *self-organization*, because *everybody's using them*. But they don't understand the origins of those words, and what this means for Agile software development. That's why I believe it's time for my own stake in the ground....

The Complexity Pamphlet

I believe people should recognize that it is human to prefer simple answers, but that the world is more complex than we usually think. And therefore I offer these suggestions....

Each Problem Has Multiple Solutions

There's not just one way to solve the Rubik's cube. There's not one best way to run a business. There's not one best strategy to win at Risk. And there is not one best way to run a software project. We are human, and we like to be the ones who are right. But we admit that others may be right as well.

Solutions Depend on the Problem's Context

The form of each species depends on its environment. The best strategies in football depend on the team and its opponents. The best marketing depends on the customers. And the best software development practices depend on the project's environment. In software development there are many nobles, but context is king.

Changing Context Requires Changing Solutions

When environments change, so do species. And good strategies for social networking today are different from what they were last year. (Follow me on Twitter, and we will see how things have changed next year.) Therefore, when software project environments change, the projects must change accordingly.

Each Strange Solution Is the Best One Somewhere

Antarctic krill are the most successful species in the world. And tit-for-tat is one of the most prevalent survival strategies in game theory. But the silly looking blob fish has its place in the world, too. And no game strategy is always superior. Likewise, some software development practices are popular, but they can never replace the exceptions that will always be there.

Solutions Change the Context and Themselves

Some new movies change the playing field of the movie business itself—and any subsequent movies that are made. The memes in our mind change the way we think, and which new memes we are willing to adopt. Similarly, our software practices change our environment and the way we can apply other practices.

Simplicity Necessitates Understanding Complexity

Biologists, businesses, and governments have done much harm by not understanding the complexity of the world. Those who don't understand the way things work have a hard time anticipating which simple solutions might work in solving complex problems.

We Cannot Predict the Best Solution

Anticipation is valuable; but it is impossible to know for sure which solution will work and which won't. Only with empirical findings in a real context can we make any claims about the success of a solution. We admit what we don't know, and that we have to try things to know if they work in our context.

The *Complexity Pamphlet* (see Figure 16.3) does not invalidate any existing values, principles, guidelines, or practices (or manifestos). On the contrary, it emphasizes that *all are valuable*, when seen in their proper context. In software development, discussions should not be about who is right and who is wrong. Instead, people should concern themselves with what is useful in which environment. We should not be overly interested in user stories versus use cases, Agile versus CMMI, Scrum versus Kanban, or Agile versus Lean. We should be interested in when to use what. Simple wrong-versus-right debates only serve popularity, not understanding.

> *It is simplicity that makes the uneducated more effective than the educated when addressing popular audiences.* [Aristotle]

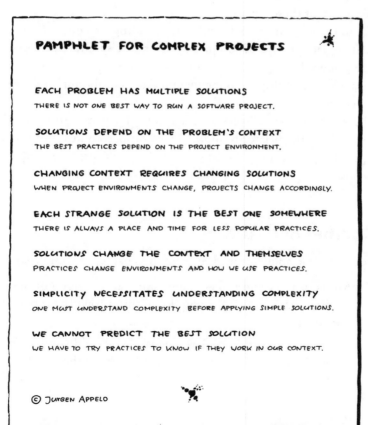

FIGURE 16.3

The Complexity Pamphlet.

I hope that software developers and managers around the world learn to understand that there's no need to flame each other over methods, frameworks, principles, and practices. In a complex world, there's a time and place (small or big) for every idea. It makes no sense discussing which idea is wrong, because they all are. The real challenge is in finding out which idea is useful in what context.

> All models are wrong, but some are useful. [Box, Draper 1969]

I know my book is "wrong," but I sincerely hope you found it useful.

Summary

The six views of the Management 3.0 model are *Energize People*, *Empower Teams*, *Align Constraints*, *Develop Competence*, *Grow Structure*, and *Improve Everything*. All practices for Agile managers should contribute positively to at least one of these six views.

But in the end, all models will fail, including this one. No model can paint a complete picture of complex systems, like software projects. That's why all models are wrong; although some can be useful. And that's why it's useful to have multiple complementary and conflicting models for different occasions.

The same applies to software methods. They can all be useful; although each of them is only useful in its proper context. In a complex world, nothing is simple. And in the end there's just one simple truth: It depends.

Reflection and Action

Let's see if you can apply some ideas from this chapter to your organization:

- Are your tasks and projects addressing all six views of the Management 3.0 model? Are you doing things that the model does not cover?

- Evaluate what this book has meant to you. Did you like it? If yes, then please tell others how it may help them, too.

Bibliography

Abilla, Pete, "Zero Defects Is Wrong Approach" <http://www.shmula.com/376/zero-defects-is-wrong-approach> *shmula.* April 3, 2007.

Abran, Alain and James Moore. *Guide to the Software Engineering Body of Knowledge.* Oxford Oxfordshire: Oxford University Press, 2004.

Adams, Cecil. "Why do we nod our heads for 'yes' and shake them for 'no'?" *The Straight Dope.* March 14, 1986.

Adkins, Lyssa. *Coaching Agile Teams.* Reading: Addison-Wesley Professional, 2010.

Alleman, Glen B. "Self Organized Does Not Mean Self Directed" <http://herdingcats.typepad.com/my_weblog/2008/12/self-organized-does-not-mean-self-directed.html>. *Herding Cats* December 24, 2008.

Allen, David. *Getting Things Done.* New York: Penguin Books, 2003.

Ambler, Scott "The Discipline of Agile" <http://www.ddj.com/architect/201804241>. *Dr. Dobb's.* September 5, 2007.

Ambler, Scott "Generalizing Specialists: Improving Your IT Career Skills" <http://www.agilemodeling.com/essays/generalizingSpecialists.htm>. *Agile Modeling.* 2010.

Anderson, Carl and Elizabeth McMillan. "Of Ants and Men: Self-Organized Teams in Human and Insect Organizations" *Emergence* Vol. 5 Iss. 2 2003.

Anderson, Chris. *Long Tail, the, Revised and Updated Edition.* New York: Hyperion, 2008.

Anderson, David. *Agile Management for Software Engineering.* Upper Saddle River: Prentice Hall Professional Technical Reference, 2004.

Anderson, David. *Kanban.* City: Blue Hole Press, 2010.

Arrow, Holly et.al. *Small Groups as Complex Systems.* Thousand Oaks: Sage, 2000.

Augustine, Sanjiv. *Managing Agile Projects.* Upper Saddle River: Prentice Hall Professional Technical Reference, 2005.

Austin, Robert. *Measuring and Managing Performance in Organizations.* New York: Dorset House, 1996.

Austin, Robert and Lee Devin. *Artful Making.* New York: Financial Times/Prentice Hall, 2003.

Avery, Christopher et.al. *Teamwork Is an Individual Skill.* San Francisco: Berrett-Koehler Publishers, 2001.

Beck, Kent. *Extreme Programming Explained, Second Edition.* Boston: Addison-Wesley, 2005.

Bennet, Alex and David Bennet. *Organizational Survival in the New World.* Amsterdam: Elsevier, 2004.

Berkun, Scott. *Making Things Happen: Mastering Project Management.* Sebastopol: O'Reilly Media, Inc., 2008.

Blanchard, Kenneth and Spencer Johnson. *The One Minute Manager.* New York: Morrow, 1982.

Bobinski, Dan. "Gardening and Management: What They Have in Common" *Hodu.com* <http://www.hodu.com/garden.shtml>. 2009.

Bobinski, Dan. "Performance appraisals don't work" *Management-Issues.* <http://www.management-issues.com/2010/7/8/opinion/performance-appraisals-dont-work.asp>. 8 July 2010.

Bond, Michael. "Critical Mass." *New Scientist* 18 July 2009 (b). <http://www.newscientist.com/article/mg20327171.400-why-cops-should-trust-the-wisdom-of-the-crowds.html>.

Bond, Michael. "Three degrees of separation." *New Scientist.* 3 January 2009 (a) <http://www.newscientist.com/article/mg20126881.600-how-your-friends-friends-can-affect-your-mood.html>.

Bowen, D.E. and Lawler, E.E. "Empowering service employees." *Sloan Management Review,* Summer 1995.

Box, George and Norman Draper. *Evolutionary Operation.* New York: Wiley, 1969.

Brahic, Catherine. "All at sea over mystery currents." *NewScientist.* 19 April 2008.

Brooks, Frederick. *The Mythical Man-Month.* Reading: Addison-Wesley Pub. Co, 1975/1995.

Brooks, Michael. "Born believers: How your brain creates God." *New Scientist,* Feb 4, 2009. <http://www.newscientist.com/article/mg20126941.700-born-believers-how-your-brain-creates-god.html>.

Brown, Tim. "Strategy by Design" <http://www.fastcompany.com/magazine/95/design-strategy.html>. *Fast Company.* June 1, 2005.

Buchanan, Mark. "Another kind of evolution" *NewScientist.* 23 January 2010.

Buchanan, Mark. "The curse of the committee" *NewScientist.* 10 January 2009.

Buckingham, Marcus and Curt Coffman. *First, Break All the Rules.* New York: Simon & Schuster, 1999.

Business Week. "Jack Welch Elaborates: Shareholder Value" *Business Week.* 16 March 2009.

Caudron, S. "Create an empowering environment." *PersonnelJournal,* 1995 74-9.

Chrissis, Beth, Mary et.al. *Cmmi.* Boston: Addison-Wesley, 2007.

Chui, Glennda. "Unified Theory is Getting Closer, Hawking Predicts." *San Jose Mercury News,* January 23, 2000.

Cilliers, Paul. *Complexity and Postmodernism.* New York: Routledge, 1998.

Cilliers, Paul. "Knowing Complex Systems" Richardson, K.A. *Managing Organizational Complexity: Philosophy, Theory and Application.* Greenwich: Information Age Publishing, 2005.

Cilliers, Paul. "Why We Cannot Know Complex Things Completely" *Emergence.* Vol. 4, Issue 1/2, 2002.

Clegg, Brian and Paul Birch. *Instant Creativity.* London: Kogan Page, 2006.

Cockburn, Alistair. "Process: the 4th dimension" <http://alistair.cockburn.us/index.php/Process:_the_fourth_dimension>. 2003.

Cockburn, Alistair. *Agile Software Development, Second Edition.* Boston: Addison-Wesley, 2007.

Cohn, Mike. *Succeeding with Agile: Software Development Using Scrum.* Reading: Addison-Wesley Professional, 2009.

Collins, James. *Good to Great.* New York: HarperBusiness, 2001.

Coplien, James and Neil Harrison. *Organizational Patterns of Agile Software Development.* Upper Saddle River: Pearson Prentice Hall, 2005.

Corning, Peter A. "The Emergence of "Emergence": Now What?" *Emergence,* Vol. 4, Issue 3, 2002.

Corning, Peter. *Nature's Magic.* Cambridge: Cambridge University Press, 2003.

Covey, Stephen. *The 7 Habits of Highly Effective People.* New York: Free Press, 2004.

Cropley, Arthur J. "Definitions of Creativity" *Encyclopedia of Creativity.* Boston: Elsevier/Academic Press, 1999.

Cross, Rob et.al. *The Hidden Power of Social Networks.* Boston: Harvard Business School Press, 2004.

Culbert, Samuel and Lawrence Rout. *Get Rid of the Performance Review!* City: Business Plus, 2010.

Curry, Andrew "Monopoly Killer: Perfect German Board Game Redefines Genre" <http://www.wired.com/gaming/gamingreviews/magazine/17-04/mf_settlers>. *Wired.* March 23, 2009.

Curtis, Bill et.al. *People Capability Maturity Model.* Boston: Addison-Wesley, 2001.

Davila, Tony et.al. *Making Innovation Work.* Upper Saddle River: Wharton School Pub, 2006.

Davis, Mark. "Living with aliens." *NewScientist.* 26 September 2009.

Dawkins, Richard. *The Blind Watchmaker.* New York: Norton, 1996.

Dawkins, Richard "The Purpose of Purpose" <http://richarddawkins.net/articles/3956>. June 18, 2009.

Dawkins, Richard. *The Selfish Gene.* Oxford Oxfordshire: Oxford University Press, 1989.

De Geus, Arie. *The Living Company*. Boston: Harvard Business School Press, 1997.

De Wolf, Tom, and Tom Holvoet. "Emergence Versus Self-Organisation: Different Concepts but Promising When Combined." *Engineering Self Organising Systems: Methodologies and Applications, Lecture Notes in Computer Science,* volume 3464, pp 1-15, 2005.

Deci, Edward L. and Richard M. Ryan. *The Handbook of Self-Determination Research*. Rochester: University of Rochester Press, 2004.

DeMarco, Tom and Timothy Lister. *Peopleware, Second Edition*. New York: Dorset House Pub, 1999.

Deming, W. *Out of the Crisis*. Cambridge: Massachusetts Institute of Technology, Center for Advanced Engineering Study, 1986.

Dennett, Daniel. *Consciousness Explained*. Boston: Back Bay Books, 1992.

Dennett, Daniel. *Darwin's Dangerous Idea*. New York: Simon & Schuster, 1995.

Dent, Eric B. "Complexity Science: a Worldview Shift" *Emergence*. Vol. 1, Issue 4, 1999.

Derby, Esther. "Performance Without Appraisal: Addressing the Most Common Concerns" 12 July 2010 <http://www.estherderby.com/2010/07/performance-without-appraisal-addressing-the-most-common-concerns.html>.

Derby, Esther and Diana Larsen. *Agile Retrospectives*. Boston: Twayne Publishers, 2006.

Eliot, Lise. "We are all from Alpha Centauri" *NewScientist*. 17 July 2010.

Eoyang, Glenda and Doris Jane Conway "Conditions That Support Self-Organization in a Complex Adaptive System" <http://amauta-international.com/iaf99/Thread1/conway.html>. *IAF* January 14-17, 1999.

Falconer, James. "Emergence Happens! Misguided Paradigms Regarding Organizational Change and the Role of Complexity and Patterns in the Change Landscape" *Emergence*. Vol. 4, Issue 1/2, 2002.

Fonseca, José. *Complexity and Innovation in Organizations*. New York: Routledge, 2002.

Forrester, Jay W. "System Dynamics, Systems Thinking, and Soft OR" Massachusetts Institute of Technology, August 18, 1992.

Fox, John. "Employee Empowerment: An Apprentice Model" 22 June 1998. <http://members.tripod.com/j_fox/thesis.html>.

Friedman, Milton "The Social Responsibility of Business is to Increase Its Profits" *New York Times Magazine* September 13, 1970

Gall, John. *The Systems Bible*. Ann Arbor: General Systemantics Press, 2002.

Gat, Israel. "A Social Contract for Agile" <http://theagileexecutive.com/2009/02/03/a-social-contract-for-agile/>. *The Agile Executive*. February 3, 2009.

Gell-Mann, Murray. *The Quark and the Jaguar*. Clearwater: Owl Books, 1994.

Gilb, Tom et.al. *Software Inspection*. Boston: Addison-Wesley, 1993.

Gladwell, Malcolm. *Outliers: Why Some People Succeed and Some Don't*. Little: Little, 2008.

Gladwell, Malcolm. *The Tipping Point*. Boston: Back Bay Books, 2002.

Glass, Robert. *Facts and Fallacies of Software Engineering*. Boston: Addison-Wesley, 2003.

Gleick, James. *Chaos*. Harmondsworth Eng.: Penguin, 1987.

Godin, Seth. *Tribes: We Need You to Lead Us*. City: Portfolio Hardcover, 2008.

Gould, Stephen Jay. "Full House: The Spread of Excellence from Plato to Darwin." Three Rivers Press, 1997.

Gould, Stephen Jay. *The Structure of Evolutionary Theory*. Cambridge: Belknap Harvard, 2002.

Granovetter, Mark. "The Strength of Weak Ties" *American Journal of Sociology* 78 (6): 1360–1380, May 1973.

Hackman, J. *Leading Teams*. Boston: Harvard Business School Press, 2002.

Hamel, Gary. *The Future of Management*. Boston: Harvard Business School Press, 2007.

Hartzog, Paul B. "Panarchy: Governance in the Network Age" <http://panarchy.com/Members/PaulBHartzog/Papers/Panarchy%20-%20Governance%20in%20the%20Network%20Age.pdf>. 2009.

Heath, Chip and Dan Heath. *Made to Stick*. New York: Random House, 2007.

Heathfield, Susan M. "Team Building and Delegation: How and When to Empower People" *Michigan State University M.E.N.T.O.R.S. Manual: Monthly Conversation Guide #9* 2003-2004.

Heathfield, Susan M. "The Darker Side of Goal Setting: Why Goal Setting Fails...." <http://humanresources.about.com/cs/strategichr/a/aadark_goals.htm>. *About.com*. 2010 (a).

Heathfield, Susan M. "360 Degree Feedback: The Good, the Bad, and the Ugly." <http://humanresources.about.com/od/360feedback/a/360feedback.htm>. *About.com*. 2010 (b).

Heathfield, Susan M. "Performance Appraisals Don't Work." <http://humanresources.about.com/od/performanceevals/a/perf_appraisal.htm>. *About.com*. 2010 (c).

Herzberg, Frederick. *One More Time: How Do You Motivate Employees?*. Boston: Harvard Business Press, 2008.

Highsmith, Jim. *Adaptive Software Development*. New York: Dorset House Pub, 1999.

Highsmith, Jim. *Agile Project Management, Second Edition*. Boston: Addison-Wesley, 2009.

Highsmith, Jim. "Does Agility Work?" *Dr. Dobbs*. June 1, 2002. <http://www.drdobbs.com/184414858>.

Hofstadter, Douglas. *Gödel, Escher, Bach*. New York: Basic Books, 1979.

Holland, John. *Hidden Order*. Boston: Addison-Wesley, 1995.

Hunt, Andrew. *Pragmatic Thinking and Learning*. City: Pragmatic Bookshelf, 2008.

Hunt, Andrew and David Thomas. *The Pragmatic Programmer*. Boston: Addison-Wesley, 2000.

Jacobson, Ivar "Enough of Processes: Let's Do Practices." <http://www.ddj.com/architect/198000264>. *Dr. Dobb's*. March 12, 2007.

Jaques, Elliott "In Praise of Hierarchy" *Harvard Business Review*. January-February 1990.

Jaques, Elliott. *Requisite Organization*. Oxford Oxfordshire: Oxford University Press, 1998.

Jensen, Eric. *Enriching the Brain*. San Francisco: Jossey-Bass, A John Wiley & Sons Imprint, 2006.

Jones, Capers. *Software Assessments, Benchmarks, and Best Practices*. Harlow: Addison-Wesley, 2001.

Kao, John. *Innovation Nation*. New York: Free Press, 2007.

Kaplan, Robert and David Norton. *The Balanced Scorecard*. Boston: Harvard Business School Press, 1996.

Kauffman, Stuart. *At Home in the Universe*. Oxford Oxfordshire: Oxford University Press, 1995.

Kaye, Beverly and Sharon Jordan-Evans. *Love 'Em or Lose 'Em: Getting Good People to Stay*. San Francisco: Berrett-Koehler Publishers, 2008.

Keizer, Kees, et.al. "The Spreading of Disorder" <http://www.sciencemag.org/cgi/content/abstract/1161405>. *Science*. December 12, 2008.

Kelly, Kevin. *Out of Control*. Boston: Addison-Wesley, 1994.

Kruchten, Philippe. "Voyage in the Agile Memeplex" *ACM Queue*. August 16, 2007.

Lane, David et.al. *Complexity Perspectives in Innovation and Social Change*. Berlin: Springer, 2009.

Larman, Craig. *Agile and Iterative Development*. Boston: Addison-Wesley, 2004.

Larman, Craig and Bas Vodde. *Scaling Lean & Agile Development*. Boston: Addison-Wesley, 2009.

Leffingwell, Dean. *Scaling Software Agility*. Oxford Oxfordshire: Oxford University Press, 2007.

Lencioni, Patrick. *The Five Dysfunctions of a Team*. San Francisco: Jossey-Bass, 2002.

Le Page, Michael. "Evolution: A guide for the not-yet perplexed" *NewScientist*. 19 April 2008

Levitt, Ted. *Ted Levitt on Marketing*. Boston: Harvard Business School Press, 2006.

Lewin, Roger. *Complexity*. Chicago: University of Chicago Press, 1999.

Lewin, Roger and Birute Regine. *Weaving Complexity and Business*. Mason: Texere, 2001.

Liker, Jeffrey. *The Toyota Way*. New York: McGraw-Hill, 2004.

Lissack, Michael R. "Complexity: the Science, its Vocabulary, and its Relation to Organizations" *Emergence*. Vol. 1, Issue 1, 1999.

Lundin, Stephen et.al. *Fish!*. New York: Hyperion, 2000.

Maguire, Steve. and Bill McKelvey. "Complexity and Management: Moving from Fad to Firm Foundations". *Emergence*. Vol. 1, Issue 2, 1999.

Macleod, Mairi. "You are what you copy" *NewScientist*. 1 May 2010.

Mandelbrot, Benoit and Richard Hudson. *The (Mis) Behavior of Markets*. Cambridge: Perseus Books Group, 2006.

Manns, Lynn, Mary and Linda Rising. *Fearless Change*. Boston: Twayne Publishers, 2005.

Marick, Brian "Six years later: What the Agile Manifesto left out" <http://www.exampler.com/blog/2007/05/16/six-years-later-what-the-agile-manifesto-left-out/>.

Marion, Russ and Mary Uhl-Bien. "Paradigmatic Influence and Leadership: The Perspectives of Complexity Theory and Bureaucratic Theory" in Hazy, K., James et.al. *Complex Systems Leadership Theory*. Goodyear: ISCE Pub, 2007.

Maxwell, John. *The 21 Irrefutable Laws of Leadership*. Nashville: Thomas Nelson Publishers, 1998.

McConnell, Steve. *Professional Software Development*. Boston: Addison-Wesley, 2004.

McConnell, Steve. *Rapid Development*. New York: McGraw-Hill, 1996.

McGregor, Douglas and Joel Cutcher-Gershenfeld. *The Human Side of Enterprise*. New York: McGraw-Hill, 2006.

McKelvey, Bill. "Complexity Theory in Organization Science: Seizing the Promise or Becoming a Fad?" *Emergence*. Volume 1 Issue 1, 1999.

Middleton, Peter and James Sutton. *Lean Software Strategies*. Portland: Productivity Press, 2005.

Miller, John H. and Scott E. Page. *Complex Adaptive Systems*. Princeton: Princeton University Press, 2007.

Minsky, Marvin. *The Society of Mind*. New York: Simon and Schuster, 1986.

Mintzberg, Henry. *Managers Not Mbas*. San Francisco: Berrett-Koehler Publishers, 2005.

Mintzberg, Henry. *Managing*. San Francisco: Ignatius Press, 2009.

Mitchell, Melanie. *Complexity*. City: Oxford U Pr, N Y, 2009.

Nonaka, Ikujiro. *The Knowledge-Creating Company*. Boston: Harvard Business School Press, 2008.

Norberg, Johan. *Financial Fiasco*. Washington D.C.: Cato Institute, 2009.

Norman, Don. "Simplicity Is Highly Overrated." <http://www.jnd.org/dn.mss/simplicity_is_highly.html>. *Jnd.org*. 2007.

O'Donogue, James. "Look at the SIZE of those things!" *NewScientist*. 21 March 2009.

Pettit, Ross <http://www.rosspettit.com/2008/06/agile-made-us-better-but-we-signed-up.html>. *The Agile Manager*. June 29, 2008.

Phillips, Jeffrey. *Make Us More Innovative*. United States: iUniverse, Inc., 2008.

Pink, Daniel H. *Drive: The Surprising Truth About What Motivates Us*. Riverhead, 2009.

Pmi, Pmi. *Guide to the Project Management Body of Knowledge*. Drexel Hill: Project Management Institute, 2008.

Poppendieck, Mary. "Unjust Deserts" *Better Software*. July/August 2004.

Poppendieck, Mary et.al. *Implementing Lean Software Development*. Boston: Addison-Wesley, 2007.

Poppendieck, Mary et.al. *Leading Lean Software Development*. Boston: Addison-Wesley, 2009.

Prigogine, I. and Isabelle Stengers. *The End of Certainty*. New York: Free Press, 1997.

Pulford, Kevin et.al. *A Quantitative Approach to Software Management*. San Francisco: Ignatius Press, 1996.

Pundir, Ashok K, et.al. "Towards a Complexity Framework for Managing Projects" *E:CO*. Vol. 9, Issue 4, 2007.

Quinn, R.E. & Spreitzer, "G.M. The road to empowerment: Seven questions every leader should consider." *Organizational Dynamics*, 26-2, 1997

Rand, Ayn and Nathaniel Branden. *The Virtue of Selfishness*. New York: Signet, 1970.

Reinertsen, Donald. *Managing the Design Factory*. New York: Free Press, 1997.

Reiss, Steven. *Who Am I? the 16 Basic Desires That Motivate Our Actions and Define Our Personalities*. City: Berkley Trade, 2002.

Reynolds, Craig (1987), "Flocks, herds and schools: A distributed behavioral model.", SIGGRAPH '87: Proceedings of the 14th annual conference on Computer graphics and interactive techniques (Association for Computing Machinery): 25-34, doi:10.1145/37401.37406, ISBN 0-89791-227-6.

Richardson, K.A. "Managing Complex Organizations" *E:CO* Vol. 10 No. 2 2008.

Richardson, K.A. "Systems theory and complexity: Part 1" *E:CO* Vol. 6 No. 3 2004 (a).

Richardson, K.A. "Systems theory and complexity: Part 2" *E:CO* Vol. 6 No. 4 2004 (b).

Rico, F., David et.al. *The Business Value of Agile Software Methods.* New York: McGraw-Hill, 2009.

Roam, Dan. *The Back of the Napkin (Expanded Edition).* City: Portfolio Hardcover, 2009.

Rothman, Johanna and Esther Derby. *Behind Closed Doors.* Raleigh: Pragmatic Bookshelf, 2005.

Runco, Mark and Steven Pritzker. *Encyclopedia of Creativity.* Boston: Academic Press, 1999.

Satir, Virginia et.al. *The Satir Model.* Palo Alto:Science and Behavior Books, 1991.

Saviano, Roberto and Virginia Jewiss. *Gomorrah: a Personal Journey into the Violent International Empire of Naples' Organized Crime System.* New York: Picador, 2008.

Schwaber, Ken. "Agile Processes and Self-Organization" <http://www.controlchaos.com/storage/scrum-articles/selforg.pdf>. 2001.

Schwaber, Ken. *Agile Project Management with Scrum.* Redmond: Microsoft Press, 2004.

Schwaber, Ken and Mike Beedle. *Agile Software Development with Scrum.* Englewood Cliffs: Prentice Hall, 2002.

Senge, Peter. *The Fifth Discipline.* San Francisco: Ignatius Press, 2006.

Sheedy, Tim. "People Management is Fundamental to the Success of Large Systems Integration Projects." *Forrester,* June 11, 2008. <http://www.forrester.com/rb/Research/people_management_is_fundamental_to_success_of/q/id/46112/t/2>.

Shore, James. "Why I Don't Provide Agile Certification." *The Art of Agile,* March 31, 2009. <http://jamesshore.com/Blog/Why-I-Dont-Provide-Agile-Certification.html>.

Sivers, Derek. "Shut up! Announcing your plans makes you less motivated to accomplish them" <http://sivers.org/zipit> 16 June 2009.

Skyttner, L. *General systems theory: Ideas and applications,* River Edge, NJ: World Scientific. 2001.

Snowden, David. "Knowledge sharing across silos: Part II" *CognitiveEdge* <http://www.cognitive-edge.com/blogs/dave/2010/01/knowledge_sharing_across_silos.php> 2010 (a).

Snowden, David. "Multi-ontology sense making: a new simplicity in decision making" *Management Today.* Yearbook 2005, Vol 20.

Snowden, David. "The origin of Cynefin (part 1)…(part 7)" *CognitiveEdge* <http://www.cognitive-edge.com/blogs/dave/2010/07/origins_of_cynefin_part_7.php> 2010 (b).

Sokal, Alan and Jean Bricmont. Intellectual Impostures: Postmodern Philosophers' Abuse of Science. Economist Books, 1998.

Solé, Ricard et.al. *Signs of Life.* New York: Basic Books, 2000.

Spagnuolo, Chris. "Discipline versus Motivation." <http://edgehopper.com/discipline-versus-motivation/> *EdgeHopper.* 9 October 2008.

Spanyi, Andrew. "Beyond Process Maturity to Process Competence." *BPTrends*, June, 2004. <http://processownercoach.com/To%20Process%20Competence.pdf>.

Spolsky, Joel. "In Defense of Not-Invented-Here Syndrome." *Joel on Software*, 14 Oct. 2001. <http://www.joelonsoftware.com/articles/fog0000000007.html>.

Spolsky, Joel. "The Law of Leaky Abstractions." *Joel on Software*, 11 Nov. 2002. <http://www.joelonsoftware.com/articles/LeakyAbstractions.html>.

Sprangers, Chris "Verkeer zonder regels is veiliger" <http://www.intermediair.nl/artikel.jsp?id=644129>. January 11, 2007 Intermediair.

Stacey, Ralph D. Strategic Management and Organisational Dynamics: The Challenge of Complexity, First Edition. Upper Saddle River: Prentice Hall, 2000 (b).

Stacey, Ralph D. et.al. *Complexity and Management.* New York: Routledge, 2000 (a).

Stack, Jack. *The Great Game of Business.* Oxford Oxfordshire: Oxford University Press, 1994.

Stallard, Michael L. *Fired Up or Burned Out.* Nashville: Thomas Nelson, 2007.

Starcevich, Matt M. "Coach, Mentor: Is there a difference." <http://www.coachingandmentoring.com/Articles/mentoring.html>. *Center for Coaching & Mentoring.* 2009.

"The State of Agile Development Survey 2009" *VersionOne*, August, 2009. <http://pm.versionone.com/StateOfAgileSurvey.html>.

Stephenson, Karen. *Quantum Theory of Trust.* Harlow: Pearson Education Ltd, 2005.

Sterling, Chris. "Focus on Value: How to create value-driven user stories." <http://www.volaroint.com/pages/Focus_on_Value.html>.

Strogatz, Steven. *Sync.* New York: Theia, 2003.

Suzuki, Shunryu et.al. *Zen Mind, Beginner's Mind*. New York: Weatherhill, 1980.

Tapscott, Don and Anthony Williams. *Wikinomics*. City: Portfolio Hardcover, 2008.

Testa, Louis. *Growing Software*. San Francisco: No Starch Press, 2009.

Thomas, Kenneth. *Intrinsic Motivation at Work*. San Francisco: Berrett-Koehler Publishers, 2000.

Van Vugt, Mark. "Triumph of the Commons" *NewScientist*. 22 August 2009.

Wailgum, Thomas "The Best Way to Implement Agile Development Processes: Your Own Way" <http://www.cio.com/article/111400/> *CIO.com*. May 21, 2007.

Waldrop, M. *Complexity*. New York: Simon & Schuster, 1992.

Wallis, Steven E. "The Complexity of Complexity Theory: An Innovative Analysis" *E:CO* Vol. 11, Issue 4, 2009.

Webb, Richard. "I want what she wants" *New Scientist*. 20/27. December 2007.

Weinberg, Gerald. An Introduction to General Systems Thinking: Silver Anniversary Edition. New York: Dorset House, 2001.

Weinberg, Gerald. *Quality Software Management*. New York: Dorset House Pub, 1992.

Wilson, James Q. and George L. Kelling "Broken Windows." <http://www.manhattan-institute.org/pdf/_atlantic_monthly-broken_windows.pdf>. *The Atlantic Monthly*. March 1982.

Wolfram, Stephen. "Universality and Complexity in Cellular Automata" *Physica D*, January 10, 1984, 1–35.

Yourdon, Edward. *Death March*. Upper Saddle River: Prentice Hall Professional Technical Reference, 2004.

Index

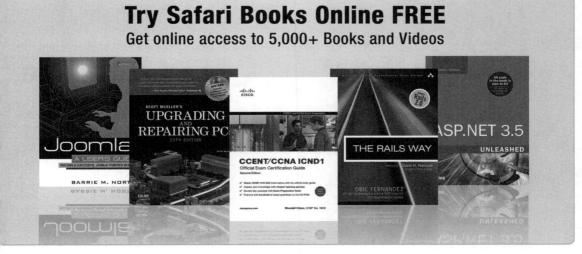

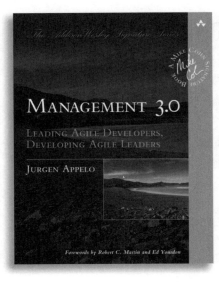

FREE Online Edition

Your purchase of **Management 3.0** includes access to a free online edition for 45 days through the Safari Books Online subscription service. Nearly every Addison-Wesley Professional book is available online through Safari Books Online, along with more than 5,000 other technical books and videos from publishers such as Cisco Press, Exam Cram, IBM Press, O'Reilly, Prentice Hall, Que, and Sams.

SAFARI BOOKS ONLINE allows you to search for a specific answer, cut and paste code, download chapters, and stay current with emerging technologies.

Activate your FREE Online Edition at www.informit.com/safarifree

> **STEP 1:** Enter the coupon code: QRIZWWA.

> **STEP 2:** New Safari users, complete the brief registration form.
> Safari subscribers, just log in.

If you have difficulty registering on Safari or accessing the online edition, please e-mail customer-service@safaribooksonline.com